JOURNAL

OF THE

ROYAL ASIATIC SOCIETY

China

Journal

OF THE

Royal Asiatic Society China

Vol. 78 No. 1, 2018

EDITOR
Julie Chun

Copyright 2018 RAS China

The Journal of the Royal Asiatic Society China is published by
Earnshaw Books on behalf of the Royal Asiatic Society China.

———∞———

CONTRIBUTIONS
The editor of the Journal invites submission of original unpublished
scholarly articles and book reviews on the religion and philosophy,
art and architecture, archaeology, anthropology and environment,
of China. Books sent for review will be donated to the Royal Asiatic
Society China Library. Contributors will receive a copy of the Journal.

SUBSCRIPTIONS
Members receive a copy of the Journal, with their paid annual membership
fee. Individual copies will be sold to non-members, as available.

LIBRARY POLICY
Copies and back issues of the Journal are available in
the library. The library is available to members.

www.royalasiaticsociety.org.cn

Journal of the Royal Asiatic Society China
Vol. 78 No. 1, 2018

978-988-8552-32-0

EB 121

© 2018 Royal Asiatic Society China

The copyright of each article rests with the author.

Designed and produced for RAS China by Earnshaw Books Ltd.
17/F, Siu Ying Commercial Building, 151-155 Queen's Road Central, Hong Kong

All rights reserved. No part of this book may be reproduced in material form
by any means, whether graphic, electronic, mechanical or other, including
photocopying or information storage, in whole or in part. May not be used to
prepare other publications without written permission from the publisher.

*The Royal Asiatic Society China thanks Earnshaw Books
for its valuable contribution and support.*

In memoriam.
The 2018 RAS Journal is dedicated to
David F. Bridgman (1932-2018)

CONTENTS

RAS CHINA COUNCIL 2016-2018   *1*

Foreward
By Julie Chun   *5*

Introduction
By Julie Chun   *7*

SECTION 1: RECLAIMING THE PAST

The Formative Years Of The North China Branch Of The Royal
Asiatic Society In Shanghai
By Peter Hibbard   *13*

Defying Tradition:
Eliza Bridgman, Foreign Feminist And The Awakening Of Women
In China
By David F. Bridgman   *41*

An Irish Policeman In Shanghai:
From Constable To Commissioner Of The SMP, 1904-1939
By Andrew David Field   *71*

And What Do We Know About China?
The International Labour Office, Albert Thomas And Republican
China, 1919 – 1930
By Christian Mueller   *101*

A Czechoslovak Founding Father In China
An Account Of The November 1918 Visit By Czechoslovakia's Milan
Rastislav Štefánik
By Lukáš Gajdoš   *123*

A Most Foreign Hutong:
Beijing's Kuei Chia Chang In 1922
By Paul French   *154*

The Cooperators War:
The Chinese Industrial Cooperatives, The China Defence League,
And Internationalism In The Sino-Japanese War
By Evan Taylor   *176*

Facing The Foreign: Media Myths In China And Japan
By John D. Van Fleet 199

Political Power And Memory In The Han Dynasty:
The Career Of Huo Guang Re-Considered
By J. Benjamin Askew 228

SECTION 2: CONSIDERING THE PRESENT

Dragon Marble Reliefs From The Imperial Palaces, Temples And
Mausoleums In Ming And Qing Dynasty
By Jimmy Nuo Zang 253

Hawkers In Hong Kong:
The Informal Sector In A Contemporary City
By Parul Rewal 285

Analysis Of Mexican Foreign Policy. The Case Of The Diversification
Of Foreign Relations:
A Look At The Relationship With The People's Republic Of China
By Edith Yazmin Montes Incin 320

YOUNG SCHOLAR ESSAY

Rewriting The Future:
The Conflict And Compromise Of China's Script Revolution
By Athena Ru 350

BOOK REVIEWS

When True Love Came to China
By Lynn Pan
Reviewed by Dagmar Borchard 364

Half the Sky: Conversations With Women Artists In China
By Luise Guest
Reviewed by Niamh Cunningham 367

RAS CHINA 2017-2018

Hon President
John Edwards – British Consul General Shanghai

Hon Vice Presidents
Carma Elliot CMG, OBE
Peter Hibbard MBE
Liu Wei
Tess Johnston

RAS COUNCIL 2017-2018

Vice President
Julie Chun (also Art Focus Convenor)

Secretary
John Van Fleet

Treasurer
Robert Martin

Membership Director
Parul Rewal

Programme Director
John Villar

Journal Editor
Julie Chun

Co-Librarians
Carolyn Robertson
Sven Serrano

Council Members
Connor Bralla (Non-fiction Book Club Convenor)
Furkan Erdogan (History Club Convenor)
Sue Morrell Stewart (Events Booking)
Johan Uusitalo (IT Support)
Ted Willard (THOR Liaison)
Tracey Willard

Ex-officio
Alan Babington-Smith (Vice President, Beijing Chapter)

RAS CHINA 2016-2017

Hon President
John Edwards – British Consul General Shanghai

Hon Vice Presidents
Carma Elliot CMG, OBE
Peter Hibbard MBE
Liu Wei
Tess Johnston

RAS COUNCIL 2016-2017

President
Spencer Doddington (November 2016 - April 2017)

Co-Vice Presidents
Julie Chun (also Art Focus Convenor)
Marcia Johnson

Secretary
Sandra Strand

Treasurer
Ted Willard

Membership Director
Tracey Willard

Programme Director
John Villar

Journal Editor
Richard de Grijs

Librarian
Kyle Pulsifer

Council Members
Connor Bralla (Book Club Convenor)
Furkan Erdogan (History Club Convenor)
Duncan Hewitt
Carolyn Robertson
Johan Uusital (IT Support)

Ex-officio
Alan Babington-Smith (Vice President, Beijing Chapter)

FOREWARD

THE YEAR 2017 marked a significant turn in the Royal Asiatic Society China's tradition and history. After five years in residence at the Sino-British College on Fuxing Middle Road, the RAS Library was relocated in June 2017 to the third floor of the House of Roosevelt on 27 Zhong Shan Dong Yi Lu, reviving the Society's presence on the Bund. This move was hardly simple as it took the Library Search Committee over a year-long pursuit, followed by lengthy discussions, of where the Library was to be housed when our time at the Sino-British College came to an end. Through a kind mediation by the British Consul-General in Shanghai, John Edwards, Tim Tse of Shanghai's House of Roosevelt agreed to provide a spacious site to house our Society's collection of over 4,000 books that has been growing incrementally since RAS was re-instituted in 2007. On 23 September 2017, just one day shy of the 160-year anniversary of the founding of the RAS China in 1857, the RAS Library was re-dedicated with many of the 2007 RAS founding members present, including Peter Hibbard (President 2007-2011) who continues as advisor and consultant with his wealth of knowledge about the Society's history.

In personal ways, 2017 was also a historical moment. While the Society had the honour of inaugurating Katy Gow as the first female President from 2011-2014, I stepped up from Co-Vice President as the first Asian female Vice President to counter any claims that RAS remains a colonial organization. With the appointments of greater numbers of women and wider ranges of age and ethnic demographics of Council Members and Conveners, we strive to foster and promote a Society that embraces a culture of diversity. As we have been operating without a President the past year and a half, I could not have carried on the duties of re-establishing the Library at the House of Roosevelt and keeping the Society operational without the efforts of our dedicated Council Members who I acknowledge as 'Team RAS.' They are all listed by name and position in the pages above. In 1857, when the Society was established, it was international in membership and outlook and we remain as such to this day in this immensely cosmopolitan metropolis of Shanghai, which we are all honoured to call home as temporary guests. In an era of post-modernism and post-internet, as History is continually being reclaimed and revised, we are doing our part to take the Society into the future while upholding our tripartite mission of providing a library, publishing the Journal and programming lectures to promote the understanding, knowledge and scholarship of China and Asia to a diverse array of the members of Shanghai's foreign community. May this foundational endeavour, begun in 1857, endure for another one hundred and sixty years, and longer.

Julie Chun
RAS Vice President 2017-2018

INTRODUCTION
RAS Journal Editor 2017-2018
BY JULIE CHUN

SINCE THE RE-ESTABLISHMENT of the RAS Library on 23 September 2017 at 27 Zhongshan Dong Yi Lu, on the third floor of the House of Roosevelt (originally the headquarters of Jardine Matheson under the name EWO Building), we have had the honour and pleasure of being called upon by visiting scholars from various parts of the world including Cologne, Germany; Sydney, Australia; Rochester, USA and Sabah, Malaysia. The most surprising visitor and researcher to arrive at the RAS Library during my shift was an older gentleman by the name of David Bridgman from Orlando, Florida, USA. He was introduced by our life-time member Betty Barr as one of her schoolmates from the Shanghai American School in Shanghai. After an hour that stretched into two and then three, I learned that David was the fourth generation descendent of Henry Augustus Bridgman. Henry was the elder brother of Elijah Coleman Bridgman. To those well versed in the Society's history, Elijah was the first American missionary to China and the Society's first president. David had been returning to China on several occasions to conduct research on Eliza Jane Gillett Bridgman, who was not only the wife of Elijah Bridgman but also an instrumental pioneer who started the first school for girls in Shanghai and later in Beijing. I had a working knowledge of the Bridgman's history in China but as David filled in the gaps by revealing the wealth of his research, I knew this unique narrative needed to be written and archived. It took several attempts to convince David to compile his research into a working draft, but as the manuscript progressed, he became emboldened and genuinely excited with how the article was taking a life of its own. As we were about to lay out the final draft, I received an email from David's daughter of his passing on 9 August 2018. It was with such a heavy heart that I literally dropped my phone while reading the message. I cannot bring David back, but David has brought Eliza back to us with his carefully researched article of a singular woman who was a visionary, an educator and a proponent of women's rights at a time and in a society when she was viewed as an outlier. David's article is timely in honouring an unsung hero who deserves recognition.

The 2018 Journal pays tribute to people of today and yester years - to individuals and collective body of people. This aspect of focusing on the achievements of people who made contributions to China and Asia has been one of the critical contents of the *Journal of the North China Branch of the Royal Asiatic Society*, which have featured profiles of RAS members as well as its speakers, including many who were explorers conducting geographical surveys in China, Japan, Formosa (Taiwan) and Southeast Asia. What began as a literary and scientific study group in 1857 as the formation of Shanghai Literary and Scientific Society composed of learned men with Elijah Cole Bridgman as the President, broadened in scope and prestige with the receipt of the Royal Charter from King George the IV in 1858, to mark the inauguration of the Royal Asiatic Society China. Eventually occupying a two-storey building on 20 Huqiu Lu, the Society and the building continued to evolve and expand to accommodate the foreign and the Chinese community in Shanghai to offer an extensive holding of its library, the establishment of a natural history museum and a lecture hall where speakers from various parts of the globe arrived to deliver lectures on their discoveries and research.

To uncover the obscure protagonists and occasional antagonists who have been slumbering quietly under the veil of time, present-day scholars, researchers and authors have lifted the layers to reclaim the men and women who have defined and defied history in China. The body of original and unpublished articles that follow cast probing inquiry upon former members of Shanghai's community who did not have the distinction of becoming household names, yet are deserving of distinction in their own right. In Part 1, 'Reclaiming the Past,' we delve into the history to revive people and events. Peter Hibbard opens with an introduction relaying the twilight years of the Society's formation. This provides the context for David Bridgman's extensive research on his aunt four generations removed, Eliza Jane Gillett Bridgman. As the wife of Elijah Bridgman, Eliza held her own position as she championed the rights of girls and women by instituting China's first all-girls school. Andrew Field, likewise, reacquaints us with Stewart Cromie Young, a twenty-two year old Irish recruit who joined the Shanghai Municipal Police as a second-class constable and worked his way up to become the Deputy Commissioner in 1934. Christian Mueller contributes a carefully researched article on Albert Thomas, who between 1919 and 1930, endeavoured to integrate China into the

League of Nations' labour regime known as the International Labour Organisation. Mueller's account of Thomas underscores the challenges in the complex discourse of China's striving for modernisation. Lukáš Gajdoš recounts a detailed historical meeting in November 1918 between Slovak-born Milan Rastislav Štefánik and Li Chia Ao (Li Jia'ao) that resulted in the establishment of the Czechoslovak legionnaires, the Czechoslovak Consulate, and the wider Czechoslovak community in Harbin. Paul French outlines another foreign community that was formed in Beijing's Keui Chia Chang hutong in 1922. Evan Taylor's investigative research examines a rare topic that has received very little attention in Asian Studies - the Chinese Industrial Cooperatives and the China Defence League, two related organisations founded in the spring of 1938 that provided material and medical support to China in its resistance against Japanese occupation. Taylor fills the lacunae in the historical canons by documenting the origins and the background of the key people who founded the organisations. His research strives to re-examine history to locate a renewed viewpoint and voice. John Van Fleet's article also intersects with Japan as he narrates the creation and nurturing of sensationalist anti-foreign myths that circulated in China and Japan's mid-nineteenth century mass media. Lastly, J. Benjamin Askew reaches back into Han Dynasty to reconsider the career of Huo Guang against extant historical records. Through a renewed examination, Askew critically questions the assumptions ingrained in traditional writings that rely on Confucianist historical methodology.

Part 2 reveals articles under 'Considering the Present' in which the authors negotiate the past through the contemporary lens of the present. Jimmy Nuo Zang offers a detailed examination of dragon marble reliefs located in Beijing. The careful categorization and scrutiny, which is accompanied by primary photos taken by Zang on site, will serve to assist future art historians in dating and placement of these monuments. Parul Rewal's fascinating urban study research explores how the past conditions and historical legislation governing Hong Kong's hawkers (informal street vendors) have evolved in today's current society. Through a carefully excavated research with supporting source materials, Rewal highlights an important segment of the marginalised members of the urban community who contribute in enlivening the economic and social relations on the streets. Similarly, Edith Yazmin Montes Incin investigates the value of past and present foreign relations between Mexico and China. Incin advocates diversification as key strategy fostering and improving diplomatic ties across borders in present global conditions rife with instability driven by tensions of incomprehension and misunderstandings. Bilateral talks and collaborative negotiations should be one of the primary tasks for humanity in our present epoch of difficult and contentious times as we transition into the next century. Our tomorrow relies on the future generation. In order to celebrate and honour our young scholars, a new seminal section has been established with the assistance of Kate Massey, the Spouse of the British Consul-General in Shanghai, who worked closely and tirelessly with me to launch the Young Scholar Essay, which aims to encourage young students to carry the torch as the next generation of thinkers and researchers. Lastly, in keeping with our tradition of reviewing books, Beijing RAS member Niamh Cunningham discusses her take on *Half the Sky: Conversations with Women Artists in China,* an art historical survey of female Chinese artists penned by Luise Guest who was invited as the RAS China Art Focus guest speaker on 19 April 2018. Guest kindly donated a copy of her book, which is now available in the collection of the RAS Library. Our Fiction Bookclub Convener Dagmar Borchard reviews *When True Love Came to China* by Lynn Pan, who is another long-time member of the RAS China and a contributor to Shanghai's circle of literary and chamber music societies.

My deep gratitude is thus owed to all our writers who worked professionally to meet the requirements of the deadline. Without the benefit of a time-travel machine, they have proved to be time travellers as they excavated and examined artefacts, waded through archives and revisited the scenes of action. I would also like to thank all the RAS China Council Members for their support and am grateful to Council Members Carolyn Robertson, Tracey Willard and John Van Fleet, who assisted in copy-editing the first draft of the articles and for being a sounding board for me to bounce off ideas. Also, a word of thanks is due to Graham Earnshaw, our publisher, who in his years of publishing the RAS China Journal since 2010 has been invaluable with his insight and wit. Finally, an immense gratitude is due to each and every one of Royal Asiatic Society China members without whom our annual publications would not be possible.

Section 1:
Reclaiming the past

THE FORMATIVE YEARS OF THE NORTH CHINA BRANCH OF THE ROYAL ASIATIC SOCIETY IN SHANGHAI

BY PETER HIBBARD

ABSTRACT

Whilst homes had been created for the commercial, spiritual and recreational needs of Shanghai's small foreign, predominantly British, population by the early 1850s, scant provision for the engagement of the mind through intellectual or cultural pursuits existed. In 1852 some elders of the community proposed an all-encompassing commercial and cultural centre, far greater than their numbers could afford. However, those numbers and the city's intellectual life was greatly influenced and enhanced, by swarms of naval visitors over the years of the Taiping Rebellion (1850-64). They, alongside a huge influx of Chinese into the English Settlement escaping the conflict set the scene for the formation of a foreign literary and scientific society in 1857. In 1858 the organisation became the North China Branch of the Royal Asiatic Society. Many of its original ambitions and ideals were fulfilled in 1872 upon completion of its own building, housing a library and later a museum. This article examines the environment within which the RAS was born as an international institution.

NOURISHMENT OF THE BODY AND THE MIND

In the seven years following the city's opening to foreign trade in 1843, Shanghai's predominantly British community had made great strides in bringing order to their new society. Priority had been given to religion through the erection of an Anglican church, to benevolence in the form of a hospital and to leisure and entertainment in the form of a racecourse and recreation ground. Home comforts were plentiful. The front page of the city's own newspaper, the *North-China Herald* (NCH), first published in 1850, regularly carried advertisements for everything from Yorkshire hams, Cheddar cheese and gooseberry jam to a wide range of fine champagne, sherry and other intoxications, including Allsopps Pale Ale. English coal burned in the hearths of imposing colonial homes built in 'compradoric' style, featuring wide verandas with columns.

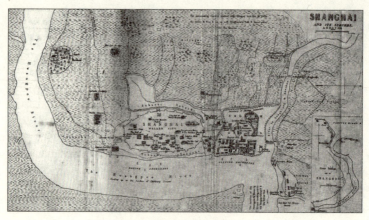

Figure 1: Map of Old Shanghai

However, as Henri Cordier, the incumbent librarian of the North China Branch of the Royal Asiatic Society (NCBRAS) remarked in 1873 when reflecting on the cultural development of Shanghai in the 1850s, stated:

After the foundations of a city have been laid-after the butcher, the grocer and the inevitable chemist have opened their shops-the newcomers very soon find that the mind requires feeding and healing no less than the body, and they establish clubs to exchange their views, institute societies to bring forth their ideas, and create libraries to obtain the science which, with the knowledge derived from experience and observation, forms the basis of these views and ideas.[1]

The first such move towards the cultural enrichment of the small foreign community came with the institution of the Shanghai Library, funded by public subscription in March 1849.[2] In the same year a Dramatic Corps was formed, providing light musical entertainments, farces and burlesques.[3]

The foreign population of the English Settlement rose from just 50 in 1844 to 175 in 1849.[4] At that time, the Settlement extended westwards from the Bund to today's Tibet Road Central and was bounded by today's Yan'an Road East to the south and Suzhou Creek to the north. A rare insight into the demographic composition of this population was given in the first issue of the *North-China Herald* on 3 August 1850, in which 157 male individuals or heads of households, 31 resident with family, were listed. Of those 157, around 120 were occupied with some form of merchant activity, and 16 missionaries and five medical practitioners were enumerated. In March 1851, the paper recorded 256 residents as British citizens, but more importantly gave a breakdown by age, revealing a youthful population. Among the 218 males, 91 were between the ages of 25 and 30, while only 30 were 36 years or older. Of the small female population of 38, 34 women were 35 years old or younger, including 12 children.[5]

Nonetheless, the true nature of foreign life in Shanghai was not reflected in such statistics, as seafaring visitors vastly outnumbered its small resident population. An analysis published by the *North-China Herald* in December 1851 estimated 'conservatively' by their account that 17,000 sailors on merchant vessels alone had visited the port since 1844 on 607 British ships, 187 American and around 40 ships of other nations. The author reported that 'during their short period of liberty they are so apt to partake to excess of the most pernicious description of intoxicating drinks and noted that, of the 79 foreign burials at the Shanghai cemetery, 54 were sailors.[6]

The resident community was also transient. Whilst the British emulated the manners and appearances of home, Shanghai was not home. As one merchant proclaimed:

In two or three years at farthest I hope to realize a fortune and get away. And what can it matter to me if all Shanghai disappear afterwards in fire or flood? You must not expect men in my position to condemn themselves to prolonged exile in an unhealthy climate for the benefit of posterity. We are money-making, practical men. Our business is to make money, as much and as fast as we can.[7]

Despite advances in sanitation, Shanghai remained an unhealthy place to live and it certainly was so for young children, the majority of whom formed part of missionary families. There were frequent epidemics of cholera, smallpox and typhoid. Another serious challenge facing the foreign community was the maintenance of law and order in the face of the unruly behaviour of some of its seafaring visitors. Many men had been at sea for months. The journey from London was around 110 days and a large industry catering to their liberty had emerged in the Hongkou district where grog shops, selling homemade gin, taverns and brothels abounded. In the absence of an organised police force, Consular constables and native watchmen tried to prevent assaults on person and property, and jail spaces were scarce. However, there were much greater battles to come, as Shanghai was threatened at various times during the ebbs and flows of the Taiping Rebellion, a civil war of unparalleled destructive and cruel magnitude that spanned the years from 1850 to 1864.

On the intellectual front, a chess club was established in July 1851. The move drew wry criticism from Henry Shearman, the editor of the *North-China Herald* who scarcely thought it well suited. He derided the sedentary nature of chess as undeserving in a community that needed more physical exercise than that which was found in Shanghai's billiard room, its fives court (a racquet sport) and bowling alley.[8] One anonymous resident in favour of the club retorted that 'if bodily lethargy is a bad thing, mental stagnation is a worse.'[9]

However, considering talk of combining the library with the chess club in a new building, Shearman suggested a scheme, wider in scope, to include a public meeting and lecture room.[10] An ambitious plan to create a public building of use to all of Shanghai's clubs and societies, as well as a commercial exchange and newsroom for its mercantile members, with Shearman as a leading advocate, was announced in September 1852.[11] The building was also to house the billiard club and the Masonic Lodge. A prospectus and a building plan was drawn up where commerce would sit alongside departments of 'an intellectual or social character.[12]

Compounded by a lack of public interest in financing such a scheme, the project came to a halt in July 1853 when a request to grant land for the building was refused by the British government. The committee remarked, though it was desirable connecting 'the commercial and what may without impropriety be termed the social portions of their scheme there is no necessary dependence of the one upon the other.' They suggested that an enlarged library building, with public meeting rooms might form a focus 'for further additions tending to promote public recreation and social intercourse.'[13] Clearly commercial concerns took pride of place.[14] Such a judgment foretold of the schism between public and private, between commerce and culture that would prevail throughout Shanghai's Treaty Port era. Interpreting this paradigm in the years that followed, the RAS developed as a popular public institution, whilst the Shanghai Club opened in 1864 to fulfil the commercial and recreational needs of an exclusive membership that barred Chinese and women.

Shanghai felt the first major impact of war in late 1853, following the capture of the native walled city by the Small Swords Society, a triad organisation. The nature of foreign life in the Settlement changed dramatically and irrevocably as a swelling torrent of Chinese escaping the conflict found refuge in its confines. At that point, the need for improved sanitation and public hygiene became more urgent, as did the need for public order. Consequently, the Shanghai Municipal Council, incorporating a police force, was formed in 1854. On 4 April of that year, British and American marines, supported by a local militia known as the Shanghai Volunteer Corps, formed in 1853, had successfully fought off imperialist troops battling the Taiping rebels in the first real threat to foreign life and property in the Settlement. Regulations allowing the Chinese to reside and to rent or buy land in the Settlement were introduced, fuelling a boom in property speculation. Tens of thousands of refugees were recorded in the early months of 1854 and hundreds of thousands followed. While swathes of China were ravaged by war in the succeeding years, the English Settlement was not directly troubled again in the 1850s, laying the foundations for Shanghai's rise as a great international city that afforded tangible safety and security to all its residents.[15] A new cultural milieu and order was melded as two civilisations collided in close physical proximity. The foreign, largely British community, who were making huge fortunes on the back of contraband trade in opium and on housing migrants appositely faced the might of China and an ignorance they had of the nation. Visitors from across the globe also enriched the cultural and social life of resident foreigners. Professional theatrical touring companies began visiting the city in 1856, when an American company performed a minstrel show.[16] Later that year, a leading French musician performed what was described as the 'first professional concert and introduced the Saxophone to Shanghai.'[17] However it was yet again those seafaring visitors, and particularly the proliferation in the number of British and American men-of-war that were often stationed in Shanghai for considerable periods of time, which would have a major influence on the city. Many had their own theatrical and musical companies, as well as on-board stage facilities.

In October 1857, around 75 merchant ships and four British warships, including the *HMS Pique* and the American steamer *San Jacinto*, were in harbour.[18] The Union Theatre Company of the *San Jacinto* regularly performed entertainments aboard ship, and its band performed on many occasions around town.[19]

The frigate *HMS Pique* with her crew of 350 had been in harbour since September 1856, and remained there for over 18 months, 'protecting British and other foreign interests in this immediate neighbourhood' until its departure in March 1858.[20] The *USS San Jacinto*, with 218 crew, had been in Shanghai since at least July 1857, and left in early November 1858. With such long sojourns, captains, officers and crews melded into the routines of Shanghai life, becoming important members of the foreign community.

Whilst some navy ships were acting as Shanghai's unofficial social centres, a scheme for a Central Public Building, housing the library and reading room, the chamber of commerce, the billiard room and the Masonic Lodge, as well as a large public room, was announced in February 1858.[21] The proposal to erect an imposing three storey building on the Bund failed to evoke a public response. It appears that prestige in finding the right address on Shanghai's prime real estate took pride of place over substance in catering to the needs of the small foreign community.[22]

MIND OVER MATTER - THE SOCIETY IS BORN

Whilst that plan, like the one from 1852, focused on building extravagant premises as a prerequisite, the nascent Shanghai Literary and Scientific Society focused on matters within the precincts of the heart and the mind. This first incarnation of the North China Branch of the Royal Asiatic Society (NCBRAS) was established as an institution – not a landmark. There was no mention of a building in its early years – just a belief that whenever there was a need for financial assistance it would be 'cheerfully afforded' by the Shanghai community.[23] The Society generally held its meetings in rooms of the Shanghai Library. Its first meeting, attended by 18 men, was held there on 24 September 1857. A full report of the proceedings, from which the following account was taken, appeared in the pages of *the North-China Herald*.[24]

Sir Frederick Nicolson, captain of *HMS Pique*, was elected to take the chair, and the Reverend Edward W. Syle proposed the case for the foundation of the new society. Syle, a British-born graduate of the Virginia Theological Seminary, reached out to all corners of foreign society in a quest to venture beyond the self-interests they held in commerce or religion. He stated 'what so natural then, as that the gradual development of public life of Shanghai should demand some provision for cultivating the intellectual tastes and acquirements which must be supposed to exist in a community numbering some two hundred or more, who have found their way here from cultivated homes of Europe and America?'

Syle noted that certain intellectual members of the community could prepare papers to be read before the new society – its medical community comprised a body of scientific men, and its missionaries who were able 'to bring to our knowledge matters of interest in a field of research little explored as yet.' He continued, 'there was also a succession of distinguished strangers connected with our Ships of War, among whom we can always count upon finding some lovers of science and literature.' Syle also singled out the large number of young men in Shanghai, 'who bring from home intellectual tastes and habits which ought not to be dissipated here but rather cherished and cultivated. The moral welfare of Shanghai's youthful population was of particular concern to Syle.[25]

Syle also had grand plans for Shanghai, remarking that: 'We, who identify ourselves with Shanghai's interests and reputation, shall not be content till the apparatus of social cultivation and intellectual improvement be made complete by the establishment of a musical Society and a public gallery of the fine arts.'[26] For the present, however, the founding of a literary and scientific society was the matter most immediately demanded. Referring back to the proceedings of the meeting, in support, Thomas Moncrieff, a businessman and one of the original proposers of the Shanghai Library in 1849, viewed any attention to literary or scientific pursuits as a refreshing of the mind from the ordinary occupations and considerations of daily life.

The name Shanghai Literary and Scientific Society, was adopted, though the idea of some form of affiliation with the Asiatic Society of London had been proposed at the outset. Mr W. G. Howell said he could hardly doubt that the Asiatic Society would gladly recognise the formation of such an institution as that now projected. Reverend Joseph Edkins noted that the West was now moving to the East, that it was consequently becoming more necessary than ever to study the East's literature and civilisation. Concluding the meeting the Reverend Elijah Coleman Bridgman was elected as the first president of the Society. Bridgman became in 1830 the first American missionary to reach China. He established himself as an accomplished Sinologist and founder and editor of the *Chinese Repository*, a scholarly monthly magazine dedicated to examining Chinese culture and society, first published in 1832.

Bridgman's inaugural address at the Society's first formal meeting, on 16 October 1857, was recorded in the Society's first journal. Therein he predicted that Shanghai would soon become:

> One of the greatest centres of interest and of influence, perhaps the greatest, in the Eastern hemisphere, As surely as it becomes such by the presence and the agency of the educated men of Christendom, all active in their various professions and callings, so surely will literature and science, under the hallowed influences of revealed truth, here find a nursery and a home, and shed forth healthful influences on all sides of us, and to the remotest limits of this vast empire.[27]

Figure 2: Elijah Bridgman

Bridgman continued by outlining three pillars on which the society would stand. Primarily he spoke about people, firmly believing that the society would be able to inspire 'a large measure of enthusiasm' and attract those who love literary and scientific studies and regard their intellectual pursuit, 'not as to irksome toil, but as to sources of real pleasure and rich entertainment.' Secondly, Bridgman envisaged that an 'extensive apparatus' would be needed to support the society's endeavours.

At that meeting, Captain Nicolson of HMS Pique read the first paper to the Society, on 'Cyclones, or the Law of Storms.' That paper was printed in June 1858 in the Society's first journal, the only one published in the original name of the Society, which included articles on such diverse topics as meteorology, numismatics, Buddhism, Japan and Sino-foreign relations.

The Society received an enthusiastic welcome, as 24 new members were admitted that evening, bringing the total up to 42.

Founding member Edkins recalled:

> The room was filled with captains and first officers of ships, with commercial men and missionaries. That so many seamen were in town, at a time the Taipings were

still in Nanking and Admiral Seymour was preparing to bombard Canton, shows that trade at Shanghai never ceased. Two years later Peking was taken by the British and French forces. All through the intervening time the political atmosphere was seething with disturbances. It was during that period of almost universal commotion in China that this society was founded. With the peaceful design of conducting useful research into the history, the industry, the philosophy, the literature, the language and the manners of the Chinese people. We were determined to understand both their religion and their want of religion. We wished to know what makes the Chinese hate us and how far they love us.[28]

Given the immediate success of the organisation, Edkins penned a letter, dated 2 December 1857, to Professor Horace Hayman Wilson, President and Director of RAS in London, informing him:

Of the recent formation of a Society here for investigating the literature, arts, antiquities and social life of China and the neighbouring nations, and conducting researches in the same field. Taking such a province of inquiry it desires to be affiliated to the Royal Asiatic Society of Great Britain, which is engaged in similar labours but over a wider surface. [He concluded that] if the Royal Asiatic Society should see fit to adopt us as one of its branches, we beg to suggest a suitable name for our Society as the North China Branch of the Royal Asiatic Society.[29]

The London-based Royal Asiatic Society annual report of 1858 recorded:

In February last, the Council had before it a letter from the Rev. J. Edkins of Shanghai, announcing the formation of a new Literary and Scientific Association at the place, and expressing, on the part of its members, a desire to be affiliated to this Society under the appellation of The North China Branch of the Royal Asiatic Society.

Edkins' request was accepted on the 35th anniversary meeting of the RAS, on 15 May 1858, presided over by Professor Wilson. In recommending that the Literary and Scientific Society should be incorporated as a branch, Wilson noted that they were indebted to Edkins for some interesting communications on the subject of ancient Buddhist books from India, brought to China many ages before and translated into Chinese. 'The proposition was agreed by the meeting, *nem. con.*'[30]

As the Vice-President of the NCRAS in 1902, Edkins gave an address detailing the Society's history on its 45th anniversary. He revealed that there had been much debate over which name the society should adopt. Many of the mercantile community, who worked with facts and figures, wished to retain the original name whilst those students of Chinese, including Alexander Wylie who was elected a member in November 1857 favoured affiliation with the Royal Asiatic Society. As Edkins remarked, the benefits of the affiliation 'secured ... a sisterly relationship with the Indian, the Straits and the Japanese branches of the Asiatic Society of London.'[31]

London's decision was formally announced at the annual general meeting of the Shanghai Literary and Scientific Society on 21 September 1858. Reverend Bridgman gave notice 'that at the next general meeting he should propose the change in the name of the Society.[32] That he did on 26 October and it was unanimously adopted 'the Society is therefore for the future, the North China Branch of the Royal Asiatic Society.'[33]

At the next meeting, on 23 December, 'after considerable discussion it was unanimously resolved, that the Council of this Society, having the power to invite ladies to the general meetings, they be requested to exercise the same on all suitable occasions.'[34] Unfortunately, no record of the discussion exists, but presumably the fact that most women in Shanghai were married to missionaries who were members of the Society, and indeed were missionaries themselves, had a bearing on the decision. The committee was soon informed of the fragility of life in Shanghai as Syle's wife unexpectedly passed away five days later.[35] Syle had already lost two children to disease and his son Arthur, who was apparently very healthy, suddenly passed away on 30 September 1857.[36]

Most prominent RAS members, including Syle and Bridgman, were also involved with a host of other community and philanthropic activities. Bridgman was chair of the Shanghai Library Committee.[37] Syle was behind various endeavours helping to train and educate blind people in the Chinese community. In response to an article in the *North-China Herald* in December 1858 damning the absence of any respectable accommodation for the recreation and refreshment of seafarers, Bridgman, Syle and NCBRAS librarian the Reverend John Hobson, among others, met to discuss establishing a 'sailors home.'[38]

Like Captain Nicolson, Shadwell also contributed to the NCBRAS Journal with a "Memorandum on the Present State of some of the Magnetic Elements in China," appearing in Issue No. 2, dated May 1859. In fact, due to a shortage of funds the journal wasn't issued until two months later following a successful public appeal that resulted in a large increase in the number of subscribers. By the time the third volume was published in December 1859, Bridgman had stepped down as president with Thomas Taylor Meadows HBM British Consul, being elected as his successor in September of that year. (Meadows was the first of a long line of British Consuls who would preside, informally positioning the Society in the colonial realm.)

Whilst the journal had proved a success, no headway had been made on the establishment of a museum. With regards to the library, Henri Cordier remarked that it had a very modest beginning with books donated by Syle and copies of the *Chinese Repository* presented by Bridgman in January 1858, when Benjamin Hobson, a distinguished medical missionary, was appointed librarian.[39] Dr MacGowan donated Chinese volumes later that year.[40] Some valuable books had been secured through links with learned societies in Europe, such as the Imperial Geological Institute of Austria, and copies of the Journal entitled *Transactions* of RAS in London had been secured by 1860.[41] No mention was made of the whereabouts of the collection, and it might have held little interest to the Shanghai public, who had recourse to a wide selection of popular books in the Shanghai Library.

As nothing had been heard of the Society since a regular meeting in January 1860, its efficacy was publicly questioned by an unnamed correspondent in August 1860, who lambasted the society for its 'ponderous style [and] excessive antiquarian tendencies' and suggested the papers read at meetings might 'be brought to bear a little more on things that interest us, and have actually to do with the engagements of the Shanghai community.'[42]

An acknowledgment by President Meadows that the continuance

and growth of the Society would rely on it having more popular appeal was made at the annual general meeting in September 1860. Thoughts on achieving this aim included encouraging more discussions on practical matters and securing volunteers to deliver lectures on subjects of general interest such as banking, the book trade, postal service, horticulture and music. The most progressive proposal was the formation of a translation department so that new works under the auspices of the Society on the arts and sciences could be offered to the much larger Chinese public eager to keep up with modern developments.

At the time of that meeting The Society's fourth journal, Vol. 2, No. 1, was nearly ready for distribution.[43] Whilst the meeting featured a regular academic topic - the grammatical structure of the Japanese language, a novel and interesting paper on the dissection of a Japanese criminal appeared in the Journal. Over the rest of the year there were lectures by Edkins on Suzhou and Bridgman on the language of the Miao minority.

Reflecting the Society's desire to have a more popular appeal the 1861 season began with an engaging talk on Chinese agriculture by William Howard , not a Sinologist or missionary, but the Chairman of the Municipal Council.[44] What may have sounded like a conventional subject for the Society – that of a journey from Shanghai to Nanking, followed next. However, the talk and the journey were far from ordinary. The paper, about the journey of two missionaries, had been translated by the Reverend W. Cunningham. It was far from a travelogue, rather a vivid and melancholy description of the savage effects of the Taiping Rebellion on humanity, as documented by the missionaries' companion – a Chinese Christian.[45] For the first time a Chinese voice was heard within the Society and it seemed that had an immediate impact as in October, a Chinese publication committee, composed of three members was established. They were to oversee 'the publication of historical, scientific and other treatises, in the Chinese language and the endeavour was to become one of the leading objects of the Society.'[46] A programme of lectures solely on Chinese subjects was also designed that would 'enlighten us upon the ethnology of the Chinese.'[47] The Society pushed ahead with the printing of the fifth number of its journal in August, which was due to be ready by the end of the year.[48]

Despite British Consul Thomas Meadows having been transferred to Newchwang in Liaoning province in April 1861, a renewed vigour was found within the proceedings of the Society's annual general meeting in October, with the Reverend John Hobson, vice-president, in the Chair.[49] A report prepared by the Council reasserted the Society's original objectives in collecting original papers, the publication of the journal and the expansion of the library. It stated that urgency was to be given to 'devising ways and means for bringing into our library every valuable work accident on China, with a complete collection of Chinese authors. ... Our library should be made as complete as possible.'[50]

With the hope of gaining more subscribers from the increasing foreign population, greater frequency in the publication of the journal was also called for.[51] The report also called for by a move to popularise lectures, focusing on all aspects of life in China, as well as its geology, botany and natural history. For the very first time the question of the Society having its own premises was mentioned in the report as it was thought impractical to obtain the 'proper accommodations', for larger audiences. With the election of newly appointed British Consul Walter Henry Medhurst as President and with Bridgman remaining on the Council as a director, the report concluded that the 'conditions of success' of such an enterprise should be 'looked forward to at no distant period.'[52]

Within a week that excitement and expectation was transmuted into a stunned silence as Bridgman passed away on 2 November 1861. The Society disappeared from the pages of the *North-China Herald* and the accounts of its members until March 1864. The Society's historical accounts from 1864 on attribute its two-plus-year dormancy to Bridgman's death in particular, but also to its inability to appeal to a wider public. However, given that arrangements had already been made for a new lecture series and that the Society's journal had already been printed, but never distributed, it seems highly unlikely that Bridgman's death alone would have stopped the Society in its tracks. In fact, a renewed threat to safety in early 1862 disrupted the routines of the Society, as well as the daily lives of foreigners in the Settlement.

The British had maintained a policy of neutrality during the Taiping Rebellion, and military forces had interceded only on those occasions when foreign life in Shanghai was under threat in April 1854 and August 1860. British policy changed toward intervention in 1862, when British military forces engaged the Taiping rebels. Consul

Medhurst now had pressing affairs of state to deal with. In January 1862, rebel forces overran the countryside around Shanghai and a British military force of around 700 men was stationed in the city, supplemented by around 500 French and others, totalling 1,500.[53] The foreign Settlement was again bloated with Chinese refugees, and Medhurst urged the need for action by British forces in clearing the neighbouring areas in order to maintain supplies for all those within its confines.[54]

The campaign went on until the summer, when the city witnessed its first massive cholera attack, which killed countless thousands. With the recapture of Suzhou at the end of 1863, and the Taiping destruction by mid-1864, hundreds of thousands of Chinese left Shanghai, but its foreign population began to swell again. The first Municipal Council census, in 1865, recorded around 2,300 resident foreigners and 1,000 seafarers, some of whom surely jumped ship to find fortune in the city, in the recently created International Settlement, and around 400 foreigners in the French Concession – as well as over 1,800 British army and navy personnel.[55]

MINDFUL PROCEEDINGS[56]

The conditions were now propitious for the Society's revival. On 1 March 1864 by Dr James Henderson, of the Shantung Road Hospital, presided over a meeting at the Shanghai Library, where it was decided that a gathering 'of the former members of the Society and those desiring membership" should be held on 9 March.[57] At the 9 March meeting, the attendees reaffirmed that the original mission of the Society in that it was to be involved with the investigation of subjects connected with China and the surrounding nations, the publication of papers in a journal and the formation of a library and museum.[58] Perhaps having learned lessons from the past, the attendees outlined no temporal constraints.

The distinguished Sir Harry Parkes, having replaced Medhurst as British Consul in Shanghai and subsequently appointed British Minister to China, was elected as the Society's President. The Society's monthly lecture series resumed in May, and an augmented edition of the journal that had been printed in 1861 was bound and released as the *Journal of the NCBRAS*, New Series, Volume 1, 1864. In its preface there was an admission that the death of Dr Bridgman was a severe shock and that the Society's vitality had been damaged, but no detail of the consequences or indeed the mechanics of its reinvention were disclosed. However, it appears that it was the tireless efforts of Parkes himself that laid the foundations for the Society's success that followed. A letter of thanks on his departure for Japan, dated 22 June 1865, appeared in that journal on pages 184-185.

The total number of members of the Society reached 211 in 1865. Although the breakdown by nationality is not available, a review of surnames in the membership list suggests that over ten per cent were of European or Macanese heritage. By securing premises for the Society in the Shanghai Taotai's house on Ningbo Road, Parkes had located a building for the Society to grow and fulfil its ambitions, outside those related to the Journal and its lectures. Just before Parkes departure, the Society engaged a clerk and curator, who would reside on the premises. Parkes hoped 'that the members of the Society would assist in the contemplated work of forming a good museum and library.'[59] However, it was recognised from the outset that the Society would need its own permanent premises at some juncture.

Figure 3: Harry Parkes

A brick from the Porcelain Tower at Nanking (Nanjing) and some Shanghai snakes were the first recorded donations to the RAS museum in 1865. Whilst several members had promised interesting specimens, the RAS Council was hesitant in seeking large collections. In contrast, the library had a sizeable collection of 1,045 volumes in 1865, largely donated, with the most prized coming from the Foreign Office, the Admiralty and the Smithsonian Institution. In the following year a large collection of books was donated by Thomas Hanbury, one of the founding members of the Society. In fact, these volumes were part of the old library that the Council reported had been 'lost sight of during the lapse in operation following Dr Bridgman's death.'[60]

The Society was obliged to move in 1867, and rooms were taken up in the new Masonic Hall on the Bund (on part of the site where The Peninsula hotel is today).[61] In the expectation that a suitable room could be leased there, the Society proposed an ambitious scheme to establish a public library, of which its collection of books would form the nucleus. In 1868, the efforts to establish a library became imperative as a rare opportunity arose to purchase the magnificent library of one its esteemed members - the missionary scholar Alexander Wylie, who was leaving Shanghai. A public appeal was made for that purpose and the library comprised of important work on the language, geography and history of China. Highlighting the wider scope of the Society's efforts, the offices of Librarian and Curator of the Museum was added to the RAS Council. The Society had an assurance from the British government before the appeal was launched, that a strip of land for the purpose of building a library, museum and lecture room, on Gnaomen Road had been granted at a nominal rent (no record of how much). Former British Consul Sir Rutherford Alcock had been instrumental in securing the land for the Society.[62] But at that moment, acquiring Wylie's library took precedence. Following a successful appeal, largely due to the efforts of F. B. Forbes, one of the partners of Russell and Co., Wylie's library comprising 718 English-language volumes and 1,023 Chinese-language, was purchased by the RAS Council in April 1869, by which time Syle had been elected as the librarian and J. G. Bisset as the curator. Syle remained in office for only a short period before being replaced by Mr Karl Himly, interpreter to the German Consulate. On his return to Europe, the NCBRAS Council resolved that he could 'act on its behalf in whatever manner might seem to him calculated to promote the objects of the Society.'[63]

Upon the purchase, the bare and cold room in the Masonic Hall, which a writer in the *North-China Herald* called a 'chamber of horror' was transformed into a comfortable room with 'the best furniture and a well selected collection of rare and valuable books fills the shelves which cover the walls.'[64] However, the sense of achievement was short-lived as the Society was dealt a major setback around a year later when the premises became unavailable. The Society reverted to renting a large room in the Commercial Bank buildings on Nanking Road (present day Nanjing Road). Its first meeting was held in May 1870 and yet again 'an effort was made to render the meetings of the Society more popular than they had hitherto been.'[65] On visiting the building after being elected librarian in April 1871, Henri Cordier found the library 'in a most dilapidated state' and straightaway set about cataloguing its contents.[66]

Figure 4: Alexander Wyle

28

Clearly, there was a need for the Society to push ahead with plans for their own building, particularly as the British government's offer of land was under the condition 'that it never be diverted from the purpose for which it is granted; and should the Society be dissolved, or circumstances occur which might prevent the erection of any building within three years, that it then revert to Her Majesty's Government.'[67]

In early 1871, President Charles Wycliffe Goodwin, assistant Judge of the Supreme Court of China and Japan, alerted the Society to the three-year clause. An attempt was therefore made to raise the 2,700 taels needed for construction of a building, and an additional 300 taels for fittings. Thomas Kingsmill, scholar, architect, Council officer and later President, who gave his time and expertise without charge, designed the two-storey building. It was a utilitarian structure, which Kingsmill remarked, 'economy had been consulted.'[68] Indeed the cost was over double the 1,300 taels that the Society had paid for Wylie's library.

Again, the public was called upon to support the venture. The appeal was received with a 500 tael gift from Thomas Hanbury who had re-gifted the Society's volumes back to the Society, and who acted as corresponding secretary when the Society reformed. Whilst it seems that some of the funds needed had been secured by May 1871, it was reported at a meeting of the failing Shanghai Debating Society that 'a struggle is being made at the last moment to raise the necessary funds, and that there is every chance of a house being built within the stipulated time.'[69] The Debating Society decided to donate the balance of their funds, 230 taels, to the building project on the condition that if the Society was reconstituted, they would have the privilege of meeting in the NCBRAS Library.[70]

Another highly important development occurred in October when a preliminary agreement was reached with the Shanghai Library to fund a building for their new premises as a wing adjoining the NCBRAS building. There would be no immediate financial reward for the Society, but it was hoped that they would benefit from the services of their librarian who would live on the premises.

The NCBRAS building, completed in a very short time in late 1871, came in under the 3,000 tael budget. The building opened on 11 January 1872, when a pioneering Scottish photographer John Thompson treated the Society to a showing of photographs of the ancient cities of Cambodia. Though there was no mention of Wylie

Figure 5: RAS Building

attending, he had returned to Shanghai and served as Vice President of the Society.[71] Only two other founding members of the Shanghai Literary and Scientific Society were still on the NCBRAS Council, Messrs MacGowan and Syle.

The ground floor meeting room and the library on the upper floor both measured 35 by 28 feet. The library featured new bookcases, and cases for specimens were laid out in the middle of the room.[72] Cordier completed the library catalogue in 1872, listing over 1,300 standard works in Western languages, but not including 'the 1,023 Chinese volumes of Mr Wylie and the transactions of learned societies and periodical publications which form one of the most important parts of the library.'[73]

On the opening day it was announced that the Shanghai Library plans would be going ahead soon. An agreement was made whereby the NCBRAS would pay the cost of the building with the Shanghai Library being granted a ten-year free lease and a lease at an undisclosed nominal cost for a further ten years. A meeting of the Shanghai Library committee in late April 1873 reported that the building in the same style as the NCBRAS building was nearing completion. The building's eventual appearance left some members of the committee underwhelmed. Mr Alabaster regarded it as in 'bad taste' and in some way less than decent or respectable.[74] It was a matter of prestige that plagued the proceedings - not being on the Bund was inconceivable to some members. The library had been housed at the palatial Shanghai Club on the Bund since 1865, but the Society simply could not afford to pay the rent there.

The Library's secretary, Mr L. J. Mullins had to remind its subscribers that they did not have enough money for aesthetic details and 'after all the building was not the principal essential, but the books which were in it.' With a sense of déjà vu he also announced that a chess club connected with the library had been established.[75] The prospect of combining the library with the chess club in a new building including a public meeting and lecture room, called for in 1852, was in prospect again. The library was moved from the Shanghai Club to its new building (as stated above adjoining the NCBRAS building in December 1872 and opened in early 1873, by which time the chess club had disbanded, mainly on account of the unattractiveness of the new premises. Still discontent Mr Alabaster futilely called for a return to the Shanghai Club, 'or suitable accommodation in some more convenient location.'[76] Although the library was just a ten-minute walk from the Shanghai Club, its committee reported that many members found it 'anything but convenient to go to the other end of the Settlement, to the building whither it had now been removed' and decided to set up their own library instead.[77]

Inhibited by any opportunity to employ a skilled taxidermist, plans for a museum had been on hold until the Society secured the services of Mr Wong, former assistant to the famous missionary Father Armand David, on 25 March 1874. Mr W. B. Pryer was elected as honorary curator, and a team of 16 members was organised to oversee the development of various branches of the enterprise. Whilst the majority of those were related to natural history, a department of industry and products and one of archaeology and numismatics, administered by Wylie, was formed. The first exhibits featured a collection of ducks, 'just about all the obtainable ducks in the Shanghai district.[78] With the advent of the museum, the Society's original objectives were fully realised. with the Rev. Syle witnessing this accomplishment just before his posting to Yokohama as Consular Chaplain in the following month.[79]

OPENING NIGHT INVITATION

The North-China Herald recorded some details given by Thompson of the photographs of the Nakor Wat temple (present day Angkor Wat) he presented using a limelight projection lantern on 11 January 1872. Fortunately, hundreds of Thompson's photographs of China and

Figure 6: Entrance to the RAS Library and Museum

Asia are preserved at the Wellcome Library and many can be viewed online (https://wellcomelibrary.org/collections/digital-collections/john-thomson-photographs), though most of those of the temple I inspected did not bear accurate or expansive descriptions. However, I have, with some confidence, been able to match Thompson's descriptions in the newspaper to five photographs in the collection that were shown to the Society that evening.

JOHN THOMPSON'S PHOTOS OF THE BUND SHANGHAI BUND 1

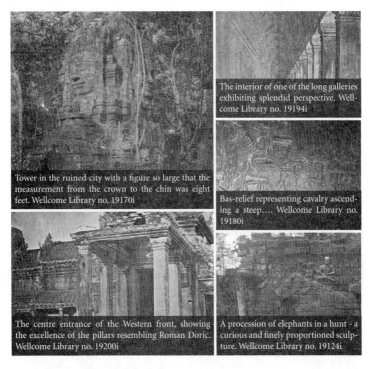

The Bund in 1869. At that time the NCBRAS rented premises in the Masonic Hall, completed in 1867 (the second building from the right on the waterfront). Appears in *Illustrations of China and its People*, London, 1874, Vol. III. Plate IV, 7. *Courtesy the Wellcome Collection.* https://wellcomelibrary.org/collections/digital-collections/john-thomson-photographs/ (accessed 16 April 2018)

The Bund in 1869. At that time the NCBRAS rented premises in the Masonic Hall, completed in 1867 (the second building from the right on the waterfront). Appears in *Illustrations of China and its People*, London, 1874, Vol. III. Plate IV, 7. Wellcome Library no. 19322i

BUND 2

Buildings of the Comptoir d'Escompte de Paris, the Masonic Hall in the centre and the Pustau & Co. building, with the memorial to the 'Ever-Victorious Army' in the foreground. Around 1871. Possibly taken on his visit to Shanghai when he talked to the Society. *Courtesy the Wellcome Collection.* https://wellcomelibrary.org/collections/digital-collections/john-thomson-photographs/ (accessed 16 April 2018).

Buildings of the Comptoir d'Escompte de Paris, the Masonic Hall in the centre and the Pustau & Co. building, with the memorial to the 'Ever-Victorious Army' in the foreground. Around 1871. Possibly taken on his visit to Shanghai when he talked to the Society. Wellcome Library no. 19320i

ABOUT THE AUTHOR

Peter Hibbard, historian and author, was president of the RAS China in Shanghai from 2007-2011.

———◇◇◇———

Endnotes

1 *North-China Herald*, 13 March 1873, p. 234.

2 For an early history of the library see *North-China Herald*, 13 March 1873, pp. 233-4.

3 *North-China Herald*, 27 November 1852, p. 66.

4 F. L. Hawks Pott, *A Short History of Shanghai* (Kelly & Walsh, Limited, Shanghai, 1928), p. 21.

5 *North-China Herald*, 3 May 1851, p. 159.

6 *North-China Herald*, 27 December 1851, p. 86.

7 C. A. Montalto de Jesus, *Historic Shanghai*, The Shanghai Mercury Limited, 1909, p. 102.

8 *North-China Herald* 19 July 1851, p. 202.

9 *North-China Herald*, 26 July 1851, p. 207.

10 *North-China Herald*, 26 June 1852, p. 190.

11 *North-China Herald*, 2 October 1852, p. 34.

12 Shanghai Municipal Archives, U1-1-155.

13 Ibid.

14 That sanctity would endure until 14 August 1937, when bombs fell in the International Settlement for the first time. See Paul French, *Bloody Saturday*, Penguin Books, 2017.

15 *North-China Herald*, 9 August 1856, p. 6.

16 *North-China Herald*, 20 September 1856, p. 30.

17 *North-China Herald*, 10 October 1857, p. 44.

18 *North-China Herald*, 1 August 1857, p. 2, reported a performance on the Hongkew Bund just after Wills Bridge across Suzhou Creek had just been built.

19 *North-China Herald*, 27 September 1856, p. 34.

20 *North-China Herald*, 3 April 1858, p. 143.

21 *North-China Herald*, 20 February 1858, p. 118

22 NCH, 21 January 1860, p. 11.

23 E. C. Bridgman inaugural address, in the *Journal of the Shanghai Literary and Scientific Society*, No. 1, June 1858, p. 13.

24 *North-China Herald*, 10 October 1858, p. 42.

25 An entry in Syle's journal dated 24 September 1857: 'I participated

in the formation of a Literary and Scientific Society, the effect of which I trust will be to keep up the tone of Christian cultivation in the community generally, both mercantile and missionary. In view even of present influence (to say nothing of the future), it is of great importance that all the means and appliances which distinguish our civilization from that of the Chinese, should be provided for those - especially the younger men - whose position here is apt to become an isolated one, and who are exposed to deteriorating influences on all hands.' *Journal of Rev E. Syle,* Syle Papers, Hagley Museum and Library, Wilmington DE. Found in *The Protestant Episcopal Church of the United States of America, in China and Japan, 1835-1870. With references to Anglican and Protestant Missions.* Ian Welch, Australia National University, 2013. Part 13, Shanghai and Japan, 1857, p. 1157.
https://openresearchrepository.anu.edu.au/bitstream/1885/11074/34/Welch_PEC2013_Pt13.pdf) (accessed16 April, 2018)

26 It is interesting to note that the establishment of some form of public art gallery was one of the first stated aims of the Society – one, despite many attempts, that was never fulfilled – see Peter Hibbard, More Than A Stuffed Bird Show - Showcasing the History of a Cultural Institution in *Time Traveler Album*, Rockbund Art Museum, 2012 and Unanswered Questions: Notes on the Life of Arthur de Carle Sowerby in the *Journal of the Royal Asiatic Society*, Vol. 74, No. 1, April 2010, pp. 22-31.

27 *Journal of the Shanghai Literary and Scientific Society,* No. 1, June 1858, pp. 12-13.

28 Proceedings, *Journal of the North China Branch of the Royal Asiatic Society*, Vol. 35, 1903/4, pp. iii-iv.

29 Despite failed attempts by the author in the past to locate Edkins letter, it and the original Constitution only recently surfaced as part of an overhaul of the RAS Archive in London. Many thanks to librarian Ed Weech and archivist Nancy Charley for their assistance.

Edkins's communication was accompanied by a copy of the rules and regulations of the Shanghai Society and the names of its officers,
Articles in the original Constitution included:
Art 1 The name of the Society shall be the "Shanghai Literary & Scientific Society": and its objects shall be,
1st The investigation of subjects concerned with the Empire of China

and the surrounding nations.

2nd The Publication of Papers in a Quarterly Journal

3rd The formation of a Library and Museum

Art 3 Officers. The Officers of this Society shall be – A President, Vice President, Treasurer, Three Directors, a Corresponding and a Recording Secretary, to be chosen annually by Ballot

Art 5 Meetings. Regular meetings shall be held on the third Tuesday evening of every month, at eight o'clock

By Laws

1. Publications

Sec 1 An editorial committee of three shall be appointed by the Council to superintend the publication of papers approved by the Council.

Sec 2 A Record of Occurrences in China shall be inserted in the Journal as well as Scientific tables & miscellaneous contributions, at the discretion of the Council

Sec 3 Twenty Five (crossed out) and Ten inserted above copies of each paper shall be placed at the disposal of the author as soon as printed.

Sec 4 Each Resident & Corresponding Member shall be entitled to a copy of the journal, any remaining copies of which may be sold to the public at One Tael a number.

2. Library and Museum

1 Gifts of book suited to the nature of the Society and objects of Scientific & Literary interest shall be accepted and preserved for the use of members.

2 Chinese and foreign works can be purchased at the discretion of the Council. Copies of important monumental inscriptions may also be procured, in like manner.

30 *Proceedings of the Royal Asiatic Society of Great Britain and Ireland*, 1858, p. ix.

31 For those wishing to look at concise histories of the NCBRAS this and other accounts, celebrating anniversaries, are found in the Society's Journal. Edkins address and another account by Henri Cordier are printed in Volume 35 (1903/04). The account of the 50th anniversary, which was purportedly published in the journal in 1907 does not appear in copies held in Shanghai or in London

– but a short account can be found in the *North-China Herald*, 18 October 1907, pp. 138-39. The last account, drawing heavily on Edkins account, by Isaac Mason was published in Volume 59, 1928. The first retrospective account by Old Mortality, Henri Cordier's nom de plume, was printed in the *North-China Herald*, 30 October 1873, pp. 361-2. Cordier was fortunate to have recourse to the original minute books to maintain accuracy, as not all of the Society's activities were documented in its journals, apart from those at Annual General Meetings. Mason noted in 1927 that the minute books and records, 'apart from a very few have been lost.' The *North-China Herald* printed substantive reports of its regular meetings detailing papers delivered, as well as details on the activities and development of the Society itself.

32 *North-China Herald*, 25 September 1858, p. 31.

33 *North-China Herald*, 30 October 1858, p. 50.

34 *North-China Herald*, 1 January 1859, p. 86.

35 *Syle Journal*, op. cit., 1 January 1860.

36 *Syle Journal*, op. cit., 30 October 1857.

37 *North-China Herald*, 16 January 1858, p. 98. NCH 29 January 1859, p. 102.

38 *North-China Herald*, 25 December 1858, p. 82.

39 *North-China Herald*, 30 October 1873, p. 361-2.

40 *North-China Herald*, 20 March 1858, p. 135.

41 *North-China Herald*, 23 April 1859, p. 150; *North-China Herald* 1 October 1859, p. 35 and *North-China Herald*, 29 September 1860 p. 154.

42 *North-China Herald*, 11 August 1860, p.126. Such criticisms of the Society's work continued throughout its career as it fought to keep pace with Shanghai's development and rapidly changing tastes and preferences.

43 The Society's four journals can be downloaded as one pdf document from the Haiti Trust Digital Library website: https://babel.hathitrust.org/cgi/pt?id=mdp.39015027916397;view=1up;seq=1

44 *North-China Herald*, 19 January 1861, p. 10.

45 *North-China Herald*, 2 March 1861, p. 35.

46 *North-China Herald*, 19 October 1861, p. 167.

47 *North-China Herald*, 26 October 1861, p. 170.

48 *North-China Herald*, 24 August 1861, p. 135.

49 *North-China Herald*, 19 October 1861, p. 167.

50 Ibid.

51 Although the original constitution stipulated the quarterly production of a journal, this was changed following its reincarnation as the NCBRAS at a meeting on 26 October 1858, to it 'will not take a quarterly form, but be published whenever sufficient papers and funds are at command. It was now hoped that it should appear at least once a quarter.' NCH, 30 October 1858, p. 50.

52 Medhurst, a British diplomat, was the son of his namesake father of the London Missionary Society who had worked with Bridgman, Edkins and Williams in the past. He later became the British Consul and presided over the Society for the first time in 1869. Even though his election was recorded at the time, retrospective historical accounts assume that Meadows was still president.

53 For an approachable account of these events see J. S. Gregory, *Great Britain and the Taipings*, The St Ann's Press, 1969.

54 Ibid.

55 *North-China Herald*, 1 April 1865, pp. 50-1.

56 Fortunately from 1864 on the Society's new journal published 'Proceedings' of its activities, informing its membership of developments and it is from these that the ensuing succinct account of the how its objectives were fulfilled is largely based.

57 Summary of Proceedings in *Journal of the NCBRAS*, New Series, Volume 1, 1864 p.175

58 Isaac Mason, *Three Score Years and Ten*, *Journal of the NCBRAS*,Volume 59, 1928, pp. 5-6

59 *North-China Herald* 17 June 1865, p. 94

60 *Journal of the NCBRAS*, New Series, Volume 3, 1866, p. 4

61 The building, which stood on the site that The Peninsula Shanghai currently occupies was demolished in 1927 - around 50 metres away from where the RAS China Library is housed today.

62 See Peter Hibbard *The Bund Shanghai, China Faces West,* Odyssey Books and Guides, Hong Kong, 2007. The plot of land was originally part of an extensive British Consulate site that was auctioned off in 1862, bounded by a ditch that became Gnaomen Road. The road name was changed to Upper Yuenmingyuen Road around 1873 and renamed with deference to the Society as Museum Road in 1886. Today it is known as Huqiu Road and the Society's second building opened in 1933 still stands there, currently in use as the

Rockbund Art Museum.

63 For an account of Wylie's life, see Ian Gow, The Scottish Shanghailander Alexander Wylie (1815-1887): Missionary, Man of Letters, Mathematician, *Journal of the Royal Asiatic Society China*, Vol. 75. No 1, April 2013, pp. 77-102.

64 *North-China Herald*, 13 April 1869, p. 186.

65 Report of the Council, *Journal of the NCBRAS*, New Series, Vol.6, 1869 &1870, p. x.

66 Henri Cordier, letter to NCBRAS, 8 August, 1902 in Proceedings, *Journal of the NCBRAS*, Vol. 35, 1903 &1904, p. x.

67 'Isaac Mason, 'Three Score Years and Ten,' *Journal of the NCBRAS*, Vol. 59, 1928, p. 8.

68 *North-China Herald*, 18 January 1872, p. 40.

69 Cordier in his 1902 historical account, op. cit., said a prospectus was issued by the Council as late as 1 June 1871 making a public appeal for funds.

70 Agreed at a meeting on May 23[rd,] 1871, NCH, 26 May 1871, p. 374. In fact it wasn't until January 1882 that an embryonic reincarnation of the Society met there - the Shanghai Young Men's Institute (NCH, January 1882, p. 77), later becoming the Shanghai Literary and Debating Society in June 1883 (NCH, 15 June 1883, p. 675.)

71 *North-China Herald*, 18 January 1872, p. 39-40.

72 Henri Cordier in the Preface to the *NCBRAS Library Catalogue*, 1872.

73 For an overview of the history of the library see Harold M. Otness, 'The One Bright Spot in Shanghai', A History of the Library of the North China Branch of the Royal Asiatic Society, *Journal of the Hong Kong Branch of the Royal Asiatic Society*, Vol. 28, 1988, pp. 185-197. http://hkjo.lib.hku.hk/archive/files/b151ef206a1d384b-0689036e145c12d6.pdf

74 *North-China Herald*, 4 April 1872, p.307)

75 *North-China Herald*, 20 April 1872, pp. 307.

76 *North-China Herald*, 20 March 1873, pp. 251-2.

77 *North-China Herald*, 6 March 1873, p. 207.

78 Report of the Council, *Journal of the NCBRAS*, Vol. 9, 1874, pp. xi-xii.

79 *North-China Herald*, 20 April 1872, p. 299 and *North-China Herald*, 4 May 1872, p. 342.

DEFYING TRADITION:

Eliza Bridgman, Foreign Feminist And The Awakening Of Women In China

BY DAVID F. BRIDGMAN

ABSTRACT

'At the beginning of the century education was the right of none, the privilege of few. With rare exceptions, woman accepted as a matter of course her position as the drudge or the toy of men.'[1]

In 1845, feminism was still in its infancy in America and England. Nevertheless, for the first time, unmarried women defied tradition to enter China against cultural norms as pioneer missionaries with a compelling call to teach girls to read and write. Mary Ann Aldersey 艾迪綏 (1797-1868) of London was the first Christian missionary single woman to serve in China. She founded a school for girls about 1843 in Ningbo, Zhejiang. Aldersey was followed by Eliza Jane Gillett 贝满夫人 (1805-1871) from Massachusetts who arrived in Canton in 1845. Later that year, Gillett married Elijah Coleman Bridgman and the couple adopted two young Chinese girls, whom they took with them to Shanghai in 1847. She subsequently opened the first school for girls in Shanghai in 1850 and another one in Beijing in 1864, which survived nationalization following China's revolution of 1949 to thrive today as top-tier secondary school to honour their founder. This article presents the consequences of these humble efforts that merits serious study not only for scholars of Asian studies but anyone interested in the topic of social change.

"Woman is sitting in darkness, without love to shelter her head, or hope to illumine her solitude, because the heaven born instincts ... having been stifled by social necessities, now burn sullenly to waste, like sepulchral lamps amongst the ancients."[2]

—Elijah Coleman Bridgman

"In China, as in other countries, woman's influence is immense. It is so in the family, and in the state, in morals and in religion. But what God has ordained for the best and noblest of purposes, is in China exercised for evil."[3]
—Eliza Gillett Bridgman

INTRODUCTION

In 1907, a large assembly of missionaries to China gathered in Shanghai to celebrate the centennial of Protestant missionary endeavors in China. Papers and memorials were read, and resolutions were adopted. One of the most significant reports concerned educational work for Chinese women, delivered by Luella Miner of Beijing, chairperson of the special committee. Miner had worked on behalf of women's education and became Eliza Jane Gillett Bridgman's successor. Miner took the remnants of Bridgman's Academy for girls in Beijing (first established in 1864) and reopened and rebuilt it after it had been demolished during the Boxer Rebellion to guide its expansion until it became the Women's College of Yenching University.

The introduction to Luella Miner's report provides an illuminating assessment of the status of women in China at the time:

When the history of the twentieth century is written, and the historian selects from every country its most epoch-making events, and notes for every race its marked tokens of progress, for this first decade of the century he will record nothing more marvelous than the awakening of the women of China. At the beginning of the century education was the right of none, the privilege of few. With rare exceptions, women accepted as a matter of course her position as the drudge or the toy of man. If a girl studied the few books generally prepared for her, she learned that from infancy to old age three chains would hold her in thralldom, first obedience to father, then obedience to husband, and obedience to her own son, and that unhappy was the lot of the woman for whom Providence did not supply the proper masters. 'For a woman to be without ability is her virtue', said the wise men, hugging to their own bosoms the treasures of learning, rejoicing that the crippled feet of their wives and sisters kept them from travelling in some dangerous but, to themselves, very delightful paths of knowledge and experience. Now and then a woman burst the chains, seized the treasures of learning, tasted the fruits of power, and was enrolled among the rulers, the poets, or the heroes of China, but did she not too often prove the converse of the proverb of the wise men by sacrificing virtue to knowledge or fame?[4]

Following the 'storm and agony' caused by the Boxer Rebellion and its aftermath, the outpouring of anti-foreign resentment and the awakening of many minds to the progress and developments occurring in the rest of the world, Chinese women sought to lay off their shackles. Even fathers, husbands and brothers began to say, 'Take the bandages from the feet of our women, and the veils from their eyes, let them be our companions, let them be fitted to fill their duties as wives and mothers, for in the home lies the roots of the empire. How can a nation be intelligent and prosperous when half of its people are ignorant and oppressed?'[5]

BACKGROUND

The nineteenth and early twentieth centuries were scarred by many events. A brief review of these key events in the history of China during the period of 1845 to 1910 provides the context for this article. The Bridgmans lived in Canton (Guangzhou) only briefly before Shanghai was opened from the 'Unequal Treaties' and the establishment of the treaty ports along China's eastern coast. With Macau, Canton was the only city open to foreigners and foreign

Figure 1: Eliza Gillett Bridgman, part of historical display, Shanghai Huangpu School
Credit: Shanghai Huangpu School

Figure 2: Mary Ann Aldersey.
Credit: http://bdcconline.net/en/stories/aldersey-mary-ann

trade until the end of the First Opium War in 1842. Canton was the principle venue for the work of Robert Morrison from England in 1807 and Elijah Bridgman in 1830.[6]

In 1832, the British East India Company had explored Shanghai and the Yangtze River as a potential trading center for tea, silk, and opium, but was rebuffed by local officials. The British then imposed on the Chinese the import of opium (produced in British India) waging the First Opium War between 1839 and 1842. The Qing military forces proved no match for the British. The war finally ended with the Treaty of Nanking, and Shanghai was one of five Chinese cities to be opened up to British consuls, merchants, and their families. Soon settlers from France, the USA, Germany and other foreign nations began to move into Shanghai, carving out for themselves sovereign 'concessions' where they were not subject to Chinese laws, establishing their autonomous territories.

With the opening of the Treaty Ports, Shanghai, which had been little more than a fishing village, now emerged as a major center for foreign interests. The American Board of Commissioners for Foreign Missions (ABCFM) also relocated much of its operations to Shanghai, and the Bridgmans moved on June 4. 1847. Michael Lazich notes that 'Bridgman could not possibly have imagined how quickly this relatively undistinguished Chinese city on the delta of the Yangzi River would emerge as China's major coastal metropolis – nor could [they] have guessed that Shanghai would remain [their] home and the focal point of [their] labors for the remainder of [their] life.'[7]

An understanding of the Opium War and the Unequal Treaties is an essential element that informs the historic, economic and moral conditions, which the early pioneers of Christian missions faced. One American denomination singled out the opium trade as the principal obstacle to missionary endeavors, which included the establishment of schools:

The contraband trade of opium, is at this time the greatest barrier of the Gospel in China. ... What a spectacle is presented here! The government of a nation not possessing the Bible, and unblessed by the light of the Gospel, laboring to protect their people from a moral pestilence, which is carrying dismay and poverty and wretchedness through the land ... and the merchants of other governments, nominally Christian, employing ships and capital and bribes to force that very evil upon them.[8]

Additionally, as stated by G. Thompson Brown:
Problems began with the rapid expansion of trade through the port of Canton, which outgrew the merchant guild system. Exports from China, principally tea and silk, were of great demand in the West. Indian cotton was needed in China for its infant textile industry and the trade was mutually beneficial. All went well until China's domestically grown cotton began to take care of its needs. What could now be used for import into China to pay for silk and tea? British merchants came up with an ideal product – readily available in India, easily transportable, in great demand in China, and – enormously profitable: opium![9]

The imperial government took frequent steps to outlaw the trade but with little success. Open importation appeared to increase after the 1842 Treaty of Nanking. The link between foreign exploitation and the arrival of missionaries is a key to understanding the anti-foreign resentment, including the antagonism by the Chinese to Christianity as a foreign religion. This strong sentiment was no doubt one more factor that inhibited Eliza Bridgman's efforts to introduce education for girls to China where she experienced opposition with chants 'foreign devil (洋鬼子)' in Canton and Shanghai. (The author vividly recalls his own experience hearing these same words as a child when traveling through the countryside.)

EDUCATION AND THE STATUS OF WOMEN IN CHINA
Wong Yin Lee writes:
It was only towards the end of the Qing Dynasty (1644-

1911) that new girls' schools were established by the imperial reforms in China. This development caused a profound social change. Prior to this period, the aim of women's education was limited to teaching social ethics and family tradition with emphasis on how to behave as a virtuous wife and good mother. In the present education system, it can be said that there is equal opportunity for men and women, and that the aim of women's education goes beyond the traditional function.[10]

Margaret Ernestine Burton, in her book *The Education of Women in China*, states 'Probably no nation of the world has ever reverenced education more profoundly than has China. "Education is the highest pursuit a man can follow" is a favourite maxim, and the genuineness of the people's belief in this statement is the respect everywhere accorded to the educated man.'[11] One's highest achievement came from passing the annual civil examination to receive the coveted degree, which entitled one to become an elite member as a court official. The examination was democratic, because it was open to all men, not just the wealthy class, yet it was not open to women.

According to Chester Holcombe in *The Real Chinese Question*:

[Men] originate, shape and control public opinion. It would be difficult to overstate the respect in which they are held and the deference shown them everywhere and by all classes. They are the unofficial judges, the arbitrators in village or family differences, the disseminators of public news and commentators upon it, the authority in matters of etiquette and propriety, the leaders in feasts and amusement, the censors of morals, the writers and readers of letters for the illiterate, the teachers of the village schools. They draw contracts, business agreements of all sorts, and petitions to the authorities. They are the leaders of thought and action.[12]

All these privileges were for the man's world, from which women were excluded. It is not that the subject of women's education was neglected altogether. But it so radically differed in both content, quality, and goal. The earliest book about woman's education in

Chinese was written by Lady Tsao, over 1800 years ago as *Nu Ke (奴课)* or Rules for Women. She wrote 'The virtue of a female does not consist altogether in extraordinary abilities or intelligence, but in being modestly grave and inviolable chaste, observing the requirements of virtuous widowhood, and in being tidy in her person and everything about her; in whatever she does to be unassuming, and whenever she moves or sits, to be decorous. This is female virtue.' [13]

Five hundred years before Lady Tsao, Confucius wrote 'Women are as different from men as earth is from heaven... Women indeed are human beings, but they are of a lower state than men and can never attain to full equality with them. The aim of female education therefore is perfect submission, not cultivation and development of the mind.' [14] Women's status took a further setback during Song Dynasty (960-1279) as Confucian ideology prevailed. [15] Lü Kun 呂坤 (1536-1618), a Neo-Confucian scholar of the Ming Dynasty said 'Few people teach their daughters to read and write nowadays for fear that they might become over ambitious.' [16]

Margaret Burton in her book *The Education of Women in China* in 1911 writes:

> At this time, moreover, the Chinese were not simply indifferent, but often strenuously opposed to the education of their daughter. Some of the literary men, it is true, considered it benefitting their daughters' station to have some smattering of knowledge of music, poetry, the classics and the like, but they were a very small proportion of the nation. Whatever theories her literature might contain, China as a whole saw no value in women's education and was strongly suspicious that its effect on women would be undesirable.' [17]

It was not until 1895 that the issue of establishing girls' schools was seriously discussed and only in the late 1920s were girls officially enrolled at Beijing University. [18]

Wong Yin Lee in her article for the Women's History Review writes:

> People of the Ming Dynasty (1368-1644) abhorred the thought of women reading and writing since female literacy had always been associated with the idea of moral

corruption in women. This was because of the fact that courtesans and female singers, who were looked upon virtually as prostitutes, had mainly come from the rank of literate women.[19]

The campaign for women's education in China began between 1894 and 1898 occurred during the same time as the fight to end the practice of foot-binding.[20]

Now all of this pertains to the status of women who belonged to the higher classes. For them, life was segregated and confined to the inner courts of the Chinese home, from which women could not easily venture out. The inner chambers may be sumptuously furnished and decorated with its own courtyard and garden. But within this world they remained as if prisoners. There may be fine suites and accommodations for the wives and concubines, for the children, and even for the servants who attended them. But it was a segregated world of women, into which only the husband could enter, and from which the male children were removed at an appropriate age, not to return.

A woman's life consisted of simple domestic tasks, of her toilette, of needle work, and entertainment.[21] On a harsher level, her feet were bound, a terribly painful ordeal, with daily changes of the bandages and massaging of the tortured appendages. Walking and standing were awkward and painful, and added to the severity of her crippling confinement. Still she was expected to move with grace and dignity. The first recorded foot binding occurred in the 10th century. According to the story, an emperor had a favorite concubine, a dancer who built a gilded stage in the shape of a lotus flower. She bound her feet into a hoof-like shape and danced on the lotus. Foot binding started with the royal court and then spread throughout China. In the 12th century, foot binding had become much more widespread, and by the early Qing Dynasty (in the mid-17th century), every girl who wished to marry had her feet bound. [22]

The status of the poor and the peasant women of the rural classes was even worse. She lacked the amenities of a fine home and luxury in either clothing or accommodation. Certainly, any form of literacy was completely absent.

The whole Chinese system of ethics required females to be so secluded that their opportunities of meeting or engaging with foreign ladies were rare. When they did meet, however, their address was singularly confiding and affectionate, and they entered conversation with sprightliness and vivacity.[23] But what did they talk about? Your age; the number of your children; your ornaments; the style of your dress; and your large feet.[24]

PIONEER WOMEN MISSIONARIES TO CHINA

Robert Pierce Beaver, author of *American Protestant Women in World Mission: A History of the First Feminist Movement in North America* has written a definitive work on this theme in 1968. British single women were the first arrivals. The Society for Promoting Female Education in the East sent one of its original members, Mary Jane Aldersey 艾迪綏 (1797 – 1868), the first Christian missionary single woman to serve in China proper.[25]

In 1837 Aldersey went to Surabaya, Indonesia, where she started a school for Chinese girls, [26] then transferred to Singapore, then Hong Kong and finally to Ningbo in 1843, where she opened a school for girls.

In 1845, Eliza Jane Gillett was the first unmarried American woman to arrive in China, commissioned by the Protestant Episcopal Church in the United States. She never reached her assigned post, but was married that same year to Elijah Coleman Bridgman, the first American Protestant Missionary to China. She transferred from the Episcopal mission to his mission, the American Board of Commissioners for Foreign Missions.

Her arrival as an unmarried woman seems to have been forgotten due to her marriage that occurred so soon, and as such Lydia Fay, an Episcopalian, became designated as the first single American woman missionary to China. Fay opened a school for boys in Shanghai, which ultimately developed into St. John's College, and then St. John's University.

Mission Boards and Societies were reluctant to employ single unmarried women and to give them freedom as to where they lived, or to permit any work beyond educational activities. Once having commissioned them, however, they did not seek to bind them to celibacy.

Eliza Gillett's assignment was to be a teacher. Her vision was to teach girls to read, and to advance the cause of women's education in China. This is the world into which Eliza Jane Gillett entered when she disembarked from her ship the *Horatio* that April 1845, in Canton,

China.

The life and times of Eliza Jane Gillett

Eliza Jane was born at Derby, Connecticut on 6 May 1805, the youngest of the nine children of Canfield and Hannah Gillett. Her father, of French Huguenot descent, was a prosperous merchant. He died when Eliza was ten years old. Her mother and the young girls moved to New Haven. There she completed her education in a boarding school, graduating at the age of sixteen. She had been baptized in St. James's Episcopal Church in Derby as an infant. She was confirmed in Trinity Episcopal Church, New Haven in 1821, following a profound personal experience at a revival. For two years she stayed on as an assistant teacher in the school where she had studied.

Two years later with her mother, Eliza moved to New York where one of her sisters was living. Young Eliza continued her teaching career, and at age twenty-two became the principal of an unnamed boarding school for girls. She held that post for seventeen years. After becoming a member of St. George's Episcopal Church in New York, she was persuaded to teach a Bible Class for the church school for many years. Dr. James Milnor, the influential rector, treated her as a daughter.

After reading the 1811 publication of *Christian Researches in Asia* by Claudius Buchanan, a sense of missionary vocation was born that was further stimulated by other readings and her participation in a farewell party for the second group of missionaries going to the Hawaiian Islands. Dr. Milnor was a leading member of the Foreign Committee of the Board of Missions of the Protestant Episcopal Church, serving as its first secretary. His influence prompted an increasing sense of Eliza's own vocation as a missionary.

About this time the Episcopal Church organized its China Mission, begun in 1836. The Rev. William J. Boone was consecrated as the missionary bishop, and began to recruit a staff of new missionaries, including three single female teachers, of which Eliza Gillett was one. She was appointed Nov. 14, 1843. The party of new appointees sailed from New York in the ship *Horatio*.[27]

In her own words Eliza Gillett describes that emotional, pivotal departure for China:

It was the last day of the week, the 14th of December 1844, a cold and frosty morning, when a company of missionaries were to take their last adieu, and for four months, or more, have a home upon the ocean's waste. The call from the land of Sinim had been heard and responded to. ...

Collected in the cabin for the concluding services were two, who 'shone in my heart's depths,' that accompanied me to the ship, – a sister dear to whom I clung, and that venerated pastor whose 'praise is in all the churches.' With these my history was deeply interwoven; I felt I had their approbation in going to China. For years, no sorrow or joy had been mine which they had not shared. Others there were whom I loved dearly and tenderly, and from whom I could not separate without a pang; but these two were associated with me in hours of affliction and bereavement, in all that makes life precious and responsible. ...

The venerable pastor, whose head was whitened with the snows of seventy winters, stood in our midst. With a countenance always beaming with benevolence, and uplifted hands, he invoked the divine protection and care; a hymn was sung; and then the grasping hand – the last farewell – and the steamer (the tug boat tender guiding their ship through the channels and out to open waters) was plowing her way back to the city. ...

I ran to the stern of the Horatio. I still discerned my venerable pastor straining his eye and waving his handkerchief; it was the last look of my mortal gaze upon the beloved Dr. Milnor.

After a voyage of one hundred and thirty-one days, a good part occupied in the study of the Chinese language, we arrived at Hong Kong, April 24th. Our large company were hospitably entertained, for some days, by the different missionary families and that of the English chaplain in Victoria.[28]

It had been a long and arduous journey from New York, and it was in May 1845 that Eilza, in company with other missionaries, made her first visit to Canton. They were confined to a small district in which were located the foreign factories, their places of business and trade, and their residences. Perhaps the most visible and influential of these factories was that of the East India Company, notorious for its trafficking in opium brought from Bombay to sell in China although not all merchants supported or encouraged such commerce. One of these was an American, D. W. C. Olyphant, who provided not only passage on his ships but residence for a growing number of missionaries. Olyphant was in effect the patron for Elijah Coleman Bridgman in 1830. Olyphant had enjoyed a close relationship since 1820 with Robert Morrison, and his firm was known for its avoidance of the opium trade.[29]

Eliza Gillett, having just arrived in Canton in mid-May, was afforded her first glimpse into a Chinese home through the kindness of Dr and Mrs Peter Parker in June 1845. The visit described here took place just before her marriage to Dr Elijah C. Bridgman.[30] Eliza wanted to learn as much as possible by studying the character of the people among whom she hoped to find a permanent home. Thanks to the Parkers, opportunities were not lacking. While a visit to Dr Parker's hospital provided an impact, it was the people she wished to study, and it was the condition of the Chinese women that most interested her. She tells of her first visit to meet Chinese ladies who were confined according to the rigid classic tradition to the 'inner apartments' of their homes. No such visit was possible until strict forms of etiquette were carefully observed. These included sending several successive messengers to carry their request the day before the visit.

On Friday, 3 June, Eliza together with Dr and Mrs Parker, the Carrs of Hong Kong and some English gentlemen set out for the home of Mrs Pwan, the lady of Pwan Tingkwa, a wealthy salt merchant. Pwan Tingkwa was employed in the services of the government. He had ten wives. Traveling by sedan chairs they arrived at the home. The gate was opened, and the men and women separated, going to different apartments except for Dr Parker who acted as interpreter for the ladies. It is noteworthy that Dr Parker was admitted into the women's quarters, contrary to proper etiquette. Perhaps his fluency and his relationship to Pwan Tingkwa afforded this rare exception. Parker was present only for the initial introductions, and then retired to rejoin the men. The room was filled with about thirty women and girls including nurses, maids and older women. At the sight of the foreign guests, these women began at once to examine every part of their attire, commenting on it all including their complexion. As Eliza writes 'This was done without the least thought of being impolite.'[31]

The apartments were elegantly furnished and with baskets of flowers suspended from the ceiling, each apartment opening onto a court or a garden. At length Mrs. Pwan entered. Miss Gillett wrote in her journal:

> She was a beautiful young creature, not over twenty-one years of age. … A repast was prepared, consisting of jellies, fruits, nuts, etc., which in the East is called Tiffin; the Chinese call it 'a bit for the heart.' It was easy to distinguish the lady of the house: she moved us to be seated, while she presided, the others standing, and the servants fanning us while we partook of the delicacies. Mrs. Pwan passed some fruit or jelly on her fork or with her chop-sticks to each lady, and we would return the compliment, she, rising very gracefully and receiving it; they even go so far as to put it into your mouth.
>
> Her private bed-room was furnished with a mirror, bureau, bedstead with mattress, the bed-clothes neatly laid in folds, and put aside in the back part of the bed. We followed Mrs. Pwan, all the attendants accompanying us, through the different apartments of this spacious building, still unfinished. The carving was elegant. The rooms were furnished with divans, centre-tables, mirrors, and chandeliers. The ceilings were beautifully painted with

Figure 3: 1937 site of Bridgman Academy, Shanghai, photo from historcal display
Credit: Shanghai Huangpu School

birds and flowers. A gallery was appropriated to the 'Sing-song' (theatre).[32]

Eliza then adds 'I could not learn that one on Pwan Tingkwa's household knew how to read.' It was some months later she learned of the death of Mrs. Pwan, and that her husband was never pleased with her. Mr. Pwan, when asked how he passed his time, replied: his wives were all over his house, and he amused himself with them.

When Eliza arrived in Canton, accommodation was arranged for her and another couple by Bishop Boone in the home of Elijah Bridgman. Bridgman was single but had recently given up his intention to remain celibate. He had been praying for God to present him with a suitable bride. The arrival of Eliza Jane was interpreted by him as God's providential answer. He proposed, she accepted, and the couple were married in the colonial chapel by the resident chaplain on 28 June 1845, less than two months after her arrival in Canton. She was forty years of age, and he was forty-four.

Eliza had come to China under appointment as an unmarried female, to be a teacher of Chinese girls, and it seems the committee of the Domestic and Foreign Missionary Society assumed she was to remain single. But even though at the time of her commissioning she had no thoughts of marriage, and had attained the age of forty, she reacted 'with spirit' against what she felt to be the arbitrary restriction of both her personal freedom and her Christian liberty. The Bishop may have considered her commissioning as her taking a vow to become a part of a missionary order. A further issue of concern, Elijah Bridgman served under the American Board of Commissioners for Foreign Missions, not the Foreign Missionary Society of the Protestant Episcopal Church.

Nevertheless, upon Eliza's marriage to Bridgman, Bishop Boone 'lost his head' out of pique over the loss of this promising recruit. He charged her with a 'breach of contract with the great Head of the Church.' She held firm. She reminded the Bishop that she had 'explicitly refused to promise to maintain celibacy and had not bound herself by a monastic vow.' After all, it was the Bishop himself who made the arrangement for her to meet Dr. Bridgman, and to be lodged along with the other new missionary couple at Dr. Bridgman's home. As far as she was concerned, her marriage to Bridgman did not hinder her original calling at all, but rather was an advantage to her work's

Figure 4: The Bridgman Girls School classroom at Wangka-Moda.
Credit:Eliza Bridgman, Daughters of China

success. She refused to accept that she had violated her covenant with God.[33]

Becoming now the wife of the senior and respected American missionary in China, she had her relationship transferred from the Episcopal Missionary Society to the American Board of Commissioners for Foreign Missions, with whom she remained until her death. Her church membership was changed to Congregational from Episcopalian and Bishop Boone soon got over his annoyance since he and Bridgman were friends.[34]

In 1847, the Bridgmans relocated to Shanghai, bringing their two adopted young ten-year-old girls, Ah-yee and A-lan with them from Canton.[35] The girl on the frontispiece of Eliza Bridgman's book, *Daughters of China* is Jin Mei ("Golden Sister"), the twelve-year-old Chinese who was the first girl to enroll in Shanghai joining Ah-yee and Al-lan at the day school initiated by Eliza. Soon other Chinese girls were recruited from the neighborhood as a nucleus of a small girls' day school.[36] The Bridgmans found a larger home from which to begin a boarding school. In 1850, Eliza opened her boarding school for girls located in the Wongka Moda, at the site of the Episcopal Mission in the southeast of Shanghai with a capacity for fifty students.[37]

Shanghai and the bridgman female school

The two young Chinese girls (Ah-yee[38], and A-lan[39]) adopted in Canton and brought to Shanghai, together with Jin Mei, were the nucleus of a school which was established as a boarding school in 1850, Bridgman Female School (裨文女塾). Funding for the school was provided through their mission agency, but Eliza also supplemented from her own resources. This allowed pupils to enter without cost to their families.

In his report for the American Board of 15 April 1851, Elijah Bridgman gave a brief survey of the school during the first year of its existence:

> As no mission school for Girls has been established in this city, and as no specific instructions had been given us, for opening such a one, I would premise that, in what has been undertaken and accomplished, on the score of female education, we have had in view two distinct objects. To do all the good we possibly could, to the people immediately around us, with the means at our disposal, was our first and principal object; our second was, to ascertain what, hereafter, might be practicable, in this important department of missionary labor.
>
> The establishment of the school was an experiment, -- a simple process, to ascertain from actual trial, what could be done, and what safely anticipated for future enterprise.
>
> The results of the experiment, thus far, are such, I am sure, as will meet approbation. ...
>
> A better field than this could hardly be desired. Thousands of families are accessible, within a few minutes' walk of our door, chiefly of the middling and lower classes – the industrious working people. ... In the whole of these suburbs, comprising 60,000 or more inhabitants, there is only one protestant mission family, and that is our own.
>
> *Opening of the school.* To prepare the way for the long-desired work, Mrs. Bridgman accompanied by the two little Canton pupils, commenced visiting the neighboring families, going from house to house, making known to them the project designed for the benefit of their children, and inviting all who pleased to send their daughters.[40]

Bridgman's report is lengthy and includes many details regarding how it began as day school, then adding a boarding school in September

Figure 5: 7. This photograph is part of a visual display of the school's history now located in the lobby of the new "Shanghai Huangpu School"
Credit: Shanghai Huangpu School.

1850, with twelve students. The total number of children enrolled was not less than forty. The report gives the terms of admission, the character of the pupils, discipline, course of instruction, and superintendence. A married Chinese woman with two children of her own was engaged as a helper for Mrs Bridgman.[41]

The school has had a continuous existence and is known today as the Shanghai Huangpu School, a coeducational government school since 1951.[42] The Shanghai Huangpu School is now located in spacious facilities adjacent to the OB/GYN Hospital of Fudan University near what used to be the 'Old City' of Shanghai. In fact, the school has always remained in this vicinity, though changing sites seven times between 1926 and 2003. The school was nationalized in 1951.

Eliza directed the Bridgman Female School for twelve years until her husband's death in 1862 when she turned it over to the Presbyterian Mission. After seventeen years of marriage, when Eliza returned to the United States after her husband's death, her school was absorbed into the Presbyterian Girl's School (opened in 1855) and continued to operate until the 1951 transition following the Liberation under the new Chinese Communist government in 1949 and was nationalized in 1951 as the Shanghai City Number Nine Female Middle School. In the year 2000, the school celebrated its 150th anniversary. It relocated to its current site in 2003, changing its name to the Shanghai City Huangpu School. There is a historical display of the school's many iterations at this location.

One noteworthy alumna of the Bridgman School is Madame Soong (Ni Guizhen倪桂珍), the wife of Charlie Soong (宋嘉樹) and mother of the Soong sisters: Soong Ai-ling (the wife of K. H. Kung), Soong Qing-ling (wife of Sun Yat-sen), and Soong Meiling (wife of Chiang Kai-shek). Madame Soong would have attended the Bridgman school sometime between 1875 and 1884.

The school was in operation after the War and has remained so since. After Liberation, the Bridgman name was no longer used. An alternate name was Blessing Girl's School (榀荸荸)女塾).

My visit to the Shanghai Huangpu School in November 2017 (I had made an earlier visit in November 2010) gave me a fuller picture of the school as it is today. The current principal, Qian Hong, has served for only fifteen months. She brings a strong vision for the school, its mission, and its function as a major contributor to this urban community, including one of China's top medical centers, the OB/GYN Hospital of Fudan University.

The Shanghai Huangpu School, now co-educational, has 130 teachers and 850 students enrolled in grades 1-9. Occupying a state-of-the-art campus, it continues to expand. An institution striving for excellence, athletics is now pursued. The soccer coach was brought in from Spain. I visited their archives, with many early photographs and documents, and a copy of the 1936 school yearbook, much of which we were permitted to photograph.

Figure 6: Current site Shanghai Huangpu School. Built 2003.
The School continues to be enlarged.
Credit: David Bridgman

Figure 7: These images are photographic copies made from the annual, by Bridgman. Credit: Shanghai Huangpu School archives

The school is near the location of the old walled city whose wall was demolished in 1912, and most of the old city has submitted to the destruction of urban renewal, now replaced with replicas of old style shops, the Yu Garden, restaurants, a rebuilt Confucian temple and other structures. During our 2010 visit, we were taken to see several of the former school sites or what remains of them. A tree had been planted by Eliza Bridgman at the original site, and has been preserved as an historic remnant, but unfortunately, we were unable to find it in 2017. The school houses a photo display giving a visual history of the schools past, with many evidences of its founder, who we were told wrote the school song (words and music) still used today. Principal Qian was accompanied by Huang Ying, director of 'moral education' and a science teacher who has been teaching there for 21 years and is fluently bilingual.

An interesting detail emerges as to Eliza Bridgman's connection with Shanghai and schools for girls about nine years after her death in 1872. It was a bequest she had left for a further school for girls in Shanghai housed in premises known as 'Bridgman Home.' The story begins in 1860 when the Woman's Union Missionary Society of America (W.U.M.S.A., an outgrowth of the American Church Mission of the Episcopal Church) based in New York was organized as the pioneer women's advocacy society. In 1868, the WUMSA appointed three female missionaries to establish a boarding school for girls in Peking. This further bequest from Eliza Bridgman led to the relocation of that school from Peking to Shanghai in 1881, to occupy the premises known as Bridgman Home (裨文堂). Without interruption, a boarding school for girls was maintained with an average attendance of thirty-five pupils. Graduates of those early days lived useful and productive lives, many serving as teachers, a few distinguishing themselves in medical work. Pupils came from Shanghai and surrounding provinces.

After 1900, a step toward self-sustainability was taken. Charlotte M. Johnson, arriving on the field in October 1904, took over as superintendent.[43] Meanwhile the work initiated by Eliza Bridgman continued, particularly during the Boxer Rebellion and the collapse of the Qing Dynasty and the rise of Japanese occupation. Four day-schools were also sustained by the WUMSA with over two thousand students, taught by former pupils of the Bridgman Memorial School. The 1907 Centennial Conference report comments:

> The distinguishing feature of these schools is that the pupils have been girls between the ages of five and fifteen years. Recently a new day-school has been opened for older girls and young women of literary families, which gives promise of success. Wives, too, and daughters of official families are in attendance. The day-school work has afforded a medium through which a force has been at work in the awakening of the old China. "Cast thy bread upon the waters and thou shalt find it after many days.[44]

Eliza Bridgman's efforts were uninterrupted except for a brief furlough in America in 1852-53. It was during this time she wrote her book, *Daughters of China: Sketches of Domestic Life in the Celestial Kingdom*. Her years in Shanghai on behalf of the education of China's girls continued for 15 years, which was her passion in life.

Henry Blodget writes in her obituary in 1872:

> No one who knew Mrs. Bridgman need be told of her ardent zeal and abundant labors on behalf of this school. It was her one concern, the greatest object of her life. Nor were her labors without reward. A good number of her

pupils became Christians and were married to members of different churches. Almost every mission church in Shanghai has received accessions either from her pupils, or from those more or less remotely connected with them, their mothers or other friends. As her older pupils left the school, several of the more promising ones were employed by her to open day schools of girls under her own supervision. One or both of the parents were usually associated with the youthful teacher. At one time in 1859 Mrs. Bridgman had three such schools under her care, one south-east of the city of Shanghai, another in the city, and a third in a hamlet one or two miles north of her residence. Besides these schools, she had also a class of poor women who came to her for instruction upon the Sabbath, and also upon one of the week days. At that time there could scarcely have been less that seventy-five women and girls who were regularly taught by her. Many of her pupils retain a lively sense of gratitude for the labors put forward in their behalf, and some of them learned to look at her as on a mother.

The period of Mrs. Bridgman's life was one of almost uninterrupted happiness. God had given her useful employments, a comfortable measure of health, and a happy home. The death of Dr. Bridgman, which occurred in 1861 caused a great change in her circumstances. Her health gave way, and much against her own wishes, she was obliged to give up her school and return to America. This happened in 1862.[45]

Eliza left her school at the height of its prosperity and the little church connected to it and transferred them to the American Presbyterian Church, which took up her task and continued the school. Though still grieving, and trying to recover her health, Eliza wrote her biography of her husband, *The Life and Labors of Elijah Coleman Bridgman*, published following her return to China in 1864.

The Beijing Years

Though her health had declined, she managed to address meetings of ladies in England and America. She had the security of sufficient support, both for her livelihood and her work. But she was now a widow and while she was still in China, without any relative on whom she could depend. She had now reached the age of fifty-nine, and her health, naturally delicate, suffered the erosion of her years in China. Loving friends received her in New York, and she was given good medical care. But her heart was in China. This was what she had consecrated her life to, and she was eager to complete her task.

Passage back to China on a new steamer had been offered Eliza Bridgman by a Mercantile House. She accepted, but then before departure nearly lost her life in an accident in New York. Thrown down in the street by a runaway horse, the sleigh went right over her injuring her severely. She almost despaired of returning. But recovering gradually, and just before the steamer's sailing, her physician reluctantly gave permission for her to travel. Still convalescing and in bed, she ventured forth alone. However, that passage began under great danger. The United States was in the midst of the Civil War, and the CSS *Alabama*, a Confederate ship secretly built in 1862 as a screw sloop-of-war, was deployed as a commerce raider harassing Union merchant and naval ships over the course of her two-year career. The *Alabama* was prepared to attack her steamer as it left port, but the CSS *Alabama's* anchor was mired in the mud, and it took so much time for it to break free and to follow the signals of Eliza's steamer's departure, that she and her fellow passengers evaded any attack, reaching neutral waters.

On her return to China she relocated to Peking in 1864. The work

Figure 8: Photos from the School by Bridgman from copies in the archives.

in Shanghai had been successfully turned over to the Presbyterians. The ABCFM had closed its office in Shanghai and moved to Peking (Beijing). Peking, the Imperial City, had just reluctantly opened its doors to foreign residents for the first time. It is possible therefore that Eliza Bridgman may have been the first foreign female resident of that city, though this is not certain. The move made it necessary for the third time for Eliza to learn a new dialect of Chinese: Mandarin. She had first to learn Cantonese (the standard language of Guangdong Province), then the local Shanghainese (the Hu dialect of the Wu language of the Shanghai region).

With money from her own resources she purchased the property on Tengshihkou in the Tartar city of Peking, in a residential district, not far from the east gate of the Imperial city. Later she made an additional gift for the lot and building nearby, which was used many years as a mission center. The main compound was a fine old Chinese establishment, with two well built houses and many smaller ones. These, altered and enlarged as the years went on, were the homes of her workers and their pupils until they were destroyed by the Boxers in 1900.

Despite many difficulties, Eliza again opened her small school for girls. In time it grew into the predecessor to the Women's Union College, soon part of Yenching University. Others gave generously for the mission and school buildings, and combined with funds remaining from her estate, years after her death her successors erected the Women's Union College.

Opposition to female education was more intense in Peking than Shanghai. She initially could only enroll beggar girls, to whom Eliza offered primary education. Enrollment never exceeded eighteen students these years because of her requirement that students buy their own clothes and abandon foot-binding.[46] She received no salary during her last eight years. In fact, she donated $12,500 towards the new American Board of Commissioners for Foreign Missions (ABCFM) facilities in Peking.

Eliza Bridgman devoted four years to this latest endeavor. In 1869, due to exhaustion and her frail condition, Eliza Bridgman was obliged to go to Shanghai for recuperation. She later did return but died 10 November 1871 at the age of 66 and was buried beside her husband in Shanghai. That cemetery was demolished in 1912. I am told that the tombstones and other markers, including those within the church that was part of the old city, have been preserved, and removed to some site for storage, but their exact whereabouts are unknown, despite many efforts to locate them.

On her retirement in the autumn of 1868, the care of the girl's school came to M. H. Porter, who continued her role until her move in 1882. In the meantime, J. E. Chapin arrived in 1872, and Ada Haven in 1879. Chapin took over direction of the school after the departure of Porter, until her furlough in 1900. Haven rendered invaluable service from her arrival until the Boxer storm.

The School suffered its most serious set-back during the Boxer Rebellion of 1899-1901. The Bridgman Academy was destroyed, and a third of the students were killed. The rest found security within the British Legation. The Boxer Rebellion was a violent anti-foreign, anti-colonial and anti-Christian uprising, comprised of several disparate groups, that took place between 1899 and 1901. Perhaps as many as 100,000 people died because of the rebellion. Many foreigners suffered. A total of 136 Protestant missionaries and 53 children were killed, and 47 Catholic priests and nuns. 30,000 Chinese Catholics, 2,000 Chinese Protestants, and 200 to 400 of the 700 Russian Orthodox Christians in Beijing were estimated to have been killed.[47] Most Christians (foreign and Chinese) had been secured inside the British legation, which was under siege.

Upon the settlement of the Boxer Rebellion, the school managed to reopen. Porter returned in the spring of 1901 to the Bridgman School after twenty years' absence and M. E. Sheffield in 1899, strengthening the faculty. She and Grace Wyckoff gathered the pupils who had passed with them through the siege at the British Legation, into a temporary home to carry on the first few months of the school's renewed life.

But it was Luella Miner who as principal in 1904 to 1913, took the school to full recovery and restored the campus, giving the school new prominence. During the reconstruction period following the Boxer Rebellion she turned her attention to education for girls. Miner had been among the many who endured privations when the foreign legation district was under siege during the Boxer Rebellion. Miner was one of the heroines of the Boxer Rebellion in 1900 and later wrote a book entitled *Two Heroes of Cathay*, dealing with that uprising.

The girls' school remained under the American Board of Commissioners for Foreign Missions. Miner brought experience from years spent with the North China College and helped raise academic standards and gained greater support for the school. Bridgman Academy was brought into the North China Educational Union in 1904. In 1905 the buildings for the Women's Union College were erected, and a kindergarten began its operation in a special building. Miner expanded the Academy by adding college level courses. As the North China Union College for Women, the school offered a few college level courses, and in 1909 graduated four students who completed the college course. The college continued to be small and had only eight pupils in 1910 and twenty in 1912. Despite doubts about the advisability of co-education in China, union with the new Yenching University was accepted in 1919-1920. This college was the first college for women in China, becoming part of the Yenching University. Miner was the college's president until 1920, then served two more years as dean. She retired in 1933, and in 1936 died in Jinan, Shandong.

Beijing No. 166 Middle School is today a premier exemplary institution of distinction located near the Forbidden City. With a student body of some 2,000 students, the school is coeducational and occupies a state-of-the art campus, recently renovated and expanded not far from the original site of the Bridgman Academy. Beijing No. 166 is among the first group of schools known as 'Centennial Schools', known for excellence of academics, social reputation, quality of programs and resources. It was ranked even in the 1950s and 1960s as one of the Top Ten Schools of Beijing, and has pioneered the introduction of mathematics, physics, and chemistry as independent subjects in secondary curriculum.

The outstanding list of alumnae include:[48]

Yong Chongrui, founder of a healthcare network for women and children
Li Dequan, first Minister of Public Health in New China
Bing Xin, premier female literary figure of the 20th Century
Xie Xide, first female president of Fudan University, member of the Chinese Academy of Sciences (CAS)
Wang Xiuying, first Chinese to win the Nightingale Prize
Wang Chengshu, nuclear physicist, founder of the theory of uranium isotope separation,member of the CAS;
Hu Maohua, dean of radiology diagnostics, founder of Clinical Radiology in China

Fei Lulu, one of the first generation of female judges in new China

Jin Lijin, founder of photochemistry in China, member of the CAS

Sun Weishi, first female drama director in new China

Cheng Tongyun, a Chinese traditional physician

Pan Jie, one of the first generation of female announcers

Zhang Houcan, founder of psychology in China

Zhang Zhongye, member of the CAS

Xie Youyu, first woman scientist to visit both North and South Poles

Bao Huiqiao, concert pianist

Zhang Linqi, chief scientist in developing innovative mucosal vaccines

Li Xingwang, expert in infectious disease treatment

In October 2014, the School celebrated its 150th Anniversary, honoring its founder, creating a museum in one of the older buildings which features the heritage of Eliza Bridgman as a pioneer of school for Chinese girls. Over fifty alumnae from pre-1950 came from across China and the United States to celebrate the school's heritage and achievements. They unveiled an original bronze sculpture affirming the school's role in advancing education among women. There is also a bronze sculpture of Bing Xin (1900-1999), a prominent Chinese female writer of the twentieth century.

Eighty percent of the graduates today are admitted to top tier universities in China. Many have qualified for advanced study in colleges and universities throughout the United States. The current principal, Wang Lei, brings a depth of vision, excellence in administration and quality of curriculum, and a desire to promote the values of service to humanity and preparing students to 'give back to society', rather than seeking simply to prosper, succeed and achieve fame, believing that these are values inherited from the founder, Eliza Bridgman.

CONCLUSION

Examined against this background, in the face of powerful forces of opposition, frequent set-backs, warfare, frail health, all the limitations imposed by the strictures of culture, and prejudice, Eliza Bridgman presents us with a model of a woman of uncanny strength of character, determination, vision, and ability to 'get things done.' She was truly a pioneer who defied insuperable odds with persistence. Other women have gained approbation greater than hers. But, she must be numbered among the most influential educators of women in China. Her passion to serve and her unshakable conviction in the capacity and rights of girls has opened a door for many Chinese to develop and achieve success. Her brief years have stimulated the birth of a movement to elevate the dignity and worth of every child of God, female and male. That vision is still alive. Well done! Good and faithful servant!

ABOUT THE AUTHOR

David F. Bridgman was a fourth generation descendent of Henry Augustus Bridgman, the elder brother of Elijah Coleman Bridgman, the first American Protestant missionary to China. He was born in China of missionary parents and has travelled to China frequently since 1998, recently visiting the two schools established by Eliza Bridgman.

E-mail: dbridgman1932@gmail.com

—∞—

Endnotes

1 Luella Miner, 'Women's Work: Educational', *China Centenary Missionary Conference Records Report of the Great Conference*, 159ff. (New York: American Tract Society, 1907).

2 Elijah Cole Bridgman, Preface, p. *vi* in Eliza J. Gillett Bridgman, *Daughters of China, or Sketches of Domestic Life in the Celestial Empire China* (New York: Robert Carter & Brothers, 1853).

3 Eliza J. Gillett Bridgman, *Daughters of China*, p. vii.

4 *China Centenary Missionary Conference Records*, American Tract Society, 1907, p.159

5 *Ibid.*, p. 160

6 Morrison died in 1834 and Bridgman became his successor and the senior foreign missionary in China.

7 Michael C. Lazich, *E. C. Bridgman (1802-1861), America's First Missionary to China* (Lewiston, NY: The Edwin Mellen Press; New York: Robert Carter & Brothers, 1853), p. 251.

8 Jame E. Jr. Bear, *1st Annual Report if the BFM, PCUSA, May 1938, in James E. Bear, Jr.*, 'The Mission Work of the Presbyterian Church

in the United States in China: 1867-1962,' 5 vols, unpublished manuscript in Union Presbyterian Seminary Library, Richmond, VA, 1963, 1, p. 51.

9 *Ibid*, pp. 25-26

10 Wong Yin Lee, *Women's Education in Traditional and Modern China*, *Women's History Review*, Volume 4, Number 3, 3 November, 1995, p. 345.

11 Margaret E. Burton, *The Education of Women in China*, (New York: Fleming H. Revell Company, 1911), p. 11.

12 Chester Holcombe, *The Real Chinese Question, Methuen, London, 1901*, p. 63, as quoted in Margaret E. Burton, *The Education of Women in China*, p. 12

13 S. W. Williams, *The Middle Kingdom*, Vol. I, 574 (New York: Charles Scribner's Sons, 1882), cited by Margaret E. Burton, *The Education of Women in China*, 1911, p. 17.

14 Quoted by Burton, *The Education of Women in China*, p. 19f

15 Lee, *Women's Education in Traditional and Modern China*, p. 346

16 Lu Kun, *Gui Fan* (Norms of Boudoir), as quoted in Lee, *Women's Education in Traditional and Modern China*, p. 346

17 Burton, *The Education of Women in China*, p. 28.

18 Lee, *Women's Education in Traditional and Modern China*, p. 353

19 *Ibid*, p. 354

20 *Ibid*, p 355

21 Eliza Bridgman, *Daughters of China*, p. 27

22 M. Schiavenza, Matt, 'The Peculiar History of Foot Binding in China,' *The Atlantic*, 16 September, 2013, https://www.theatlantic.com/china/archive/2013/09/the-peculiar-history-of-foot-binding-in-china/279718/ .

23 Eliza Bridgman, *Daughters of China*, p. 29

24 *Ibid*.

25 'Mary Ann Aldersey', retrieved from 'https://Wikipedia.org/w/index.php?title=Mary_Ann_Aldersey&oldid=783787385' https://en.wikipedia.org/wiki/Mary_Ann_Aldersey.

26 Burton, *The Education of Women in China*, p. 35

27 This data has been retrieved from the article concerning Eliza Bridgman in Edward T. James, Janet Wilson James, Paul S. Boyer, *Notable American Women, 1607-1950: A Biographical Dictionary, Volume 1* (Harvard: Harvard University Press, 1 January 1971), p. 239.

28 Eliza Bridgman, *Daughters of China*, pp. 11-13.

29 Lazich, *E. C. Bridgman (1802-1861)*, p. 49.

30 In March 1841, the degree of Doctor of Divinity was conferred on Elijah Cole Bridgman, by the Chancellor of the University of New York. Bridgman, *The Life and Labors of Elijah Coleman Bridgman.* 115

31 Eliza Bridgman, *Daughters of China*, p. 21

32 *Ibid.*, pp. 21-26.

33 Robert Pierce Beaver, *American Protestant Women in World Mission: A History of the First Feminist Movement in North America* (1969; Reprint Grand Rapids, Mich:W. B. Eerdmans Pub. Co., 1980).

34 *Ibid.*, p. 82ff.

35 The girls were not legally adopted. It was a verbal agreement with their parents for them to have the girls as long as they were not taken out of China. A-lan had been pledged by her father to an arranged marriage, and he later demanded her return to Canton to fulfil this pledge.

36 Eliza Bridgman, *Daughters of China*, p. 183, p. 224. Bridgman's list of girls' names 8 day-scholars, and 12 boarders, including their ages. King-meh is the same as Jin Mei, 'Golden Sister'. Her selection to travel with them is described on pages 223ff. A-lan was first chosen, but she could not go due to her mother's request that 'she must not go to a foreign country.'

37 Ibid, 179. "The name of the place where the school is situated, is called in the local dialect *Wongka Moda*; literally, 'King's family's horse's head' or the 'Horse's head of the King family.' By the phrase 'horse's head,' the Chinese denote a landing place or jetty; this one was built by the King's family and is situated in the south-eastern suburbs of Shanghai."

38 Eliza Bridgman. *Daughters of China*, p. 78, p. 183. Ay-yee was required to return to Canton since she had been promised by her father in an arranged marriage, p.170.

39 Ibid, p. 80, p. 183

40 Ibid, p. 178f, p. 180.

41 Ibid, pp. 184-194.

42 Donald MacGillivray (ed.), *A Century of Protestant Missions in China (1807-1907): Being the Centenary Conference Historical Volume* (New York: American Tract Society; Shanghai: American Presbyterian Mission Press, 1907), p. 381. The Rev. W. M. Lowrie of the Presbyterian Mission who arrived in China to serve on

the Bible translation team, was killed by bandits in 1847 while crossing Hangchow Bay. That task was taken over by Reverend M. S. Culbertson, D.D. (1845-62) and Elijah Bridgman of the ABCFM until its completion in 1862.

43 MacGillivray, p. 469.

44 Ibid.

45 Henry Blodget, *The Chinese Recorder and Missionary Journal*, 1862, p. 262.

46 Jessie Gregory Lutz, *China and the Christian Colleges, 1850-1950* (New York: Cornell University Press, 1971), p. 132.

47 Roger R. Thompson, 'Reporting the Taiyuan Massacre: Culture and Politics Jesse Gregory in the China War of 1900", in Robert A. Bickers and R. G. Tiedemann (eds.), *The Boxers, China, and the World* (Lanham, MD: Rowman & Littlefield, 2007), pp. 65–92, p. 184.

48 *A Brief Introduction to Beijing No. 166 Secondary School*, 2017, brochure published by Beijing No. 166 High School. No. 3 Tong Fu Jia Dao, Dong Cheng District, Beijing, China 100006, www.bi166z. cn.

AN IRISH POLICEMAN IN SHANGHAI:
From Constable To Commissioner Of The SMP, 1904-1939
by Andrew David Field

ABSTRACT

In 1904, Stewart Cromie Young, a 22 years old recruit from Ireland, joined the Shanghai Municipal Police (SMP) of the International Settlement as a second-class constable. Over the next 34 years, he made his way patiently and methodically up the ranks, achieving the position of Deputy Commissioner in 1934 and serving as a leading spokesman for the SMP in Shanghai. By the time he retired from the force in 1938, S. C. Young had served a long and distinguished career as the only policeman to start at the bottom of the force and work his way up to near the very top of the SMP. During that period, he played an important role in keeping the public order and detecting and preventing crime in a city notorious for its gangs and their rackets, all as the city and country underwent an often violent and unpredictable period of war and revolution.

One of the keys to the rise of S. C. Young lies in his civic engagements and religious and family life. He was a valued member and leader of many social and civic groups. His English wife Elizabeth Ellen also distinguished herself as a leader of the Girls' Friendly Society. Together,

Figure 1: S. C. Young and family in mid-1920s.
Photo courtesy of Peta Catto

71

the two Britons raised three sons and integrated themselves completely into the society of British Shanghailanders during their long sojourn in the city. Assembled from a combination of newspaper articles and photos and memorabilia from the Young family, this review of S. C. Young's life sheds further light on the workings of the SMP and the Shanghailander society during a vital period of the city's history.

Between 1904 and 1938, while serving as a policeman with the Shanghai Municipal Police (SMP) of the International Settlement, Stewart Cromie Young rose within the ranks. He began his career as a constable on the beat, handling quarrels with drunken sailors in the dingiest and most dangerous dives of the city. He ended his 35-year sojourn in Shanghai as the Deputy Commissioner and, for a time, the temporary Commissioner of the SMP, when he was in charge of a force of around 5,000 men from many different countries, and a spokesman on crime and policing for the city.

Along with his English wife Elizabeth Ellen, known to the public as Mrs. S. C. Young, he was also a leading figure in the civic life of the city. During their many years in Shanghai, S. C. Young and his wife, known to him as Betty, raised three sons: William Brian, the first born, arrived in December 1913, Stewart Terence was born in June 1915, and Albert Norman followed a few years later (exact date of birth unknown). All three were eventually sent to England to a public boarding school in Weymouth to complete their educations. Second son Terence attended Cambridge University, where he majored in Oriental Studies. He became a filmmaker, notably directing the three of the first four James Bond films in the 1960s, Bond being a character that shared Cambridge as an alma mater with Terence. One surmises that while helping to create one of the most memorable spies in filmdom, Terence was inspired by his own childhood in Shanghai and by his father's career as a crime fighter.

S. C. Young was born in Queens County, Ireland in 1882, according to his granddaughter Peta Catto, whom I met in Sydney in 2006. She and her daughter Annabel, who was my student at University of New South Wales, shared with me an extraordinary collection of photos and personal memorabilia handed down to them through her father William Brian, which had once belonged to her grandfather S. C. Young and his wife. Among the collection is a photograph of a gravestone dedicated to S. C. Young's parents William (d. 1930) and Mary Ann Young (d. 1928), which also confirms that S. C. Young died in 1968.

The gravestone also memorializes S. C. Young's brother Herbert John Young who was killed in action in France in 1917.

Catto remarks, 'My grandfather [S. C. Young] was from Northern Ireland; I believe that his father [William Young] was a policeman. I clearly remember him telling me that he decided to join the Royal Ulster Constabulary [RUC] as it would be more exciting than working for Guinness in Dublin, as in those days the RUC sent people to China, Hong Kong etc."[1] S. C. Young's adventurous choice to join the RUC took him to Shanghai, where he spent the next 35 years of his life, confronting and bearing witness to some of the greatest revolutionary movements, struggles, and battles of the twentieth century.

POLICING, CRIME, AND POLITICS IN THE CRUCIBLE OF REPUBLICAN SHANGHAI

S. C. Young and his family were members of a small yet influential society consisting of several thousand Britons who made their homes in Shanghai during the Republican Era (1912-1949), calling themselves 'the Shanghailanders'.[2] Established soon after the First Opium War between Britain and China (1839-1842), with the signing of the Treaty of Nanking in 1842, the treaty port system of which Shanghai was a part, was characterized by extraordinary privileges and powers granted to the thousands of Britons and other Westerners living in the concessions or settlements, where they established governments, police forces, churches, schools, hospitals, newspapers, and modern urban infrastructure. The settlements also housed a far greater Chinese population of sojourners and refugees hailing from all over the country. Shanghai served as the flagship port city of the entire treaty port system, which encompassed over one hundred ports of trade in China by the early twentieth century. Control of Shanghai and its population became a key international conflict among empires and nation-builders in Asia, including the British, French, Chinese, and Japanese.

The SMP was the policing body of the British-controlled International Settlement, one of Shanghai's two foreign settlements, the other being the French Concession. While the details of the SMP and its changes over time will be covered further in this article, generally speaking the SMP was a modern Western-style police force run by British officers and staffed by Britons, Sikhs, Chinese, Japanese and other foreigners. It was charged by the Shanghai Municipal Council

(SMC), the governing body of the International Settlement, with the task of keeping public order in the International Settlement, of detecting and preventing crime in a notoriously lawless semi-colonial Shanghai.[3] S. C. Young was one of the many policemen recruited from his homeland to serve on the force.

The SMP contributed to the maintenance of public order during several key events and movements in the history of modern Chinese nationalism, including the Xinhai Revolution of 1911-12, the May Fourth Movement of 1919, the Nationalist Revolution of 1927 and the so-called White Terror of 12 April 1927. The SMP also instigated one major movement, known to historians as the May Thirtieth Movement, catalyzed on 30 May 1925 when a unit of armed police fired on a crowd of Chinese demonstrators who had gathered on the streets in front of the police headquarters. The police killed several Chinese students with their gunfire, spurring a nationwide protest movement against British imperialism in China and helped to precipitate the Nationalist revolution of 1927.[4] While Chinese modern historians look back on these movements and struggles as major watersheds for the Chinese people, the SMP viewed them as riots, public disturbances and threats to the social, economic and political order and stability of the Settlement.

S. C. Young and his compatriots bore witness to the rise of the Kuomintang (KMT), the Nationalist party formed soon after the collapse of the Qing dynasty in 1912 under the leadership of Sun Yat-sen (1866-1925) and his self-chosen successor, Chiang Kai-shek (1887- 1975). On the bloody day of 12 April 1927, the Nationalist army, stationed outside the city, joined forces with the criminal organization known as the Shanghai Green Gang (*qingbang*) to rout and exterminate hundreds of suspected Chinese Communists. In 1928, Young witnessed the creation of the Special Municipality of Greater Shanghai (*da shanghai tebie shi*), run by the KMT, overseeing the areas of the city that lay beyond the two foreign settlements. As Frederic Wakeman relates in his book *Policing Shanghai*, this new municipal government tried to bring order to the city but ultimately failed to do so.[5] One of the key reasons for their failure was that they had entered into an entangling and corrupt pact with the Green Gang, a precarious and unstable alliance with the most powerful crime organization in China.

During his long career with the SMP, S. C. Young and his colleagues

Figure 2: S. C. Young and members of the SMP posing with leaders of the KMT's Great Shanghai Special Municipality including Mayor Wu Tiecheng, c. 1935. The Mayor stands to Young's left.
Photo courtesy of Peta Catto.

tracked the rise of the infamous Green Gang. This was the Chinese criminal syndicate led by 'Big Ears' Du Yuesheng which controlled the city's rackets and monopolized its illicit opium trade in the 1920s and 1930s.[6] Much of the SMP's police work involved dealing with members of this and other criminal organizations as well as countless petty criminals from the 'floating class' of urban migrants. S. C. Young must have been familiar with the leaders of the Green Gang, or at least he knew who they were. He also participated in the discussions and negotiations that underlay the cooperation of the SMP with the KMT's own police force, known as the Public Security Bureau (PSB or *gongan ju*). As Wakeman discusses in *Policing Shanghai*, these two police forces cooperated to root out suspected Communists, who after their vicious purge from the Nationalist movement in 1927 were now operating underground in the city into the 1930s.[7]

One undated photo from Young's personal collection, likely taken in the late 1930s, shows him tall and dapper, by this time a Deputy Commissioner of the SMP, standing next to Shanghai's Nationalist Mayor Wu Tiecheng, who was appointed by Chiang Kai-shek to establish the new municipal government. They appear along with several other Chinese Nationalist officials and one other SMP officer. They are standing on the steps of the city's new municipal building, which housed the Mayor's office. There is also a small collection of colored postcards among his memorabilia, showing the new municipal buildings and swimming pool that made up the new Civic Center in the northern district of Kiangwan (Jiangwan).

During the Republican Era, fighting crime in Shanghai was a difficult task to say the least. As Wakeman, Martin, Christian Henriot, and other Republican Shanghai historians have shown, the difficulty of crime prevention was exacerbated by the complex jurisdictional structure of the city with its two foreign settlements, which gave criminals and gangsters the opportunity to take advantage of the situation by moving into one or another district depending on circumstances.[8] This was especially the circumstance in the French Concession. As Brian Martin's work on the Green Gang reveals, the French Concession Police made a 'devil's pact' with the crime syndicate in an effort to establish some control over the criminal elements of their part of the city.[9]

Shanghai was not only a cauldron of political activity and the opium trade, but also a leading center of carnal vice in Asia and the world. Prostitution was an extremely well developed industry in Shanghai during the Republican Era.[10] Thousands of Chinese and foreigners disported themselves in nightclubs, cabarets, and dance halls, to the tunes of jazz orchestras nightly with the aid of tens of thousands of young Chinese and Russian dance hostesses.[11] Although gambling and opium were illegal in the settlements, underground gambling parlours and opium dens sprang up like 'bamboo shoots in spring rain' (*ru yu hou chun sun*, to use a popular Chinese saying). Throughout the Republican Era, the Shanghai police struggled to at least to keep tabs on them, but many policemen ended up indulging in the readily available vices of the city, and the SMP consequently had a reputation for drunken, cabaret-going bobbies.[12]

S. C. Young's own story stands in stark contrast to the largely negative image of the SMP during this age. Young steadily rose not only in the ranks of the SMP, to the top ranks of the force, but also into the upper echelons of Shanghailander society. Perhaps the best historical account of the Shanghai Municipal Police appears in historian Robert Bickers's book *Empire Made Me*, the story of British policeman Richard Maurice Tinkler, a very different sort of character from S. C. Young. At the beginning of Tinkler's short career as a policeman, he reported to S. C. Young, who in 1919 ran the depot on Gordon Road where Tinkler and other new members of the force were trained in combat, languages, and other necessary skills.[13] What becomes apparent when perusing his public record in the newspapers of the age is that S. C. Young was on a very different trajectory from Tinkler and the myriad others who joined the force at the lowest level. His career reflects an extraordinary rise to the top or near top of the force and also into the upper echelons of Shanghailander society. This rise must be accounted for not only by Young's accomplishments in his chosen profession, but also by his civic engagements and family life as well. It is to this story that we now turn.

S. C. Young's early years in shanghai

The historian must look back on S. C. Young's long career as a Shanghai policeman mainly through the prism of his later years. Scant records remain of his early years of service. A scattering of news articles from his early days in the 1900s highlight certain aspects of his life in Shanghai, particularly his sporting life. Some of his personal records give us additional glimpses into this formative period of his long stint in Shanghai. Taken together, these sources provide a composite picture of an ambitious young man making a name for himself as a hard worker, a gifted athlete, a good hunter and marksman, an emerging leader, and a valuable team player.

On the eve of his retirement, a few articles published in the city's English newspapers provide a rather detailed account of his rise within the force. In one, S. C. Young recalled arriving in Shanghai in 1904, during the height of the Russo-Japanese war, and seeing damaged Russian ships in Chinese waters.[14] He also recollected shooting pheasant in the open fields that originally lay near where the Bubbling Well Police Station stood by that time in the late 1930s (Bubbling Well Road is now Nanjing Road), suggesting the rapid development and urbanization of Shanghai during his many years there.

At first, Young's rise in the force was not so rapid when compared to others who joined in later years. When he joined the SMP as a second-class constable, he 'had to slave to make the grade of first class constable.'[15] He served eighteen months before he was promoted to first class. Then it took him thirteen more months to become a probationary sergeant and another three months to achieve the grade of third class sergeant. Twenty-one months later, he was promoted to second class sergeant on 1 June 1909. He had been eight years on the

Figure 3: S. C. Young and other men of the SMP ready themselves for a 120-yard dash in 1909, which Young won.
Photo courtesy of Peta Catto.

force before he became first class sergeant on 1 June 1912.[16]

Early on, S. C. Young was posted to Hongkew (Hongkou) Station, north of the Bund. This was a district known for its large Japanese community, eventually earning the moniker 'Little Tokyo.' It was also notorious for the presence of foreign soldiers and sailors stationed in Shanghai or on shore leave, who frequented a range of seedy bars in an infamous stretch of street known as 'the Trenches.'[17] Young later claimed that his most difficult job in those days was dealing with foreign sailors. He was called upon to 'subdue the toughest bluejackets of various nations in order to save the limbs and property of the residents.'[18] According to a report in the *China Press*, in an episode that sounds like a scene from a movie, he recalled 'a tussle he had in Hongkew with an American negro sailor of gigantic proportions, which resulted in the policeman and the sailor going together through the wall of one house into the adjoining building to the complete dismay of the unsuspecting residents.'[19] Broken noses and torn uniforms were daily events in spots like the Trenches, which was known for drunken and sometimes quite violent behavior among the soldiery and even civilians living in Shanghai.

S. C. Young was also remembered as an outstanding athlete who held police championships in running and jumping, and took prizes in international walking competitions. A member of the Police Rifle

Club, he played cricket and later the gentler game of lawn bowls. Photos of his earliest days in Shanghai attest to his prowess as a sportsman. He appears in one photo lining up with other runners and readying himself for a sprint on the lawn of the Recreation Ground in the International Settlement. The photo is labeled with the year 1909 and states that he won a 120-yard dash during the Police shorts—that is, short sprints. In other photos, he poses with groups of rugged-looking mustachioed men, each holding a rifle, backgrounded by the stark Chinese countryside. One such photo (see Figure 4) is labeled 'rifle team for Shanghai international police' and lists the names of the individuals in the photo.

The earliest reference in the newspapers to S. C. Young's sports record is in 1906, when he played for the SMP in a cricket match against the Shanghai Recreation Club.[20] He was a member of the police cricket team from 1905-1920, and the captain of lawn bowls in 1931-1933.[21] In May 1908, Young won the Sergeant's Prize in the SMP Spring Rifle Meeting and First Club Prize for the B Class Monthly Cup and came in fifth place with total 178 in the Grand Aggregate Competition.[22]

The most prominent news about S. C. Young from his early years is his marriage. On 18 February 1911, he married an Englishwoman named Elizabeth Ellen Long. Peta Catto, their granddaughter, told me that her grandmother was probably from Suffolk and had come

Figure 4: SMP Rifle Team. Front from left: Goddard, Young, Barrett, Mackintosh, Wilson. Back: Bourke, McDowell, Coghlan.
Photo courtesy of Peta Catto.

to China via the Trans-Siberian Railway to look after a couple of children in Shanghai as their nursemaid. In other words, like Young, she was from a modest family background, yet she possessed a good upbringing and a proper education. According to the 24 February 1911 edition of the *North-China Herald*:

> The marriage took place at Holy Trinity Cathedral on Saturday afternoon of Sergt. S. C. Young, of the Shanghai Municipal Polie Force, to Miss Elizabeth Ellen Long, the ceremony being performed by the Rev. A. J. Walker, M. A. The bride, who wore a dress of white satin, with wedding veil surmounted by orange blossoms, and carried a bouquet of white carnations, was given away by Mr. H. C. Gulland and Mrs. Gulland acted as matron of honour. She [the bride] was attended by two little pages—Masters Gulland and Lee—who were dressed in sailors' costumes. Mr. D. Marshall acted as best man and Messrs. J. McDowell and P. Reeves fulfilled the duties of ushers. After the ceremony, a reception was held at the residence of Mr. and Mrs. Gulland, No. 9 Nanyang Road, where a large number of friends assembled to offer their congratulations.[23]

The memorabilia treasured include the wedding invitation corroborating that Mr and Mrs Gulland sent the invitations and received the married couple and their guests at their home on 9 Nanyang Road. There is also a group photo showing the bride and groom posing in the garden with the two boys in sailor's costumes

Figure 5: Young wedding party in 1911.
Photo courtesy of Peta Catto.

along with the wedding party. One surmises Mr and Mrs Gulland, who probably stand beside the bride and groom, were the caretakers or employers of the bride and that the 'little pages' or at least one of them was under Miss Long's care. As revealed many years later in his obituary, Mr H. C. Gulland had arrived in Shanghai in 1897 as an accountant for the Chartered Bank of India, Australia and China and then joined the International Banking Corporation. He was then stationed in Yokohama for a few years and returned to Shanghai in 1909, where he and his wife raised two sons and a daughter. The Gullands must have called for help from an English governess, and Elizabeth Ellen Long had answered the call, not knowing at the time that she would marry a dashing young policeman, raise a family with him and spend over two decades of her life in Shanghai.[24]

RISING THROUGH THE RANKS

Now that he was married and raising a family, S. C. Young dedicated himself to rising up in the force. He became a sub-inspector in October 1912. It took another four years to become an inspector in 1916, then another five years to reach the rank of chief inspector in 1921. He became an assistant commissioner on 1 April 1927, when he 'performed a valuable service to the force and community during the civil war of that year,' - a reference to the Nationalist revolution that brought Chiang Kai-shek to power in Nanjing.[25] He served as personal assistant to Major Gerrard from 1 April 1931 to 24 April 1934. He was promoted to deputy commissioner on 1 January 1934 and had his own personal assistant. He took charge of the Crime Branch of the SMP on 7 April 1935 and of the Special Branch from 9 to 29 August 1936 1936, and again from 30 August to 6 September 1937 at height of the war between Japan and China. When Commissioner K.M. Bourne left Shanghai for a well-earned rest in the seaside resort town Weihaiwei in Shandong Province, Young took over as temporary Commissioner of the SMP. This was S. C. Young's career in a nut shell, as reported on the eve of his retirement.[26]

Looking at his career in detail through the newspaper archives, it becomes apparent that the Chinese Revolution of 1912 and the so-called Second Revolution of 1913 provided some key opportunities for an ambitious policeman to prove his mettle and begin to rise up the ranks, as did subsequent periods of unrest. During a 'strong demonstration' in Chapei (Zhabei), when a hostile crowd gathered around Honan road extension police station, Captain Barrett of the SMP was threatened by a rifleman and a little later his motorcar was fired upon with him inside it.[27] After the Shanghai Volunteer Corps (SVC) vacated the area under orders, only Inspector Young and a detachment of two officers remained bravely behind. Reinforcements later arrived in the form of the Shanghai Light Horse and Artillery.[28]

S. C. Young seems to have been adept at handling himself in court, and he appeared as a witness to testify in numerous court cases throughout his long career. In October 1913, Sub-Inspector Young appeared at a Mixed Court hearing involving the case of a dead suspect who was believed to have been making a bomb that exploded, killing him instantly before he had a chance to dispatch it for nefarious usage. The man, Zung Tse-van, had apparently been working with the revolutionaries who deposed the Qing dynasty, since he had a photograph of Sun Yat-sen and also one of Chen Chimei (Qimei), the revolutionary who led the movement to depose the Qing dynasty in Shanghai. The accident took place in the Hongkew District near Range Road at a house on 16 Haskell Road. The newspaper characterized this event as a 'rebel plot.'[29]

In a case that shocked the foreign community of Shanghai in 1914, S. C. Young was also involved in the investigation of a gruesome murder. The investigation took place after a German woman named Mrs Neumann was found in her bed hacked to death with knives and an axe by apparent robbers, who stole $35,000 worth of precious jewels and other items. Her fingers had been cut off to remove the rings, and her head was found hanging by a thread to the rest of her body. The newspapers provide a very long and involved description of the case, which was eventually resolved. The *mafoos* or Chinese man-servants of the houses were among the suspects, as was her husband for a spell.[30] Indeed, it was later discovered that with the aid of the house boy who provided the key to the house, members of the Green Gang had committed the heinous crime. Both of these horrifying events must have left a deep impression in the minds of S. C. Young and his compatriots in the force, not to mention shaking up the society of the Shanghailanders.

In 1916, five Chinese were brought before the Shanghai Mixed Court, charged for unlawfully carrying explosive articles within the limits of the Settlement. Sub-Inspector Young was on duty at the Police Box on Ferry Road when he noticed a four-wheeled dray approaching with five Chinese driving it and two foreigners, of whom one was a German, following behind. They were taking ammunition to the Kiangnan Arsenal. Although the German told him it was 'none of your business,' young and his colleague confiscated the cart and detained the men.[31]

Another job that S. C. Young took on was the task of training others in the force – not just his own countrymen, but also men from other countries who joined the ever-growing body of policemen in the International Settlement. That same year, Sub-inspector Young met thirty Japanese policemen from the Metropolitan Police of Tokyo who had just arrived from Tokyo to join the SMP. He personally supervised their training at the Gordon Road station. The police were well educated and spoke English but needed to learn the local dialect and urban geography as well as land regulations, police procedures and practices in Shanghai. They were assigned to duty in Hongkew because of the large number of Japanese residents there.[32]

In 1918, the SMP put out a call for volunteers from many countries to fill the gap caused by policemen heading back to the homeland to serve in the war. Inspector Young and Sgt Major Fairbairn led instruction of the volunteers at Gordon Road Depot to bring them up to speed on police practices as well as knowledge of the city and taught them to use revolvers and batons and some basic *jiujitsu* techniques. This was the time when Maurice Tinkler, the subject of Robert Bickers' book *Empire Made Me*, was in training under the supervision of S. C. Young.

Young was granted the title of Inspector on 6 April 1920.[33] As he rose up in the force, Young became more aware of the constant temptation of corruption that plagued the city's policemen, particularly in light of the criminalisation of opium during the Great War years and Shanghai's role as a key port for smuggling the illicit and lucrative substance in and out of the country. 'It is common tea-shop gossip that there is a big conspiracy on foot against the forces of law and order in the Settlement. The authorities are well aware that Chinese constables are being bribed by opium vendors', said Inspector Young during a Mixed Court case involving a Chinese tailor accused of bribing a policeman.[34] In 1922, Inspector Young appeared at the French Mixed Court for a case involving H. Austlander, a runner for Thomas Cook & Son, charged with smuggling 376 pounds of opium worth $30,000 into Shanghai. The defendant denied knowledge of what he was transporting. Young called upon two Chinese coolies to provide testimony.[35]

As a policeman on the rise, Young had mentors. One was his former boss, Inspector Lynch. In 1926, Chief Inspector Young spoke at a retirement party for Chief Inspector Lynch, relating to his colleagues how when he first joined the police force he was attached to Wayside station with Inspector Lynch in charge. Mr. Lynch 'was a father, a perfect father, from whom one could get advice at any time. Off and on the cricket field, Mr. Lynch was always the same, he never delivered an "angry ball."'[36] Young's skills and composure as a sportsman must have helped him gain the attention and admiration of his seniors during his rise, but it was his professionalism and bravery, as well as his leadership, communication, and teamwork skills, that enabled him to rise to the top of his profession.

DEPUTY COMMISSIONER AND PUBLIC SPOKESMAN FOR THE SMP

As the SMP grew in size and complexity, skilled and experienced men like S. C. Young were needed to take key positions of leadership in the force. In 1929, the SMP announced important changes in the divisional structure under Major FW Gerrard, Commissioner. Under the new scheme, there were four divisions instead of two, with each under command of an assistant commissioner, and also assistant commissioners in charge of Crime, Special, and Traffic branches. Assistant Commissioner S. C. Young was put in charge of Sinza (Xinzha), Bubbling Well, Gordon Road (present day Jiangning Road) and Pootoo Road (present day Putuo Road) along with Detective Superintendent Kay.[37] Five years later, Assistant Commissioner Young was promoted to Deputy Commissioner along with T. P. Givens, starting 1 January 1934.[38] Thus began the final phase of the Irish policeman's extraordinary career, in which he now served not only as a leader in the force but also an important public spokesman and liaison with the greater community of Shanghailanders.

In June 1936, Deputy Commissioner Young gave a speech at the International Arts Theater, 55 Yuen Ming Yuen (Yuanmingyuan) Road.[39] His speech focused on the science of finger-printing. According to Young, this crime detection method 'was first used for identification purpose in 1858 by an Indian Civil Service official. Starting our file in 1910, we now have over 430,000 finger-prints in Shanghai and the number increases at the rate of 35,000 annually. The efficient manner in which they are filed is indicated by the fact that it takes only two minutes to find a given one.' Photographs also played an important role in crime detection in a city with countless thousands of drifters and grifters coming from all parts of China and beyond. As Young stated during his speech:

> We encounter many difficulties in police work here that are peculiar to this country. Most beggar boys, for example, are potential thieves, and we have a large non-professional criminal class of persons who commit crimes only when a very good opportunity is offered. Almost anything might be stolen here: there have been thefts of entire households of furniture, grand pianos and even a bridge. The only thing which probably never might be stolen is a municipal steamboat.

In a speech to the community of Shanghailanders, Deputy Commissioner Young also mentioned several different classes of criminals, armed robbers and kidnappers who terrorized wealthy Chinese and organized embezzlements and confidence games. He pointed out that criminals were more scientific than they had been before, so science must be used to catch criminals. Finger-printing, he noted, was a powerful system of classification developed by Galton and Henry and introduced to Scotland Yard in 1901, and had since helped to solve countless crimes. These lectures served to show the Shanghai public that, despite the apparent futility of solving crimes in a city ridden with gangsters and floating migrants, the city's police force was keeping up with the latest techniques and technologies and exerting every effort to do so.[40]

It was also important to educate the public on the workings and scope of the SMP. In 1937, Deputy Commissioner Young gave a talk on the history of the SMP to the British Residents' Association, during a meeting held at the Cathedral School for Boys. His talk described the successive stages of the force since its origins in 1854, when it started out with eight members. By the time of his speech, the number of men on the force was nearly 5,000, with 452 foreigners, 272 Japanese, 555 Sikhs, and 3,452 Chinese. The leadership consisted of the Commissioner, five Deputy Commissioners of the regular police, and one Volunteer Deputy Commissioner. There were four divisions, labeled A, B, C, and D. An Assistant Commissioner or Superintendent was in charge of each division, with a Divisional Detective Officer responsible for the investigation of crimes. Divisions consisted of three or four police districts. All crime reports were transferred from the stations to each Deputy Commissioner. The Special Branch dealt with political matters including unions, labor strikes and disturbances to peace and order in the Settlement. The Traffic branch dealt with traffic issues and issued tickets and licenses to vehicles and drivers. A Training Depot opened in 1910, and every man enlisted went through courses of three to four months training in arms and combat techniques. In addition, he noted the Reserve Unit and Specials, which he claimed was too complicated to explain in such a short speech.[41]

In 1936, Deputy Commissioner Young also gave a speech to members of the Shanghai Rotary Club in the Metropole Hotel during a tiffin address (tiffin was the Shanghailander term for lunch). In his speech, he compared the crime situation in Shanghai at the time to that of New York 50 or 60 years previously. '[Shanghai] is a mecca for populations throughout China and its streets, theoretically paved with gold, attract thousands from nearly all the provinces. Many of these are from the so-called criminal class but they come here with clean records and it is frequently impossible to obtain information on their past careers.'[42] He once again stressed finger-printing as a key crime detection method. He also mentioned the arms identification unit through which police could identify a pistol found at a crime scene. He mentioned a recent shooting at Bearn Apartment and a pistol used in an attempted murder, in which bullets were examined to identify the weapon. He also mentioned the existence of a large floating class of petty criminals that made crime prevention all the more difficult.[43]

In 1938, Deputy Commissioner Young lectured to an audience at the Foreign YMCA on Bubbling Well Road:[44] 'Crime may be roughly defined as a war against society', he told his audience.[45] He cited a combination of factors leading to crime including heredity, upbringing and social and economic conditions. The huge influx of war refugees had added to the complexity of crime detection and prevention in the previous year.

CIVIC DUTIES AND FAMILY LIFE

One of the keys to S. C. Young's rise lies in his civic engagements, which made him an ideal spokesperson for the SMP. During their decades in

Shanghai, S. C. Young and his wife Elizabeth were active members of their church, the Holy Trinity Cathedral on Kiukiang (Jiujiang) Road, which played a central role in their civic lives and their identities. S. C. Young was a member of the Vestry of Holy Trinity Cathedral and also served on the committees of the Cathedral Boys' and Girls' Schools, and Lester Chinese Hospital. He received high honors in the Masonic Fraternity and was also active in the Rotary Club.[46] Mrs S. C. Young was a founding member of the Girls' Friendly Society and played an important role in the development and leadership of that organization throughout her long years in Shanghai. At one point, S. C. Young was even appointed to a board of film censors created by the SMC possibly to limit influence of American films in the British-controlled Settlement.[47]

One club that S. C. Young identified very strongly with was the St Patrick's Society, a society of Irishmen, which had a branch in Shanghai. He joined the Society early on and became an active member. In 1915, during a meeting of the Society, Inspector Young recommended that something be done for Irish soldiers in the war in Europe, but was voted down since others believed that all should be equally recognized for their contributions to the war effort.[48] In 1928, the St Patrick's Society claimed a total of 219 members, with S. C. Young serving on the executive committee.[49] In 1936, during the height of his career as a policeman, S. C. Young was elected the new President of the Society, at the Astor House Hotel. He had served as Vice President in the previous year.[50]

Later that same year, at the Shanghai Club on the Bund, President Macgregor and members of the Scottish St. Andrew's Society entertained three other Presidents, including S. C. Young of the St Patrick's Society, M Reader Harris of the Royal Society of St George and S. P. Simpson of the Anzacs, along with other distinguished guests from British Shanghailander society. As the article published in the *North-China Herald* reporting this gathering noted:

> Mr. Young said it was a pleasure to note that the British national societies were working in closer accord than was the case in his earlier days in Shanghai, and he thought this was an indication of the feeling that membership of the British Empire should instill in every member of it. In Shanghai they had a marvelous opportunity to set forth the

things for which the Empire stood, but hitherto they had not taken advantage of it. He looked forward to something very particular being done next year on the occasion of the Coronation of King Edward VIII.[51]

Serving in this Society brought S. C. Young together with other British Shanghailander elites to celebrate their common identity and love of king and country in a time of increasing uncertainty as the power of the Nazis and Fascists grew in Europe and talk of another world war was rife.

Young and his wife also showed great devotion to their church. They were married in the Holy Trinity Cathedral in 1911, and took on active roles in church activities in subsequent decades to the very end of their Shanghai sojourn. In 1920, during the Holy Trinity Cathedral annual meeting, Inspector Young proposed the acceptance of the Vestry's budget for 1920 and the movement was seconded by Mr. Lake.[52] S. C. Young later served as warden, and in April 1934, he was reelected as warden of the Holy Trinity Cathedral, an office he shared with several other men. During their meeting, an $876 deficit was reported and 'Mr. Young urg[ed] the churchmen to do all they can towards placing the Cathedral on a sound financial basis.'[53] Two years later, S. C. Young served as Secretary to the Vestry. At the time, the Holy Trinity Cathedral was in dire financial straits and issued an appeal for funds. Donations were needed to wipe out a large deficit. Young and others worked to raise $28,414.80 for repair and renewals to fabric of the Cathedral and vital repairs to the Cathedral's organ. The report on the church's financial situation in the *China Press* cited the Depression in Shanghai as having an adverse effect on the church's finances.[54]

Elizabeth, Young's wife, also played a leading role in civic and social affairs for Shanghailander women in the Settlement. Mrs Young was a longstanding member of the Girls' Friendly Society (GFS), and in 1937 she was Chairman [sic] of this organization of around 70 members. She had served as secretary as early as 1915.[55] In 1932, a news article summarized the GFS:

On Saturday the Shanghai branch of the Girls' Friendly Society had to be congratulated on attaining the age of 21 years. With those congratulations was associated the name of Mrs. S. C. Young who has been the moving spirit in the Society's work here throughout its infancy, childhood and adolescence. The Society functions as an institution which creates a bond of fellowship among young women in Shanghai, on recognized lines prescribed by the faith of the Church. It was started by Mrs. Young in modest yet courageous vein—its initial debt of some $30 was wiped out by a helpful boy scout who organized a magic lantern entertainment.[56]

In 1935, the GFS held its 25th anniversary party on Saturday night with a dance at the American Women's Club at 577 Bubbling Well Road, with Mrs Young serving as official hostess along with Mrs. Ottwell, the Vice President.[57] On 26 June of that year, the GFS held its annual festival at the Holy Trinity Cathedral followed by afternoon tea in the home of Mrs Young to mark the 26th anniversary of the society.[58] The members presented the GFS banner to the Cathedral, which was received by Dean Trivett. Home for the Youngs at that time was located on 540 Avenue Haig, 'where a tremendous tea was served in the dining room and verandah at two long tables.'[59] Mrs. Trivett cut a cake with the initials GFS made in frosting on the top. Mr and Mrs Weaver, Mr and Mrs L. Ottwell, Dean and Mrs. Trivett, and S. C. Young attended. 'After tea, the guests drifted out to the lawn to have their pictures taken, and then separated upstairs and down to play ping-pong or skittles, or any of the other games Mrs. Young had arranged for their amusement.'[60]

The private records from the Young/Catto family indicate that S. C. Young and his wife led an exemplary family life in Shanghai. Together they raised and educated three boys in the tumultuous environment of Republican Era Shanghai. The boys attended the Henry Lester Endowment Cathedral School, attached to the Holy Trinity Cathedral on 219 Kiukiang Road. Like their father they were tall and athletic and excelled in sports such as cricket and rugby. They were also known for their good manners and bright, inquisitive outlooks on life—especially the youngest son Albert Norman, who was the last to leave home in 1937. The Reverend Matthews of the Cathedral School wrote a heartfelt letter of gratitude to the boy's mother.[61] Their parents took them on regular excursions and holidays outside the city. They enjoyed numerous social and sports activities with their compatriots.

Together, whether on boat, bicycle, or automobile, they explored their surroundings to the extent limited by concerns for safety—after all, China in the warlord era of the 1920s and 1930s was never a safe place for foreigners to venture too far into the country, even for policemen and their families. Nevertheless, there are many photos showing S. C Young with family and friends exploring the countryside, often posing together with the Chinese.

Photos from the Young collection show the Young family at leisure in many different locations. Family photos show the boys growing up in elegant homes finely furnished and decorated with a combination of Chinese and foreign items. One photo shows the Youngs with an automobile, but others suggest they also took more humble conveyances including bicycles and rickshaws. One calling card for Mrs S. C. Young in the collection indicates that the Youngs lived on 80 Bubbling Well Road. Years later they moved to another residence at 540 Avenue Haig. Mr and Mrs Young played tennis, and they enjoyed many other recreational activities including boating. He and his colleagues in the force pursued hunting while Mrs Young and the members of the GFS appear in many photos having lawn picnics or with playing children or playing tennis. A few photos show Mrs Young posing with a Chinese housemaid, an *amah*, who took care of the children.

Like many elite Shanghailanders, the Youngs must have had a team of Chinese servants catering to their needs. In their later years, they are dressed for lawn parties or dinner parties and pose elegantly with other members of British Shanghailander society. Clearly on the eve of their departure, the Youngs were enjoying the fruits of their Shanghailander life, living in relative splendor and socializing with a variety of other elite Westerners, just as the semi-colonial system that supported these luxurious lifestyles was about to come crashing down

Figure 6: Mrs Young and baby with a Chinese amah.
Photo courtesy of Peta Catto.

Figure 7: S. C. Young, Deputy Commissioner of the SMP. Photo appears in the *North-China Herald*, 25 Aug. 1938. Courtesy of the Xujiahui Library in Shanghai.

around them.

Retiring from the force and returning home

S. C. Young's retirement from the force coincided with the rise of a new and even more violent and unpredictable era following the savage attack on Shanghai by Japanese military forces and their occupation of the city and surrounding countryside in 1937. By 1938, it was clear that the reign of the Shanghailanders over the International Settlement of Shanghai was beginning to come to an end. Prior to leaving Shanghai in 1939, S. C. Young agreed to serve as liaison officer for the SMC between the Settlement police force and the Chinese community. The decision of the SMC and SMP to appoint him to this role in an era of high crisis, when the Settlement was besieged by the forces of war, is a testament to his high stature in Shanghai society at the time as well as his role as a diplomat explaining the mission and methods of the police force to the general public. His stature also extended to the neighboring French Concession. In September 1938, at the French Police Club (FMP), the officers held a farewell dinner in honor of Deputy Commissioner Young, where the SMC officers were also present.[62] The SMP also entertained him at the Police Club, where they presented him with a silver cigarette case as a token of valuable services rendered.[63]

Only upon his retirement did the newspapers print his full name,

Stewart Cromie Young. The *North-China Herald* announced the news, claiming that 'one of Shanghai's most popular and most senior police officials retires tomorrow from the post of Deputy Commissioner of the SMP after 34 years' service in the course of which he rose through the various ranks and distinguished himself repeatedly in dealing with crime and political unrest.[64] By that time Young had been decorated with a Police Long Service Medal with two bars, a Chinese Government Police Medal (Class I, Grade III) presented in March 1937 for services rendered in the arrest of important criminals, and the SMC 1937 Emergency Medal.[65] All of these medals testify to his important contributions to the safety and security of the Settlement during the period of the most intense conflict that raged outside Settlement boundaries, the vicious war between Japanese and Chinese forces from August to October 1937.

Considered one of the most violent clashes during the eight-year war between China and Japan, this conflict took place largely in the northern districts of Zhabei and Hongkou and beyond, well outside Settlement boundaries.[66] The only major incidents of violence inside the International Settlement took place on 14 August 1937 when Chinese planes aiming to drop bombs on Japanese ships in the harbor accidentally dropped them in some of the busiest intersections of the city. One bomb dropped at the confluence of Avenue Edward VII (currently Yan'an Road) and Yu Ya Ching Road (present day Xizang Road), near the famed amusement center known as the Great World (*da shijie*), killing thousands of residents and refugees in an instant. Another bomb dropped on Nanjing Road near the Cathay Hotel (present day Fairmont Peace Hotel) and also a bomb caused damage to the Sincere Department store - in all killing hundreds of innocent bystanders.

S. C. Young and the SMP and SMC had to deal with the aftermath of these horrific incidents, which involved cleaning up the wreckage and rubble while collecting the thousands of dead bodies and body parts and carting them off for disposal elsewhere in the city. Young's descendants' collection of memorabilia includes several photos showing the carnage on Nanjing Road that followed the accidental bombing, such as bodies being placed in carts. There are also several photos of burning and gutted buildings and a few of bombs blasting and smoke billowing in the northern district during the 1937 conflict. These must have been among the most violent episodes that S. C.

Young witnessed and handled during his decades in the force.

In 1939, S. C. Young and his wife took their leave of Shanghai to sail to England, where their three sons waited for them. The aged couple received a warm and cordial farewell from the Shanghailander community, whose ranks were now beginning to dwindle. Captain W. G. Clarke, President of the St Patrick's Society, and Mrs. Clarke gave them a farewell garden party on 28 May at 260 Route Dupleix, with 120 guests attending. During the party, Captain Clarke remarked on

Figure 8: Dean Trivett presents a painting of the Holy Trinity Cathedral Chancel to the Youngs.
Photo courtesy of Peta Catto.

Figure 9: S. C. Young and companion on a ship (exact date unknown).
Photo courtesy of Peta Catto.

S. C. Young's long career and his achievement of one of the highest ranks in the SMP and presented him with yet another cigarette box inscribed by members of the Society. Mrs. Young received linen teacloths and handkerchiefs as a parting gift. On 4 June, at Holy Trinity Cathedral, Dean Trivett officiated a simple ceremony to thank the Youngs for their service to the church, and P. W. Massey also remarked on his long and distinguished career in the police. The Youngs were given a painting of the Cathedral's Chancel and now they were set to leave for England on 6 June on the HMS Ranchi.[67]

One intriguing photo in the Young family collection shows S. C. Young lounging in a chair on the deck of a ship along with another European male of similar age. He is wearing short pants with socks pulled up almost to his knees, and looking very relaxed.

One wonders if this photo was taken on his long voyage home. On the way back to England from Shanghai, the Youngs stopped in Bombay. As reported in the *Times of India*, '[S. C. Young] has seen Shanghai grow from an insignificant place to a large city, thoroughly international in character, the gateway of China's commerce.'[68] He had to face a rise in crime after the war with Japan started in 1937 and also the big problem of one million refugees pouring into the Settlement. According to the interview with the retired Commissioner Young, 300,000 refugees in Shanghai had found means of making a living, but 70,000 homeless remained in city at the time of his departure.[69] Among the photos in the Young family collection are one showing thousands of poor Chinese refugees streaming into the Settlement with their belongings, and another showing Chinese refugees blocked from entering the Settlement boundaries by barbed wire emplacements. Overall, my feeling as I perused this unique and remarkable collection is of one set of images showing the halcyon early years of Young's Shanghai experience being gradually replaced by a much darker and more menacing portrait of a city besieged.

Upon his return to England, S. C. Young and family faced yet another menace: Hitler and the Nazis. His reaction was not to sit on the sidelines, but to take decisive action. He enlisted in the volunteer reserve services to defend his country. In 1941, the *North-China Herald* featured a letter from the former Deputy Commissioner, which is the last news item about S. C. Young to appear in the collection of Shanghai's English-language newspapers from that era. S. C. Young had sent the city a letter from Guildford, stating that he was now a

Figure 10: Chinese wartime refugees barred from entering the International Settlement by a fence of barbed wire erected by Settlement authorities (this could either be 1932 or 1937, as the photo is not dated.)
Photo courtesy of Peta Catto.

Flight Lieutenant in the Volunteer Reserve of the RAF. His letter helped buoy the spirits of British Shanghailanders who were also being besieged –and soon, unbeknownst to them at the time, to be confined to Japanese-run prison camps outside the Settlement. S. C. Young's missive 'gives some indication of the spirit and determination with which Britons are meeting the air menace at home.'[70] The *North-China Herald* article features a long quote from his original letter describing the involvement of his entire family in the war effort and highlighting his optimism about the eventual outcome:

> 'We are all well, and happy to be in England during these great days. Brian is a Lieutenant, Terence is a Company Sergeant Major, and Norman is in an Officers Training Unit...Betty is in the Women's Voluntary Service, and I have been lucky enough to get into the Volunteer Reserve of the RAF, in which I am now a Flight Lieutenant; I am naturally glad to be allowed to do something towards winning the war. It looks like being a long job, but there is no doubt about the result here.'[71]

CONCLUSION

Through the kaleidoscope of personal images and records and public news articles taken from the 35 years of their life in China, I can discern a couple who carefully built a family and a professional and civic life and cautiously crafted a public and private identity for themselves and their family as they staked a claim in Shanghai's settler society. Over their many years there, with an almost missionary zeal, they earned stellar reputations for their integrity, their achievements, their love for socializing, their zest for competition, their commitments and sacrifices, their love of home, church, king, and country, and their adherence to the rules of decorum and propriety that characterized British Shanghailander society.

Although the Youngs were not from elite family or financial backgrounds, they nevertheless earned a coveted place in Shanghai society, hobnobbing with men and women of means who played significant roles in the city's semi-colonial power structure. Then again, Shanghai was a paradise of adventurers, which afforded people from myriad backgrounds the opportunity to advance or even reinvent themselves and to seek a higher social standing among their peers. Still, it was not easy for British men and women of modest backgrounds to integrate themselves so completely into the fabric of elite social and political life in British Shanghai, and so the Youngs stand out as an exceptional couple in the Shanghailander community.

The treaty port system of China, with its semi-colonial governments and police forces run by the British, French, and Americans and other foreigners, was arguably racist, corrupt, unstable, and unjust –

Figure 11: The Youngs at a dinner party c. 1938.
Photo courtesy of Peta Catto.

certainly so in the eyes of contemporary Chinese leftist nationalists and later very much so in the historiography of the Chinese Communist Party. Within this milieu, and in a Chinese city most notorious for its corruption, S. C. Young and family shine as beacons of exemplary Christian values, bringing peace and order, light and wisdom to the city and to their community of Shanghailanders. That they did so in a society that was increasingly tottering precariously on the edge of obliteration through the forces of nationalism, war, and revolution makes their story even more compelling. Not long after their departure from China in 1939, the Japanese occupation of Shanghai's two foreign settlements in 1941-1945 and the Communist Revolution that followed in 1949 shattered the precious vase of British Shanghailander society. By that time, the Youngs had contributed to the building of an enduring and cherished legacy for the city in terms of its built environment and modern infrastructure, if not its political system and civil society.

ABOUT THE AUTHOR

Andrew David Field is a historian and scholar of modern and contemporary Chinese society. He has published three books including *Shanghai's Dancing World, Mu Shiying: China's Lost Modernist*, and *Shanghai Nightscapes*. He currently lives in Shanghai with his family and serves as an administrator and adjunct professor for Duke Kunshan University.

E-mail: Andrew.field@dukekunshan.edu.cn

—∞—

Endnotes

1 Peta Catto, personal correspondence with author, August 2006.

2 Robert Bickers, 'Shanghailanders: The Formation and Identity of the British Settler Community in Shanghai 1843-1937', *Past & Present*, no. 159, 1998, pp. 161–211.

3 A fairly comprehensive summary of the history and workings of the SMP may be found in Robert Bickers, *Empire Made Me: An Englishman Adrift in Shanghai* (London, Penguin Books, 2003), pp. 64-94. Another good source is Frederic Wakeman Jr., *Policing Shanghai, 1927-1937* (Berkeley, University of California Press, 1995); *The China Quarterly*, no. 115, 1988, pp. 408–440.

4 This event and its background is detailed in Nicholas Clifford,

Spoilt Children of Empire: Westerners in Shanghai and the Chinese Revolution of the 1920s (New Hampshire, Middlebury College Press, 1991), pp. 97-112.

5 Wakeman, *Policing Shanghai.*

6 The best account of the rise and operations of this crime syndicate in Shanghai is Brian Martin, *The Shanghai Green Gang: Politics and Organized Crime, 1919-1937* (Berkeley: University of California Press, 1996).

7 Wakeman, *Policing Shanghai*, pp. 132-167.

8 In addition to Wakeman's, *Policing Shanghai.* and Martin's, *The Shanghai Green Gang,* for studies of vice cultures and their regulation and control by municipal authorities and police in Republican Shanghai, see Christian Henriot, *Prostitution and Sexuality in Shanghai: A Social History 1849-1949* (Cambridge: Cambridge University Press, 2001) and Gail Hershatter, *Dangerous Pleasures: Prostitution and Modernity in Twentieth-Century Shanghai* (Berkeley, University of California Press, 1996) and Frederic Wakeman, Jr., 'Licensing Leisure: The Chinese Nationalists' Attempt to Regulate Shanghai, 1927-49' in *The Journal of Asian Studies*, vol. 54, no. 1, 1995, pp. 19–42.

9 Brian Martin, 'The Pact with the Devil: The Relationship Between the Shanghai Green Gang and the Shanghai French Concession Authorities, 1925-1935' in Frederic Wakeman, Jr. and Wen-hsin Yeh, (eds.), *Shanghai Sojourners* (Berkeley: University of California Press, 1992).

10 Christian Henriot, *Prostitution and Sexuality in Shanghai,* Gail Hershatter, *Dangerous Pleasures.*

11 Andrew David Field, *Shanghai's Dancing World: Cabaret Culture and Urban Politics, 1919-1954* (Hong Kong: Chinese University Press, 2010).

12 Bickers, *Empire Made Me.*

13 Ibid., p. 72.

14 *North-China Herald*, 28 September 1938

15 Ibid.

16 *China Press*, 25 August 1938, p. 2.

17 An account of the Trenches during this period can be found in Field, *Shanghai's Dancing World*, pp. 39-43.

18 *China Press*, 25 August 1938

19 Ibid.

20 *North-China Herald,* 27 July 1906, p. 200.

21 *North-China Herald,* 30 May 1908, p. 540.

22 *North-China Herald,* 16 May 1908 p. 407.

23 *North-China Herald,* 24 February 1911 p. 442.

24 *North-China Herald,* 19 April 1932.

25 *China Press,* 25 August 1938.

26 Ibid.

27 *North-China Herald,* 2 August 1913 p. 351.

28 Ibid.

29 *North-China Herald,* 4 October 1913.

30 *North-China Herald,* 31 January 1914, p. 318-321.

31 *North-China Herald,* 28 March 1916 p. 7.

32 *North-China Herald,* 25 November 1916, p. 424.

33 *Shanghai Gazette,* 26 February 1920.

34 *North-China Herald,* 23 April 1921, p. 275.

35 *North-China Herald,* 22 July 1922, p. 272.

36 *North-China Herald,* 01 May 1926, p. 201.

37 *North-China Herald,* 9 November 1929 p. 220.

38 *China Press,* 2 February 1934: 7 also published in *North-China Herald,* 7 February 1934, p. 232.

39 The following information and quotations in this paragraph are from *North-China Herald,* 24 June 1936, p. 530.

40 *China Press,* 19 June 1936, p. 9; *North-China Herald,* 24 June 1936, p. 530.

41 *North-China Herald,* 3 March 1937, p. 370.

42 *China Press,* 3 July 1936.

43 Ibid..

44 *China Press,* 17 March 1938, p. 3.

45 Ibid.

46 *North-China Herald,* 28 September 1938.

47 *China Weekly Review,* 24 September 192, p. 87.

48 *North-China Herald,* 5 February 1915, p. 4.

49 *North-China Herald,* 4 February 1928, p. 186.

50 *China Press,* 21 January 1936, p. 9; *North-China Herald,* 29 Jan 193,6 p. 181.

51 *North-China Herald,* 1 April 1936, p. 20.

52 *Shanghai Gazette,* 13 February 1920, p. 6.

53 *China Press,* 11 April 1934, p. 3.

54 *China Press,* 25 June 1936, p. 9.

55 *Shanghai Times,* 18 February 1915, p. 6.

56 *North-China Herald,* 30 November 1932, p. 328.

57 *North-China Herald,* 1 December 1935, p. 440.

58 *North-China Herald,* 30 June 1937, p. 546.

59 Ibid.

60 Ibid.

61 This letter appears in the collection of Peta Catto that also contains the photos used in this article.

62 *China Press,* 27 September 1938.

63 *China Press,* 24 September 1938.

64 *North-China Herald,* 28 September 1938, p. 538.

65 Ibid.

66 For an account of this battle, see Wakeman, *Policing Shanghai,* pp. 277-288. See also Peter Hamsen, *Shanghai 1937: Stalingrad on the Yangtze,* (Casemate, 2015).

67 *North-China Herald,* 7 Jun 1939, p. 416.

68 *The Times of India,* 27 June 1939.

69 Ibid.

70 *North-China Herald,* 5 March 1941.

71 Ibid.

'AND WHAT DO WE KNOW ABOUT CHINA?'

The International Labour Office,
Albert Thomas And Republican China, 1919 – 1930

BY CHRISTIAN MUELLER

ABSTRACT

The integration of Republican China in the 1920s into the League of Nations' labour regime under the leadership of the International Labour Organisation (ILO) was a profound challenge that Western modernity posed to modernising China. From its very beginning in 1919 and 1920, the ILO put the Chinese labour question on the agenda, yet without directly engaging with the Chinese conditions until the seminal field trip mission by its director, Albert Thomas, in 1929 and 1930. This article argues that Thomas, as one key actor in the ILO, was very much interested in understanding the situation of workers in China and the development of political parties and labour associations that could be integrated into the ILO system of correspondents. The article illuminates the fragile political framework of the Republic under which new standards of labour law were established in China and raises questions as to the integration of China and its emerging labour law under the auspices of industrial modernisation. It also evaluates the ILO efforts to integrate China and its labour conditions into the international system of the League of Nations and its agency, the ILO, while asking how far Chinese actors were interested in actively promoting their inclusion in the global labour regime in the late 1920s.

EUROPEAN INTERNATIOANLSM IN SOCIAL ENGINEERING AND CHINA

In April 1918, Stephan Bauer, head of the old International Labour Office in Basle until 1919, showed optimism about a new peak of social reform associations in the years after the First World War. Bauer did so with a view to a post-war order in which labour relations within nations and in the international society should become the work of peaceful compromises and treaties, and not of heated labour struggles. This 'peace' in solving labour questions would provide the foundations for a lasting international peace between nations for decades to come. 'The renewal and systematic extension of the protection of labourers is a pressing and international necessity, an internal question of peace of primary order which will give international peace its full human and economic weight', said Bauer.[1] Since the 1860s, Bauer and similarly minded social reformers had focused their work on attempts at social engineering to argue that a labour regime spanning the whole world and not only Europe would be essentially shaped by states and private actors alike, thus moving from European NGO efforts in social engineering towards a global regime of labour legislation.[2]

However, Bauer believed this global regime should adhere to certain universal and normative standards that had a strong Euro-centric bias.[3] Before 1919, Bauer and other leading proponents of the international movement for social reforms and social engineering perceived the matter with a strong focus on European and North American labour. Although many examples of the effects of transnational regimes of labour legislation and knowledge transfer existed in different regions of the world, particularly in the imperial zones of contact in the extra-European world, China had few such examples and was not very prominent in Euro-centric discussions about the legislative standards of labour. This changed only gradually during the 1920s with the activities of the ILO as part of the project to establish a global order of peace in politics and social legislation.[4] However, research so far has less inquired into the ways in which Chinese labour legislation and labour standards has been perceived and conceptualised in the ILO.[5] European experts on social questions like Louis Varlez, head of the unemployment division under Albert Thomas in the ILO, identified the problematic tradition of stressing differences in social matters between countries and regions, yet saw the need in the ILO for an inclusive approach to nationally framed labour questions that would possibly bring about global solutions. 'Certainly, the West is the West and the East is the East, and it shall remain so, but it is quite as certain that the world is one world, and that upon it each people can and must develop its own task for Humanity's Happiness and Justice.'[6]

This article therefore explores the ways in which the West perceived and conceptualised Chinese labour regimes, and in how far the mission of Thomas in 1929 and 1930 can be interpreted as an approach to 'Westernise' Chinese labour questions according to a European-conceived global standard that dealt primarily with specific European aspects of modernisation. International social policy and engineering were essential to the establishment of the International

Labour Organisation within the League of Nations framework in 1919. Extensive efforts from European private associations had been made since the early 1860s to frame labour legislation and support of labour issues in a Euro-centric context.[7]

China emerged as a rather passive participant and a centre for labour export before 1914. Perceptions of China as part of a global labour regime had been mainly focused on the investment and trade opportunities and issues of labour recruitment and labour forces before 1918. It is not surprising that China, especially the Yangtze region, became a focus for foreign investment in China, while Chinese labour was mainly of interest when referring to the 'humble, industrious and enduring' character of Chinese workers that could be exploited in transitional or migratory labour regimes.[8] While China was perceived until 1919 mostly through Orientalist stereotypes of a passive market for investment, production and supply of labour forces, one can see a new focus on East Asia or the Far East in the first decade of the interwar period, culminating with the first official mission of the head of the ILO, Albert Thomas, to China and Japan in 1929 and 1930. This new situation, involving diverse new personal in organising labour legislation and labour regimes more generally, new associational and organisational actors in the international sphere to some extent mirror the trend of certain peaks in the rise and fall of waves of internationalism. The shift of interplay between nationalist issues and international cooperation is particularly complex when looking at the rising prominence and presence of Japan and China in the inter-war period, as the tensions between a politics of national(ist) interests in the League of Nations and also – to some extent – in the ILO is countered with a more diverse discourse and acknowledgement of global regimes of labour that is mirrored both in the codification on slavery and forced labour through the League of Nations and the ILO in 1926 and 1930 and the implementation of European normative standards as global regimes for labour rights and legislation more generally in the 1920s.

This article argues that the expansion of internationalism in social engineering, emanating from Europe after 1919, can be seen as an active export of local and national experience and frameworks as well as national ideological outlook of labour legislation that was deeply rooted in foremost Belgian, French, English and German perceptions. Internationalism, as understood by European powers, in the 1920s was still the 'crown of the national edifice' to alleviate the status of great powers and their cultural capital in terms of the international community of states.[9] Therefore the transfer of labour issues from the main actors in the International Labour Office, arguably Albert Thomas with a French socialist background and Louis Varlez with a mixed labour and liberal Belgian background, prefigured the lenses of how China and its labour regimes were perceived in the 1920s. In referring to Pierre-Yves Saunier's 'circulatory regimes of the social', this article argues that European functional and thematic discourses account for the increasing interest in Chinese labour legislation and labour issues since the mid-1920s, but that the main categories of understanding Chinese labour regimes remained Euro-centric.[10] Thus, it is vital to see how the mission of Albert Thomas had an effect on the ways in which China was perceived but also its limitations. Some of the functional and thematic reasons for an increased interest of the ILO in China can be narrowed down to the vital interest of Japanese politics in Manchuria and the role Japan played in the League of Nations and the International Labour Organisation.

The ilo as a european 'epistemic community' in the interwar period? Limitations of a contested concept

With the establishment of the ILO as a specialised agency for labour regimes and labour legislation under the League of Nations, regulation of labour issues received a strong and centralised international force after the First World War. Hopes for a new peak in internationalism lay now within the new International Organisation that superseded the old private associations of experts.[11] Albert Thomas insisted that the ILO would provide solutions where the previous associations were still 'sleeping and being taken over by reactionary forces.'[12] However, the ILO was closely linked to the older European private associations and was composed of representatives from the trade unions, employers and national governments. The main efforts of these representatives were to draft, elaborate, and create international conventions on issues of labour and employment with the aspiration to provide universal rules and regulations. In terms of their personnel, they remained closely related to the older pre-war network of experts.[13] Among these older experts, perhaps the most prominent examples that were hired for the ILO were Louis Varlez as Head of the ILO's Unemployment and Migration department (1920 – 1929), and Arthur Fontaine as Chair of the ILO Governing Body (1920 – 1931).[14] Under the French socialist and former labour activist Albert Thomas, the ILO soon became the leading actor in the 1920s on international labour regimes, aiming to set the social agenda on a global scale by incorporating pre-1914 efforts of the diverse international NGOs in social engineering.

To understand the mind-set that the ILO employed towards integrating large parts of Asia and Africa into their social agenda that was framed by European expertise and experiences, historians have used the concept of 'epistemic communities' to explain how networks within institutions develop, adopt and transform scientific knowledge.[15] Many of the social reformers shared a common worldview (*Weltanschauung*) that placed the hopes on academic deliberation of social engineering that would eventually deliver academic results of a perfectible global social regime. The prime movers within those epistemic communities are supposed to possess shared knowledge and a common worldview. This poses a problem for historical research. The concept of 'epistemic community' presupposes an ideal-type of a close-knit and tight network of a homogenous select assembly of like-minded ideological actors who are purely interested in knowledge transfer and dissemination. Yet this ideal-type established by Peter Haas to describe international expert committees in the 1980s often does not match the historical reality. We can find that in the 1920s, the actors used their membership in the ILO or other associations also for ideological, internationalist, nationalist, local or party-political purposes.[16] In essence, worldviews could interfere with or even dominate the production of knowledge.

Further, and this is a new criticism, the concept of 'epistemic communities' implies that the quest for knowledge does not contradict with a worldview that the members of the community share. This assumption would mean that a worldview that tends to be political and biased towards national, regional, religious, party or other allegiances do not influence a specific quest for knowledge or the knowledge that the community produces. When this concept of 'epistemic community' is located in the context of the ILO, it becomes obvious that the actors shared experiences of social policies in Europe in the pre-war period as much as specific national allegiances. This entrenchment in Euro-centric thinking and party-political as well as national settings very much influenced the process of creating knowledge about labour regimes, and it defined the nature of the

Euro-centric created knowledge about labour regimes and labour legislations in Asia or in other parts of the world. It is therefore necessary to treat 'epistemic communities' as an ideal-type that shaped knowledge according to political bias, and thus counters the rhetoric of the ILO that the new beginning towards a universal labour regime was free from Eurocentric assumptions and national aspirations. This assumed and political 'epistemic community' on social engineering in the ILO that created knowledge about labour conditions to draft universal or global legislation regimes in the 1920s was clearly biased towards the European experience.[17] The revived and strong interest in China, despite its notable silence within the ILO in the first years and the conceptualisation of China's labour regime under the Republican government, clearly illustrates this bias.

EUROPEAN EXPERTS TURNING EAST - THE ILO AND ITS INTEREST IN CHINESE LABOUR REGIMES, 1919 – 1924

The officials setting up the International Labour Office after the war with a standing International Labour Conference tried to combine the expertise on all labour issues that was promoted by its member states and adherent countries. With the notable exceptions of the Soviet Union and the United States of America, neither of which joined the League of Nations, the main countries and continents of reference were Europe and the Americas, especially Latin America. The United States of America found itself in the odd position that although congress voted against joining the League of Nations in 1919, it became an essential part of the ILO. The strong labour movement including the American Federation of Labour under Samuel Gompers made an important contribution towards forging labour rights. China joined the League of Nations in 1920, but remained notably absent from the ILO in the first years, in contrast to Germany who could not join the League of Nations until 1926 but was active in the ILO from the beginning in 1919.[18] The effects of the Washington Conference on International Labour in 1919 were short-lived, and it appears that the negotiations in Peking about what to do with or how to become active in the forming ILO were long drawn out and inconclusive until 1923.[19]

The ILO promoted social peace as its universal goal, adhering to the preamble of the ILO statutes that 'the League of Nations has for its object the establishment of universal peace, and such a peace can be established only if it is based upon social justice.'[20] According to common ILO thinking, an essential part of universal social peace was the establishment of universal rules and legislations for labour protection, insurances and working conditions. In this respect, the ILO promoted the normative regulations of the earlier private associations related to unemployment, eight-hour workdays, women and child labour, and as the first case for health and safety at work, the banning of white phosphorus from the matchstick industry. Those were adopted in the first International Labour Conference in Washington in 1919.[21]

While conceptually the international labour conventions should extend to all states, including the ones who were not yet members of the ILO, this proved difficult in practice during the 1920s.[22] The ILO could not claim to have any authority over non-member states and depended on the good will of those governments. Yet, more problematic, the ILO governing body struggled with the amelioration of labour conditions in the United States despite Samuel Gompers, the long-standing leader of the AFL, being both an organisational leader in the ILO and an ardent correspondent with Albert Thomas. Further, Africa's colonial territories were subject to their colonial home countries. Asia – with the notable exception of India – was a relatively unknown continent to the ILO in 1920. Japan had joined the ILO in 1919, but little was known as to labour regulations in Japan until the mid-1920s. At the first International Labour Conference in Washington in 1919, this led to the assumption that both Japan and China had good claims to opt out of the agreement for a 48-hour working week to set a precedent for 'exceptions' of universal labour regimes regarding Asia.[23] In relation to the new Republic of China, the most prominent aspect that the ILO addressed first was the opium trade in the broader remit to tackle drugs and narcotic trade. The ILO followed the international initiatives taken before the First World War, and urged for the renewal of the International Opium Convention signed in 1912 on the ban of opium trade. The commission for fighting the opium trade was established within the League of Nations in 1921 and it became necessary because the United States of America and China abandoned the old Convention in 1919 as part of a global regime of health relating to labour conditions. China was surprisingly one of the first nations to join the commission, next to France, Great Britain, Portugal, Italy, Japan, Germany, India, Siam and Bolivia.[24] Yet, the main problem appeared to be that the League of Nations, as much as the ILO urged it to establish the commission to fight against any kind of opiates and drugs, took over the commission so that national interests of trade and regional influence superseded a genuine belief in internationalising health regulations. As much as Asian expertise was wanted, it was not used to establish international or transnational regimes of health, labour and social justice, but rather placed in a commission to control and regulate trade.

The notable absence of prominent Asian expertise or knowledge on labour regimes did not change drastically in the early 1920s despite the fact that Siam and Japan joined the ILO consecutively. The Chinese Republic took up formal communication with the ILO only in 1923 when the Minister of the Republic of China at Berne, by presidential decree, established a permanent liaison office with the ILO in Switzerland.[25] Chi-Yung Hsiao, the First Secretary of the Chinese legation in Berne and delegate to the 4th session of the International Labour Conference was designated as Chief of Service on 23 March 1923.[26] The new liaison officer also responded to questionnaires sent out by the ILO in 1921 to gather information about the status of labour legislation in all non-member countries and to identify major issues and problems that the ILO should address in the future.

The Chinese response to the questionnaire issued by the ILO regarding labour legislation was more evasive than informative. The Chinese Diet discussed a possible labour bill in 1923, yet no clear communication was made to the ILO as to the status of working hour regulations, protection against accidents, old age and invalidity pensions or the right of association for the workers.[27] The ILO questions indicated that those topics had been the struggles of European internationalist private associations before the First World War and appeared high on the agenda in 1919, when the ILO was re-organised under the League of Nations. Yet, China would not respond to those questions, partly because the government itself had no answer, and partly because those questions suggested a Euro-centric labour regime that the Republican Government was not willing to adopt in all its details. Where China could adhere was to the 'golden yardstick' of internationalism for workers' rights – the ban of white phosphorus in the match stick industry as adopted at the Berne convention in 1906,[28] and to the ban of using white lead in the painting industry.[29] But the more concerning issues that mattered to the Europeans oriented toward the standards of the ILO were the minimum age of child labour, the right of association for workers, and the age of children working both in Chinese and foreign factories and on ships as trimmers and stokers.

All those questions remained unanswered in 1923-1924, until the Chinese Republic signed the Amendment to Article 393 of the Versailles Treaty and the corresponding articles of the other peace treaties.[30] For China, the whole new system of internationalism emerging from the Versailles Treaty posed a dilemma that could not easily be solved, and the European powers were well aware of it. One the one hand, the League of Nations and the reinforcement of national interests in the committees and commissions appeared to be strengthened instruments of old great power diplomacy. On the other hand, new international organisations like the ILO seemed to offer a possible way to pursue back doors policy making with and within the West.[31] The second approach was taken up reluctantly because it remained uncertain whether the ILO offered new opportunities to influence aspects of global governance, or whether it would just mirror the flipside of old power diplomacy. As much as this was fought in practice among the European nations in the early 1920s, the space for new opportunities to participate as equal member in the international system remained unclear to the leaders of the young Chinese Republic. Certainly, the Chinese nationalist protesters in 1919 and 1925 claimed the new global order was nothing more than old imperialism in disguise.[32] However, Chinese collaboration with the ILO seemed to offer chances to become an active member in the international system and be recognised by the Western powers. One way to move forward was to foster closer ties within the ILO to influence the new world order in terms of labour and social justice from within, and to make sure that nationalist aspects were recognised at the forum of nations in Geneva.[33]

GROWING AWARENESS OF CHINA UNDER THE ILO LABOUR REGIME, 1924 – 1929

Therefore, it does not come as a surprise that the first time the ILO noticed the unsecure labour conditions and the necessity for the ILO to inquire further into labour regimes in China, it depicted a rather dull and pessimistic image of Republican China. Following the Chinese comments on the report regarding working hours that was sent around after the First International Labour Conference in Washington, D.C., in 1919, Albert Thomas stated in his article *Labour Legislation in China* in 1924 that 'China was still very largely an undeveloped country, that it was faced with special difficulties ... that made it impossible for China to conform to Western standards.'[34] Although Thomas applauded the Chinese government that it supported in principle the protection of labour by factory legislation, the ILO insisted that it would now have a closer eye and more direct communications with China to understand the real problems and issues in a vast territory where the government had no tariff autonomy, where factory legislation had no predecessors, and where foreign settlements and leased autonomous territories were not necessarily subject to national labour legislation.[35]

As mentioned above, while the Chinese government ardently adhered to the older labour legislations that banned certain dangerous substances from factories such as white lead and white phosphorus, the actual labour regime of working hours, resting days and pension schemes were largely ignored. Those legislative norms designed to protect the health of the workers were considered as 'Western' impositions that would not take root in China. In this sense, the Republican government strictly questioned an international labour regime that was promoted as a universal concept of social justice and peace by the European experts in the ILO. Implicitly, the 'epistemic community' of the governing body of the ILO was accused of exercising European imperialism in the field of labour protection. China found itself 'unable to accept the principle of a weekly rest day, because tradition and custom in China are not the same as in Western countries.'[36] The Presidential Decree issued by the Republican Government concluded that Chinese workers would not need to rest one day a week, and that, if they wanted to, the government might consider a random resting day or two.[37] The government's evasive rhetoric of exceptionalism to avoid adopting ILO rules was duly criticised in China by the *North-China Herald* that claimed there was still 'much room for progress in labour legislation in this country and for the betterment of social conditions.'[38]

Alarmed by the Chinese official accusations of exercising Western imperialism by neglecting asserted 'cultural differences' among Chinese workers, the ILO governing body under the leadership of Arthur Fontaine inquired further into China's labour conditions and working hours, especially in Shanghai and Manchuria. They found that proposals for limiting working hours and protecting children at work had not been aptly recognised by the Chinese government.[39] The ILO director Albert Thomas had just led the first fact-finding mission to Shanghai in early 1924 to investigate the conditions of child employment in Chinese factories.[40] The investigation thus helped to direct international attention to the labour conditions in China for the first time.[41] Thomas was subsequently commissioned to approach competent authorities in China, to draw their attention to the allegedly precarious situation of overwork and undue child labour in China, and to report back to the ILO governing body with any news on steps taken in amelioration of the situation.[42]

It was only in the early 1930s that the International Labour Conference, together with the governing body of the International Labour Office, finally decided that the Asian countries, among them Japan and China, needed their own voice to raise labour issues that might not fit the matrix of the close-knit network of former European activists and experts in social engineering. Opening up the rather closed 'epistemic community' of experts in the ILO, the governing body of the International Labour Office decided in its 55th session (12 – 17 October 1931) at Geneva under the chairmanship of Ernest Mahaim the 'convocation of an advisory conference of Asiatic countries' to the International Labour Office in Geneva.[43] The governing body suggested that all Asian states that were members of the ILO, as well as all European states with possessions in Asia, should join together in an advisory conference to provide the 'epistemic community' in Geneva with the necessary knowledge that the community lacked.[44] It was to some extent a necessary step in understanding the labour regimes in Republican China, triggered by Thomas' travels to China in 1929 and 1930, to note the shortcomings of a purely European community of experts relying on colonial knowledge and assumptions about the Far East. The advisory conference was intended to be a first step towards this undertaking.

UNDERSTANDING LABOUR REGIMES IN REPUBLICAN CHINA – THE MISSION OF ALBERT THOMAS IN 1929 AND 1930

As the Director of the International Labour Office from 1919 until his death in May 1932, Albert Thomas was highly important in shaping the course of action of the ILO in international labour legislation and formulating global regimes for the regulation of labour. Thomas did not perceive 'international labour legislation as a collection of texts, but as a living reality the development of which he watched' and actively influenced.[45] His obituary claimed that the 'desire to be always directly and accurately informed upon social questions led him [to] the Far East' in 1929 and 1930.[46] Thomas had a vision to promote and eventually achieve social justice among all classes, yet in the 1920s, not necessarily across all nations. However, he embodied the spirit of a particularly European pre-1914 belief in unlimited social progress that international labour legislation and social engineering in the ILO model between government experts, employers and workers promoted. Thomas' efforts forged the ILO into a central organ of scientific understanding of industrial and labour conditions of different countries.'[47] He personally promoted this core as essence of liberal and labour internationalism that had its roots in the late 19th century as an institution that longed for social progress through universal knowledge.[48]

The historian Jasmien van Daele has described this trend of the ILO in the 1920s to finalise and regulate transnational labour legislations and labour regimes with the dichotomy of 'internationalising the national – nationalising the international.'[49] Certainly Albert Thomas was keen on internationalising the national labour regulations, but he remained deeply rooted in his national understanding of European and French politics in particular. Until 1928, the topics in his correspondence rarely reached beyond the scope of European and American topics and focused on negotiating with socialist and labour activists in the Northern hemisphere of the 'West' and the European governments. Albert Thomas was an ardent opponent of the colonial regimes in Africa and Asia, especially regarding labour regimes and the neglect of workers' rights. However, he was, to some extent, unable to look beyond the idea that internationalising or universalising national regulations in the ILO would structurally similar to European efforts of imperialism in slavery and forced labour regimes in the interwar period. This normative yardstick was heavily influenced by European experiences and ultimately European expertise that evaluated the outcome of the second industrial revolution in Europe and its effects on European national societies and universalised those towards a global labour regime.

This problem of European 'labour' imperialism that the Chinese government had already addressed inadequately in 1924 became more prominent in the late 1920s. As Director and intellectual leader of the

ILO, Albert Thomas was already involved in Chinese labour affairs before his departure to the Far East in summer of 1929. Under his leadership, the ILO had developed a somewhat critical stance against the extra-territoriality of parts of China, especially in Shanghai, and the problems that extra-territoriality posed for a uniform labour regime in China that could protect workers across the vast territory. The China correspondent of the London *Times* criticised Thomas and the ILO for being at odds with the interests of the British, French and other imperial nations who had gained such extra-territoriality from China in the Treaty of Nanking in 1842, a statement that Albert Thomas took pain to publicly deny in early 1929.[50] But as much as Thomas opposed the imperial principle of extra-territoriality manifest in the Treaty system, he concluded that labour regimes in China exploited labour under the guise of Chinese exceptionalism. The rhetoric that Chinese workers would not understand the concept of a weekly day off ran counter to his view that a free day per week was needed to recover from an eight to ten hour labour day.[51]

In 1928, the International Labour Office made a two-fold attempt to address its social mission under the League of Nations system in Asia. Thomas was eager to understand the problems that came with the diversification of labour in the different provinces and the extra-territorial and leased parts of China, while Louis Varlez was supposed to focus on migrations in East Asia. Neither of the two phenomena was new in the 1920s, but it was only then that the Europeans took notice of the problems that came with extra-territoriality and intra-Asian labour migration for a universal labour regime under the ILO. As neither Thomas nor Varlez had worked on those issues before, the two men set in 1929 a double mission to map theretofore unchartered territory for the ILO.[52] Despite Varlez' retirement that year, he embarked on the mission that he shared with Thomas.[53] In January 1929, Thomas insisted that Varlez attend the Third Conference of the Institute of Pacific Relations in Kyoto in the autumn of that year. Varlez was supposed to talk about land lease and migration labour in Asia.[54] For both men, the travels in East Asia were supposed to be an insight into a different world of labour regimes, but personal motives and concepts of Orientalism prevailed. Varlez and Thomas wanted to 'see interesting countries by getting into close contact with their people, ... prepare university lectures on international institutions ... and working towards the realisation of my social and political ideals within my strengths and limits.'[55]

Although the topics at the Conference were of a more technical nature, both men were aware already that their presence in Asia could be construed in a more political sense under the rising tensions between Japan and China regarding Manchuria. Thomas had already seen that his presence in Shanghai in 1924 and his statements in late 1928 could be considered as interfering with the colonial policies in China. Varlez' mission to comment on intra-Asian migrant labour was equally political in the context of Manchuria. The Chinese Northeast was one of the more heavily industrialised parts of China with traditional intra-China labour migration present, and Japan was propagating a more belligerent pan-Asianism directed towards Manchuria. Thus, questions about labour legislation and migration were ultimately political as they touched upon the organisation of industrial labour forces in the Asian colonial context. In this context, Varlez and Thomas promoted the neutrality of their missions by highlighting the official ILO nature of their travels. Varlez pointed out that he travelled 'as an [sic] European professor and a free man' to indicate the independence of his mission, his opinions and his expertise.[56] The idea that the ILO and its experts were part of a fact-finding and not a political mission is contradicted by the fact that the ILO had already included more Japanese into their ranks, due to the elevated status of Japan during and after the Versailles peace talks in 1919. When Varlez was paired on behalf of the ILO among other Europeans together with Junshiro Asari, director of the ILO correspondence office in Tokyo, his mission was instantly perceived as highly political.[57]

Not surprisingly, the Pacific conference itself also took a rather political character in the heightened tensions between Japan and China over Manchuria even if the Institute of Pacific Relations tried to adhere to its promoted stance of neutrality.[58] While Thomas travelled directly from Europe to Asia, Varlez took the transatlantic route via New York, San Francisco and Hawaii, then to Yokohama and Kyoto.[59] The Conference itself, as much as Thomas' experiences in China towards the assumed defence of Manchuria, were characterized less by pacific notions but by belligerent conflicts that had little to do with social peace and harmony or with world peace.[60] As the ILO claimed to achieve the world peace through social peace and harmony, one might wonder if Varlez and Thomas saw at the end of their lives their mission doomed to fail. Certainly, Varlez commented with a pun that his impressions of the Pacific Congress were 'much less peaceful' than he had hoped for.[61] The rising tensions between Japan and China, and also within China, were duly noted by both, who realised that technical and scientific questions such as demographics, nutrition, or trade were strongly politicised by both sides. Especially the conflicting interests in Manchuria barred the two nations from a more objective and scientific deliberation that was the aim of the International Labour Office.[62] The European middle-class concept of internationalism, social peace, and universal justice met its limits in Asia in 1929 and 1930.

THE ILO AND CHINA: ORIENTALIST VISIONS OF ASIAN LABOUR UNDER UNIVERSAL DISGUISE, 1919 – 1931

The International Labour Office, and its leading personnel Albert Thomas and Louis Varlez, embodied the aspirations of working middle-class experts to promote social peace through systems of deliberation, expansion of factual knowledge and the rise of universal legal regimes that should capture problems of labour legislation. This 'epistemic community' of political experts with a universal mission, yet divided by government interests in Europe, set out in the 1920s to discover East Asia, in particular China and its internal and transnational labour regimes. While not much was known, yet much assumed about the new Republic in 1919 and 1920, the ILO actively tried to incorporate China into its system of labour laws, international conventions and regulations. However, technical or 'epistemic' discussions, labour legislations and social engineering took a turn towards the political. In China, nationalists claimed that the International Labour Organisation was merely another instrument of the League of Nations system that only represented the old great-power imperialism in disguise. This made it difficult for the ILO to get into close contact with Chinese labour officials or effectively implement long-standing European standards of working hours, insurances, pension schemes, off-work days and other elements that should promote and enhance the well-being of workers regardless of nation, language or continent.

The social engineering discourses featuring the dichotomy between undeveloped Orientals vs. benevolent and developed Occidentals intruded so dominantly in the colonial visions of China before 1914 and prevailed to a large extent in the 1920s. Thus, the claims towards disinterested universalism and internationalism embodied in the labour legislation and conventions of the ILO were met by Republican China with distrust. China's representatives claimed that Western social engineering and labour regimes would not be applicable in China because China had a completely different approach to workers and workers' rights. In essence, Republican China claimed an early version of 'cultural exceptionalism' to escape the universalising force of the ILO in global labour regulations, to some extent rightly arguing that the universal regime relied to a large extent on colonial representations of benevolently educating the 'Orientals' and including them in a philanthropic mission. Assuming that all European legislation would rely on Western-biased concepts of work, industriousness, and leisure, China feared a constant intrusion of Western ideology behind the measures suggested by the ILO. On the other hand, the ILO naturally assumed that the effects of industrialisation and modernisation in East Asia would be the same as was in Europe fifty years before, and therefore to some extent considered itself the tutor of an undeveloped country that needed to learn and catch up to avoid the problems and massive social costs that the industrial revolution in its second phase had caused in Europe. Failing to embrace China's specific needs as a country that had to bridge the gap between different provinces, come to terms with a weak and increasingly failing central government, leased and extraterritorial parts of the country, and a belligerent imperial neighbour on its northeastern doorstep, the ILO suggested mainly measures that addressed social peace and justice within a progressive and stable society. China in 1929 and 1930 was far away from this European ideal of a 'stable progressive society' that mirrored the ideology of progress in decades both before and after the Great War.

The rise of nationalism and racial expansionism in East Asia would fundamentally question the global mission of the ILO, and the individual missions of Albert Thomas and Louis Varlez conducted in 1929-30. The increase in international labour legislation during the interwar period, promoted by organised inter-governmental internationalism with powerful national representatives, had very little to offer to a country where nationalism was the dominant rising force against both the Europeans and continental neighbours. To some extent, the basic assumption that East Asia, and China in particular, would adhere to a universal standard promoted by the experience of European social experts assembled in the 'epistemic community' in and around the ILO proved to be futile. Yet this assumption shows both the limits of global universalism in the realm of labour legislation and social engineering in the 1920s, and the conflicts that arose from an international system that strengthened the interests of nations instead of embedding and including them in a genuinely new international order after 1919.

ABOUT THE AUTHOR

Christian Mueller is Associate Professor in History at the University of Nottingham Ningbo China and Visiting Research Fellow at The Rothermere American Institute and St Antony's College, University of Oxford. He specialises in global and transnational history of political ideas, associations and institutions 1770 – 1950. He holds an MSt from the University of Oxford and an MA and a DPhil from the University of Heidelberg.

E-mail: Christian.Mueller@nottingham.edu.cn

Endnotes

1 Stephan Bauer, *Arbeiterschutz und Völkergemeinschaft* (Zürich: Orell Füssli, 1918), p. 3.

2 Christian Müller and Jasmien van Daele, 'Peaks of Internationalism in Social Engineering: A transnational history of International Social Reform Associations and Belgian Agency, 1860-1925', *Revue belge de philologie et d'histoire*, 90, no. 4, 2012, pp. 1297-1319.

3 Jürgen Osterhammel, *Die Verwandlung der Welt. Eine Geschichte des 19. Jahrhunderts* (Munich: Beck, 2009), pp. 723-4, 726.

4 See F. P. Walters, *A History of the League of Nations* (Vol. 1, Oxford: Oxford University Press, 1952), p. 328.

5 Tellingly, one of the main books on the ILO work in the process of development and decolonization mentions Thomas' mission merely as an anecdote. See Daniel Roger Maul, *Human rights, development and decolonization: The International Labour Organization, 1940-1970*, (Basingstoke: Palgrave MacMillan, 2010), p. 17f.

6 *International Labour Office Archives, Geneva*, D 600/1000/30/2, Letter from Louis Varlez to J. Merle-Davis, Geneva 9 October 1928.

7 See Müller and van Daele, 'Peaks of Internationalism'; Pierre-Yves Saunier, 'Les régimes circulatoires du domaine social 1800-1940: projéts et ingénierie de la convérgence et de la difference', *Genèses* 71.

2008, pp. 4-25, 7, 13; Sandrine Kott, 'From Transnational Reformist Network to International Organization: The International Association for Labour Legislation and the International Labour Office (1900-1930s)' in Davide Rodogno (ed.), *Shaping the Transnational Sphere. Experts, Networks, and Issues (c.1850-1930)*, (New York; Oxford: Berghahn, 2015), pp. 239-258; Madeleine Herren, *Internationale Sozialpolitik vor dem Ersten Weltkrieg. Die Anfänge europäischer Kooperation aus der Sicht Frankreichs* (Berlin: Duncker & Humblot, 1993); Ursula Ratz, *Sozialreform und Arbeiterschaft: die Gesellschaft für soziale Reform und die sozialdemokratische Arbeiterbewegung von der Jahrhundertwende bis zum Ausbruck des Ersten Weltkrieges*, (Berlin: Colloquium, 1980).

8 Georg Wegener, 'Die wirtschaftliche Bedeutung des Yangtse-Gebietes', in *Verhandlungen des deutschen Kolonialkongresses 1905* (Berlin: Reimer, 1906), pp. 989-1006; August Bebel in *Stenographische Berichte des Deutschen Reichstages* (Vol. 1, Berlin: Reichsdruckerei, 1898), p. 903; Otto Goebel, 'Asiatische Arbeit', *Die Grenzboten*, Leipzig, 69, no. 3, 1910, pp. 280-283.

9 Alfred H. Fried, *Das internationale Leben der Gegenwart* (Leipzig: Teubner, 1908), p. V and pp. 31-33.

10 Saunier, 'Les régimes circulatoires du domaine social 1800-1940', p. 7, p. 13.

11 Müller and van Daele, '*Peaks of Internationalism in Social Engineering*', p. 1311.

12 Albert Thomas, in *International Labour Office Archives, Geneva*, CAT 6c-1, 'Historique du congrès de politique sociale' (Note for the Director), Annexe 5, Plenary Session of the International Association for the Legal Protection of Workers, 14 October 1922, p. 10.

13 Kott, 'From Transnational Reformist Network to International Organization'.

14 See in particular Jasmien van Daele, *Van Gent tot Geneve. Louis Varlez. Een biografie* (Gent: Academia Press, 2002).

15 Peter Haas, 'Epistemic Communities and International Policy Coordination', *International Organisation* 46, no. 1, 1992, pp. 1-35, pp. 10-11; Madeleine Herren, *Internationale Organisationen seit 1865. Eine Globalgeschichte der Internationalen Ordnung* (Darmstadt: WBG, 2009), p. 10; John Ruggie, 'International Responses to Technology. Concepts and Trends,' *International*

Organisation 29, no. 3, 1975, pp. 557-583, 558.

16 See for critical accounts on the concept of epistemic community: Yves Viltard, 'L'étrange carrier du concept d'épisteme en science politique', *Raisons politiques* 23. 2006, pp. 195-201; Sandrine Kott, 'Une communauté épistemique du social? Experts de l'OIT et internationalisation des politiques sociales dans l'entre-deux-guerres', *Genèses* 71, 2008, pp. 26-46; Sandrine Kott, 'Constructing a European Social Model. The Fight for Social Insurance in the Interwar Period', in Jasmien van Daele (ed.), *ILO Histories: Essays on the International Labour Office and Its Impact on the World During the Twentieth Century*, (Berlin: Lang, 2010), pp. 173-195; Chris Leonards and Nico Randeraad, 'Transnational Experts in Social Reform, 1840-1880', *International Review of Social History* 55. 2010, pp. 215-239; Müller and van Daele,'Peaks of Internationalism in Social Engineering'.

17 Mark Mazover, *Governing the World. The History of an Idea, 1815 to the Present* (New York: Penguin, 2012), p. 148.

18 Herren, *International Organisationen seit 1865*, p. 67.

19 Walters, *League of Nations*, I, p. 329.

20 *International Labour Office, Official Bulletin*, Vol. I, 1919-20, p. 94 and 269.

21 Walters, *League of Nations*, I, pp. 79-80.

22 *International Labour Office, Official Bulletin*, Vol. I, 1919-20, p. 441.

23 *North-China Herald (Shanghai)*, 15 November 1919, p. 402.

24 Hans Wehberg, *Die Völkerbundsatzung, erläutert unter Berücksichtigung der Verträge von Locarno etc.*, (3rd edn, Berlin: Hensel und Co, 1929), p. 147.

25 Presidential Decree 3 February 1923, in *International Labour Office, Official Bulletin*, VII, 1923, p. 97.

26 *International Labour Office, Official Bulletin*, VII, 1923, p. 97.

27 *International Labour Office, Official Bulletin*, VII, 1923, p. 97; *Ibid.*, VIII, 1924. pp. 7-8.

28 Prohibition by the Chinese Ministry of Agriculture and Commerce 30 January 1923, in *International Labour Office, Official Bulletin*, VIII, 1924, p. 5. See also *ibid.*, IX, 1924, p. 99.

29 *International Labour Office, Official Bulletin*, VIII, 1924, p. 7.

30 Chinese report on the draft conventions from the Geneva session of the International Labour Conference, 1921, Letter from the Chinese Presidential Office, 21 June 1923, quoted in *International*

Labour Office, Official Bulletin, VIII, 1924, pp. 7-8. See also letter from Than Chi Jui, Minister for Foreign Affairs, Peking 10 February 1924, in *Ibid.*, XI, 1926, p. 125.

31 Herren, *Internationale Organisationen seit 1865*, p. 67; Thomas Davies, *NGOs. A New History of Transnational Civil Society* (London: Hurst, 2013), p. 89.

32 'A League of Peace', *North-China Herald (Shanghai)*, 3 May 1919; Lu Xun, '"Sudden Notions' – Reactions to the May Thirteenth Incident, 1925', in Janet Chen, Pei-Kai Cheng, Michael Lestz, Jonathan D. Spence (eds.), *The Search for Modern China. Documentary Collection* (3rd edn, New York; London, Norton, 2014), pp. 247-249; Shinkichi Eto, 'China's International Relations, 1911-1931', in John K. Fairbank and Albert Feuerwerker (eds.), *The Cambridge History of China. Vol. 13: Republican China 1912-1949, Part 2* (Cambridge: Cambridge University Press, 1986), pp. 74-115, pp. 106-7.

33 Herren, *Internationale Organisationen seit 1865*, 67; Akira Iriye, *Cultural Internationalism and World Order* (Baltimore; London: Johns Hopkins University Press, 1997), p. 69.

34 [Albert Thomas], 'Labour Legislation in China', in *International Labour Office, Official Bulletin*, VIII, 1924, pp. 47-49, here 47-48.

35 *Ibid.*, p. 48.

36 Chinese Presidential Decree 225, 29 March 1923, in *International Labour Office, Official Bulletin*, VIII. 1924, p. 49.

37 *International Labour Office, Official Bulletin*, VIII, 1924, pp. 49-50.

38 'If Only It Were So', *North-China Herald (Shanghai)*, 30 August 1924, p. 328.

39 *International Labour Office, Official Bulletin*, VIII, 1924, pp. 49-50.

40 See Isabella Jackson, *Shaping Modern Shanghai. Colonialism in China's Global City* (Cambridge: Cambridge University Press, 2018), p. 210.

41 Jean Chesneaux, *The Chinese Labor Movement 1919-1927* (Stanford: Stanford University Press, 1968), p. 385; Jackson, *Shaping Modern Shanghai*, p. 210.

42 26th session of the International Labour Office' Governing Body, 2 April 1925, report in *International Labour Office, Official Bulletin*, X, 1925, p. 51.

43 *International Labour Office, Official Bulletin*, XVII, 1932, p. 22.

44 *Ibid.*, 22.

45 *International Labour Office, Official Bulletin*, XVII, 1932, p. 96.

46 'Albert Thomas,' in *International Labour Office, Official Bulletin*, XVII, 1932, pp. 95-97, p. 96f.

47 *International Labour Office, Official Bulletin*, XVII, 1932, p. 97.

48 *Ibid.*. Müller and van Daele, 'Peaks of Internationalism in Social Engineering'.

49 Jasmine van Daele, 'Industrial States and Transnational Exchanges of Social Policies: Belgium and the ILO in the Interwar Period', in S. Kott and J. Droux (eds.), *Globalizing Social Rights: The International Labour Office and beyond*, (Basingstoke: Palgrave MacMillan, 2013), pp. 190-209.

50 *The Times (London)*, 2 January, 22 February and 26 April 1929. See also Jackson, *Shaping Modern Shanghai*, p. 210.

51 Thomas, 'Labour Legislation in China', p. 48.

52 Van Daele, *Van Gent tot Genève*, p. 202

53 *International Labour Office Archives, Geneva*, P 6/8: Extract of a note of Albert Thomas (Director) to Harold Butler, 29 October 1928; Extract of the report of the administrative commission, 6 December 1928.

54 *International Labour Office Archives, Geneva*, CAT 7-712: Letter Louis Varlez to Albert Thomas, Geneva, 19 January 1929; and Letter Louis Varlez to Secretary of Albert Thomas, Geneva, 10 April 1929.

55 *International Labour Office Archives, Geneva*, CAT 7-712: Letter Louis Varlez to Albert Thomas, Geneva, 8 March 1929.

56 *International Labour Office Archives, Geneva*, D 600/1000/30/2, Letter Albert Thomas to J. Merle-Davis, Geneva 26 September 1929.

57 *International Labour Office Archives, Geneva*, D 600/1000/30/2, Letter Albert Thomas to J. Merle-Davis, Geneva 26 September 1929; *International Labour Office Archives, Geneva*, CAT 7-712, Cabinet note by Thomas, n.d.

58 Van Daele, *Van Gent tot Genève*, 207-209; Susan Pedersen. *The Guardians. The League of Nations and the Crisis of Empire*, (Oxford: Oxford University Press, 2015), p. 289.

59 Van Daele, *Van Gent tot Genève*, p. 207.

60 Brian Masaru Hayashi, 'From Race to Nation: The Institute of Pacific Relations, Asian Americans, and George Blakeslee from 1908 to 1929', *The Japanese Journal of American Studies*, 23, 2012, pp. 51-71, 65-66; Priscilla Roberts, 'The Institute of Pacific Relations: pan-Pacific and pan-Asian visions of international order', *International*

Politics, 2017, n.p., https://doi.org/10.1057/s41311-017-0108-y, (accessed 1 July 2018).

61 Louis Varlez, letter to unknown, Kyoto, 31 October 1929, quoted as in: Van Daele, *Van Gent tot Genève*, p. 207.

62 *International Labour Office Archives, Geneva*, CAT 7-712, Letter Louis Varlez to Albert Thomas, n.p., 16 January 1930; *International Labour Office Archives, Geneva*, D 600/1000/30/2, The Third Biennial Conference of the Institute of Pacific Relations, Kyoto, Japan, n.d., pp. 8-12.

A CZECHOSLOVAK FOUNDING FATHER IN CHINA

An Account Of The November 1918 Visit By Czechoslovakia's Milan Rastislav Štefánik

BY LUKÁŠ GAJDOŠ

ABSTRACT

Slovak-born Milan Rastislav Štefánik (1880-1919) lived many lives - as an astronomer, he was in charge of the Janssen Observatory on Mont Blanc and participated in scientific expeditions to a number of far-flung places including North Africa, Central Asia, Ecuador, the Galapagos, and Tahiti. As an aviator and soldier, he fought with the French Air Force and was responsible for the creation of the Czecho-Slovak Legion. As a diplomat and leading member of the Czecho-Slovak National Council, he was instrumental in winning support among the Entente Powers, especially France, for the idea of independent Czechoslovakia.[1] As a politician, he was one of the three co-founders of Czechoslovakia and became its first Minister of War. It was in this capacity that following the outbreak of the Russian Civil War, the involvement of Czecho-Slovak troops therein, and the creation of Czechoslovakia on 28 October 1918, while en-route from Japan to Siberia, Štefánik made a brief sojourn in China in November 1918.

This article explores Štefánik's brief visit, drawing on a number of sources from the Czechoslovak Foreign Ministry and military archives, press, and various memoirs of first-hand witnesses to provide a detailed account of his stay in Harbin and meetings with Li Chia Ao (Li Jia'ao, 李家鰲, 1859-1926), the *daoyin* (道尹, often translated as 'intendant') of the three north-eastern provinces and Commissioner for Foreign Affairs for Harbin, who later became Minister of the Embassy of the Republic of China in the Soviet Union.[2] The historical significance of this meeting – the very first between a high-ranking Czechoslovak and Chinese officials - has thus far largely been overlooked and should be commemorated, especially in the year of the 100th anniversary of Štefánik's visit. The article concludes with a brief overview of the aftermath of the visit, including the presence

Figure 1: Astronomer Štefánik (first right) during a scientific expedition in Samarkand, 1907. Arnošt Bareš, Štefánikův memoriál (Štefánik's Memorial) (Praha: Památník odboje, 1929).

of Czechoslovak legionnaires, Czechoslovak Consulate, and the wider Czechoslovak community in Harbin.

MANY LIVES OF MILAN RASTISLAV ŠTEFÁNIK AND THE RUN-UP TO THE CHINA VISIT

Milan Rastislav Štefánik was born on 21 July 1880 in Košariská, village in the then Austro-Hungarian Empire and present-day western Slovakia. He attended primary school in his home village and Šamorín and Lutheran high schools in Bratislava and Sopron, graduating from yet another Lutheran school in Szarvas (the latter two places are located in present-day Hungary). He abandoned his studies of structural engineering at the Prague Polytechnical Institute (in 1920 renamed to the Czech Technical University) after a mere two years and started to pursue a degree in mathematics and astronomy at the Charles University in Prague instead, obtaining his PhD in 1904. Štefánik's youth had a formative influence on the rest of his life – his father was described as a 'nationalist and Slavophil' and while in Prague, he attended lectures of Professor Tomáš Garrigue Masaryk, who later became the first President of Czechoslovakia. Štefánik was also active in the Slovak student society Detvan, which was then headed by Vavro Šrobár, the future Czechoslovak Minister for Slovakia and senator.

After graduation Štefánik moved to France, becoming an assistant to the famous astronomer Jules Janssen, who discovered the solar chromosphere and headed the prestigious Paris-Meudon Observatory. In 1905, Štefánik conducted the first in a series of ascends of Mont Blanc and an expedition in Spain. From 1905 to 1906, he served as the co-director of the Mont Blanc observatory. He was subsequently awarded the *Prix Jules Janssen*, the highest award of the *Société Astronomique de France*. After Janssen's death, Štefánik was relieved of his positions but tasked by the French government to conduct astronomical and meteorological observations in a wide variety of places, including Turkistan (1906-1907 – while passing through Russia, he visited Leo Tolstoy and his Slovak doctor Dušan Makovický), North Africa (1907, 1909 - Algeria, Morocco, Tunisia), the Pacific (1911 – Tahiti, Tonga, Fiji, Australia, New Zealand), and South America (1912 – Panama, Brazil, Ecuador, the Galapagos Islands). In 1912, Štefánik was granted a French citizenship.

Following the outbreak of the First World War, Štefánik joined the military aviation school in Pau, graduating as corporal and flying as ensign MFS-54 planes for the 10th Army on the Western Front in Artois. Given his scientific background, he was offered the position of commander of the Air Force meteorological bureau. However, he turned this down and asked for a transfer to the Serbian front instead, which he joined in September 1915. Štefánik suffered from lifelong ailments, which he mentions in 'The Ecuador Diary' that he kept during one of his numerous scientific expeditions, writing about his 'lost health', i.e. stomach, kidney, and liver pain.[3] His chronic condition was exacerbated while serving on the Serbian front, especially after the crash during the evacuation of the Niš Airport. Subsequently he became the first-ever person in history to be 'medi-vacked' – this happened in November 1918,

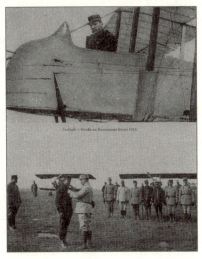

Figure 2: Aviator Štefánik being decorated with the Croix de Guerre, 1915. Arnošt Bareš, Štefánikův memoriál (Štefánik's Memorial) (Praha: Památník odboje, 1929).

Figure 3: Diplomat Štefánik (centre) in Washington, D.C., 1917. Arnošt Bareš, Štefánikův memoriál (Štefánik's Memorial) (Praha: Památník odboje, 1929).

when he was evacuated by air by the French pilot Louis Paulhan (they flew over 200 km through the ravine of the *Beli Drim* Valley, which is only 200 metres wide) and Štefánik was then transported to Rome to recover.[4]

Štefánik began gradually taking advantage of his good connections in the top echelons of the French society for diplomatic work, in which he became fully immersed after his return from Serbia. He met Edvard Beneš, who later became Prime Minister (and eventually President) of Czechoslovakia, in December 1915, offering his services and connections to the Czecho-Slovak cause (which was then in its infancy). Using his connections, especially with Claire Boas de Jouvenel, Štefánik was received by Aristide Briand, the Prime Minister of France, who just over two months later, on 3 February 1916, received Štefánik along with Masaryk. Masaryk, using the rhetoric of self-determination, proposed the division of the Austro-Hungarian Empire along national lines. *Conseil national des Pays Tchèques* (later renamed to the Czecho-Slovak National Council) was created ten days later, with Masaryk as its chair and Štefánik and Beneš as his deputies.[5] Štefánik undertook further diplomatic missions to Italy, Russia, and Romania with the goal of gaining support for the formation of the Czecho-Slovak Legion – an armed force comprised of Czech and

Slovak prisoners of war and volunteers from the ranks of Czech and Slovak migrants in the US. It was during his mission to Russia in August 1916 that Štefánik first met French General Maurice Janin, who was at that time posted to the Russian Central Command. Janin described Štefánik as 'short, slim, with a very thin, shaven face with blue eyes, bald head, short hair on the sides. He looks intelligent, passionate, and nervous. His French is lightly accented. Even though he talks in a slightly roundabout manner, he is always exact and precise.'[6] It was a successful meeting, as Janin 'promised to wholeheartedly support the Czecho-Slovak cause.'[7] The two were to meet again.

First Czecho-Slovak units were formed in Russia in late 1916 and early 1917, with the Czecho-Slovak Shooting Brigade earning much respect during the Battle of Zborov in July 1917. Štefánik himself sailed to the United States on 2 June 1917, promoting the Czecho-Slovak cause and raising 3,000 volunteers to join the Legion on the Western Front (with President Wilson's approval) and was given the rank of general in the French Army on 20 June 1917. Two entire divisions with approximately 40,000 men were created in Russia in October 1917 and the 'Decree on the Creation of the Czecho-Slovak Army in France' was signed by French President Raymond Poincaré on 19 December 1917.[8] The Army answered to the Czecho-Slovak National Council and from February 1918, headed by General Janin as its commander and Štefánik as his deputy, who had by this time also been promoted to the rank of general. Following successful diplomatic missions, the Army was recognised by Entente powers, in France as part of the *Armée*'s divisions, but in Italy as fully sovereign and autonomous. This major diplomatic triumph had been proposed by Štefánik during his first meeting with Italian Prime Minister Vittorio Emanuele Orlando on 6 March 1918 and concluded several weeks later on 21 April 1918. Military colours were presented to Czecho-Slovak troops in front of the *Altare della Patria* in the centre of Rome on 24 May 1918.[9]

Events took an even more dramatic turn after the Russian Revolution in November 1917 – Czecho-Slovak troops on the Eastern Front became redundant once the Treaty of Brest-Litovsk was concluded. The newly established Bolshevik regime demanded that they hand in their heavy weapons and sizeable part of their light weapons and become 'travelling civilians.'[10] This was accepted by the Russian Branch of the Czecho-Slovak National Council in the

Figure 4: Armoured train of the Czecho-Slovak Legion, 1918. The Czechoslovak Review, v. 3, no. 1, p. 14.

Penza Agreement, penned on 26 March 1918 (on the Soviet side by Joseph Stalin). Their evacuation started one day later and was to be carried out in 63 trains with 40 carriages each. Their progress towards Vladivostok was, however, slow and tensions became more and more frequent. The Chelyabinsk Incident of 14 May 1918 was the inevitable spark – a group of Hungarian prisoners of war injured a Czecho-Slovak legionnaire and the perpetrators were lynched. The local Soviet reacted by arresting 10 legionnaires and was in turn attacked by Czecho-Slovaks, who took over 2,800 rifles and several pieces of artillery from the Red Guards. Lev Trotsky's command to disarm the Legion and the Red Guards' unsuccessful attempts to enforce it turned scuffles into open confrontation. A successful Czecho-Slovak offensive resulted in the capture of the Tsarist gold reserves in Kazan in early August and the Trans-Siberian railway in its entirety by the end of the month. Czecho-Slovak troops effectively controlled the vicinity of the railway from the right bank of river Volga to the shores of the Pacific Ocean in Vladivostok. Their leaders were Bohdan Pavlů, Stanislav Čeček, and Radola Gajda.[11]

It was within this context that Štefánik and Janin hurried to Siberia. They had arrived in New York on 2 September 1918, meeting Masaryk in Washington, D.C. on 6 September, leaving San Francisco on 24 September aboard the *Korea Maru* and arriving to Yokohama (after a brief stopover in Honolulu) on 12 October. The choice of

Figure 5: Štefánik (sitting, third left) and Janin (sitting, third right) in Japan shortly before leaving for China and Siberia, 1918. Dušan Kováč, Štefánik a Janin – príbeh priateľstva (Štefánik and Janin – Story of Friendship) (Bratislava: Dilema, 2001), p. 122.

this destination was no coincidence, as Japanese Ambassador in Paris Kenshiro Matsui wrote to his superiors, 'following agreement with the French government, he [Štefánik] is to travel to our Empire to coordinate Japanese and Czechoslovak armies in Russia.'[12] On 15 October, General Štefánik was received by the Japanese Deputy Foreign Minister Kijūrō Shidehara, who later became Japan's second post-World War II Prime Minister. One day later, he was received by Prime Minister Hara Takashi, and on 5 November by Emperor Taishō. It should be noted that Czechoslovakia was established on 28 October 1918 and Štefánik was named its Minister of War.[13] His debilitating bouts of stomach pain made his stay in Japan much longer than planned but still enjoyable. As General Janin wrote in his memoirs, 'the friendly welcome [he received] in Japan and the days he spent there seemed to him – and also to me – like a clear stretch of sky amidst dark days.'[14] The party boarded *Taichu Maru* in Moji and left for Vladivostok on 13 November, where it disembarked on 16 November.

Štefánik in Harbin

Štefánik left Vladivostok for Harbin in the late hours of 18 November, accompanied by Bohdan Pavlů, by now the Plenipotentiary of the Czechoslovak Republic to Russia based in Omsk, and French military

Figure 6: Some of the characters described in the article, including General Syrový, General Janin, and Plenipotentiary Pavlů. The Czechoslovak Review, v. 3, no. 2, p. 368.

escort. General Janin, the commander of the Czechoslovak Legion, was due to follow one day later, but was forced to stay in Vladivostok in the aftermath of Admiral Kolchak's *coup d'etat*, which took place in Omsk on the day of Štefánik's departure from Vladivostok. Styling himself 'Supreme Ruler of Russia', Kolchak demanded that the commander of Czechoslovak forces in the Urals, General Jan Syrový, gave commands in the name of Kolchak to Russian soldiers that were in the Czechoslovak ranks. The acceptance of this demand would be tantamount to breaking the order of Czechoslovak President Masaryk of not intervening in Russian domestic affairs, and Janin had to stay behind to deal with this delicate situation.[15]

Štefánik arrived to Harbin on 20 November 1918 at 8:00 am. He was greeted at the local train station by a guard of honour of the Harbin-based Czechoslovak Fifth Infantry Regiment, but ignored by the local Russian officials, who left as soon as they learned that Štefánik was not accompanied by Janin. This behaviour did not go unnoticed by Czechoslovak officers and Štefánik himself.[16] It is also important to note that Štefánik was not the first high-ranking Czechoslovak to pass through Harbin – Tomáš Garrigue Masaryk, arrived on 1 April 1918 while en-route to the USA for a meeting with President Woodrow Wilson.[17] The then head of the Czecho-Slovak National Council did not, however, disembark from his railway carriage. Still, while on the railway tracks in Harbin, he received Ferdinand Erml, Czech founder of the local brewery, thus honouring his active support of the Czecho-Slovak cause.[18]

General Štefánik then proceeded to the local telegraph office, where he received a message from General Janin, informing him about Kolchak's demands and sending him the following draft of orders for

General Syrový, 'As far as any interference in [Russian domestic] politics is concerned, reply that President Masaryk ordered to refrain from any such acts. The only persons these matters can be referred to are myself and especially General Štefánik, the local political representative of the [Czechoslovak] national government.'[19] Štefánik failed to send a message to General Syrový, whose telegraph connection was cut by forces of Ataman Semenov, but his friendly demeanour towards Czechoslovak rank and file made a favourable impression on Russian employees of the telegraph bureau.[20] In the afternoon, he paid a visit to the French vice-consul M. Lépice[21] and Japanese General Takeuchi and at 4:00 pm approved Janin's draft orders, which he received earlier in the day.[22] His evening automobile ride to Pristan (Russian for quay), Harbin's commercial district and most densely populated area, and the subsequent telegraph exchange with Janin were both cut short by Štefánik's notoriously poor health.[23] Štefánik insisted on leaving Harbin at the earliest possible convenience, while Janin argued that he stayed put, recovered and that they maintained telegraphic connection in order to deal with the Kolchak crisis. This exchange was cut abruptly – an unnamed third person concluded the conversation by noting, 'the General has left, he is having another seizure.'[24]

Štefánik's health improved overnight and in the morning he paid a visit to Li Chia Ao (Li Jia'ao, 李家鏊, 1859-1926), the *daoyin* (道尹, often translated as 'intendant')[25] of the three north-eastern provinces (東三省) of Heilongjiang, Kirin, and Mukden and concurrently Commissioner for Foreign Affairs for Harbin and Director of the Bureau of Foreign Affairs of the Kirin Railway.[26]

Intendant Li's life was no less interesting than that of his counterpart General Štefánik Born in Shanghai shortly before the end of the rule of Xianfeng Emperor, Li received classical Confucian education and went on to work in the famous Chiangnan (Jiangnan) Arsenal (江南機器製造總局). The Arsenal which was established by Zeng Guofan, the famous anti-Taiping general and the late-Qing era reformist Li Hongzhang, was directly linked with the Self-Strengthening Movement of the late nineteenth century.[27] Young Li Chia Ao was 'highly esteemed by his superiors for his activities in the reform of the administration' and in 1886, sent to study at a Russian military high school in St Petersburg. After graduating, he joined the Chinese Legation as attaché, spent a grand total of ten years in Russia (both in St Petersburg and Vladivostok) and undertook an adventurous voyage

Figure 7: Li Chia Ao, General Štefánik's Chinese counter-part. John Benjamin Powell, Who's Who in China (Shanghai: The China Weekly Review, 1925), p. 452.

back to China, which lasted 109 days and which took him (by carriage and by boat, as the Trans-Siberian Railway had yet to be constructed) through Western and Eastern Siberia as well as Russo-Chinese borderlands. He published his 'Memoirs on the Travel in Siberia' in two volumes, reportedly impressing Li Hongzhang himself and leading Li Chia Ao to further promotions. He was put in charge of Tianjin's foreign affairs, made the *daoyin* of Binjiang, and then became the Commissioner for Foreign Affairs for Harbin and Director of the Bureau of Foreign Affairs of the Kirin Railway. He was twice decorated by Emperor Nicolas II (the Second Class Order of Stanislaus and the Order of St. Ann), retired due to health reasons (but continued working as a businessman in the gold mining industry) and returned to public administration in 1918.[28]

Given Li Chia Ao's background, we may presume that the actual meeting was conducted in Russian – one author claims that he 'was famous for his fluent Russian.'[29] The only surviving account of the meeting by the Czechoslovak side was recorded by František Kubka:

> The conversation with Chinese general [*daoyin*] was of political-diplomatic kind. It mainly concerned the deep reservations of the Chinese side with certain blunders by Major-General Gajda and Lieutenant Kadlec (at the beginning of October). Štefánik used gentle diplomacy to soften the stubbornness of the Chinese side. When the conversation changed to private talk, Štefánik greatly surprised well-educated general [*daoyin*] Li Chia Ao by his ability to count in Mandarin and by his knowledge of the Chinese zodiac. It was a magnificent sight – suddenly one astronomer sat next to another one and the difference

of races and opinions disappeared. The Chinese general [*daoyin*] was so impressed with the Czech[oslovak] general's knowledge of astronomy that he commemorated the occasion by gifting him his photograph – a friendly gesture that was reciprocated by Štefánik.[30]

Ivana Bakešová, a leading Czech sinologist, argued that Štefánik's attitude was deeply pragmatic – 'differing from most of our soldiers and politicians, Štefánik did not overlook the fact that Harbin was despite its Russian feel, a Chinese city, and he realised that the presence of [the Czechoslovak] army may lead to the beginning of economic cooperation between Czechoslovakia and China.'[31] She adds he emphasised that 'the companies, which were located, [following the collapse of the Austro-Hungarian Empire] in 1918, on the Czechoslovak territory, had significantly participated in commercial contacts of the Austro-Hungarian monarchy (up to 70 per cent) with north-eastern China and it was necessary to continue in these links.'[32]

The most vivid account of the meeting was recorded by Li Chia Ao himself, who wrote the following dedication on the back of his photograph, which was sent to the Czechoslovak Foreign Ministry by the Czechoslovak Office in Harbin on 4 March 1919:

> Mr. Štefánik is a great Czechoslovak astronomer and military Minister of a newly established country in Central Europe. Last winter he passed through Harbin. We spoke in a very candid manner about global events. What he said was true. Speaking both modestly and seriously, he enquired about various topics from Chinese history and astronomy. Answering his questions, I was unable to finish what I wanted to say. How saddened was I when he said farewell. I cannot help but desire for another meeting with him. Looking at his photograph, I always feel that I am in his presence. And now I send him my photograph as a sign of my gratitude and pleasant memories.[33]

Unfortunately, this dedication survives only as a printed account in Czechoslovak press, and it is unclear whether the letter ever reached its recipient, who died a mere three months later. The letter's current whereabouts are also unknown. The Czechoslovak Foreign

Figure 8: A selection of items that Štefánik most likely purchased in China (Harbin or Shanghai) – brocade garment (left) and silk cover (right). Image courtesy of the Slovak National Museum.[37]

Ministry Archive, however, holds a letter from the Czechoslovak Office in Harbin, signed by Plenipotentiary Hesse, which was dispatched alongside the photograph. This letter briefly sums up the meeting in November 1918 and specifies that the photograph was delivered via the French consul in Harbin and that Li Chia Ao's dedication was written in both Chinese and English, with an additional Czech translation enclosed by the Office.[34]

Judging from the aforementioned personal recollection of the meeting by František Kubka, we may assume that this was the second photograph of himself that Li Chia Ao gifted to Štefánik. Sadly, neither has been located, neither in the Archive of the Czechoslovak Foreign Ministry in Prague nor in the Slovak National Archive, which inherited Štefánik's correspondence. The same applies to Li Chia Ao's photograph of Štefánik, which has yet to be found. Much time has been spent on consulting Chinese official sources and press coverage of the meeting – unfortunately, without any tangible results.[35]

It is, however, worth noting that the *Associated Press* (AP) noticed his visit and the *New York Times* printed an article titled 'Czechs (*sic*) to Stay in Russia – Stefanik, Their War Minister, Pays High Tribute to America,' which was published on 26 November 1918. The article noted that 'the General was in Harbin today on his way to the Volga front' and quoted his tribute to the role of the United States: 'America by this [First World] war has not gained provinces nor indemnities, but has gained the love of the free peoples of the world. President Wilson's pronouncement gave the first practical solution to the problems of our oppressed people.'[36] It remains unclear at which stage of his visit Štefánik spoke to the AP correspondent.

Following the morning meeting with Li Chia Ao, General Štefánik headed to Fujiadian, a city adjacent to Harbin and the seat of the Chinese Bingjiang County Office since 31 October 1905.[38] Here, he was welcomed by a 'horn-blowing' Chinese guard of honour and had a meeting with the commander of the First Chinese Division, a certain General Dao, who hosted a banquet to honour his guest.[39]

After the visit, Štefánik once again visited the telegraph office for a further discussion with General Janin and Lieutenant General Čeček, who were still in Vladivostok. Štefánik expressed his wish to leave Harbin and join Czechoslovak troops, led by General Syrový, in Omsk in order to avoid their possible demoralisation as the troops were increasingly worried by the uncertainty surrounding their predicament in Russia – the combination of an escalating civil war coupled with the slow pace of their evacuation from Russia.[40] At 3:30 pm, Štefánik received Li Chiao Ao, General Dao, and their interpreter in his railway carriage. Afterwards, he made calls on British, American, Russian, and Japanese consuls as well as on (White) Russian generals Dmitri Horvath and Mikhail Pleshkov – the latter a former competitor for Russia in equestrian jumping at the 1912 Stockholm

Figure 9: Czechoslovak and Chinese soldiers in Harbin. *Ivana Bakešová, Legionáři v roli diplomatů: československo-čínské vztahy 1918-1949 (Legionnaires as Diplomats: Czechoslovak-Chinese relations 1918-1949) (Prague: Filozofická fakulta Univerzity Karlovy, 2013),* p. 206.

Summer Olympics. After dinner with French consul Lépice, he visited a performance in the Chinese theatre of Fujiadian that was held to commemorate his visit. A Chinese guard of honour was lined up along the entire street, on which the theatre was located.[41] Naturally, Chinese hosts Li Chiao Ao and General Dao as well as Bohdan Pavlů, Plenipotentiary of the Czechoslovak Republic to Russia, and M. Lépice, French Consul in Harbin, joined the performance and were later given yet another banquet at an unspecified Chinese hotel in Fujiadian.[42] Judging from the generous treatment the Chinese side gave to the Czechoslovak delegation, it can be concluded that they held them in high esteem, most likely as the result of the impression that General Štefánik made on Li Chia Ao.

The train of General Štefánik left Harbin at 5:30 am on 22 November 1918 and headed west.[43] Before leaving, he issued one more command, which was read out to Czechoslovak troops in Harbin by Captain Hříbek two days later, 'Brother General Štefánik was very pleasantly surprised by the welcome he received here at the train station and upon his departure told me to send his regards and also those of Professor [President] Masaryk to all [Czechoslovak] volunteers.'[44]

The aftermath of the Harbin visit

General Štefánik's subsequent visit to Siberia was physically and mentally draining – he made repeated visits to Yekaterinburg and Omsk (stopping in smaller cities with Czechoslovak presence along the way, including Chita, Tyumen, Samara, Irkutsk) to inspect Czechoslovak troops and increase their morale, which was severely tested by the uncertainty about their future. On the one hand, the troops, as the most potent military force in the region, were a valuable bargaining chip for newly established Czechoslovakia in her dealings with the victorious powers at a time when the post-World War I global order had yet to be created. On the other hand, the troops desired to secure their early withdrawal from the Ural front and an early return to their homeland. Štefánik was also reunited with General Janin, met with Admiral Kolchak (with whom he had many heated exchanges), French representative Regnault, British representative Elliot, and many others.[45] According to memoirs of Dr. Josef Mandaus, Štefánik's already poor health suffered another blow in mid-January because of draining work and poor diet and he himself started talking of death ('I am not scared of death, only of slow dying').[46] While in Omsk, General Janin decorated him on 14 January 1919 with the *Ordre National de la Légion d'Honneur* (Third Class – *Commandeur*).[47] Throughout his time in Siberia, his medical problems intensified further as did the predicament of Czechoslovak troops – Štefánik concluded that they were unable to attack the Bolsheviks and that he should return to Paris, either to secure reinforcements or their complete withdrawal from Russia.[48]

Figure 10: General Štefánik (left) with General Gajda (right) in Yekaterinburg on 10 December 1918 – just three weeks after his visit of Harbin. The Czechoslovak Review, v. 3, no. 2, p. 369.

Upon learning that *Porthos*, a French ship that was due to leave Shanghai for Marseille on 1 February, he left Omsk on 16 January 1919 at 1 a.m. Doctor Mandaus recalled that 'we headed eastwards as fast as we could, stopping only to get new locomotives.'[49] Štefánik's train arrived in Harbin on 25 January at 6:00 am. According to one witness, Štefánik was 'seriously, mortally ill' and did not leave the carriage to greet the assembled guard of honour.[50] He did not receive any visitors either, but dispatched the local Czechoslovak commander along with French Mayor Fournier to pay a visit to French Consul Lépice and French Military Mission's Lieutenant Defontain. The train left for Changchun at 11:15 am, where Štefánik, 'completely exhausted and physically broken,' was transferred onto a first class carriage to Shanghai, passing through Peking on 28 January and arrived to Shanghai on 30 January.[51] While in Shanghai, his planned to meet with representatives of local companies, the municipality, and Czechs and Slovaks were cut short as his health further deteriorated. He only managed to meet with the French consul, with whom he reached an understanding that an elected representative of the local Czechoslovak community would work at the French consulate as an advisor for Czechoslovak affairs.[52] Štefánik spent most of his time in Shanghai in bed, and according to one direct witness 'stood up only one hour before the departure of *Porthos*, with strong will and determination

Figure 11: Czechoslovak community in Harbin, 1938. *Ivana Bakešová*, Legionáři v roli diplomatů: československo-čínské vztahy 1918-1949 (Legionnaires as Diplomats: Czechoslovak-Chinese relations 1918-1949) (Prague: Filozofická fakulta Univerzity Karlovy, 2013), p. 21.[55]

saying "My quest is extremely important, I have to arrive [in France]!" and left for the port.'[53]

Štefánik never returned to China, dying in an air accident while landing in Bratislava just three months later, on 4 May 1919. The cause of the accident remains unknown.

The *North-China Herald* reflected on his departure from Siberia and the wider ramifications of the decision to leave under a headline 'Deadline in Siberia – Information Upon the Czech (*sic*) Problem' in an article 'From Our Own Correspondent', written on 6 February and published on 22 February 1919. The article stated the following:

> The sudden return of General Stefanik, the Czecho-Slovak War Minister who had accompanied General Janin, as Chief of Staff from France to Harbin from the Ural Front, naturally created surprise among those living in these parts. The initiated felt something was in the air when it was announced that Stefanik was not returning to Western Siberia. The cat is now out of the bag, and though no official announcement has yet been made, it is practically certain that all the Czech (*sic*) troops now at the Eastern front are to be withdrawn as quickly as possible and are to

be transported to their native soil. The higher Czech (*sic*) authorities on the spot have come to the conclusion that further interference into Russia's intestine affairs has now become inadvisable.[54]

Prior to leaving China, Štefánik made several important decisions concerning Czechoslovakia's future relations with China. On 23 January 1919 he named Lieutenant-Colonel Miloš Hess as head of the newly created Czechoslovak Representative Office in Harbin – his full title was 'Plenipotentiary of the Czechoslovak Government for Russia (eastwards of Lake Baikal), China, and Japan' and the Office was opened on 28 January 1919.[56] Hess titled himself 'chargé d'affaires' despite the lack of diplomatic relations between China and Czechoslovakia (his stamp said '*Republique Tchécoslovaque, chargé d'affaires pour Extréme-Orient, Harbin*'), later changing it to 'Plenipotentiary.'[57] Further Offices were opened in Shanghai in February 1919 (headed *pro bono* by a Czechoslovak citizen – an equivalent of Honorary Consul) and Beijing in May 1920, but diplomatic relations were not established until 5 December 1930 as the two sides could not reach an agreement on contentious points of extraterritoriality and tariffs. Moreover, Czechoslovak policy towards China was marred by a number of blunders, especially with regard to its personnel, which were largely responsible for the long delay in establishing diplomatic relations.

The Czechoslovak community in Harbin also deserves some attention. The first Czechs in Harbin appeared during the construction of the Chinese Eastern Railway at the end of the nineteenth century, including musicians, craftsmen, small businessmen, engineers and even brewers.[59] The most successful of them was aforementioned Ferdinand Erml, who ran a local brewery and whose role as the speaker of the Czech community was acknowledged even by Professor (later President) Masaryk, who passed through Harbin in April 1918. The Czechoslovak community developed further in the 1920s,

Figure 12: 'Slovak Voices' – a newspaper published in Harbin for Slovak legionnaires.[58]

roughly echoing the growth in trade between Czechoslovakia and this region of China, including the opening of commercial office of Škoda Plzeň, a leading provider of railway machinery and equipment, in 1924.[60] The company also participated in the refurbishment of the Chinese Eastern Railway in 1928, building two railway bridges near Harbin and supplying other machinery. Zbrojovka Brno, leading Czechoslovak manufacturer of light weapons, started selling arms to local warlord Zhang Zuolin in 1927. The story of their arrival to China was rather adventurous; they left Europe on ship *Praga*, which initially flew a German flag but upon reaching the Indian Ocean switched to a Czechoslovak flag. The Kuomintang learned of the ship's existence before its arrival to Manila and tried to bribe its crew to hand over the ship. This attempt was unsuccessful and Zhang Zuolin's cruiser escorted it from Manila to one of his ports. According to reports, Zhang Zuolin himself welcomed the ship and inspected the newly delivered weapons. He could not hide his satisfaction, immediately ordering another 30,000 rifles and 500 machine guns and concluding a contract for another 100,000 rifles and 1,500 machine guns.[61] Contacts also continued under his son Zhang Xueliang. Zbrojovka Brno sold him an Š-31 plane accompanying it with a gift of a chrome-plated automatic rifle. He was supposedly so pleased that he ordered

Figure 13: Slovak legionnaires from the 12th Shooting Regiment of General Milan Rastislav Štefánik transferring via Harbin, 13 June 1920. This particular regiment was created in the aftermath of Štefánik's visit of Siberia and composed (primarily) of Slovak soldiers. Photo courtesy of the Institute of Military History, Bratislava.

another 100 pieces as 'gifts for his dignitaries.'[62]

Fortunes of the Czechoslovak diplomatic mission varied with its Representative Office in Harbin, which was opened following Štefánik's visit in early 1919 was closed for financial reasons (despite protests from the local Czechoslovak community) in 1925. Ferdinand Erml served as liaison between the Czechoslovak community and the Czechoslovak legation in Peking.[63] Following the establishment of diplomatic relations between the two countries in 1930, a full-fledged Czechoslovak Consulate was opened in Harbin on 18 September 1931. It was headed by former legionnaire Rudolf Hejný and housed in a classist villa that was built and previously owned by a rich Russian merchant.[64] One week later, Japanese troops invaded Manchuria.

Czechoslovak Foreign Minister Edvard Beneš strongly denounced Japan's actions during his speech at the League of Nations in Geneva in December 1932. Czechoslovakia refused to recognise Manchukuo, but the Consulate remained operational until the second half of 1938. The Japanese occupation had an adverse effect on the local Czechoslovak community – its numbers fell from approx. 500 citizens to 250 and only the poorest remained – those who could ill-afford the journey back to Europe.[65] One of the last, highly symbolic major events organised by Consul-General Hejný and the Czechoslovak community in Harbin was the unveiling of a memorial made by sculptor Vinkler to fallen Czechoslovak legionnaires at the local Orthodox cemetery on 31 October 1937, just three days after the nineteenth anniversary of the establishment of Czechoslovakia.[66] One Czechoslovak newspaper reported that the event started at 3:00 pm and was attended by Harbin's Orthodox Archbishop, Consul-General Hejný, French Consul-General Reynaud, the entire Czechoslovak community, members of the Yugoslav community, and Russian émigrés. The memorial was destroyed during the Cultural Revolution.

Following the departure of Consul-General Hejný in 1939, Czechoslovak authorities received no news from the Harbin community until December 1946, when a list of 117 Czechoslovak citizens living in north-eastern China (mainly in Harbin), expressing their desire to return home, were delivered to the Czechoslovak Embassy in Moscow.[67] The list was compiled by the Soviet consul and Václav Pensa, leader of the local Czechoslovak community. The Czechoslovak Embassy in Nanjing managed to establish regular contact with the community in February 1949, after the restoration of postal service

Figure 14: Memorial to Czechoslovak legionnaires in Harbin, unveiled in October 1937 and destroyed during the Cultural Revolution. Image from Legionářský týden, *Legionaries' Weekly*, no. 5, 16 January 1938.[69]

between the Freed Territories and Nanjing government. Václav Pensa confirmed that the community had 110-120 members, mostly workers, musicians, and employees of small businesses. They were without Czechoslovak passports, which were taken away from them by the local authorities after the break-up of Czechoslovakia in 1939. Repatriation of all Czechoslovak citizens occurred from 1952 to 1954 on Polish ships and the community ceased to exist.[68]

published in Harbin for Slovak legionnaires.[58]

Li Chia Ao stayed in his posts until March 1919, when he resigned and rejoined the Foreign Office. In September 1919, he assumed the position of the High Commissioner to Siberia and concurrently sat on the board of the Trans-Siberian Railway.[70] He returned to Peking in August 1920, becoming Acting Chief Justice of the Special High Court for the Eastern Provinces in September 1921 and serving in this role until March 1923.[71] In October 1923, Li Chia Ao was appointed Chinese Envoy to Russia and one month later, he was given the rank of Envoy Extraordinary and Minister Plenipotentiary to Russia, reaching the peak of his career.

Li was in Moscow at pivotal times in early Sino-Soviet relations and was directly involved in the process of the establishment of diplomatic relations and renunciation of Tsarist privileges on the Chinese territory, which occurred on 31 May 1924. His diplomatic work has been acknowledged by several historians of early Sino-Soviet relations. Firstly, Li was involved in negotiations concerning the issue of the control of the Chinese Eastern Railway, during which he liaised with Lev Karakhan, the Soviet envoy to China, just before the establishment of diplomatic relations, and helped to convince Foreign Minister Wellington Koo to accept the proposal of joint Sino-Soviet management of the northern branch of CER.[72] Secondly, he led the subsequent protests of the Chinese government against the

Figure 15: Detail of a note verbale signed by Li Chia Ao in his capacity of Chinese Minister of Finland. Image courtesy of the Ministry of Foreign Affairs of Finland.

Soviet decision to conclude a secret supplemental agreement with warlord Zhang Zuolin, who effectively controlled the site of the CER and engineered the October 1924 coup in Beijing.[73] Thirdly, Li also participated in difficult discussions with Soviet Foreign Minister Chicerin over the status of (Outer) Mongolia, which took place in May 1925, insisting that the territory formed an integral part of China, as stated in the 1924 Sino-Soviet Treaty, and meeting with a less than amicable answer (thinly veiled threats of Soviet intervention should China enforce its claim over Mongolia).[74]

The Finnish government issued *agrément* to Li Chia Ao on 24 August 1925, and he thus became China's Minister to Finland.[75] A note verbale sent by the Chinese Legation to the Finnish Ministry of Foreign Affairs in late July 1926 informed of Li Chia Ao's illness, the onset of which was not sudden – in yet another note verbale from April 1926, he informed the Finnish Foreign Minister E. Setälä that Li had 'been advised by doctor to go to the South of France for recreation for some time.'[76] Li passed away in Helsinki on 1 September aged 67 and his remains were transported to China on 28 September 1926.[77] An obituary by Tsai Ting Kan, Minister of Foreign Affairs of the Republic of China, was subsequently transmitted to the Ministry of Foreign Affairs of Finland, praising his 'excellent record of public services to China [and] frankness, straightforwardness, sincerity, faithfulness and sympathetic attitude.'[78]

The ultimately tragic fate of Li Chia Ao's family has also been pieced together. His son Li Pao Tan (Li Baotang, 李寶堂, 1888 - ?), known in Russia as Vladimir Aleksandrovich, worked in 1924 as Second Secretary at the Embassy of the Republic of China in Moscow and married a woman called Maria Filippovna Marks.[80] They lived in Harbin and Peking in the 1930s, where Li Pao Tan taught Russian at Tsinghua, moving to the National Southwestern Associated University (Lianda) in Kunming after the Second Sino-Japanese broke out and to the Shanghai Jiao Tong University in the late 1940s.[81] They had three children - son Valentin, who committed suicide in his youth while living with his father in Peking; daughter Ariadna, who was born in Paris, lived in Shanghai, served in the army but was maltreated during the Cultural Revolution, dying some years later; and another daughter Rita, who was four years younger, born in Berlin and described as 'stunning', moved to Hong Kong to marry a businessman of mixed Chinese-British descent.[82] She died of cancer in Hong Kong. Whether Rita and her husband had any further descendants remains unknown.

This article briefly introduced Milan Rastislav Štefánik, the circumstances of his brief visit of China in November 1918 and February 1919, and his amicable meeting with the Li Chia Ao, the *daoyin* of the three north-eastern provinces and Commissioner for Foreign Affairs for Harbin. It also explored the aftermath of Štefánik's visit, especially the presence of Czechoslovak community in Harbin, which continued for another three decades, and explored the equally fascinating career of Li Chia Ao and the fortunes his descendants.

The historical significance of Štefánik's meeting with Li Chia Ao is

Figure 16: *The Li family, date unknown – Li Chia Ao, Rita, Li (Vladimir Aleksandrovich) Pao Tan, Valery, Li Chia Ao's second wife (name unknown), Ariadna, and Maria Filippovna Marks (from left to right).* Qiu Chonglu, 美女上校 (Beautiful Female Officer), 2014 http://blog.sina.com.cn/s/blog_45d4d1900102v9au.html, last modified on 25 December 2014. (accessed 22 May 2018).[79]

undoubtable and has not thus been given proper attention. What is, perhaps, more fascinating is the friendship that ensued, the evidence of which survived thanks to eyewitnesses' accounts and Li's letter, which was published in Czechoslovak press. Given the circumstances in which the meeting took place, several blank spots exist, especially in terms missing coverage of the visit in local and provincial media as well as official documents on the Chinese side. Further archival documents may eventually come to light and provide answers to yet unanswered questions.

The author dedicates this article to VK and MP, memorable conversations with whom inspired this article. I would also like to express my gratitude to Mrs. Ivana Bakešová; Mrs. Mária Halmová, Director of the Slovak National Museum in Martin; Mrs. Anna Halienová from the Slovak National Library in Martin; Mrs. Luo Huan from the National Library of China; Ms. Liu Nian from Handelsblatt; Mr. Miloslav Čaplovič, Director of the Institute of Military History and, Mr. Peter Kralčák, Director of the Military History Archive in Bratislava; Mr. Josef Žikeš, Director of the Central Military Archive in Prague; Prof. Mark Gamsa from the Tel Aviv University; and colleagues from Slovak Embassies in Prague, Helsinki, Paris, Tokyo, and our Office in Taipei.

About the author
Lukáš Gajdoš works as a diplomat at the Embassy of the Slovak Republic in Beijing.
E-mail: lgajdos@gmail.com

Endnotes

1 Prior to its creation, the term 'Czecho-Slovakia', which was also preferred by Štefánik, had been used – after its creation on 28 October 1918 the country was, however, called 'Czechoslovakia.' Terminology used in this article corresponds with this distinction.

2 Some sources state that Li Chiao Ao was in fact born four years later in 1863 – this article uses the 1925 edition of 'Who's Who in China', according to which he was born in 1859.

3 Milan Rastislav Štefánik, *Ekvádorský zápisník, The Ecuador Diary*, 1913, available at *http://zlatyfond.sme.sk/dielo/1273/Stefanik_*

Ekvadorsky-zapisnik/1 (accessed 22 May 2018).

4 *http://www.stefaniktrail.sk/en/* (accessed 22 May 2018).

5 Bohumila Ferenčuhová, 'Štefánik diplomat - medzi Francúzskom a Talianskom (1914-1919)' (Diplomat Štefánik– between France and Italy (1914-1919)), in Marián Hronský and Miloslav Čaplovič (eds.), *Generál dr. Milan Rastislav Štefánik - vojak a diplomat (General Dr. Milan Rastislav Štefánik – Soldier and Diplomat)* (Bratislava: Vojenský historický ústav, 1999), pp. 87-108.

6 Dušan Kováč, *Štefánik a Janin – príbeh priateľstva (Štefánik and Janin – Story of Friendship)* (Bratislava: Dilema, 2001), pp. 13-14.

7 Ibid.

8 Martin Hronský, Anna Krivá, Miloslav Čaplovič, *Vojenské dejiny Slovenska IV., 1914-1939 (Military History of Slovakia, vol. 4, 1914-1939)*, (Bratislava: Ministerstvo obrany Slovenskej republiky, 1996), p. 54.

9 The meeting had reportedly been arranged using Štefánik's good connections within the Masonic circles. At this stage, Štefánik was already engaged to Marchioness Giuliana Benzoni, favourite granddaughter of Ferdinando Martini, former Governor of Eritrea (1897-1907) and Member of the Italian Parliament (1876-1919). Benzoni later became a prominent anti-fascist activist. For more information, see *Banditi o eroi? Milan Rastislav Stefanik e la legione ceco-slovacca* (Bandits or Heroes? Milan Rastislav Štefánik and the Czecho-Slovak Legion) by Sergio Tazzer; František Hruška, 'O Štefánikovi z Talianska' (About Štefánik from Italy), https://zurnal. pravda.sk/spolocnost/clanok/471009-o-stefanikovi-z-talianska/, last modified on 26 May 2018 (accessed 26 May 2018).

10 This paragraph is based on Daniel Šmihula's well-written article. Daniel Šmihula, 2018, Hviezdna hodina légií, ktoré vystúpili proti sovietskej vláde (The Finest Hour of the Legions that stood up to the Soviet Government), Pravda, http://zurnal.pravda.sk/ spolocnost/clanok/470427-hviezdna-hodina-legii/, last modified on 22 May 2018) (accessed 23 May 2018).

11 Bohdan Pavlů was born in the present-day Czech Republic, but spent his childhood in present-day Slovakia and identified himself as being from 'the Slovak branch of the Czechoslovak nation.' He was elected to lead the troops on the ground in Russia during the absence of their commanders – Janin and Štefánik and as Šmihula correctly point

out, no Slovak in history has ever controlled such a vast territory. After his return to Czechoslovakia he worked as chief editor of 'The Slovak Daily' and later server as Ambassador to Bulgaria, Denmark, and Soviet Union, becoming Deputy Minister of Foreign Affairs in 1937. He died in a car crash in Yugoslavia in May 1938. Ibid.

Radula Gajda (1892-1948) was yet another colourful figure in this fascinating story – born in the picturesque Montenegrin town of Kotor, he served in the Austro-Hungarian Army (1914-15) and Montenegrin Army (1915-16), joining the Czechoslovak Legions in early 1917 and rising through the ranks to become a Major-General at the age of 26. Nicknamed 'the Siberian Ataman' or 'the Siberian Tiger', he decided to join Kolchak's forces. Part of his conversation with Štefánik was captured by his doctor Mandaus, who (rather prophetically) warned Gajda 'not to think to be a great soldier yet and not to choose the wrong path in the light of recent successes.' Gajda's time with Kolchak ended in failure and after his return to Czechoslovakia in the early 1920s he became a pro-Fascist sympathiser, cofounding the Mussolini-inspired National Fascist Community in late 1926. He was an MP for this (but paradoxically anti-German) party, took part in the so-called Židenice mutiny in 1931, refused cooperation with Germany during the occupation of the Czech lands, but was still arrested and imprisoned in the aftermath of the Second World War (1945-1947). He was freed and died in April 1948, aged 56. He remains a controversial figure. Josef Mandaus, 'S generálem Štefánikem na Sibiři (In Siberia with General Štefánik),' in by Ladislav Mazáč (ed.), *Štefánik: Kniha druhá: vzpomínky, dokumenty a jiné příspěvky (Štefánik: Book II: memories, documents, and other contributions)* (Prague: L. Mazáč, 1938), p. 285.

12 Susumu Nagayo, 'Nové poznatky z pobytu Milana Rastislava Štefánika v Japonsku (október - november 1918)' (New Findings on the Visit of Milan Rastislav Štefánik to Japan (October – November 1918)), *Historická revue* 18, no. 9 (2007), p. 14.

13 Štefánik did not take this easily – given his role within the Czecho-Slovak National Council, Janin wrote that he had expected to be the Vice-President, which 'would reflect his love for the Slovaks ... and enable him to better determine how to reach a closer union of his country with the other branches of the Czechoslovak nation.' Kováč, *Štefánik a Janin – príbeh priateľstva*, p. 80.

14 Ibid., p. 91.

15 Ibid., p. 41.

16 František Kubka, 'Generál Dr M. R. Štefánik v Charbině (General Dr. Milan Rastislav Štefánik in Harbin)', in Ladislav Mazáč (ed.), *Štefánik: Kniha druhá: vzpomínky, dokumenty a jiné příspěvky (Štefánik: Book II: memories, documents, and other contributions)* (Prague: L. Mazáč, 1938), p. 275. This published account is identical with the 'History of the Czechoslovak Armed Forces in Harbin – Since the Beginning until 29th June 1920', which was edited by František Kubka and Josef Tichý and the handwritten manuscript of which was kindly provided by the Central Military Archive in Prague.

17 Tomáš Garrigue Masaryk, *Světová revoluce (Global Revolution)*, (Prague: Orbis, 1925), p. 166.

18 Ivana Bakešová, *Legionáři v roli diplomatů: československo-čínské vztahy 1918-1949 (Legionnaires as Diplomats: Czechoslovak-Chinese relations 1918-1949)* (Prague: Filozofická fakulta Univerzity Karlovy, 2013), p. 24.

19 Telegram in Kováč, *Štefánik a Janin – príbeh priateľstva*, p. 135.

20 Kubka, 'Generál Dr M. R. Štefánik v Charbině', p. 276.

21 Czechoslovak soldier František Kubka who accompanied Štefánik in Harbin, refers to Lépice (whom he calls, phonetically, 'Lepis') as 'French consul' – email communication with *La Courneuve,* the Archive of the Ministry of Foreign Affairs of France, however identified Lépice as 'vice-consul.'

22 Telegram in Kováč, 2001, *Štefánik a Janin – príbeh priateľstva*, p. 136.

23 To give a more detailed account – 'Pristan' (Daoli or 'the area within' in Chinese; Pristan or 'wharves' in Russian) was the business centre of Harbin ... rested on the western side of the marsh and was surrounded by the tracks of the CER, tracks that roughly mirrored the concession's physical border. Less grand and less expensive that Newtown, Pristan was where most of Harbin's shops and apartments were located. The main street – called, ironically, China Street – was lined with pastel neo-classical buildings. The street earned Harbin the nickname 'the Chinese St. Petersburg'. Blaine R. Chiasson, *Administering the Colonizer: Manchuria's Russians under Chinese Rule, 1918-29* (Vancouver: University of British Columbia Press, 2010), p. 152.

A detailed account of his poor health was given my General Dr Josef Mandaus, who was at the time in charge of medical train, stationed in

Yekaterinburg at the time of Štefánik's arrival on 9 December 1918. (Then Mayor) Dr Mandaus accompanied Štefánik all the way to Changchun – until his departure for Shanghai in late January 1919 – and the two led many interesting conversations, which he captured in his diary. Mandaus, 'S generálem Štefánikem na Sibiři,' p. 279-287.

24 Telegram in Kováč, *Štefánik a Janin – príbeh priateľstva*, p. 137.

25 According to one authoritative explanation, 'an intermediate post that had existed between Governor and prefect, the circuit intendant (*daoyuan* but often *daotai* or *daoyin*) remained [after the fall of the Qing Empire] but the position of this official in the administration of the Republican period was anomalous and his authority unclear.' Michael Dillon, *Xinjiang and the Expansion of Chinese Communist Power: Kashgar in the Early Twentieth Century* (Abingdon: Routledge, 2015), p. 89.

26 František Kubka, who participated in the meeting, added that the three provinces were jointly administered since 7th April 1907. Kubka, 'Generál Dr M. R. Štefánik v Charbině', p. 277.

27 Larry M. Wortzel, Robin D. S. Higham, *Dictionary of Contemporary Chinese Military History* (Westport, CT: Greenwood Press, 1999), p. 128.

28 Based on John Benjamin Powell, *Who's Who in China* (Shanghai: The China Weekly Review, 1925), pp. 452-453.

29 Mark Gamsa, 'Mixed Marriages in Russian-Chinese Manchuria' in Dan Ben-Canaan, Frank Grüner, and Ines Prodöhl (eds.), *Entangled Histories – The Transcultural Past of Northeastern China* (Springer: Cham, 2013), p. 55. Also Kubka, 'Generál Dr M. R. Štefánik v Charbině', p. 275.

30 Kubka, 'Generál Dr M. R. Štefánik v Charbině', pp. 276-277.

31 The source of these claims is not specified. Bakešová, *Legionáři v roli diplomatů: československo-čínské vztahy 1918-1949*, p. 24.

32 Ibid.

33 *Československý týdeník* (Czechoslovak Weekly), Dopis z Charbina (Letter from Harbin), 1 April 1919.

34 Archive of the Ministry of Foreign Affairs, Prague, Siberian archives, Archive of the Harbin-based Czechoslovak Plenipotentiary for the Far East Lieutenant-Colonel Miloš Hess, dated 4 March 1919.

35 The author approached the Second Historical Archives in Nanjing, Academia Sinica in Taipei, and the Harbin Archives Bureau. Chinese-language collections of local newspapers in the National Library of

China, Heilongjiang Provincial Library and Jilin Provincial Library (namely《东陲商报》,《国际协报》,《哈尔滨新闻》- also called《哈尔滨日报》, and《新生活报》). Local Russian (《远东报》,《满洲新闻》) and Japanese-language (《盛京日报》,《泰东日报》,《生活新闻》,《北满洲》) newspapers have yet to be consulted and may reveal a mention of the visit.

36 *The New York Times*, 26 November 1918.

37 Following the death of Milan Rastislav Štefánik in May 1919, his brother Kazimír gifted the items to the Slovak National Museum (he later moved to Argentina where he passed away in 1971. He is buried in Presidencia Roque Sáenz Peña, Gran Chaco Province). Their (most likely) Chinese origin was confirmed by experts from the Náprstek Museum of Asian, African and American Cultures in Prague. They are currently exhibited in Košariská – the place of birth of Štefánik – and were kindly photographed for this article by the local branch of the Slovak National Museum. Photos of additional items are available at *http://bit.ly/MRSinCN.* (accessed 22 May 2018).

38 Chiasson, *Administering the Colonizer: Manchuria's Russians under Chinese Rule, 1918-29*, p. 39.

39 The full name of the Chinese general was not recorded. Kubka, 'Generál Dr M. R. Štefánik v Charbině', p. 277.

40 Telegram in Kováč, *Štefánik a Janin – príbeh priateľstva*, p. 136-138.

41 Kubka, 'Generál Dr M. R. Štefánik v Charbině', p. 277.

42 Ibid.

43 Josef Bartůšek, 'Cestovní data M. R. Štefánika (Travel Log of Milan Rastislav Štefánik)', in Ladislav Mazáč (ed.), *Štefánik: Kniha druhá: vzpomínky, dokumenty a jiné příspěvky (Štefánik: Book II: memories, documents, and other contributions)* (Prague: L. Mazáč, 1938), p. 384.

44 Kubka, 'Generál Dr M. R. Štefánik v Charbině', pp. 277-278.

45 Štefánik harshly criticised Admiral Kolchak's political and military circumstances – one particular exchange concluded with the following words – Kolchak: 'Vous êtes très dur, mon général' (You are very tough my general.); Štefánik: 'Non, je suis conséquent.' (No, I am thorough.) Noted in Mandaus, 'S generálem Štefánikem na Sibiři,' p. 284; Bartůšek, 'Cestovní data M. R. Štefánika', p. 387.

46 Mandaus, 'S generálem Štefánikem na Sibiři,' p. 285.

47 Štefánik previously received two lower-level *Ordre National de la*

Légion d´Honneur – Chevalier (Fifth Class) in 1914 and *Officier* (Fourth Class) in 1917.

48 Kováč, *Štefánik a Janin – príbeh priateľstva*, p. 44.

49 Mandaus, 'S generálem Štefánikem na Sibiři,' p. 285.

50 Kubka, 'Generál Dr M. R. Štefánik v Charbině', p. 278.

51 Bartůšek, 'Cestovní data M. R. Štefánika,' p. 387.

52 Bakešová, *Legionáři v roli diplomatů: československo-čínské vztahy 1918-1949*, p. 25.

53 Stanislav Kovář, '1938, Ministr M. R. Štefánik v Šanghaji (Minister M.R. Štefánik in Shanghai)', in Ladislav Mazáč (ed.), *Štefánik: Kniha druhá: vzpomínky, dokumenty a jiné příspěvky* (*Štefánik: Book II: memories, documents, and other contributions*) (Prague: L. Mazáč, 1938), p. 290.

54 *The North-China Herald*, 22 February 1919.

55 The photo is from Mrs. Věra Sýkorová, who was born in Harbin – one of the youngsters is her brother. Bakešová, *Legionáři v roli diplomatů: československo-čínské vztahy 1918-1949*, 215.

56 Ibid., p. 25.

57 Ibid., p. 27. The Chinese side called him 捷克斯拉夫共和國代辦.

58 The newspaper has been fully digitised and is available at *http://digitalna.kniznica.info/s/Nloi3YOZH5*. (accessed 22 May 2018).

59 Martin Hošek, 'A Good Pitch for Busking: Czech Compatriots in Manchuria, 1899-1918,' *Journal of the Center for Northern Humanities*, no. 3 (2010), p. 19.

60 Ibid, Bakešová, *Legionáři v roli diplomatů: československo-čínské vztahy 1918-1949*, 166.

61 Ibid., p. 169.

62 Ibid., pp. 169-170.

63 Hošek, 'A Good Pitch for Busking: Czech Compatriots in Manchuria, 1899-1918', p. 23.

64 The villa still exists and is located on Jilin Jie 52 (吉林街52号). It is a listed building, but its current state is very poor – see *http://bit.ly/CSinHB* for "then and now" photos as well as *http://bit.ly/CSinHBonBD* (Baidu 'Street View') for an interactive view its surroundings. Bakešová, *Legionáři v roli diplomatů: československo-čínské vztahy 1918-1949*, p. 69.

65 Ibid., p. 81.

66 *Legionářský týden* (Legionaries' Weekly), no. 5, 16 January 1938.

67 Bakešová, *Legionáři v roli diplomatů: československo-čínské vztahy*

1918-1949, p. 148.

68 Ibid., pp. 151-152.

69 For GPS coordinates of the memorial and its current position within the city of Harbin see *http://bit.ly/CSmemorialHB*. (accessed 22 May 2018).

70 Powell, *Who's Who in China*, p. 453.

71 Ibid.

72 Bruce A. Elleman, *Diplomacy and Deception: Secret History of Sino-Soviet Diplomatic Relations, 1917-1927* (Armonk, London: M. E. Sharpe, 1997), p. 136.

73 G. Patrick March, *Eastern Destiny: Russia in Asia and the North Pacific*, (New York: Praeger, 1996), p. 204.

74 Sarah C. Paine, *Imperial Rivals: China, Russia, and Their Disputed Frontier* (Armonk, NY: M.E. Sharpe, 1996), p. 326.

75 Ministry of Foreign Affairs of Finland, Note Verbale no. 15/2228 (24 August 1925).

76 Legation of the Republic of China in Helsinki, Note Verbale no. 233 (20 July 1926) and no. 136 (6 April 1926).

77 Ministry of Foreign Affairs of Finland, Note Verbale no. 6/2199 (28 September 1926).

78 Legation of the Republic of China in Helsinki, Note Verbale (no number/date provided).

79 I am grateful to Liu Nian's stellar research skills for locating this photo and other interesting details about the Li family. Qiu Chonglu, 美女上校 (Beautiful Female Officer), 2014, *http://blog. sina.com.cn/s/blog_45d4d1900102v9au.html*, last modified on 25 December 2014. (accessed 22 May 2018).

80 This information was kindly shared by Prof. Mark Gamsa. 'Vsia Moskva na 1924 god (Moscow in its Entirety in 1924),' *https:// archive.org/stream/AllMoscow/1924_Vsya_Moskva_1924_djvu.txt*. (accessed 22 May 2018).

81 [校史回顾]上海交通大学外语教育百年回眸 ([School History Review] Shanghai Jiaotong University's Foreign Language Education Review in the Past 100 Years), https://www.sjtu.edu.cn/info/1489/24839.htm. (accessed 22 May 2018).

82 I am grateful to Professor Gamsa for kindly sharing the original source of this information. Nina Kruk, Nam ulybalas' Kvan In" (Guanyin Smiled at Us), *Rossiiane v Azii* (Russians in Asia), no. 7 (autumn 2000), 151–197; Gamsa, 2013, 'Vsia Moskva na 1924

god', pp. 55-56. Photos of Ariadne as a soldier in the national army have also been located and are available at *http://blog.sina.com.cn/s/blog_45d4d1900102v9au.html.* (accessed 22 May 2018). Following the end of the Second Sino-Japanese War, Ariadne Li entered the northeast with the 13th Army and for nine months was responsible for liaising with the Soviet garrison in Shenyang and Manzhouli. Qiu, 美女上校.

A MOST FOREIGN HUTONG:
Beijing's Kuei Chia Chang In 1922
BY PAUL FRENCH

ABSTRACT

Kuei Chia Chang, or Armour Factory Alley in English, was a residential *hutong* popular with foreigners in Peking (Beijing) in the first half of the twentieth century.[1] Situated in the Eastern Tartar City (present day Dongcheng District), the hutong was close by the Tartar Wall with easy access to the Legation Quarter to the west, as well as the shopping, dining and socialising areas of Hatamen (Chongwenmen) and Morrison Street (Wangfujing) to the north. The 1922 edition of *The Peking Who's Who* lists a number of its foreign residents.[2] This article uncovers who they were and what they were doing in Peking that year. It looks at how this particular hutong had developed into a desirable environment for foreigners and how it changed throughout the inter-war period.

DESIREABLE HUTONGS

In the first three decades of the twentieth century, the majority of the foreign colony of Peking lived on traditional hutongs. Before the First World War and into the early 1920s, there was only a small selection of purpose-built accommodation for foreigners. In the first decade of the century, the city's first Western-style apartment building, the Cattaneo Flats, was constructed on Morrison Street.[3] In the 1920s, the Cattaneo was followed by the construction of several more Western style apartment blocks, of typically three to four floors, along Legation Street (Dongjiaomin Xiang), and around what is now Dahua Road. There were some Western-style residences constructed by the Rockefeller Foundation for the European and American staff of the Peking Union Medical College (PUMC). However, the number of foreigners in the city outstripped the construction of Western-style apartment buildings considerably. Most diplomats and their families resided in rooms within their national legation compounds. Troops stationed in Peking resided in barracks adjacent to the embassies, and missionaries mostly lived in premises attached to Christian missions and churches. This meant that the hutongs were effectively the only option for most foreigners in Peking.

Though foreigners lived in many hutongs across the city in the early 1920s, Shih-chia Hutong, Nan-chi Tze Hutong and Kuei Chia Chang Hutong were clearly the most popular. Each had specific reasons to be favoured. The quiet and leafy Shih-chia Hutong contained many well-built and large courtyard residences (*siheyuan*) close to the retail and banking centre of Morrison Street and the social centre of the *Grand Hôtel de Pékin* on the junction of Morrison and Chang'an Boulevard.[4] It was also close to the Legation Quarter. Nan-chi Tze Hutong ran parallel to the eastern wall of the old Ancestral Temple, north from Chang'an Boulevard to Donghuamen, the east gate of the Forbidden City. It was equally well situated for access to the Legation Quarter. Kuei Chia Chang Hutong, where the *siheyuan* were slightly smaller on average than those on Shih-Chia Hutong or Nan-chi Tze, was close to the Tartar Wall by the Fox Tower (Dongbianmen) with easy access to both the Legation Quarter and the retail, restaurant and socialising district along Hatamen Street. It was also a short walk from Chang'an, the *Grand Hôtel* and the Morrison Street retail district.

Each of these hutongs attracted a slightly different sort of foreign resident. Shih-chia attracted a number of Scandinavian residents due to its proximity to the former Danish Embassy building and the offices of the Danish-owned Northern Telegraph Company (the firm instrumental in establishing the cables connecting China with Russia, Japan and Hong Kong). Additionally, Shih-chia's larger than average courtyards attracted wealthy members of the foreign colony. In 1924 the American millionaire and would-be China Hand Herman Rogers and his wife Katherine moved into one of these *siheyuan* and then invited an old friend, Wallis Spencer (later Simpson, and later still the Duchess of Windsor) to stay with them for a while. Finally, due to its proximity to many Chinese government offices, Shih-chia was popular with senior officials of the former Qing Dynasty administration and the new Republican government.

But Kuei Chia Chang attracted perhaps the most varied range of foreign residents of the three addresses and was perhaps the best situated for a number of reasons. Many foreigners valued the easy access to the Tartar Wall – at this point approximately twenty feet wide – for walking, bicycle or horse riding. The wall from the Fox Tower down the side of the Legation Quarter to Chienmen (Qianmen) was effectively (though the legal status of this is hard to fully ascertain) 'foreigner only', and for supposed security reasons, ruled 'out of bounds' to the Chinese. Kuei Chia Chang also offered proximity to the Glacis open area at the eastern edge of the Legation Quarter, which was regularly used for local residents to exercise horses and for polo matches, as well as for the drilling of troops. The Glacis, from a military term meaning a piece of land kept open to provide a buffer zone, had been a no-man's land situated between Chinese and foreign Peking, between the Legation Quarter and the eastern Tartar City, to provide an easterly defence of the Quarter. By 1920, fears of another Boxer Rebellion were receding and mounted cavalry seen as a thing of the past after the Great War. Consequently, the Glacis was to become increasingly developed and built over, and by 1927, the exercise yard and the polo fields were swallowed up by development entirely. Additionally, the new Round-the-Wall steam train, whose track began by the Fox Tower, offered quick access to the Chienmen area and beyond out to western Peking and the Purple Hills.

Kuei Chia Chang ran west into Soochow (Suzhou) Hutong (then, as now, a noted food street), which continued through to the edge of the Legation Quarter at Hatamen Street. Kuei Chia Chang was close to the old imperial examination halls and had traditionally been the area where various concerns linked to the Chinese arsenal had been situated in the Ming Dynasty (1368-1744) – hence its association with armouries. It later became home to a number of papermaking factories; small family businesses that had given the warren of lanes around Kuei Chia Chang the name of the Papermakers' District. The hutong was lined with plane trees and had poplar and/or gingko trees within most of the courtyards.

Chinese property owners on Kuei Chia Chang, keen to secure the higher rents foreigners were willing and able to pay, had been quick to realise the potential of the hutong. In some cases, the traditional windows of thick translucent paper had been replaced with glass. Gradually many of the courtyard residences along the hutong were fitted out with electric lights, modern Western-style bathrooms and WCs, water boilers, modern plumbing and steam heating. The hutong, though ancient, was wide enough to accommodate both rickshaws and, when they were widely introduced, motorised taxis. Though we know little of the landlords on Kuei Chia Chang, it seems all were Chinese in the 1920s (though in the 1930s some foreigners were able to purchase their courtyard properties outright), and

Figure 1: Kuei Chia Chang, looking east, with overhanging plane trees, January 2010 *(courtesy: Jo Lusby)*

several at least were registered as overseas Chinese living in America and France. Kuei Chia Chang was a good source of income for them and, with their experience of having lived abroad, they were among the smaller group of Chinese landlords in Peking at the time able to deal relatively easily with Europeans and Americans. The American Board of Commissioners for Foreign Missions (ABCFM), or simply The American Board leased several adjacent houses on the street for several decades to house their missionaries and lay employees.[5]

However, there were some disadvantages to Kuei Chia Chang. The eastern end of the hutong was close to an old portion of the Grand Canal that had silted up. Grain barges were no longer able to transit the canal and it had become a fetid rubbish dump that stank in the hot summer months. The eastern end of the hutong could also feel somewhat more remote. Beyond was the abandoned Fox Tower, some wasteland (on what is now the Second Ring Road) inhabited largely by feral dogs and, beyond that again, several large burial grounds including the major foreign and Chinese cemeteries for Peking. Many local Chinese believed the cemeteries and burial grounds to be the home of fox spirits, a superstition so persistent and strong that, it was reported, some taxi drivers and rickshaw pullers would refuse (or require an extra financial inducement) to drop off or pick up fares on Kuei Chia Chang.

A MOST FOREIGN ALLEY

In 1922, Kuei Chia Chang probably comprised no more than fifteen, perhaps as many as twenty, dwellings (*siheyuans* of various size). We know the foreigners who lived in some of these.

The Corbetts – The courtyard at the far eastern end of Kuei Chia Chang, No.1, was, in 1922, the registered address of the Reverend Charles Hodge Corbett, his wife and their three children. Corbett, an American national, was 44 years of age, a professor lecturing in physics and chemistry at Peking University. Corbett had been born in 1881 in Chefoo (Yantai) in Shandong, the son of a prominent and strict Protestant missionary father who originally hailed from Clarion County, Pennsylvania. Corbett's father was the pioneering American Presbyterian missionary Rev. Dr. Hunter Corbett, who had come to China in 1863 and was the founder of Shantung (Shandong) Christian University, now Cheeloo University, arguably China's first Western-style university. He had also founded the Yi Wen School (also known as the Boy's Academy or the Hunter Corbett Academy) in Chefoo.

As a missionary child, a 'mishkid', Charles had attended the Chefoo School from 1889 to 1906. Also known as the Protestant Collegiate School, the Chefoo School was a Christian boarding institution that had been established in 1880 by the London-based China Inland Mission (CIM). It was mainly for British children, though American Protestant missionaries also sent their offspring there. When Corbett began studying there, the original premises had just been significantly improved and enlarged with better heating, glass windows and plumbed in WCs. Christian education was the mainstay of the Chefoo School's syllabus. The principal led daily prayers and pupils attended two services each Sunday.

After his basic education, Corbett went to America for his higher education. He gained his degree at the private Wooster Liberal Arts College in Ohio. He then went straight into teaching, obtaining a position at Huron College in London, Ontario from 1901 to 1903. Between 1906 and 1908, he taught at the Union Settlement in East Harlem, founded in 1895 by members of the Union Theological Seminary Alumni Club who had been inspired by what they had seen at Toynbee Hall in London and Hull House in Chicago. The general idea was to provide educational opportunities to low income and immigrant residents of poor urban areas. During this time, Charles gave many lectures across America with titles such as, 'Missions in China and How They are Carried on.' As with many of the American missionary-teachers, including a number living on Kuei Chia Chang in 1922, Corbett was both a qualified university lecturer and an ordained minister.

After a couple of years at Union Settlement, Corbett returned to China and spent a decade teaching physics and chemistry at the North China Union College for Men in Tungchow (now Tongzhou District, Beijing). In 1918 Corbett joined the faculty of Peking University and came to live on Kuei Chia Chang. Charles Corbett met and married Minnie Coursen Webster of East Orange, New Jersey in 1906. Minnie was also active in the First Presbyterian Church. They had two children Alfred Hunter Corbett Jr., and a daughter called Helen, who was studying at Peking University in 1922. Charles's father, the Reverend Hunter Corbett, had died in Chefoo in 1920 at 85 years of age.

Charles Hodge Corbett and his family returned to the United States in 1926 and settled in Brooklyn, where he became an Associate Minister at the Union Church of Bay Ridge. In 1955, Corbett published a history of Shantung Christian University and also contributed to a book celebrating the life of his father. Minnie died in 1958; Charles in 1963.

Miss Fischer-Togo – At No.6 lived perhaps the most mercurial of Kuei Chia Chang's foreign residents, the wonderfully named Miss Olga Fischer-Togo. Miss Fischer-Togo, an Austrian, was a soprano singer who had been appearing in concerts and light operas across Japan and northern China since before the First World War. One thing we can be sure of about Miss Fischer-Togo is that she was a strong woman – not only was she one of only a handful of women to have their own separate entry in the 1922 *Peking Who's Who* main section (as opposed to the far more brief 'Ladies List' at the end of the book), but she also seems to have survived incarceration in a Siberian prison.

Olga Fischer was born in Vienna in 1875, one of twelve brothers and sisters. She studied music at the Vienna Conservatory and then in Milan. She made her stage debut in Milan as Nedda in an early production of Ruggero Leoncavallo's *Pagliacci*, a role most famously played by Dame Nellie Melba in London several years previously. Somehow Miss Fischer ended up involved in the Russo-Japanese War (1904-1905) where two things happened – firstly, she was awarded the Austrian Red Cross (a medal usually given for services to nursing in wartime), and secondly, she adopted the stage name 'Togo', apparently in order to improve her profile with Japanese audiences. Certainly,

Figure 2: Kuei Chia Chang, looking west, with additions attached to the original building walls, January 2010 *(courtesy: Jo Lusby)*

from about 1912 she was appearing often in Tokyo and other Japanese cities, being described in the English language press in Tokyo as 'well-known' opera singer.[6] By 1913, she began appearing at concerts in northern China and Peking.

It seems the reason for Miss Fischer-Togo's trips to the Far East was that her older brother, Emil, lived in China. Emil Sigmund Fischer (born in 1865) was a banker who first came to China in 1894 and worked in Shanghai and Tientsin (Tianjin). He was also a prolific author of guides (often using his adopted Chinese name Fei-shi). His books included *Through the Silk and Tea Districts of Kiang-nan and Chekiang, Overland via the Trans-Siberian Railway, Guide to Peking: Environs Near and Far, A Trip into Anhui, The Present Outlook in Manchuria, Travels in China, 1894-1940*, and others, as well as travel journalism for a wide variety of magazines including *Collier's Weekly* in America.[7]

At some time around the end of the First World War, Fischer-Togo decided to settle in Peking and is recorded in the pages of the *Peking Gazette* as performing regularly at events at various concert halls and legations throughout the city, often appearing at charity galas. It seems that by 1919 she was attached to the Music School of the Peking School of Fine Arts. She never seems to have married and lived alone in some style on Kuei Chia Chang. She was clearly earning a decent independent living as a soprano in 1920s China.

In 1922 Olga Fischer-Togo was the biggest celebrity living on Kuei Chia Chang, thanks to her regular artistic performances in the city as well as her newly published book, *My Trip from China, via Siberia to Europe: Including Experiences in a Siberian Prison*. As with many of her brother Emil's books and *The Peking Who's Who*, Fischer Togo's book was published by the Tientsin Press.[8] Fischer-Togo had recently attempted to travel from China to Europe via the Trans-Siberian Railway, but had encountered numerous problems with over-zealous Bolshevik commissars, various officials demanding bribes and brief periods of incarceration and quarantine due to the Spanish flu pandemic and other disease outbreaks in Russia. The tone of the book is rather huffy, as though disease, revolution, the aftermath of war and rapacious officials were all specifically targeting Miss Olga Fischer-Togo.

Emil remained in China through to the Japanese occupation and was held prisoner by the Japanese in a civilian internment camp from 1941 until his death. It seems that Emil and Olga had both taken American citizenship some time around 1940 and so found themselves liable for internment as enemy aliens. Olga, who avoided internment by having left China earlier, died in the United States in 1968, aged 88.

The McFalls – In 1922, Robert Erskine McFalls and his wife lived at No.10 Kuei Chia Chang. McFalls was just 36 years old and working as a 'Representative' (or Resident Technical Engineer) for the Baldwin Locomotive Works, an American train manufacturing company. Originally from Philadelphia, McFalls had been working for Baldwin since 1905 as an engineer, but had only arrived in China in 1919. Clearly, he had quickly settled in, living in a courtyard on Kuei Chia Chang and listed as having already secured membership in the exclusive Peking Club in the Legation Quarter. His wife Margaret had accompanied him to China.

McFalls' major role was concerned with the Peking-Suiyuan Railway.[9] The line was expanding when McFalls arrived in China in 1919, with the Peking-Hankow (Hankou) Railway being amalgamated with the Peking-Suiyuan Railway that year. Baldwin Locomotive was an American firm based in Philadelphia and founded in 1831 by Matthias Baldwin. Baldwin had been very aggressive in selling trains to China and also very successful. As well as the Peking-Hankow and Peking-Suiyuan lines, they were selling trains to the Peking-Mukden (Shenyang) Railway, also within McFalls' remit as north China representative of the firm. McFalls it seems was doing well too – it's recorded that he sold three trains for Baldwin in China in

1919 and ten in 1920. McFalls worked out of the Anderson, Meyer & Company offices in Peking (Anderson, Meyer were general agents for many foreign manufacturing and engineering companies in China at the time, including Baldwins) at No.1 Da Yuan Fu Hutong (Datianshujing), just a ten-minute walk from Kuei Chia Chang off Morrison Street.[10]

McFalls died in 1936 at just 50 years of age and is buried in Arlington Cemetery, Virginia. Margaret died in 1969 and was interred with him.

William Collins – William Fredrick (or sometimes Frederick) Collins, FRGS, ARSM, M Inst M & M resided at No.13 Kuei Chia Chang, the largest single courtyard property on the hutong. Thirty-eight years old in 1922, Collins was a British mining engineer, a Fellow of the Royal Geographic Society, an Associate of the Royal School of Mines (at Imperial College, London) and a member of the Institute of Mines and Metallurgy in England. Collins had been educated at the well-regarded St Olave's Grammar School in Southwark, London (though now relocated to Orpington in outer London). From there he went to the prestigious Westminster School and then to London University. Initially after graduation he worked as an assayer in Cornwall. In 1906, he accepted the position of Engineer with the French Syndicat du Yunnan, being promoted to Manager in 1909. He spent many years in western China and corresponded with the famous *Times of London* China correspondent Ernest Morrison ('Morrison of Peking') concerning current events in Yunnan, a region plagued with warlords and uprisings, and a site of Anglo-French contestation for influence.

In 1912, Collins took the post of Director and Manager of the Anglo-French China Corporation. He resigned from this post in 1915 to return to Europe as a Staff Captain with the Chinese Labour Corps (CLC) on the Western Front. He remained with the CLC, undertaking salvage work in France and Belgium till mid-1919. He then returned to China, working on an effectively freelance basis for a number of mining companies as a consulting engineer. He was a Vice-Chairman of the British Chamber of Commerce in Peking and also wrote a number of books on mining in China (with *Mineral Enterprise in China* being generally regarded as the most informed title on Chinese mining before World War Two[11]), several highly technical academic papers presented to the Institute of Mining and Metallurgy in London, and some useful translations from French into English of documents concerning Yunnan mining and metallurgy. Collins also turned his skills in metallurgy to other ends, preparing a paper for the *Journal of the Institute of Metals* on 'The Corrosion of Early Chinese Bronzes' (published in 1931).

Collins, a Peking Club member, was also a member of the Peking branch of The Thatched House Club, Britain's Geological Society Club, which had been formed in 1824 at the Thatched House Tavern in St. James's Street. Dinners were arranged for members accompanied by discussions of matters geological. Collins, along with others in Peking working in or with an interest in geology, metallurgy and mining, gathered at their own Thatched House Club for dinners and discussion.

Though Kuei Chia Chang was quite modern in terms of many properties having steam heating, Western toilets and glass rather than paper in the windows, Collins was one of only a couple of people on the hutong in 1922 to have had a telephone installed – the directory lists him as being available on 'Peking 2670.'

Howard Galt – the Reverend Howard Spilman Galt from Shenandoah, Iowa was a graduate of the University of Chicago and the Hartford Theological Seminary. In 1922 he was employed as a missionary-teacher with the ABCFM in Peking. Though the ABCFM leased several properties on Kuei Chia Chang for their employees, it seems the Galts had rented their courtyard separately and independently.

In 1922, the Reverend Galt was 44 years old, married to Louise Alberta (née West of Tabor, Iowa) and living at No.15 Kuei Chia Chang. Howard and Louise had arrived in China in late 1899, just in time to be caught up in the Boxer Rebellion and the Siege of the Legations the following year. Being a veteran of the 1900 Siege was always something to be noted in biographies of such people in the various editions of *The Peking Who's Who*. Galt survived the siege and then went to teach at the North China Union College for Men from 1902 to 1911, when he was promoted to the position of President of the institution. In 1917, he returned to the United States for a year to be a Special Lecturer (of the Henry D. Porter Foundation) at Pomona Liberal Arts College in Claremont, California. He returned to China in 1918 to take up a new post as Professor of Education at Yenching University, the largest Christian college in Peking. It is of course impossible to imagine that Howard Galt did not know Charles Corbett and his family and the other ABCFM staff and volunteers living nearby, given that they all lived on the same hutong, were all missionaries (or of missionary stock) and all worked in either Peking or Yenching Universities.

Around the time the Galts lived in Kuei Chia Chang, Howard was involved in the establishment of the Peking Apologetic Group at Yenching University, which later renamed itself The Life Fellowship. This was a mixed Christian group of foreigners and Chinese, all with links to the Union Theological Seminary at New York's Columbia University, the oldest independent seminary in the United States. Other members of the Fellowship included John Leighton Stuart, later to become the President of Yenching and also an American ambassador to China in 1946, as well as the prominent Chinese Protestants and educators Liu Tingfang and Xu Baoqian.

Galt remained in China up until the Japanese attack in 1937, working at Yenching, where he was for a time Acting President and a long serving trustee of the university representing the interests of the ABCFM. He also found time to publish a book, *The Development of Chinese Educational Theory* (Commercial Press of Shanghai, 1930). The Galts had four children – Mabel (born 1900), Lawrence, Dorothy and Wendell. Galt and his family were eventually interned by the Japanese in the civilian assembly camp established in the grounds of the (by then former) British Embassy. The Galts were later transferred to the larger internment camp for northern China at Wei-Hsien (Weixian, Shandong).

Mme de Fontblanc – Madame de Fontblanc is listed in the 'Ladies List' section of the 1922 *Peking Who's Who* as residing on Kuei Chia Chang, yet no property number is given or any biographical details. It seems most likely that she was the widow of Assistant-Commissary General de Fontblanc, who was with the British 60th Rifles in Northern China in the 1860s. This would make Madame de Fontblanc quite aged in 1922. Sadly, no further information is available.

The Evans family – Mrs R. K. Evans is listed in the 'Ladies List' section of the 1922 *Peking Who's Who*, though there is curiously no entry for a Mr R. K. Evans. But the Reverend Robert Kenneth Evans did exist (1880-1925) and would eventually become immortalised by one of China's greatest twentieth century novelists.

Evans was a Protestant missionary-teacher with the London

164

Missionary Society (LMS). He is recorded as working with the China Continuation Committee, a group formed in 1910 at a conference in Edinburgh to foster better cooperation between the various British and American Protestant missionary organisations operating in China. Evans was a highly active missionary – he had graduated in theology from Oxford University and had been Chairman of the Student Christian Movement of Great Britain and Ireland for a time. He met his future wife when he was teaching at Mansfield Religion and Theology College in Oxford. Janet Elizabeth Rees was herself the daughter of a clergyman, the Welsh missionary and linguist W. Hopkyn Rees (1859–1924), who had weathered the Boxer rebellion.

In 1912 Evans was listed as a 'teacher' at the John Griffith College in Hankow. (Griffith was an earlier LMS missionary to China who arrived in Hankow in 1861 and stayed until 1912). After Hankow it seems that the Evanses spent time at Wuchang (now part of Wuhan) and Hwangpei (now Huangpi in Hubei). They seem to have moved to Peking in 1916, when Evans started teaching at the Peking Union Theological College (part of Yenching University), specialising in New Testament Literature and Interpretation. As part of the job he was allocated accommodation on Kuei Chia Chang, in a property rented by Yenching. One of the reasons the Rev. Evans might have neglected to get his biography in the 1922 *Peking Who's Who* is that it was a big year for him. In 1922 the World Student Christian Federation (WCSF) held its annual conference in Peking and Evans was a leading organiser of the event. As well as teaching, Evans was on the Executive Committee of the Peking Missionary Association, was one of the LMS appointed trustees to Peking University and in 1928 would publish a pamphlet, *Jesus - Lord or Leader?*

It was also probably in 1922 that Evans made the acquaintance of an ambitious young teacher Shu Qingchun, a fellow member of Haidian's Gangwashi Church board, trustee of its Neighbourhood Service Centre and Dean of Studies for the church's primary schools, where he taught classes in Moral Cultivation and Music. In the spring of 1922 Shu had been baptised a Christian, taking the name Colin C. Shu, He is now better known as the novelist Lao She.

While Evans had been informally supervising the Gangwashi Church, by December 1922, he was home in England from China after suffering 'a serious nervous breakdown' and was living with his father-in-law, Hopkyn Rees, who was now retired from the LMS to a chair of Chinese at the University of London (1921–1924). When Hopkyn Rees was looking for a candidate for an assistant lectureship in Mandarin he sought out Lao She on Evans' recommendation. Lao She was met by Reverend Evans at London's Cannon Street Railway Station on 14 September 1924. He would remain in London for four years and record his experiences in his novel *Er Ma* (1929).[12] Whether a fair portrait or not, his lampooning of Evans as the Reverend Ely in his novel *Er Ma* (*Mr. Ma and Son*) indicates Lao She's marked distancing from the British missionary endeavour:

> The Reverend Ely was an old missionary who'd spread the Word for twenty years in China. He knew everything there was to know about China ... And yes he truly loved the Chinese, and at midnight, if lying awake unable to sleep, he would invariably pray to God to hurry up and make China a British dominion. Eyes filled with hot tears, he would point out to God that if the Chinese were not taken in hand by the British, that vast mass of yellow-faced black-haired creatures would never achieve the ascent to Heaven on High.[13]

The Taylers– Like the Evans, the Taylers, John Bernard ('J B') and his wife Selina, were allocated university-rented accommodation on Kuei Chia Chang. Tayler was also attached to the LMS and taught economics at Yenching, while Selina taught at various missionary schools. J. B. had been in China since at least 1910, working first at Tungchow and for a time in Tientsin. A former chemist, he became a specialist in Chinese agrarian systems, publishing a number of articles on agriculture in journals including *Farm and Factory in China: Aspects of the Industrial Revolution.*[14] At Yenching, and through the various journals and papers of the LMS, Tayler advocated the boosting of rural industries through the creation of co-operatives to help lift villages out of poverty and raise standards of living. Tayler was the guiding light on the newly formed Industrial Commission of the Chinese National Christian Council.

Shortly before the Japanese invasion of China in 1937, the Taylers moved to Sandan (now Shantan) in Gansu province where there were a lot of industrial co-operatives active and his work was supported. Tayler's ideas on rural-industrial co-operatives had found favour with the Nationalist government.

The Taylers' youngest daughter Gladys was born in China in 1919. She later came to some prominence after falling in love with the son of a wealthy Tientsin banking family, Yang Xianyi, while at Oxford in the 1930s. In 1940 they made the perilous journey back to the wartime Chinese capital of Chungking (Chongqing) and were married there and worked as teachers and translators. Yang's family were well known and he himself had found come acclaim as a poet. After the war, Gladys and Xianyi supported the Communist revolution and stayed in China after 1949. However, come the Cultural Revolution Yang's wealthy banking childhood and Gladys's foreign heritage meant they were badly treated and suffered greatly.

Tayler left China shortly after the Japanese surrender in 1945 and is believed to have died back in England. Gladys lived on into the 1960s. The Taylers' oldest son Bernard, who joined the British army in the Second World War, was captured by the Japanese at the fall of Singapore and killed shortly before the Japanese surrender. Two other brothers, Harold and John, survived the war, as did their oldest daughter Hilda. Selina returned to England with her husband in 1945 and died in 1970 on the Isle of Wight.

The Porters – The Rev. Lucius Chapin Porter and his wife were another ABCFM family working at Peking University and living in ABCFM-provided housing on Kuei Chia Chang (similar to the Galt family). Lucius Porter was known for his familiarity with Chinese traditional belief systems and their relationship, both adversarial and complementary, to Christianity. He summarised the relationship in his book, which he was writing while living on Kuei Chia Chang in 1922, *China's Challenge to Christianity*.[15]

Porter's family had been American Board missionaries in Shandong province, and he had been born in Tientsin in 1880, where he was privately tutored by his father. He had then gone to America to study at Beloit College in Wisconsin (graduating class of 1901) before attending Yale Divinity School and Columbia University, where he gained an MA in education in 1917. Between his time at Yale and Columbia, Porter married Lillian Dudley, whom he had met at Beloit, in 1908, and they moved together to China to work for the American Board. Porter was already at that time regarded as a 'brilliant speaker.'[16]

Porter had worked for some years teaching psychology and philosophy at the North China Union College in Tungchow within the Harvard-Yenching Studies Institute. In 1922 he was a professor of philosophy at Yenching. He was a fluent Mandarin speaker and quite happy to be known by his Chinese name, Bo Chenguang. Porter was clearly a much-liked member of the faculty.

The most striking feature of the Yenching campus was its pagoda, located on the south-eastern border of the university's lake. It was a thirteen-storied replica of an ancient Tungchow pagoda and actually functioned as a water tower. Its construction was initially controversial – an obvious symbol of Buddhism in an overly Christian institution. It was Lucius Porter who led the successful argument for its construction, and consequently it was called the Boya Pagoda – the 'Bo' referring to Porter's Chinese name and 'Ya' indicating an 'elegant scholar.' English speakers simply referred to it as 'Porter's Pagoda.' The pagoda was hard to ignore on the campus due to its location and size, while constant reminders of its presence were given as the hours were announced by its two hundred-year old bronze bell, decorated with imperial dragons and ocean waves, that was made to sound like a swinging wooden beam.[17]

For Porter, 1922 was a good year. In the autumn he left Kuei Chia Chang, with Lillian and their children Henry and Elizabeth (both born in Tungchow), returning to America on furlough to teach at Columbia. He was made the Dean Lung Professor of Chinese Studies for the 1922-1923 academic year.[18] In 1925, he returned to Peking, and Kuei Chia Chang, and was made the first Dean of the new Yenching School of Chinese Studies. In furlough years when he returned home he taught Chinese studies and Christian thought at Harvard, Beloit, Yale, Claremont and Columbia (where he was made a Dean of Chinese Studies). He remained in Peking in the 1930s, teaching philosophy at Yenching and submitting academic articles to the *Chinese Social and Political Science Review* and other journals. In the aftermath of the Japanese occupation in the summer of 1937, Porter was a vocal advocate for the protection of all the city's churches. He also travelled to his home town of Tientsin during the Japanese attack in late 1937 to personally escort back to Peking a large number of Chinese Christian students trapped in the city. He also managed to gain the release of three Chinese Yenching students who had been arrested by the Japanese army in Tientsin that summer while attending a meeting of the local Oxford Group.[19] He carried on working despite the wartime conditions, publishing *Tao in the Lun Yu* (the Lun Yu being another name for the Confucian Analects) in 1939.

Lucius and Lillian were interned as enemy nationals during the Sino-Japanese war. Released in 1945, the Porters returned to Peking, and Kuei Chia Chang, but in 1949 were once again arrested, this time by the communists, before being expelled from China after nearly forty years. Back in the United States, Porter took on the role of President of the Beloit Committee on Human Rights as well as occasionally lecturing at Harvard and Columbia. He died in 1958 in a traffic accident in Beloit at 78 years of age. Lillian predeceased him. Porter remained remarkably robust into old age. As a Beloit College student, he had been a champion hurdler – at 72 he still claimed to be running two miles a day for exercise.

Miss Swann – The American Board's properties on Kuei Chia Chang included accommodation for two young women – a Miss Anne P. Swann and a Miss Anne (referred to as 'Annie' to avoid confusion) E. Lueders. They were lay volunteers with ABCFM and the only single young foreign women living on the hutong.

Anne Swann was born in 1895 in China to an American missionary family originally from Bridgewater, New Jersey. She left China to study at Vassar College (graduating class of 1917) and continued her education with graduate work in exercise therapy at Columbia University's Teachers College. Anne began her China career as a teacher in the Bridgman Academy in Tunghsien (now Antung District, Beijing), an institution started in the 1860s by the wife of the well-known early American Protestant missionary Elijah Coleman Bridgman (1801-1861).[20] Most of Anne's early time in China as a single woman was spent in Peking living on Kuei Chia Chang though, on behalf of the American Board, she did make journeys to ABCFM stations as far north as Jehol, and as far south as Changsha and Canton (Guangzhou).[21]

In 1922 Anne's life was about to change significantly – she had just become engaged to Luther Carrington Goodrich, whom she would marry the following year. Goodrich was the son of a North China missionary, the Reverend Chauncey Goodrich, and born in Peking in 1894. He was educated at the Chefoo School in Yantai, Oberlin Academy in Ohio and Williams College in Massachusetts (graduating in 1917). Luther had lived through the Boxer Rebellion and the Siege of the Legations as a young child and was eventually one of the last living witnesses to those events. Luther worked for the China Medical Board of the Rockefeller Foundation in Peking.

Figure 3: The former entrance to a siheyuan on Kuei Chia Chang, now a communal entrance, January 2010 *(courtesy: Jo Lusby)*

In 1925 Luther and Anne left Peking so Luther could join the faculty at Columbia full-time. He later became the Dean Lung Professor Emeritus of Chinese, following in the footsteps of his wife's former colleague and neighbour on Kuei Chia Chang, Lucius Porter. Anne too retained her Sinological interests after returning to America. As Anne Swann Goodrich, she wrote *The Peking Temple of the Eastern Peak*, a charming description of the Peking she had come to know.[22] During her time in China, Swann was a great collector of paper gods and created one of the finest collections in the West, most purchased from the famous Peking curio store *Ren he zhi dian* (Unity Among Men Paper Shop) situated in the traditional papermakers district adjacent to Kuei Chia Chang.[23] Anne continued to research areas that were of interest to her, publishing a number of papers and books including, *Chinese Hells: The Peking Temple of Eighteen Hells and Chinese Conception of Hell* and *Peking's Paper Gods*.[24] She became a lifetime member of the American Society of Women Geographers. Luther Goodrich is perhaps best remembered for his *Dictionary of Ming Biography, 1368–1644* (Association for Asian Studies, 1976).

The couple had two sons, Thomas and Hubbard, as well as two daughters, Sally and Anne. Luther died in 1986; Anne died in 2005 at a very respectable 109 years of age.

Miss Lueders – Anne 'Annie' Eleonor Lueders was the other 'Miss' registered with the ABCFM-related residents on Kuei Chia Chang. She had been born in 1893 in Philadelphia to a family with a Moravian background. Her older sister Emma married Richard H. Ritter, who had been a missionary with the Princeton-in-China mission as well as a professor at Yenching since 1920. It seems Annie decided to travel to China with the couple and register as a volunteer with the ABCFM. Hence, as a single woman in Peking she came to live with Anne Swann.

The Ritters left China in 1929, though Annie remained in Peking until 1941 when, due to the imminent war with Japan and the conditions in occupied Peking, she opted to return to America – thereby avoiding the internment suffered by others on Kuei Chia Chang. She remained unmarried and died in 1942 in Hartford, Connecticut aged just 49. Her sister Emma, who must have been a frequent visitor to Kuei Chia Chang, died in 1975 aged 84.

THE TRANSCIENCE OF KUEI CHIA CHANG

It is difficult to work out how long the various foreign residents of

Kuei Chia Chang recorded in the 1922 *Peking Who's Who* had already been resident on the hutong and also how long they stayed. Marriage, the return home (or to countries their parents had originally come from) and then war and internment meant a certain transience was a feature of the hutong's life.

Still, Kuei Chia Chang remained a popular location. In the later 1920s and 1930s several notable foreigners in Peking lived on the hutong. Edward Theodore Chalmers (ETC) Werner took a long lease on No.1 Kuei Chia Chang, formerly the Corbett family home, after they returned to America in 1926. Werner, a retired British diplomat turned full time China scholar and author, and widower, remained at No.1 till he was interned by the Japanese in 1942, and then returned for several years after the liberation. He stayed until October 1951, by which time he was one of the last British residents of Peking.[25]

In 1931, Dr E. T. Nystrom, a wealthy Swedish geologist, moved into one of the largest *siheyuan* on Kuei Chia Chang, No.13 (previously the home of William Collins). Nystrom knew China's steel and coal reserves to the nearest ton and had used part of his fortune to found the Nystrom Institute for Scientific Research in the coal producing base of Taiyuan in Shanxi province. Nystrom and his wife lived half the year in Sweden, as she refused to move permanently to Peking. Reputedly Nystrom retained the property until 1954, when he was expelled from China and returned to Sweden.

For a brief time in 1936 and 1937, Nystrom rented part of his large courtyard to two young American journalists, Edgar and Helen (née Foster) Snow (whose pen name was Nym Wales). With Nystrom frequently away and having made many conversions and adaptations to the property – including a conservatory running along the front two wings, stables, a tennis court, and a glassed-in pavilion for garden parties – the Snows lived in luxury with their dog Gobi. Nystrom had converted a former garden shed into a writing room. Edgar finished his best-known work, *Red Star Over China* (Victor Gollancz, 1937), working in the writing shed on Kuei Chia Chang.

THE SURVIVAL OF KUEI CHIA CHANG

Kuei Chia Chang survives today as Kuijiachang – perhaps against the odds. As well as the general destruction of the city's hutong stock, there have been several major infrastructural changes that have threatened Kuei Chia Chang. The silted up portion of the Grand Canal was converted into train tracks in the late 1950s. The tracks run into the Beijing Railway Station (completed in September 1959), which replaced the former main station (Zhengyangmen) by the Qianmen Gate at the northern end of Tiananmen Square.[26] The second major change was the construction of the Second Ring Road in the 1980s effectively at the eastern end of Kuei Chia Chang.

Of course, after 1949, by the late 1950s, all the properties on the hutong fell under state control and were repeatedly sub-divided to provide additional accommodation for multiple families. No.13 (the former Collins and then Nystrom property) was, in the 1950s, converted into a hostel for Ministry of Railroads workers before being knocked down entirely and rebuilt as the Zhongan Hotel.[27]

We may hope that Kuei Chia Chang will escape a date with the bulldozers, though neighbouring hutong have largely not survived. As Kuei Chia Chang is now a dead-end at the Second Ring Road, its attractiveness to developers may be less obvious. In 2017 an area that had been wasteland at the eastern end of the hutong, adjacent to the ring road, was landscaped into a public park - perhaps indicating a continuing future for the hutong. We can but hope.

ABOUT THE AUTHOR

Paul French is the author of the 2012 book *Midnight in Peking: The Murder That Haunted the Last Days of Old Peking* (that partly takes place on Kuei Chia Chang) and the 2018 *City of Devils: A Shanghai Noir* – both published by Penguin.

Endnotes

1 Alternatively spelt Kwei Chia Ch'ang in 1922, and today Kuijiachang.

2 Alex Ramsay (Ed), *The Peking Who's Who* (Tientsin: Tientsin Press, 1922). Sadly, the *Who's Who* was only published in 1922 and never subsequently.

3 Named after Lazzaro Cattaneo (1560-1640), an Italian Jesuit missionary who invented the first tone markings for Chinese transcription.

4 The hotel had been constructed in 1915, with a second wing completed in 1917, and is now part of the larger Beijing Hotel complex.

5 The American Board of Commissioners for Foreign Missions

(ABCFM) was among the first American Christian missionary organisations. Graduates of Williams College, Massachusetts created it in 1810. In the nineteenth century it was the largest and most important of American missionary organisations and consisted of participants from Reformed traditions such as Presbyterians, Congregationalists and German Reformed churches.

6 *Japan Times and Mail,* 30 March 1913.

7 *Through the Silk and Tea Districts of Kiang-nan and Chekiang* (New York: Journal of the American Geographical Society of New York, 1900), *Overland via the Trans-Siberian Railway* (Tientsin: Tientsin Press, 1908), *Guide to Peking: Environs Near and Far* (Tientsin: Tientsin Press, 1924), *A Trip into Anhui, The Present Outlook in Manchuria* (Tientsin: Tientsin Press, 1935), *Travels in China, 1894-1940* (Tientsin: Tientsin Press, 1941).

8 *My Trip from China, via Siberia to Europe: Including Experiences in a Siberian Prison* (Tientsin: Tientsin Press, 1922). The Tientsin Press was the book and atlas publishing arm of *The Tientsin and Peking Times newspaper.*

9 Suiyuan was a historical province of China with Guisui (now Hohhot) as the capital city.

10 Sadly, in 2010, the majority of Datianshujing Hutong, just off Wangfujing, was bulldozed.

11 William Fredrick Collins, *Mineral Enterprise in China* (Tientsin: Tientsin Press, 1918).

12 For more on Lao She's experiences in London see Anne Witchard, *Lao She in London* (Hong Kong: Hong Kong University Press and the Royal Asiatic Society Shanghai, 2012).

13 Lao She, *Mr. Ma and Son* (London: Penguin Modern Classics, 2014).

14 John B. Tayler, *Farm and Factory in China: Aspects of the Industrial Revolution* (New York: Student Christian Movement, 1928).

15 Lucius C. Porter, *China's Challenge to Christianity* (New York: Missionary Education Movement of the United States and Canada, 1924).

16 'Noted Speaker Coming to Poughkeepsie', *Poughkeepsie Evening News,* 18 November 1915.

17 The Boya Pagoda remains on the Yenching campus.

18 The chair of Chinese Studies, which was donated to Columbia in 1901 by General (of the California State Militia) Horace Carpentier,

a Columbia alumni himself who had made a fortune in building telegraph lines. It was named in honour of Carpentier's Chinese valet Dean Lung, who had accompanied him through the gold rush and on an extended trip to Asia. The bequest was USD 250,000 in 1901, worth approximately USD 6,000,000 in 2018. Herbert Giles gave the inaugural Dean Lung lectures on the rather vague and imprecise topic of 'China and the Chinese.'

19 A Christian organisation, founded by the American missionary Frank Buchman, which believed that the root of all problems were fear and selfishness. Further, Buchman believed that the solution to living with fear and selfishness was to surrender one's life over to God's Plan.

20 Who was also the first president of the Shanghai Literary and Scientific Society, later renamed the North China Branch of the Royal Asiatic Society.

21 Jehol (also known as Rehe) no longer exists as a separate province in China. In 1955, Jehol was divided between Inner Mongolian and the provinces of Hebei and Liaoning.

22 Anne Swann Goodrich, *The Peking Temple of the Eastern Peak* (Sankt Augustin, Germany: Monumenta Serica, 1964).

23 Anne Swann's paper gods collection is now part of the CV Starr East Asian Library at Columbia.

24 *Chinese Hells: The Peking Temple of Eighteen Hells and Chinese Conception of Hell* (Sankt Augustin, Germany: Monumenta Serica, 1981) and *Peking's Paper Gods* (Sankt Augustin, Germany, Steyler Verlag, 1991).

25 See Paul French, *Midnight in Peking* (Beijing: Penguin Books, 2012), p. 267.

26 Now the Beijing Railway Museum.

27 A semi-accurate plaque to the Snows is in the grounds of the hotel.

THE COOPERATORS WAR:
The Chinese Industrial Cooperatives, The China Defence League, And Internationalism In The Sino-Japanese War
BY EVAN TAYLOR

ABSTRACT

This paper examines the Chinese Industrial Cooperatives (CIC) and the China Defence League (CDL), two related organisations founded in the spring of 1938 to provide material and medical support to China in its resistance to Japanese occupation. Although their organisers included such well-known figures as the American journalist Edgar Snow and the Chinese revolutionary Soong Chingling (Song Qingling), the two organisations are rarely mentioned in histories of the wartime period. This study attempts to fill that gap by giving an introduction of the origins of both organisations and the background of some of their key founders. It then explores how organizers of the CIC utilised the overseas Chinese population in the Philippines and elsewhere in Southeast Asia to channel covert aid to the Chinese Communist Party. More theoretically, by looking at the variety of motivations that factored into such support among both the Western and Chinese participants, this article attempts to reorient narratives of ideology and transnationalism in the war, pointing to the global nature of the movement and the unlikely connections that it fostered.

INTRODUCTION

On March 4th, 1939, Rewi Alley sat down after a months-long trip through the snowy wilds of Sichuan and Shaanxi provinces. He was on an inspection tour for the Chinese Industrial Cooperatives (CIC) - for which he was the field secretary - and his stops included a grassroots machine shop in the town of Fengxiang, an umbrella factory in the city of Hanzhong and an audience in Yan'an with Mao Zedong. Upon returning to Baoji, the regional headquarters of the CIC, Alley composed his usual mass of letters to his family, friends and fellow Cooperative organizers in China. But among his many letters was one to a rather strange set of recipients - Alfonso Sycip (Xue Fenshi, 薛芬士) and Dee C. Chuan (Li Qingquan, 李清泉), two leading Filipino business magnates of Chinese descent. Dee and Sycip were prominent in Manila's Chinese Chamber of Commerce, had founded the Chinese Banking Corporation and were now receiving updates from leftist Westerners on the progress of tiny factories in the hinterlands of North China.

Although this may seem like an unlikely connection, between wealthy businessmen in Manila and rural industry in northern China, it represents exactly the type of relationship fostered by the CIC and its sister organisation, the China Defence League (CDL). The two organisations, both founded in the spring of 1938, were meant to support China's resistance to Japanese occupation through the development of small-scale factories, producer cooperatives and medical clinics for the Chinese armies. Additionally, they were meant to publicize the war effort in China to the rest of the world, solicit foreign contributions and raise awareness of China's resistance. But, where the CIC conducted their work over all of China, the CDL focused on the areas controlled by the Communist New 4th and 8th Route Armies.

This paper will examine the origins of these two organisations and the background of the people involved in their founding. Internationalist to a great degree, the organisations highlight the ties between China and the West already present at the onset of the Second World War. The article will then look at the specific case of fundraising in the Philippines, where Filipino-Chinese businessmen such as Sycip and Dee formed an alliance with American journalists such as Edgar and Helen Foster Snow to benefit the Communist Party of China. Although this support was desired by the Communist leadership in line with their United Front policy, an in-depth examination points to a varied set of motivations behind such support.

More theoretically, while the majority of scholarship on the Sino-Japanese war focuses on divisiveness - Chinese vs. Japanese, Nationalist vs. Communist, imperialism and colonialism vs. nationalism - the world surrounding the CIC instead offers a picture of connectivity. It was an international organisation, garnering official support from the U.S. and British governments, as well as a transnational one connecting civil society actors across state borders. By following the politics and people of the Cooperatives, from Shanghai to Manila, Hong Kong to Yan'an, a more diffuse narrative of wartime ideologies and sympathies emerge.

Origins of the Chinese Industrial Cooperatives

The Chinese Industrial Cooperatives (CIC) were founded in war-torn Shanghai in the spring of 1938 by a combination of Western and Chinese journalists, financiers, political activists, and engineers. Although many of these individuals were well known, and the Cooperatives remain active today, the history of the CIC often goes unmentioned or is glossed over in studies of the period.[1] It is known by a number of names, but the official name of the organisation, which remains in use today, is the Chinese Industrial Cooperatives (中国工业合作协会). From this is derived its famous abbreviation of *Gong He,* or in the Wade-Giles romanization of the period, *Gung Ho* - the slogan that graced its logo at the time. Indusco, another name for the movement, came from its telegraphic handle, Industrial Cooperatives.

The original rationale behind the CIC was three-fold. First was its pragmatic goal of building up China's industrial capacity in order to resist Japanese occupation. One byproduct of the capitulation of Shanghai in November 1937 and Nanjing one month later was the Japanese seizure of nearly all of China's manufacturing base. During the three months of fighting in Shanghai, the Guomindang government had done little to dismantle and evacuate factories and industrial equipment in advance of Japanese troops. The CIC was imagined as a strategy to restart Chinese industry, and at the same time put it out of further Japanese reach. The author Geoff Chapple described the rationale aptly in his biography of Rewi Alley, the most famous individual associated with the CIC. As Chapple put it, the cooperatives:

> Would cheat the Japanese War Machine. Its bombers, raining destruction on concentrations of Chinese industry, would be met by the dispersal of the industry. Its infantry, on any advance inland, would be robbed of intended captures by the mobility of industry. Small-scale plant, distributed throughout the hinterland, would be picked up in front of any advance, rolling away before the enemy salient, a thousand globules of quicksilver, to settle in again, in front, to the side, or behind any new advance.[2]

Second was a related goal to employ the numerous out-of-work engineers, mechanics and others who had fled inland from the

Japanese occupation. An estimated 600,000 from Shanghai alone, organizers believed those refugees, combined with the war widows and orphans, formed a vast potential workforce to build China's resistance industries. Lastly was a social goal. Many of its organizers saw the CIC as an opportunity to influence the future direction of Chinese society. As Alley wrote in one letter, 'what the cooperator tries to build is the kind of human structure that will outlast the follow the leader psychology of fascism.'[3] Or, as it was put by a promotional book of the movement at the time, 'Cooperative industry lays the foundation for democracy in China.'[4]

Besides Alley, the two key Western organizers present at the creation of the movement were the journalist couple Edgar and Helen Foster Snow. All three had nearly a decade of experience in China. Alley, a New Zealander, had arrived in Shanghai in 1927 and worked as a fireman and factory inspector for the Shanghai Municipal Council.[5] Unlike many Western Shanghailanders of the time, Alley grew to embrace Chinese society, adopting two Chinese sons and frequently travelling outside Shanghai on weekends and holiday jaunts.

Alley's professional career made him uniquely suited to champion the cooperative cause. In his role as a factory inspector, he showed empathy for the plight of the Chinese working class, and especially the child labourers who toiled in the city's workhouses and sweatshops, while also witnessing the rapaciousness of China's factory bosses. He spent many months in 1929 and 1932 assisting famine and flood relief projects in Shaanxi and Hubei, witnessing firsthand the poverty and poor administration in the hinterland. He was also connected to Shanghai's underground Communist movement, penning articles for the Moscow funded *Voice of China* magazine and installing a secret radio transmitting signals to Communist forces from the roof of his home on 1315 Yuyuan Road.

Like Alley, Edgar and Helen Foster Snow were well-travelled in the Chinese interior and well connected to the Chinese Communist Party (CCP).[6] Edgar Snow had just published his groundbreaking *Red Star Over China* in 1937, the product of many months interviewing the Communist Party leadership in Bao'an. Snow's wife, Helen (who wrote under the pen name Nym Wales) had made her own trip to visit the Communist capital of Yan'an, spending the spring and summer of 1937 continuing Edgar's work interviewing and photographing CCP leaders. Upon her return in September, the Snows moved from Beijing to Shanghai, renting an apartment in the Medhurst Building, which still stands today, on the corner of West Nanjing Road and Taixing Road.

Chinese individuals also played a key role in the CIC's founding. Three key organizers were Liang Shishun (梁士纯), Xu Xinliu (徐新六), and Lu Guangmian (卢广绵). Liang, then usually referred to by the English name Hubert, was a 'Bailie Boy', a disciple of the American missionary Joseph Bailie. Liang and the other Bailie Boys were brought to the U.S. in the 1920s to attend the Ford School of Technology, part of the Ford Motor Company in Detroit, Michigan, where they learned engineering techniques, mixed with a dose of American cultural training.[7] But engineering was not Liang's calling, and he soon switched to journalism, and from 1926 to 1928 he was employed as a correspondent for the *Detroit News* in both Detroit and Shanghai. After returning to China, he worked for the YMCA, and then was appointed dean of the journalism department at Yenching University, where he was a colleague of Edgar Snow. Following the Japanese occupation of Beijing, Liang moved to Shanghai to undertake cultural resistance activities.[8]

Xu, known at the time as Singloh Hsu, was a banker and economist, who at the time of the CIC's formation was the general manager of the National Commercial Bank of Shanghai. Like Liang, he too had studied overseas, at Victoria University in Manchester, England. He soon entered government service, including serving as a representative for China at the 1919 Versailles conference, and rose up the ranks of the Chinese financial world, to become, as Helen Foster snow put it, 'the Dean of all Shanghai Bankers', not an insignificant role in that money-drenched metropolis.[9] In August 1938, however, Xu perished when his plane, the Kweilin, was shot down by the Japanese en-route from Hong Kong to Chengdu, the first military attack on a civilian airplane in history.

Lu, known to his Western colleagues as K. M. Lu, was the cooperative expert of the group. A graduate of Peking University, he had trained in Japan, Scotland, and London, before taking up a position at Yenching University, where he fell under the tutelage of John Bernard Tayler. Tayler was one of the earliest proponents of producer cooperatives in China, and Lu proceeded to work as a rural economic organizer, under Tayler's leadership, with the Hebei Cotton Improvement Commission.[10]

In Snow's apartment and other locations in Shanghai's still-unoccupied International Settlement and French Concession, these individuals spent March and April 1938 leading a series of meetings, where they devised a number of organisational and promotional committees and drafted a report to solicit funds for their ideas.[11] But the dreams of a working group were not enough; the planners needed money, as well as government approval. Along came an unlikely figure that played a key role - the British Ambassador to China, Sir Archibald Clark-Kerr.

Clark-Kerr had arrived in China only that February, and he was eager to call on Edgar Snow, now famed for *Red Star Over China*. Snow pushed on the ambassador his idea for the Cooperatives and the need for the approval of Nationalist leader Chiang Kai-Shek, then in the transplanted capital of Wuhan. 'And I'm your choice for the salesman job?' Clark-Kerr asked approvingly, according to Snow's recollections.[12] He brought the CIC materials up to Wuhan, and after a series of meetings with Chiang, his wife Soong Meiling, and Finance Minister H. H. Kung (Kong Xiangxi), the CIC was officially born. They were given office space on the top floor of the Yokohama Specie Bank building and $5 million worth in Chinese national currency. Rewi Alley was made official technical advisor with a passport that allowed him to travel throughout unoccupied China. In August 1938, the initial cooperative was opened in Baoji, just west of Xi'an in Shaanxi Province, the first of 1,867 cooperative societies that were to form over the next two years.[13]

Origins of the china defence league

Partnering with the Chinese Industrial Cooperatives was another little-known organisation, the China Defence League (CDL).[14] Like the CIC, the CDL was founded in the spring of 1938 and was similarly concerned with bringing war relief to China. The CDL, however, also had a more subversive goal - to support the CCP.

Officially, the organisation was founded by Soong Chingling in Hong Kong. However, its actual genesis began thousands of kilometers to the north, in Wuhan with its original planner Zhou Enlai. The occasion was the arrival in Wuhan of Dr. Norman Bethune, a Canadian surgeon well known in China today for the medical assistance he provided to the Communist armies during the war. Medical assistance was on Zhou's mind, and he held a discussion with Bethune, the New

Zealand journalist James Bertram, the American missionary Frances Roots, and the American journalist Agnes Smedley about what medical assistance was needed in the Communist-controlled areas.[15] Bertram, who had just returned from a months-long tour of 8th Route Army areas, was nominated to write a report on medical conditions in North China and take it down to Soong in Hong Kong.

Bertram put together his report, entitled 'Memo on Medical Assistance to the 8th Route Army', and carried it from Wuhan to the British island colony. Hong Kong, not yet under Japanese occupation, was in an economic war boom and filling up with Chinese leftists increasingly frustrated by the conservative nature of the Nationalist government. Soong, the widow of Sun Yat-sen and the sister-in-law of Chiang, was the leftist doyen of the island. Closest to Soong were the Liao family, He Xiangning (何香凝) and her son and daughter - Liao Chengzhi (廖承志) and Liao Mengxing (廖梦醒). Like Soong, the Liaos were Chinese revolutionary royalty, with He and her husband Liao Zhongkai being two of Sun Yat-sen's earliest comrades. When Liao Zhongkai and Sun both died in 1925 - Liao by assassination, Sun by liver cancer - Soong and He were drawn even closer together. He's two children were operatives of the Communist Party, with Chengzhi being the Hong Kong representative of the 8th Route Army and a chief organizer of the Bethune medical mission, and Mengxing Soong's secretary.

When Bertram arrived in Hong Kong, he was taken to a meeting with Liao Chengzhi, who wanted to expand Bethune's work, and 'projected a larger organisation, with Chinese and foreign officers, to make public appeals and connect with aid-China groups abroad' as claimed by CDL participant Israel Epstein.[16] Liao, previously based in Guangdong, had been sent to Hong Kong in January 1938 to open an office of the Communist Party in the British territory. The purpose of the office was to solicit the type of aid and overseas connections pursued by the CDL.[17] The meeting was held at the house of Deng Wenzhao (邓文钊), also called at the time M. C. Tang, a cousin of the Liaos and a Cambridge-educated banker who would later serve as treasurer of the CDL. Bertram suggested Hilda Selwyn-Clarke as a secretary for the League and John Leaning to be in charge of publicity. Other members who were involved in the early months of organisation include Israel Epstein and Norman H. France, who were later joined by Chen Hanseng, a famed Chinese social scientist. The president of the organization was T. V. Soong (Song Ziwen), the brother of Soong Chingling and a top Nationalist official, giving the CDL the seal of government approval, although T. V.'s actual involvement with the organisation remained small. The CDL quickly moved from talk to action, publishing their first newsletter in July 1938, a twelve-page, text-heavy report on medical conditions in the regions of Wuhan and Changsha, produced in collaboration with Smedley's Northwest Partisan Relief Committee.[18]

One main node of support for the CDL was in Beijing, where a number of administrators and professors at Yenching University and the Peking Union Medical College (PUMC) worked on behalf of the organisation. These Beijing literati took 'picnics' to the Japanese-occupied city's Western Hills, on which they would smuggle medicine, a radio vacuum tube, printing press, revolvers, and explosives for the Communist Party guerrillas. Leading this group was Ida Pruitt, head of social services at the PUMC, who would remain devoted to the cooperatives for the next decade. In her biography of Pruitt, Marjorie King wrote of a Hong Kong cocktail party where, 'Ida met a British officer whom she had known casually in Beijing. The officer asker her, his eyes twinkling, "What are the guerrillas doing for medicine now that you have left Beijing?"'[19]

Another node was in New York City. The Bethune mission, besides being an original inspiration of the type of work to be supported by the CDL, also helped solidify the CDL's United States connections. Bethune's work had originally been sponsored by the New York-based China Aid Council (CAC), a sub-organisation of the American League for Peace and Democracy, and the most prominent 'Aid China' group put together by the two North American Communist Parties, the Communist Party USA and the Communist Party of Canada. The CAC was run by Phillip Jaffe, a wealthy publisher of the leftist magazines *China Today* and *Amerasia*, who had himself visited China and Yan'an in the summer of 1937. However once Bethune arrived in China, his relationship with the CAC became frayed, due to disagreements over financial and personnel matters, and the overseas publicity and fund-raising side of his mission was soon also taken up by an organisation newly created by Agnes Smedley the Northwest Partisan Relief Committee.[20] Bethune, being a short-tempered and uncooperative individual, fell out with Smedley as well, and in his letter to Smedley, he stated he worked under one authority, 'and that authority is the 8th Route Army.'[21] Back in New York, the CAC desired to professionalize their aid work, instead of working directly through such temperamental personalities as Bethune and Smedley, and as a result, decided in August 1938 that the CDL would be the chosen repository and distributor of all the funds they received in the United States.[22] The CAC's decision solidified the CDL as a key liaison of left wing fundraising in the United States for the war in China.

What can we surmise from the origins and participants of the CIC and the CDL? First, the background of the founders was abundantly international. Nearly all had been educated or travelled internationally. The background of prominent CIC members is given above. The CDL founders were similarly globe-trotting. New Zealander Bertram was educated in Australia and England, and turned a travel grant from Oxford into an opportunity to become an expert on the CCP. Israel Epstein was a journalist and stateless, born in Warsaw, raised in Tianjin (where he was a classmate of John Hersey) and already a seasoned war correspondent at the age of twenty-three.[23] Norman H. France, born in China, was a long-time Hong Konger and professor of History at Hong Kong University, fluent in both Cantonese and Mandarin. Hilda Selwyn-Clarke, originally Hilda Browning, was a former London radical and an organizer of the Society for Cultural Relations with the Soviet Union, who had married Sir Percy Selwyn-Clarke, the director of Medical Services in Hong Kong.

On the Chinese side, Soong Chingling, the daughter of Shanghai business magnate Charlie Song and the widow of Sun Yat-sen, attended college in the American south, and fled to Moscow to escape the 1927 White Terror in Shanghai. The Liaos were born in Japan, and Liao Chengzhi, fluent in Chinese, Japanese, and English, had participated in underground organizing in Berlin, Moscow, and Amsterdam. Liao and Soong even reportedly spoke to each other in English, as it was a more comprehensible shared language than Liao's Cantonese and Soong's Mandarin.[24] Even Zhou Enlai had significant international experience, having studied in Japan and undertaken political work in Paris.

Second, the social and skillful roles of the founders crossed professional and ideological boundaries. Journalists such as the Snows, Bertram, and Epstein became activists, little concerned with the limits of 'objectivity' that might trouble journalists today. Employees of imperialist institutions such as the Shanghai Municipal Council, the British Foreign Service, and the Hong Kong Crown Colony Administration worked to support a grassroots social movement that had little benefit to Western business or political interests. Similarly, the CIC and the CDL operated in a nebulous space both in official government programs but one that was at odds with official policy. Officially, the top Nationalist leaders, especially Soong Meiling, were leaders of the movement. But as Edgar Snow wrote in a letter to James Bertram, 'Do not for a moment imagine that CIC is being backed by the [Chiangs] because they like it. It's there because outside pressure mobilized for its promotion proved too strong for them to resist.'[25] At the same time, Edgar Snow saw the benefit of such government support, writing, 'in promoting Indusco, the first thing to do is to praise Madame Chiang and H.H. K'ung for their foresight in supporting it. This will make them publicly responsible so they will lose face if it should fail.'[26] The CIC and the CDL were liminal organisations - in between China and the West, in between imperial rule and popular resistance, and in between government and the grassroots.

The chinese industrual cooperatives in the philippines and southeast asia

Although they were initially separate organisations, the CIC and the CDL almost immediately began to work together. In essence, the CDL was the CICs route to the underground, funneling aid to the Communist armies that bypassed the Nationalist leadership. Helen Foster Snow wrote to Soong in July 1938 about the idea of using cooperatives to aid the CCP armies. Snow wrote, 'I think we must begin to tie up the cooperatives with the China Defence League and the support to the guerrillas... One of the things to do along this line is to get a few 'guerrilla cooperatives' functioning near the guerrilla lines, to produce war supplies for the soldiers. And in connection with these, we can have 'medical cooperatives' with doctors and nurses-- for the guerrillas.'[27] Her husband had similar ideas. 'Nearly every step taken in the promotion of this project has been communicated to Era [8th Route Army] and its leaders'. Snow wrote in a letter to Soong Chingling in November 1938, 'In no case would I seek to divert any money that might be available for direct gifts to Era and Newfa [New 4th Army] to CIC on the contrary, my first and last hope is to get people to send money direct to those armies.'[28]

However, as the CIC became an official agency of the Chinese government, they could not openly raise money for the Communist armies. As Rewi Alley wrote to Edgar Snow in 1939, referring to areas of Communist control, 'must be careful not to give N. Shensi and Anhwei offices publicity inside China these days. They are still outlawed, more or less.'[29] Although CIC's work in the Communist areas proceeded, it couldn't be advertised or openly fundraised for.[30] The Snows soon found a solution to this problem by funding the Communist co-operatives with international donations, especially from overseas Chinese or *huaqiao*. In the fall of 1938, the Snows took up residence in the Filipino mountain town of Baguio, the Philippines being at that time the United State's only official colonial territory. Immediately upon arriving, the Snows began to organize and fundraise for the movement. Soong Chingling was receptive to the plan, and encouraged the Snows to 'deliver as many addresses in [Philippines] as possible in as your words carry great weight.'[31]

In the Philippines, the Snow's found a *huaqiao* community that had since 1931 been supporting the war effort in China, forming national salvation organisations, donating heavily to the Chinese war chest and even sending small groups of soldiers to assist in the conflict.[32] According to the historian Yung-li Yuk-wai, the Chinese community in the Philippines numbered 117,000 in the 1939 census, the smallest of any overseas Chinese population in South East Asia. Why then, were the Filipino-Chinese such ardent supporters of the war-resistance effort? One explanation is that the Philippine's *huaqiao* population was predominantly young, male, and first-generation immigrants from China, as well as being largely of a commercial class.[33] This provided them with money and an emotional connection to the mainland.

Central to the fund-raising efforts in the Philippines were the two influential *huaqiao* businessmen mentioned above: Albino Sycip and Dee C. Chuan. Sycip and Dee were longtime friends and at times business partners, having co-founded the China Banking Corporation in 1920.[34] Sycip and his brother, Alfonso Sycip (Xue Fenshi/薛芬士) were also instrumental in leading the Chinese Chamber of Commerce, the foremost organisation representing Chinese commercial and social issues in the Philippines. Past research has painted the 1930s as 'the heyday of Guomindang power in the Philippines' and pointed to the relative wealth of the Chinese population as creating a 'natural distaste for communist ideas.'[35] The Sycips and Dee, however, did not follow this trend. In her memoir, Helen Foster Snow described the extensive Filipino support for the CIC as 'a minor revolution' that hit Chongqing 'like a strike of lightning.' 'They were wild with anxiety about this revolt in the Philippines,' Snow wrote, and their acceptance of the CIC fundraising tactics in fact helped to greatly legitimize the entire CIC cause in China.[36]

According to letters from Helen Foster Snow, both men were extremely interested in the CIC, as they saw the 'value of industry as a base of future resistance.'[37] She wrote that Dee's wife held a tea for the Snows to meet the Chinese community, and that Dee, who 'liked Ed's book tremendously [was a] liberal and a progressive man, and will cooperate fully with Indusco and the CDL if the way is made easy for it.'[38] This was not a passing fancy, as Helen Foster Snow continued to describe Dee as '… very liberal. We rate with them because of *Red Star*, believe it or not! Dee C. Chuan is keenly interested in the book for instance. This week they sent $10,000 to "comfort" guerrillas in Shansi of the 8th Route Army.'[39] With these two leading the way, support groups were formed on the island, including the Philippine Association for Chinese Indusco and the Philippines Chinese Women's Relief Association. Sycip remained heavily involved in the movement, even going so far as to write United States leaders such as former President Herbert Hoover and Secretary of War Henry Stimson on Indusco's behalf.[40]

The Philippines also served as a base from which to raise funds from elsewhere in Southeast Asia. The largest effort was made by Morris Appelman, an American resident of Manila and former communist provocateur.[41] In March and April 1939, Appelman visited Saigon, Singapore, Jakarta, Bandung, and Surabaya. The trip was funded by Sycip, with a goal of raising CN$200,000. Dee C. Chuan, however, stressed that raising funds in those locations would be more difficult than doing so in the Philippines, as the overseas Chinese population would be more conservative.[42] But Appelman made progress. In Java, for example, Appelman put together a local advisory board and publicity committee that included prominent members of the Batavia Chinese Chamber of Commerce and Bank of China. Appelman also involved journalists in Indonesia, including some who had been the former students of Edgar Snow at Yenching University.[43] In Singapore, Alfonso Sycip stressed that British leaders would be key in Singapore, writing letters of introduction for Appelman to them.[44] Appelman, however, had an ulterior motive. As a letter from Edgar Snow attests, the actual purpose of his trip was to raise money for the CDL and the CCP armies. Snow wrote, 'All funds raised by you should go direct to CDL for Era [8th Route Army] and Newfa [New 4th Army] if possible. Indusco appeals only to those who don't want to help CDL or the Xians [Communists], but want to help refugees or China in general.'[45] Appelman reported his trip to be a success, having spent a few days in each city where he met with influential Chinese leaders and set fund raising goals.[46]

But, the Philippines was where the overseas Chinese made the largest contributions to the CIC, and specifically the CIC cooperatives meant to assist the 8th Route and New 4th Armies. Cooperatives in the border region areas in northwest China, under the military control of the 8th Route Army, had been under development since February 1939, when Rewi Alley visited Yan'an and discussed with Mao and others the idea of the CIC, with the Communist leaders generally receptive to the idea. By March 1939, the CIC had established a branch office in Yan'an, run by Tsao Chu-ju, the head of the Border Government Bank. Alley made sure to write to Dee and Alfonso Sycip from Baoji, where the cooperatives had their Northwest headquarters. He reassured them that the $140,000 they had raised was being well spent, and the plan was to focus on cooperatives in the Northwest and Southeast.[47] Although Alley omitted any direct reference to Communist or guerrilla armies, it was well known that these were the two regions where the CCP held military control.

Cooperatives in the New 4th Army area (roughly from Anhui through to the Yangtze delta) were also funded from the Philippines. Natalie Crouter, who had lived with her husband Jerry in the Philippines since 1927, took the early lead in fundraising for them. They hoped, as Helen Foster Snow wrote, 'to help establish an arsenal or to assist whatever arsenal the NFA may now have in operation. In fact, the Crouters have been telling everyone that they have a "guerrilla arsenal" in operation for the New 4th.'[48] Crouter was one of the leaders of the Philippines Association for Chinese Indusco, which had 100 members, including many in high ranking establishment positions on the islands. These included Polly Babcock, an international secretary for the YWCA, Elizabeth Sayre, the wife of U.S. High Commissioner for the Islands Francis Sayre, and Colonel Henry Mclean, a U.S. Army intelligence officer.

Starting in June 1939, the first of what were referred to as 'international centers' was set up at Tunxi, in Anhui province.[49] The plan was for these centers, located exclusively in areas controlled by Communist armies, to be named after the overseas association that funded them. As such, Snow recommended in December 1939 that three different units needed to be set up, a Java Unit, a Philippine Overseas Chinese Unit, and a Pioneer Unit.[50] According to Lu Guangmian, who had become head of CIC Northwest operations, the funds were all received by January 1940, and were allocated between cooperatives in Yan'an, the Jin-Cha-Ji base area, and southeast Shanxi province.[51] The CDL followed a similar strategy of naming hospital wings after their international donors. and according to Israel Epstein, the loess caves in Yan'an housed a Los Angeles Nursery, funded by donations to the CDL from L. A. based overseas Chinese.[52]

Why did the overseas Chinese population of the Philippines donate so much to the Chinese Communist Armies? The answer is multifaceted. One reason, common to many *huaqiao* phenomenon, was regional loyalty. The majority of the New 4th Army soldiers were Fujianese, as were the great majority of the Chinese in the Philippines. As Yung-li writes, 'the nationalist spirit of the Philippine Chinese could probably be regarded as parochial loyalty.'[53] For these Filipino Chinese donors, the ideology of the Chinese armies on the receiving end mattered little, and instead it was their regional origin that made them important. Another reason, an ideological attraction to the communist cause, was also present. Starting in November 1937, the Philippine Chinese United Workers' Union, an openly leftist group, organized a brigade of 28 soldiers to join the New 4th Army and sent students to Yan'an to study at the communist academies.[54]

For the wealthy Filipino businessmen who led the movement, a more complicated political motivation was apparent. It was in fact their conservative nature that drew them to supporting the Communist armies. Writing to Ida Pruitt, Helen Snow indicated that nearly all the money raised 'comes from conservative elements, especially among overseas Chinese. They want to indicate to the 8th Route that they support the United Front and present struggle for a democratic solution to the delicate political problems of China.'[55] Other letters highlight this point as well. Referring to a $20,000 donation to the New 4th Army from the Anti-Enemy Association in Manila, Helen Snow wrote, 'it is the conservative patriotic org. made up of members of the Chamber of Commerce largely. Quite a victory for the NFA to get support from such people!'[56] In fact, in July 1939 Edgar Snow had to write to Dee C. Chuan to reassure him that 'there is no grounds whatsoever for the suspicion that [the CIC] is not supported by the central government and that the purpose is only to help the 8th Route and New 4th Army.'[57]

Further confusing the narrative is the fact that some of the purportedly conservative businessmen were actually openly supportive of Communism. A letter from Albino Sycip to W. R. Babcock, one of the Cooperative activists in the Philippines, is key here. Babcock had written to Sycip concerned about outside accusations that Indusco was a communist leaning organisations. Sycip wrote, 'My idea of a "communist" is one who is willing to share what he has with others; not one who uses force to get what they want from others. Under this category, one should be proud to be a "communist" and the world would be a much happier place to live in if it is peopled by more of such kind.'[58]

Likewise, Westerners involved with the movement decided to work with the CIC and the Chinese Communist Party for a variety of reasons. While at the time these Westerners were written off as simply being pro-Communist, there was in fact more nuance to their decision-making. Illustrative here is the roundabout political logic behind British Ambassador's Archibald Clark-Kerr's support. In his biography of the ambassador, Donald Gillies states, while Clark-Kerr understood the CIC to be supporting a form of socialism, he felt it to be 'just the sort of development necessary to help prevent the spread of communism', while at the same time wishing to mask his involvement so as to prevent the Chinese Communists from perceiving the movement as rooted in British Imperialism.59

Other motivations were similarly complicated. S. Bernard Thomas, in his biography of Edgar Snow, argues that Snow's advocacy for the CIC to work exclusively in Communist-controlled areas was in fact counter to official Party policy at that point, which supported an alliance with the Guomindang. Thomas writes, 'Snow was taking a more leftist position than the prevailing Communist orthodoxy on just where the political and military center of gravity in the China conflict lay.'[60] Helen Foster Snow thought 'fear of Japan' the motivating factor among the Western population of the Philippines, which she described as 'the most conservative group of people on the face of this earth ... our die hard imperialists.'[61] But "on the question of China, people make allowances ... they have to support the vital, workable thing there, or nothing.'[62]

Regardless of the motivating factors, funds from the Philippines continued to be sent to the CIC until the Japanese occupation of the islands in December 1941. Projects they funded included chemical cooperatives in the northwest, a *Xiaogui* kindergarten for war orphans, a Bailie memorial technical school, drug making cooperatives, and a joint Chinese Red Cross/CIC project based out of the CIC Southeast headquarters.[63] As Snow wrote, the money 'is not the gift of some bank. It is not the gift of any government. It comes from the hard-earned wages of overseas Chinese, and from small contributions from patriots who work for a living ... They don't want to lose sight of it forever.'[64] Overall, Snow believed the influence of the CIC in the Philippines to be large. Writing to the United States in December 1939, he attributed the decision of Filipino president Manuel Quezon to give funding to domestic industrial cooperatives as resulting from the popularity of the CIC.[65]

CONCLUSION: REEXAMINING THE TRANSNATIONAL WAR AND THE UNITED FRONT

What are we to make of this confluence of trends: a Los Angeles nursery in Yan'an; wealthy businessmen in the Philippines donating money to the Chinese Communist Party; colonial administrators supporting grassroots industry; and Rockefeller funded professors operating underground gun-running networks to supply guerrilla armies? These can primarily be seen as the original byproduct of the Chinese Communist Party's United Front Work (统一战线工作). Although the 'United Front' is often remembered during the war years as primarily an alliance between the Communist and Nationalist Parties, it was actually a far wider effort. Argues Gerry Groot, an expert on the Front, 'The fundamental principle of United Front work is simple, to rally as many allies as possible in order to achieve a common cause, usually to defeat a common enemy.'[66] This meant casting away ideological rigidity in order to cooperate with civil and political associations that were similarly opposed to the Japanese occupation of China.

Although it long remained invisible to foreign China-watchers, today, there is a growing discussion of the United Front Work Department. This trend of reportage initially took root in Australia and

New Zealand, but it is now expanding to the United States. As Anne-Marie Brady wrote in a widely circulated paper, 'the People's Republic of China's attempts to guide, buy, or coerce political influence abroad are widespread.'[67] The *New York Times* put it more bluntly: 'China has a vast influence machine, and you don't even know it.'[68] From today's perspective, 'United Front' type activities are portrayed in a negative light, as one sided actions undertaken by the CCP on unsuspecting outside groups.

However, looking back from the perspective of the Chinese Industrial Cooperatives and the China Defence League, it is clear that during the war-era United Front activity was not necessarily defined by an active-passive dynamic. Many of the participants in the movement possessed agency, knowingly cooperating with the Communist Party, and based their actions on their own motivations. Some overseas Chinese felt regional loyalties, others desired to support political unity in China due to their allegiance with the central government, while others were partisans wanting to fight alongside the Communist Armies. Similarly, some Westerners saw the socialistic nature of the organisation as a bulwark against Communism, others were party loyalists, and others feared Japanese domination above any considerations of Chinese politics.

In this light, the CIC shows the possibility of considering United Front activity from a transnational and trans-ideological perspective. It was being undertaken in support of the Communist Party, but not only for that reason. Groups and individuals also had their own motivations at play as well, often ones that bridged Chinese and international politics. As Pauline Keating has argued, the Cooperatives 'meshed ideas from a range of different sources in different parts of the world, making it [sic] a genuinely "global" phenomenon.'[69] In a larger sense, situating the Cooperatives and the United Front within a global framework reorients our understanding of the Sino-Japanese War and the narratives around it. The global network of Indusco connected Manila to Yan'an to Shanghai to New York City, and forged an alliance between imperial bureaucrats and Chinese workers, communist party members and overseas businessmen. Participants acted out of diverse motivations, across national borders, and unrestricted by ideological boundaries. By seeing the CIC as a microcosm of the war itself, a new picture begins to emerge of a conflict far more varied than the one popularly remembered today.

ABOUT THE AUTHOR

Evan Taylor is a historian and writer. From 2014-2017, he was a researcher at Shanghai Jiao Tong University's World Anti-Fascist War Research Center.

E-mail: egtayl@gmail.com

—◦◦◦—

Endnotes

1 The only scholarly, book length work in English that directly focuses on the CIC movement that the author is aware of is a PhD dissertation written by Douglas Reynolds in 1975. Douglas R. Reynolds, 'The Chinese Industrial Cooperative Movement and the Political Polarization of Wartime China, 1938-1945', (PhD thesis, Columbia University, 1975). As part of this research, Reynolds helped process the 'Indusco Inc. Records' at Columbia University, a voluminous archival collection on life in rural wartime China.

2 Geoff Chapple, *Rewi Alley of China* (Auckland: Hodder and Stoughton, 1980), p. 101.

3 Rewi Alley, 'Some Rambling Discourses', 31 December 1942, Box 2, Folder 1942-1943 Extracts of China Material (A-I Indexed), Indusco Inc. Records, Columbia University Rare Book and Manuscript Library (From hereon Indusco Papers).

4 Nym Wales, *China Builds for Democracy: A Story of Cooperative Industry* (New York: Modern Age Books, 1941), p. 8.

5 Besides Chapple's *Rewi Alley of China*, the best sources on Alley's life are Rewi Alley, *An Autobiography* (Beijing: New World Press, 1987); Anne-Marie Brady, *Friend of China: The Myth of Rewi Alley* (New York: Routledge, 2003).

6 For information on the Snows see, Edgar Snow, *Journey to the Beginning* (New York: Random House, 1958); S. Bernard Thomas, *Season of High Adventure: Edgar Snow in China* (Berkeley, University of California Press, 1996); Helen Foster Snow, *My China Years* (New York: William Morrow and Company, Inc, 1984); Kelly Ann Long, *Helen Foster Snow: An American Woman in Revolutionary China* (Boulder, University of Colorado Press, 2006).

7 A number of other alumni of the Bailie network would play key roles in the CIC, and the movement would adopt the Bailie name in their factories and schools.

8 Nym Wales, 'The "Bailie Boys" of China's Industrial Cooperatives',

14 February 1940, Box 2 Folder 11, Nym Wales Papers, Hoover Institution Archives (from hereon NW Papers).

9 Wales, *China Builds for Democracy*, p. 41.

10 Paul B. Trescott, 'John Bernard Tayler and the Development of Cooperatives in China', *Annals of Public and Cooperative Economics*, April 1993.

11 The notes of these meetings are contained in the 'Nym Wales Papers' held at the Hoover Institution Archives at Stanford University in Palo Alto, California. Other participants in the initial planning meetings included John Alexander, a young official at the British Consulate in Shanghai who played a key role convincing Helen Foster Snow as to the viability of cooperatives, Alec Camplin, a British engineer and the roommate of Alley, the publisher J.B. Powell, the bankers Wang Tzu-hsing and an unidentified 'Mr. Sun', the publisher and political organizer Hu Yu-Chih, and the Shanghai Women's leader Huang Ting-Chu.

12 Snow, *Journey to the Beginning*, p. 201.

13 Reynolds, *The Chinese Industrial Cooperative Movement and the Political Polarization of Wartime China, 1938-1945*, p. 179.

14 Its name has been at times translated as Alliance for the Protection of China 保卫中国同盟. There is no single book, article, or thesis focusing on the CDL, but a good summary can be found in Him Mark Lai, *Chinese American Transnational Politics* (Chicago: University of Illinois Press, 2010), pp. 102-106.

15 James Bertram, 'Recollections of Soong Ching Ling,' nd, Papers of James and Jean Bertram, 94-021-03, Alexander Turnbull Library, Wellington, New Zealand.

16 Israel Epstein, *Woman in World History: Life and Times of Soong Ching Ling (Mme. Sun Yatsen)* (Beijing: New World Press, 1993), pp. 357-358.

17 Cindy Yik-Yi Chu, *Chinese Communists and Hong Kong Capitalists, 1937-1947* (New York, Palgrave Macmillan, 2010), p. 27; Chan Sui-Jing, *East River Column: Hong Kong Guerrilla in the Second World War and After* (Hong Kong: Hong Kong University Press, 2009), p. 17.

18 The China Defence League Central Committee, 'Newsletter No.1', July 1938, Box 5 Folder CDL, American Bureau of Medical Aid to China Papers, Columbia University Rare Book and Manuscript Library.

19 Marjorie King, *China's American Daughter: Ida Pruitt (1888-1985)*

(Hong Kong: The Chinese University Press, 2006), pp. 122-123. Besides Pruitt, others in the Yenching scene who helped with the Cooperatives included Ran Sailor, Ralph Lapwood, and Michael Lindsay.

20 Roderick Stewart and Sharon Stewart, *Phoenix: The Life of Norman Bethune* (Montreal: McGill's-Queen University Press, 2011), p. 257.

21 Ibid., p. 280.

22 Ibid., p. 282.

23 Israel Epstein, *My China Eye: Memoirs of a Jew and a Journalist* (San Francisco: Long River Press, 2005).

24 Mayumi Itoh, *Pioneers of Sino-Japanese Relations: Liao and Takasaki* (New York: Palgrave-Macmillan, 2012), p. 35.

25 Edgar Snow, letter to James Bertram, 15 November 1938, Box 8 Folder 87, Edgar Snow Papers, University Archives, University of Missouri Kansas City (from hereon ES Papers).

26 Edgar Snow, letter to Ida Pruitt, Box 29, Helen Foster Snow Papers, Brigham Young University (from hereon HFS papers).

27 Helen Foster Snow, letter to Soong Chingling, 24 July 1938, Box 28, HFS Papers.

28 Edgar Snow, letter to Soong Chingling, 27 November 1938, Box 1, Folder 12, ES Papers.

29 Rewi Alley, letter to Edgar Snow, 17 March 1939, Box 8 Folder 88, ES Papers.

30 For a discussion of the role of cooperatives (more than just those administered by the CIC), in the base areas, see Pauline Keating, 'The Yan'an Way of Co-Operativization', *The China Quarterly*, No. 140. December 1994.

31 Soong Chingling, letter to Edgar Snow, 8 September 1938, Box 1 Folder 12, ES Papers.

32 Yung Li Yuk-wai, *The Huaqiao Warriors: Chinese Resistance Movement in the Philippines, 1942-1945* (Hong Kong: Hong Kong University Press, 1995), p. 24. Antonio S. Tan, 'The Philippine Chinese Response to the Sino-Japanese Conflict', *Journal of Southeast Asian Studies*, vol. 12, no. 1, Mar. 1981.

33 Yuk-wai, *The Huaqiao Warriors*, pp. 8-12.

34 For a recent in-depth examination of Sycip, see Phillip Guingona 'The Sundry Acquaintances of Dr. Albino Z. Sycip: Exploring the Shanghai-Manila Connection, circa 1910-1940,' *Journal of World History* 27, no. 1, March 2016.

35 Yuk-wai, *The Huaiqiao Warriors*, pp. 66-68.

36 Snow, *My China Years*, pp. 314-315.

37 Helen Foster Snow, letter to Rewi Alley, 9 November 1938, Box 3 Folder Rewi Alley 1938, Indusco Papers.

38 Helen Foster Snow, letter to Ida Pruitt, Box 31 Folder Snow, Peg 1938-1939, Indusco Papers.

39 Helen Foster Snow, letter to Rewi Alley, 16 February 1939, Box 30 Folder 1, HFS Papers.

40 Alfonso Sycip, letter to Henry Stimson, 23 September 1940, Box 28, HFS Papers; Alfonso Sycip, letter to Herbert Hoover, 18 March 1940, Box 29, HFS Papers.

41 While war-era documents make no mention of Appelman's communist ties, he admitted in testimony before the House Un-American Affairs Committee that he had been a member of the Communist Party USA (CPUSA) from 1925-1938. In 1934-1935 he had lived in Shanghai, where he had met Agnes Smedley, Rewi Alley, and Anne Louise Strong. He had been sent back to China in 1937 to assist in the publication of the *Voice of China* magazine, but the Japanese occupation of Shanghai diverted him to Manila. *Testimony of Morris L. Appelman*, House Committee on Un-American Activities, 10 January1952. Notably, when he the Snows were on their way to Baguio, Soong Chingling wrote a letter to Edgar telling him that Appelman and James Allen, the official representative of the CPUSA in the Philippines, would help him organize meetings in Manila. Soong to E. Snow, 8 September 1938.

42 Helen Foster Snow, letter to Ida Pruitt, 24. February 1939, Box 31 Folder Snow, Peg, 1938, Indusco Papers.

43 Morris Appelman, letter to Dee Chuan, 19 April1939, Box 30 Folder 4, HFS Papers.

44 Morris Appelman, letter to Edgar Snow, 7 March 1939, Box 27, HFS Papers.

45 Edgar Snow, letter to Morris Appelman, 2 March1939, Box 8 Folder 88, ES Papers.

46 Morris Appelman, 'Promotional Tour of the South Seas Area in behalf of Indusco', Not Dated, Box 8 Folder 1, NW Papers.

47 Rewi Alley, letter to Alfonso Sycip and Dee Chuan, 4 March 1939, Box 28, HFS Papers.

48 Helen Foster Snow, letter to Rewi Alley, 10 January 1939, Box 30 Folder 1, HFS Papers.

49 Helen Foster Snow, letter to Rewi Alley, 4 May 1939, Box 31 Folder Snow, Peg 1938-1939, Indusco Papers.

50 The Java Unit was funded by a $100,000 donation from a 'Mrs. Liem' in Jakarta, the 'Philippine Overseas Chinese Unit' was funded by a $100,000 donation from the Philippine's Chinese Woman's Relief Association, and the 'Pioneer Unit' was funded by a $25,000 donation from the Philippine's Association for Industrial Cooperatives (all amounts in National Chinese currency). Edgar Snow, letter to Lu Kwang-mien, 17 December 1939, Box 8 Folder 90, ES Papers.

51 Lu Kwang-mien, letter to Helen Foster Snow, 4 January 1940, Box 1 Folder 35, NW Papers.

52 Epstein, *Woman in World History*, pp. 362-363

53 Yung Li, *Huaqiao Warriors*, p. 27.

54 Ibid., 63. Yung Li cites the Guomindang's suppression of the 19th route army (based out of the southern coastal provinces) in the early 1930s as evidence that the Filipino Chinese may have had less than warm feelings towards the central government.

55 Helen Foster Snow, letter to Ida Pruitt, 7 April 1940, Box 31 Folder Mrs. Edgar Snow, Indusco Papers.

56 Helen Foster Snow, letter to Rewi Alley, 4 May 1939, *op. cit.*

57 Edgar Snow, letter to Dee C. Chuan, 17 June 1939, Box 1 Folder 14, ES Papers.

58 Albino Z. Sycip, letter to W.R. Babcock, 28 May 1940, Box 28, HFS Papers.

59 Donald Gillie, *Radical Diplomat: The Life of Archibald Clark-Kerr Lord Inverchapel, 1882-1951* (London: I.B. Tauris, 1999), p. 93.

60 Thomas, *Season of High Adventure*, pp. 206-207.

61 Helen Foster Snow, letter to Ida Pruitt, 30 February 1940, Box 29, HFS Papers.

62 Ibid.

63 A near complete records of Filipino (and other international) donations can be found in the meeting minutes of the CIC International Committee, which met nearly monthly in Hong Kong from February 1939 through August 1941. Box 56 Indusco Papers. While the majority of Asian donations came from the Philippines, funds also came from Indonesia, Hawaii, and Malaysia.

64 Edgar Snow, letter to NW Cooperative Leaders, 31 October 1939, Box 2 Folder 15, ES Papers.

65 Edgar Snow, letter to Edward Carter, 15 December 1935, Box 8, Folder 90, ES Papers.

66 Gerry Groot, *Managing Transitions: The Chinese Communist Party, United Front Work, Corporatism and Hegemony* (New York: Routledge, 2004), p. xii. Following the conclusion of the Sino-Japanese war and the Chinese civil war, United Front work has continued to the present, with Mao Zedong proclaiming it one of China's three 'magic weapons.'

67 Anne-Marie Brady, 'Magic Weapons: China's Political Influence Activities Under Xi Jingping',
Paper presented at the conference on 'The corrosion of democracy under China's global influence', Arlington, Virginia, USA, 16-17 September 2017.

68 Yi-Zheng Lian, 'China has a Vast Influence Machine, and You Don't Even Know It', *New York Times*, 21 May 2018.

69 Pauline Keating, 'U.S.-China Cooperative and Cooperatives: The Case of American Involvement in China's Wartime Cooperative Movement', Paper presented at Shanghai Jiao Tong University, Workshop on Sino-Japanese War in an International Framework, 3-5 December 2013.

FACING THE FOREIGN:

Media Myths In China And Japan

BY JOHN DARWIN VAN FLEET

ABSTRACT

The fantastical anti-Japanese dramas we see on Chinese television have a long ancestry on both sides of the East China Sea. Since the mid-nineteenth century, when the two countries faced naval aggression (Japan) or outright invasion (China), and continuing today, popular and governmental anxiety about foreign intrusion has fostered the creation and nurturing of media myths. These myths often feature fictitious fights, either in the form of martial arts or, as we see on the TV today, pitched military clashes.

These myth-driven, often fevered conceptions can be more than just barriers to development – they can create substantial risks for both China and Japan, and therefore the region – and the entire world.

BARBARIANS AT THE GATES

Mid-nineteenth century Japan was a revolution waiting to happen. In his reflection 80 years on, the renowned diplomat and historian G. B. Sansom put the matter succinctly and was not ashamed to say so:

> The peasants were heavily oppressed by members of the knightly order, who soon in their turn were exploited by the rising class of merchants. Then, as the *daimyō* and the *samurai* attempted to transfer their burden of debt to the already overladen shoulders of the farmers, the agricultural economy broke down, and was replaced by a mercantile economy which Japan was unable to support without calling on the outside world. Her history for more than two hundred years is summarised in that brief statement.[1]

In July 1853, U.S. Navy Commodore Perry's ominous Black Ships sailed and steamed into what is now Tokyo Bay, bearing the demand that Japan open itself to trade with the United States. These Black Ships became the earthquake-triggering catalyst for the societal tectonic pressure that had been building in Japan for a few centuries.

Figure 1: With Perry's Black Ships in the offing, four peasants in this contemporary woodblock print are rather dismissive of the vertically-printed exhortation to the left that declares, 'no need to pay attention to those black ships', predating 'pay no attention to that man behind the curtain' in The Wizard of Oz by decades.
Image on display at 埼玉県現立博物館 *(Saitama Prefecture Modern Museum) from* 大江戸万華鏡 *(O-Edo Kaleidescope, 1991), p. 471.*

The cultural earthquake spawned assassinations, millennial cults and 'civil' war (a top ten term on the list of global oxymorons), and culminated in a revolution that shook the feudal structure of the Tokugawa era (ca 1600 – 1867) to the ground. It led to Japan's first written constitution, the Meiji Constitution, in 1889, and the country's meteoric rise to the level of the global imperial powers by the turn of the twentieth century.

In the 1850s and 1860s, the militant factions opposing the country's opening to foreign relations rallied to the cry of *sonno joi* (尊皇攘夷, 'honour the emperor, expel the [foreign] barbarians'). One of the primary architects of Japan's modernisation, Fukuzawa Yukichi, a target for the militants because he favoured the opening, described the time:

> Here then was the beginning of the national movement, 'Honour the Emperor and Expel the Barbarians.' It was claimed that the Shogun was not prompt enough in carrying out the desires of the imperial court which had decreed the expulsion of all foreigners without exception. From this, it was argued that the Shogun was disobedient, was disrespecting the great doctrine of the land, and moreover was catering to foreign aggressiveness.

...

The period from the Bunkyū era [early 1860s] to the sixth or seventh year of Meiji—some twelve or thirteen years— was for me the most dangerous. I never ventured out of my house in the evenings during that period.[2]

The slogan itself was an import – from China – but the anti-foreigner sentiment was deadly serious, expressing itself in sensational *samurai* attacks, such as the 1862 murder of Charles Richardson (the Namagumi Incident), which prompted the Royal Navy to shell the southwestern port of Kagoshima later that year.

In 1860, at the Sakuradamon, a gate of the shogun's palace, now Tokyo's Imperial Palace, a group of *samurai* attacked the entourage of Ii Naosuke, essentially vice shogun and a signatory of the 1858 Harris Treaty with the United States, which officially opened Japan. In what became known as the Sakuradamon Incident, *samurai* Arimura Jisaemon shot Ii in his palanquin, then dragged Ii from it, then beheaded him, then committed *seppuku*, finally having his own head removed from his shoulders by a dutiful second.

The perpetrators of the Sakuradamon Incident not only lent credence to Fukuzawa's fears – they also were a nineteenth century version of media-savvy. A printed manifesto, describing their mission, was found on the bodies of the dead:

> While fully aware of the necessity for some change in policy since the coming of the Americans to Uraga, it is entirely against the interest of the country and a stain on the national honour to open up commercial relations with foreigners, to admit foreigners into the Castle, to conclude treaties with them, to abolish the established practice of trampling on the picture of Christ, to permit foreigners to build places of worship for the evil religion, and to allow the three foreign Ministers to reside in the land . . . Our sense of patriotism could not brook this abuse of power at the hands of such a wicked rebel [Ii]. Therefore we have consecrated ourselves to be the instruments of Heaven to punish this wicked man, and we have taken on ourselves the duty of ending a serious evil, by killing this atrocious autocrat.[3]

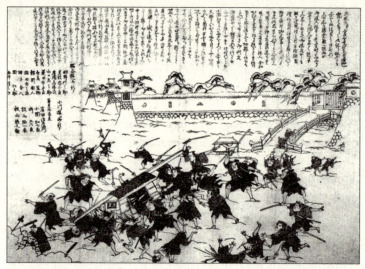

Figure 2: A popular woodblock print, a primary mass media channel of the day, about the Sakuradamon Incident. Note the gate to the shogun's palace in the background, and the various decapitated bodies in the foreground.
Public domain, image from 大江戸万華鏡 (O-Edo Kaleidescope, 1991), p. 473.

Woodblock printers, the mass media producers of the day, wasted no time in creating broadsheets featuring sensationalised graphics of the murder, along with the manifesto. The lurid descriptions and graphic representations appealed to some, appalled others, but the broadsheets became best sellers, a mid-nineteenth century equivalent of the mass media coverage we endure in our century of terrorist attacks and other disasters.

The woodblock prints of the Sakuradamon Incident had at least the virtue of being based on fact. Less so, but equally popular at the time, were prints of Japanese *sumo* wrestlers throwing foreigners. The newly opened 'commercial relations with foreigners' cited in the manifesto of the Sakuradamon assassins had led to massive economic dislocation (including currency manipulation by the United States that devalued Japanese labor and products) and an erosion of the formerly rigid class system of (in descending order) nobles, peasants, artisans and merchants – all disruptions widely seen as foreign instigated.

In a society where foreigners were increasingly present and powerful, and seemingly irresistible, the images of foreigners on their backs, defeated by icons of Japanese culture, salved bruised egos. While there may have been a few demonstrations of *sumo* wrestling, with locals (chosen for their size to showcase Japanese strength) opposing foreigners, these matches would have taken place in public plazas or such, never in an actual *sumo* ring. Such a match would have been repugnant. Even Japanese women, considered impure (a superstition that continues today – see the Appendix about women and the *sumo* ring), were barred from the ring – a foreigner would have been sacrilegious.

The media aggrandisement of these conflicts, whether in a sporting display or at the blade of a sword, are little more than a historical footnote. But one media sensation of the time has resonated down through the decades. Saitō Kichi (斎藤きち) was born in 1841, just south of Tokyo. The legend has it that she was an accomplished *geisha* by her teens, but was assigned as a concubine to the first U.S. ambassador to Japan, Townsend Harris, in 1857, where she became at the tender age of 16 the innocent victim of the tectonic forces of the time, and specifically of the presumed prodigious lust of Ambassador Harris. Faced with barbarian Harris' 'large frame and the long red beard that covered the lower part of his red leathery face' and hands like 'the hairy legs of a giant spider reaching out for her' the story has Saitō, who by then had taken the name Okichi, nobly sacrificing her pure Japanese body to foreign, er, aggression.[4]

Okichi's name would soon change again, as she became widely known as Tojin Okichi (唐人お吉) – 'foreigner Okichi' – the property of barbarians. And according to the tale, this particular foreigner rejected her. Harris supposedly sent her packing after some time – packing to a fate of loneliness and drink, and an early death by suicide, as she could not return to her true love, in her soiled condition, shunned by her own people.

Kimura Rei's 2000 retelling,

Figure 3: A uniformed foreigner getting his comeuppance from a *sumo* champion, in a depiction of a match that would never have happened in any *sumo* ring.
Public domain, source unknown.

Figure 4: One of the more popular pictures of Okichi, née Saitō, at the time of her meeting Ambassador Harris, below (figure 5). Public domain, source unknown.

Figure 5: Public domain, image from Crow, Carl, *He Opened the Door to Japan* (1939), frontispiece

Butterfly in the Wind, borrows all the melodrama, becoming a star in the category of unintentional (we may assume) comedy. But Kimura's is only one of the more recent embellishments of the Okichi myth, fodder for three-tissue movies and such for more than a century now, notably in Japanese box-office hits in the 1930s and 1950s. One of John Huston's oddest film forays demonstrated that the myth had international resonance. Huston cast John Wayne as Townsend Harris against Andō Eiko as Okichi in 1958's *The Barbarian and the Geisha*. Japan's first modern opera, a mashup of *kabuki* and the European opera tradition, was 1940's *Kurofune* ('Black Ships'), which featured the Okichi myth. In 1960, the pop song *Okichi Monogatari* ('Okichi's Story') became a big hit. Today, the town of Shimoda, Japan, Okichi's birthplace, generates a substantial amount of tourism revenue from the memorial hall that promulgates the tear-jerking tale.

Skeptics have long suggested that Okichi served in Harris' household not for years, more like days, that her services to Harris were no more than housekeeping chores (or that she may have been more of a prostitute than a geisha) and that her departure from Harris' employ was because he found her poor skin condition off-putting. The *Kodansha Encyclopedia of Japan* supports this skeptical conclusion.

But none of that has had much effect on the century-plus of myth-making. Cultural myths that endure are those that tell us not necessarily what is true, but what we prefer to be, whether it is or not. An example from the opposite side of the Pacific: media magnate Henry Luce (1898 – 1967), born in China to missionary parents, made a vast fortune and became 'the most influential private citizen of his day' in the United States by framing a view of the U.S. and the world around narratives that were more or less, often less, true.[5] In *The Publisher*, a 2010 biography of Luce, author Alan Brinkley writes, 'In an era blighted by Depression, prejudice, social turmoil and the shadow of war, Life [one of Luce's flagship publications] offered the comforting image of a nation united behind a shared, if contrived, vision of the "American Dream."'[6] Luce's promulgated vision of a consensus society, one blessed with the Manifest Destiny of divine favour, was of course quite popular – still is – despite having little basis in fact.

The media myth of Okichi similarly thrives in Japan because it echoes an image dear to many Japanese hearts – that of some idealised and essential Japanese purity supposedly lost in the transition to a modern and globalised society, dominated by foreigners. A schoolteacher at the turn of the twentieth century, Endō Takeshi, said, 'I remember the time before Shōgun Tokugawa Yoshinobu [Japan's last shogun, who abdicated in 1867], and the absolute rule of the *samurai*. Everything is changing so quickly now – for my liking, far too quickly, and too much.'[7] Endō's lament seems nearly universal – usually the whine of the aged, faced with Heraclitus' maxim that the only constant is change. But in Japan's case, the 'everything' that Endō refers to was overwhelmingly driven by interaction with the foreign. In the *sumo* ring, as in innumerable mythic examples from around the world, impurity intrudes from outside.

Okichi's imagined sacrifice for the common good, combined with the externally compelled change of Japan's Meiji era (starting in 1868) and again postwar (see below, Media Myths Supporting Policy –and Sales), have continually driven the Okichi myth to overwhelm evidence of its falsity.

Fists of harmony and justice

The China that the Manchurian Qing conquered in the early 1600s was, geographically, one of the more substantial empires on the planet. The Qing then set about making it bigger by a factor of more than two, from roughly seven million square kilometres to nearly 15,

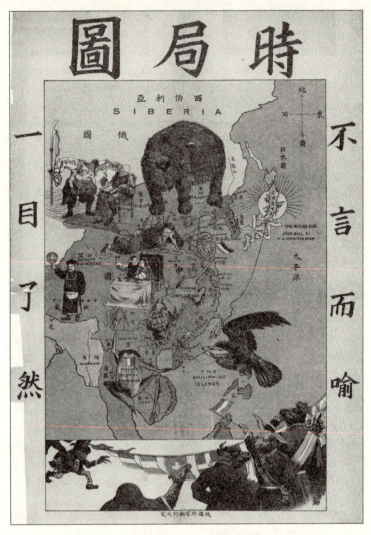

Figure 6: This popular early twentieth century poster, The Situation in the Far East, by revolutionary Tse Tsan Tai (謝纘泰) decries the territorial predations of the Russians (bear), British (lion), French (frog) Japanese (sun) and United States (eagle), with other foreigners at the bottom eager to grab their own territory, while corrupt and incompetent Chinese officials are otherwise engaged.
Tse co-founded the *South China Morning Post*.
Public domain, source unknown.

primarily by absorbing Tibet and Xinjiang in the mid 18th century, a territorial expansion similar to that of the United States with its Louisiana Purchase in 1804, which doubled the size of that young country. The eighteenth century marked the zenith of the Qing, during which century a strengthening commercial system fostered the growth of a market economy. Qing China also benefitted from steadily growing international trade, on the back of the advent of trans-oceanic shipping in the sixteenth century. Demand in Europe for Chinese goods, especially tea, silk and porcelain, brought a massive influx of silver, the 'gold standard' of the era, to China. Agricultural improvements accompanied the growth, dramatically reducing not the incidence of the age-old instigators of famine, such as capricious weather and rivers changing course, but at least the scale of the historically devastating effects.

The former CEO of Intel, Andy Grove, famously opined that success breeds complacency, which in turn breeds failure. The good fortune of the Qing in the eighteenth century led to a population explosion, to about 430 million by the mid-nineteenth century, nearly double what it had been 200 years earlier. Increased arable land, better ability to use it for agricultural production and increased exports proved to be largely one-off economic benefits. Finally, the governance structure of the Qing was revealed to be woefully inadequate for China's evolved and existential challenges of the nineteenth century – the population growth and ecological reverses combined with foreign aggression and, more importantly, 'civil' wars. Historians reckon the Taiping Rebellion (1850-64) as the deadliest internal conflict in human history, reducing China's population by 20 million or so.

In particular, Shandong Province in the late 1890s was, for millions, a devastatingly bad place to be:

> This already desperately poor, overpopulated province— the birthplace of Confucius—had been hard hit economically by the increasing tide of foreign goods flooding into China, particularly foreign textiles. New foreign technology was also wreaking havoc. The steamboats and steam launches, plying busily up China's rivers and canals, had put thousands of bargemen out of work, just as, in other provinces of northern China, railways were destroying the livelihoods of camel-men, mule-drivers, chair bearers and innkeepers.
>
> Shantung [sic] had also been wracked by successive floods and droughts. In 1898 the great Yellow River, 'China's Sorrow', overflowed its banks, flooding 2,500 square miles

of country and destroying 1,500 villages. Plagues of locusts and bitter drought followed. Such economic and natural disasters made the province a fertile recruiting ground for the Boxers, who blamed foreign influence and the Christian converts for alienating China's traditional gods and causing them to punish the land and its people.[8]

In 1899, China's North-China News reported, 'A sect has arisen whose only reason for existence is their hatred for foreigners and the foreign religion. For some occult reason they have taken the name "Boxers", and last spring they tried to drive out the missionaries . . .'[9] The uprising spread under the Chinese names *Yihetuan* (義和團, 'League of Harmony and Justice') or *Yihequan* (義和拳, 'Fists of Harmony and Justice'). Foreigners derogatorily named them Boxers, because of their group martial arts exercises.

The *Yihetuan* bragged that they were invincible to sword and bullet, and conducted demonstrations of their abilities at 'media' channels of provincial nineteenth century China – tea houses, town halls and temple grounds, where people would gather to hear the latest news and take in performances. When *Yihetuan* performers were injured in demonstrations of their supposed invincibility, injuries one might expect in a human flesh vs. metal encounter, no problem! The injury was explained away with the claim that the injured person was insufficiently diligent in following the rituals and beliefs of the *Yihuetuan*.

Figure 7: The rebel in this famous image holds a banner stating his allegiance to the *Yihetuan*. Jonathan Spence, *In Search of Modern China* (New York; London: WW Norton & Co. Inc., 1990), 228.

The *Yihetuan* and their Rebellion reached their high-water mark with the siege of about 4,000 people in Beijing's Legation Quarter in the summer of 1900.

By this point, the Qing leaders had thrown their support behind the *Yihetuan*, who in return developed the rallying cry, 'Support the Qing, Destroy the Foreign (扶清滅洋)' – a variation on the same 2,000 year

Figure 8: Another popular media myth of the time – foreign missionaries were alleged to harvest Chinese eyes (what this late nineteenth century poster warns against) and other organs for supposed medicinal purposes, a myth that encouraged membership in the foreigner-opposing *Yihetuan*. Image from Frances Wood, *No Dogs and Not Many Chinese* (John Murray, 1998), p. 112ff.

Figure 9: Beijing's Legation Quarter at the time of the siege.
Image from Diana Preston, *The Boxer Rebellion*
(New York: Walker & Company, 1999), p. 198.

old Chinese saying that the *samurai* hotheads in Japan had borrowed 50 years before.

The Eight-Nation Alliance, sent to relieve the 55-day siege, numbered about 50,000 soldiers, 40 per cent of whom were Japanese, the rest from (in order of numbers) Russia, the United Kingdom, France, the United States and a few others. Some of the results of what we commonly call in English the Boxer Rebellion:

- Empress Dowager Cixi and her court were forced to flee Beijing for Xi'an, disguised as peasants;
- The so-called Alliance occupied Beijing and Tianjin and other nearby cities for more than a year, and Tsarist Russia captured all of Manchuria;
- Demands by the foreigners for exorbitant reparations;
- Perhaps 100,000 dead, about 30,000 of them Chinese who had converted to Christianity and were therefore murdered by *Yihetuan* rebels, though many of the dead converts were derogatorily called 'rice Christians', for whom conversion was more of a gastronomical than a theological impulse.

Yet another abject defeat for the Chinese at the hands of foreigners. Given the extent of the Rebellion and its aftermath, its massive publicity in both China and abroad, and the disastrous result, it would have been hard for Chinese to create a popular myth out of the Rebellion, though the Communist Party of China (CPC) has tried to do so. In 2006, the Party closed a popular and respected weekly, *Freezing Point*, in part for an essay challenging the official view of history in mainland Chinese textbooks, by Yuan Weishi, a faculty member at Zhongshan University:

[Yuan] criticised Chinese textbooks for teaching an incomplete history of China's last imperial dynasty, the Qing, that fosters blind nationalism and closed-minded anti-foreign sentiment. For example, he challenged the textbooks for portraying the 1900 Boxer Rebellion as a 'magnificent feat of patriotism' without describing the violence committed by the rebels or their extreme anti-foreign views.'[10]

Nonetheless, by the early twentieth century the Chinese had plenty to be anxious about regarding foreigners. Before the Boxer uprising, China had been overwhelmed first in the two Opium Wars (1839-42, 1856-60), and then by upstart Japanese in the first Sino-Japanese War (1894-95), demonstrating repeatedly that the Qing were no match for

Figure 10: Captured *Yihetuan* rebels in 1900. They fared better than some of their fellows, below. Image From Jonathan Fenby, (2008), *The Penguin History of Modern China* (Michigan: Allen Lane, 2008), p. 143ff

Figure 11: Image from Frances Wood, *No Dogs and Not Many Chinese* (John Murray, 1998), p. 112ff.

the foreign and the modern, even when represented by a Japan that had only recently adopted the ways of the West.

A hero was found. Martial artist Huo Yuanjia (霍元甲, 1868 – 1910), credited with founding the Shanghai Chin Woo Athletic Federation, spent the last decade of his life supposedly accepting challenges from large Westerners to public bouts, which Huo then supposedly won, avenging claims by such media villains as one Hugh O'Brien that China was the 'sick man of Asia.' Huo's story had an additional relevant frisson, as his untimely death at 42 was widely rumoured to have been caused by poisoning at the hand of a Japanese physician.

As the myth of Okichi has resonated through the Japanese archipelago and beyond, and through the decades, the myth of Huo has resonated through modern China and the diaspora. In 1972's *Fist of Fury*, written and created in Hong Kong, Bruce Lee established himself as an international martial arts movie sensation with his role as Chen Zhen, fictitious disciple of Huo, defending Huo's honour and that of Chin Woo. *Fist of Fury* 'upgrades' the Huo myth by casting the Japanese as the primary evildoers and usurpers, with one wicked Russian in a minor supporting role. Such an angle would not likely have had much chance in the mainland China at the time, focused as the mainland was with a children-devouring revolution. Moreover, Mao had no patience for Japan-bashing. Speaking to a Japanese political leader in 1961, Mao said that, without the Japanese invasion, "We would still be in the mountains and not be able to watch Peking Opera in Beijing. If a 'thank you' is needed, I would actually like to thank the Japanese warlords."[11]

With the anti-Japanese upgrade firmly established, the myth of Huo has become massively powerful in China and beyond. 2006's *Fearless*, titled *Huo Yuanjia* in Chinese and starring Jet Li, has grossed nearly US$100 million to date, and is only one of many recent retellings of the tale, going back to a few in the 1980s, a remake of *Fist of Fury* in the 1990s, television dramas and so on. This popularity has withstood even a ruling by the mainland legal system that Li's 2006 film is 'an exaggerated and fictitious portrait of the late Huo . . ."[12]

MEDIA MYTHS SUPPORTING POLICY – AND SALES

At the end of World War II, the Japanese faced occupation by the United States military, with some token representation from the other

Allies. Given what the Imperial Japanese Army (IJA) had done around Asia, the Japanese leadership of the time had some justification in fearing occupying forces, particularly what those troops might do to Japanese women. Japanese wartime propaganda about the nature of Allied soldiers did not help.

The myth of Tojin Okichi proved of some value to policymakers. Within days of the end of the war, the surviving Japanese government established what they euphemistically called the Recreation and Amusement Association, a string of brothels around the country aimed at deflecting the lusts, real and imagined, of the occupying forces. These leaders had some experience with both institutional-level 'recruitment' for brothels, as the IJA had pressed tens of thousands of sex slaves into service around Asia in the previous ten years, and also with euphemism, as the sex slaves were referred to as 'comfort women' (慰安婦) working at 'comfort stations.' In his monumental *Hirohito and the Making of Modern Japan*, Herbert Bix writes:

> On August 19 [1945] the Home Ministry ordered local government offices to establish 'Recreation and Amusement Associations' (RAA), funded from the National Treasury. Almost overnight advertisements appeared in the national press and elsewhere informing women in need that food, clothing, and accommodation would be provided to all who volunteered to join. At the inaugural declaration of the RAA, crowds formed on the Imperial Plaza and an estimated fifteen hundred young women gathered on the street outside the temporary headquarters of RAA at Ginza 7 *chome* ['district', in the vicinity of today's Matsuzaka Department Store]. There they listened as an RAA official read a declaration stating: 'Through the sacrifice of thousands of Okichis of the Showa era [since 1926], we shall construct a dike to hold back the mad frenzy [of the Occupation troops] and cultivate and preserve the purity of our race long into the future [. . .] In this way we shall contribute to the peace of society.[13]

Poor Tojin Okichi was thus promoted from being merely a model of noble sacrifice to an image supporting governmental policy, somewhat similar to what the myth of Lei Feng (雷锋) became in mainland China a few decades later, and similar to what the Japanese military leaders had done in 1944 with the myth of the *kamikaze* (神風), 'divine winds' – actual victories repelling Chinese (led by Mongolians) invaders in the thirteenth century, credited to supernatural intervention. The IJA co-opted the well-established myth as the name for suicide pilots, hoping that the borrowing would make the pilots' missions seem less, well, suicidal. No surprise, a false hope – but one that engendered thousands more tragic, pointless deaths.

Another image of Japanese response to foreign incursion became a substantial contributor to economic growth. In 1951, a former *sumo* wrestler, Rikidōzan (力道山), joined Japan's version of professional wrestling, which as everywhere is performance rather than athletic competition. Rikidōzan became a 1950s icon for his (scripted of course) defeats of much larger Western opponents. Such was the excitement among the Japanese at seeing one of their own defeating such opponents that infirm viewers sometimes died from heart attacks when Rikidōzan's performances took unexpected turns for the worse.

Rikidōzan's performances were among the earliest television programs available in postwar Japan, and contributed massively to

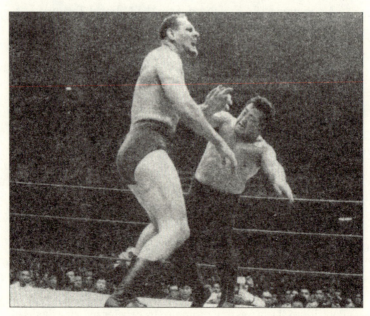

Figure 12: Rikidōzan delivering his signature karate chop move in a performance with the infamous Killer Kowalski.
Public domain, source unknown.

increases in TV sales, part of the resurrection of the country's consumer culture in the 1950s. Rikidōzan's victories were not only staged, but more or less known to be so, as were the images of *sumo* wrestlers throwing foreigners 100 years earlier. But Rikidozan's story has an additional mythical aspect, a delicious irony kept secret (officially, and none too well) by his minders, just as the singing sensation in China in the 1940s, Li Xianglang (李香蘭), had her actual Japanese identity (birth name: Yamaguchi Yoshiko, 山口淑子) shielded from the Chinese public for years, as a central part of her appeal to Chinese audiences. Rikidōzan, the defender of Japanese honour against foreigners, was himself ethnically Korean, perhaps the most despised foreign group among Japanese. Born Kim Sin-rak (김신락) in what is now North Korea, in 1924, when the entire peninsula was under Japanese annexation, Rikidōzan was therefore legally a Japanese citizen, but that hardly mattered. He went to his early grave pretending (sort of) to be Japanese – he was stabbed by a gang assailant in 1963 and died before reaching his 40th birthday. Rikidōzan played himself in a few highly popular Japanese films in the 1950s, and in 2004 a South Korean movie company made a feature film entitled Yeokdosan, the Korean pronunciation of his Japanese *nom de guerre*, about his life.

Supply and demand

By several years ago, complaints about the silly anti-Japanese dramas on mainland Chinese television had become so widespread and disparaging that even CCTV and other official entities called for restraint and reconsideration. According to the *South China Morning Post*, Ni Jun, associate professor at the Central Academy of Drama's Cinema and Television Department, told CCTV, 'I believe there should be a clear bottom line to these anti-Japanese war dramas, as they should not go as far as to insult the intelligence of audiences.[14] Viewers reacted to more than just the fanciful historiography (and physical impossibilities, such as a Japanese fighter plane being brought down by a grenade tossed into the air by a noble Chinese resistance fighter) – plenty of producers had managed to use the cover of anti-Japanese plot lines to produce salacious soft porn. One example:

> The male protagonist, a bandit leader turned anti-Japanese hero, is detained by the Japanese occupation authorities. His wife, played by actress Ge Tian, Mr. Liu's

wife, visits him in the cell. She miraculously manages to hide an elongated stick-type grenade in her vagina and passes the guards. While being watched by the Japanese military interrogator and his Chinese collaborator, the two then perform a last act of erotic intimacy while the husband insults the Japanese emperor. When the Japanese interrogator is about to shoot the man for the royal insult, the husband pulls the grenade from his wife's body, and the woman gleefully pulls the ignition pin, thus sacrificing their lives for the party and the motherland.

Their last words: 'Let's have an ecstatic moment one more time.[15]

Aside from titillation, why might such a deluge of clearly nonsensical content have been appearing on mainland Chinese television screens for years now? In 2017's *Asia's Reckoning*, Richard McGregor suggests an answer:

The debate over the Nanjing Massacre in Japan was often ugly, but it was also the product of a society with free speech. In China, by contrast, the list of taboo topics is long and the ability to enforce them formidable. [. . .] With so many topics off the agenda, Chinese journalists, writers, and filmmakers naturally gravitate to areas where they have the freedom to work and get paid for it. Ahead of the seventieth anniversary commemoration [of the end of World War II - 1945], no area of cultural output was freer, and better funded, than accounts of the war and Japan.

...

In 2013, with Chinese movie producers readying their schedules for the anniversary two years later, the state film bureau approved sixty-nine television series and about a hundred films with anti-Japanese story lines. At one stage that year, forty-eight of the anti-Japanese-themed series were being shot simultaneously at the Hengdian World Studios, one of the country's filmmaking centers [and the world's largest such facility], in Zhejiang province, adjoining Shanghai. A Chinese university professor estimated that about 70 percent of the dramas on Chinese television consisted of wartime shows, inevitably focusing on Japan and its misdeeds.[16]

McGregor addresses the supply side of the question. Elsewhere in his book he describes some Party motivations for the shift to anti-Japanese propaganda, dating back to the mid 1990s. In postwar Japan, the media myth of Tojin Okichi became a lever in postwar government policy, in that case to 'encourage' women to become prostitutes. In China, the reverse happened – the government's shift in public policy, favouring a more aggressive anti-Japanese propaganda stance, led to the creation of an entire category of media myth.

But supply is only half of the equation – why are these silly dramas so popular in mainland China, and is there any relationship to the popularity of the century-old myth of Huo, most recently portrayed as combatting the Japanese? Writing in *Newsweek* in 2008, during the media explosion of China discussion at the time of the Beijing Olympics, China scholar Orville Schell suggests an answer:

> [China's] proud prickliness has deep historical roots that involve China, the West and even Japan. [. . .] the most critical element in the formation of China's modern identity has been the legacy of the country's 'humiliation' at the hands of foreigners, beginning with its defeat in the Opium Wars in the mid-19th century and the shameful treatment of Chinese immigrants in America. The process was exacerbated by Japan's successful industrialization. Tokyo's invasion and occupation of the mainland during World War II was in many ways psychologically more devastating than Western interventions because Japan was an Asian power that had succeeded in modernizing, where China had failed.
>
> This inferiority complex has been institutionalized in the Chinese mind.[17]

Six years later, Schell had an exchange with Perry Link, co-publisher of *The Tiananmen Papers*, on the same topic. Link agrees with Schell's suggestion of an inferiority complex. In his response, Link asks:

Why do people in China's elite - the ones who have it best - want to leave? Polluted air in the cities is certainly one reason, but others relate to 'confidence'.

...most fundamentally (although people are reluctant to articulate it), legal émigré status is an insurance policy against an unpredictable future in China: life in the West offers a feeling of security that life in China, despite government expenditures of hundreds of billions of yuan per year on 'stability maintenance', cannot offer. Schell correctly notes that [the Party and its supporters] find Western criticisms of their one-party rule to be condescending. But that very fact reveals their ambivalence about the West. If they were really confident that their system is superior, they might simply pity the misguided West. That they feel 'condescended to' shows that, at one level in their minds, they are still according the West an elevated position.[18]

Considering Schell's earlier suggestion, Link might have added Japan to geographies accorded an elevated position. Given the ancient and recent history between the two countries, and Schell's assertion of an institutionalised inferiority complex, we should be surprised if such anti-Japanese dramatic excesses were not occurring.

WELCOME TO JAPAN – NOW GO HOME

Silly TV dramas notwithstanding, Japan poses no practical danger to any country but itself. In *Asia's Reckoning*, McGregor suggests that the phrase 'Japanese militarism' is 'jarringly inaccurate... Unlike in the United States, where the military is highly visible and invariably venerated, it is still rare to see Japanese officers in uniform in public.'[19]

Japan's biggest threat is not only internal; it is self-imposed – a rapidly ageing society and a labor force insufficient to meet the increasing service needs of a greying population, combined with a legendary reticence to accept immigrants who might otherwise serve such needs. In his 1931 classic, *Japan: A Short Cultural History*, a passage from which opens this essay, G.B. Sansom suggests that the mid-nineteenth century country had an 'economy which Japan was unable to support without calling on the outside world.' Japan again has such an economy, but this time the need from the outside world is for people.

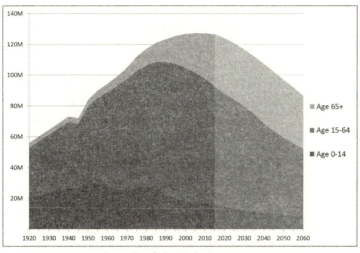

Japan: Population Projection to 2060
Jon McDonald, *Japan Statistical Yearbook* (2016) and *Population Projections for Japan*: 2011 to 2060 (2012), (https://en.wikipedia.org/wiki/Aging_of_Japan#/media/File:Japan_Population_by_Age_1920-2010_with_Projection_to_2060.png)

The country's population is on pace to shrink faster than that of any other country in history has, other than by plague or war. In July 2017, the *Financial Times* reported, 'According to projections from [Japan's] National Institute of Population and Social Security Research, the pace of decline will rise every year until 2045, by which time Japan will be losing about 900,000 residents a year — equivalent to a city the size of Austin, Texas.'[20]

Perhaps the most dramatic and threatening aspect of this decline: the working-age component of the population is shrinking faster than the overall rate – it is likely to halve by about 2040.

It seems the blindingly obvious solution to the economic *tsunami* starting to break on Japanese shores is immigration, but as anyone who knows Japan is well aware, immigration is a third rail in Japanese politics. A myth of Japanese being unique goes back centuries, based in part on the archipelago having been relatively isolated from the continental ebb and flow of populations, dynasties and the like, over millennia. Ethno-national myths of uniqueness are, of course, not unique to Japan, though the Japanese variant is particularly virulent. A natural consequence of broad acceptance of such a myth, accompanied as it usually is with the assumption that the fictitious uniqueness also equals 'better', is resistance to substantial foreign interaction, or just xenophobia.

Nihonjinron (日本人論 – theories of Japaneseness), a postwar eruption of the Japanese version of the myth, exploded in the media in the 1980s, at a time when the Japanese economy seemed invincible. Extreme versions of *Nihonjinron* claimed that the Japanese were unique genetically and linguistically, that Japanese snow is unique, so only Japanese-made skis are suitable for Japanese ski slopes, etc. In a 2017 Japan Times column, veteran commentator Mark Schreiber pointed out that such silliness continues today, with a quote from the 13 June 2017 edition of the Japanese weekly Spa!:

> For over 1,000 years, Japanese had not consumed meat, and their diet was centered on grains and vegetables rich in dietary fiber, which takes longer to digest. For that reason, compared with Westerners, they evolved intestines that are 1.5 to 2 meters longer.'[21]

Schreiber continues by reminding us that the intestines claim, along with the snow claim, was used by Japanese government leaders in the 1980s to resist imports – such myth propagation often has a commercial motivation as well.

Polls routinely indicate that about 60 per cent of Japanese citizens are opposed to any immigration other than fixed and short term, such as for those granted entry to work on construction for the 2020 Olympics, who are expected to then go away. In an interview with CNN in August 2017, Chris Burgess, a migration researcher and lecturer of Japan studies at Tsuda Juku University in Tokyo, explained:

> Japan doesn't have an immigration policy -- this is something that politicians stress. Many people in Japan believe that the country's peace and harmony is [sic] based on it being a homogenous country where there are few foreigners. That kind of thinking pervades a lot of aspects of society and underlies the no immigration principle.[22]

Even the Japanese word for 'immigrant' or 'immigration', *imin* (移民, literally people on the move) is toxic for politicians. Commenting to the *Financial Times* in 2014, Nishimura Yasutoshi, a relevant deputy minister, said, 'We don't use the word 'immigration'.'[23] Prime Minister Abe has borne this out – he assiduously avoids the word. His party, the

Liberal Democratic Party (LDP), is filled with members who oppose even talk of immigration, particularly the members from provincial and rural areas, traditional strongholds for the LDP and (more irony) the areas that are most rapidly depopulating, therefore facing the most dire economic futures.

Some in Japan attempt to address the looming demographic disaster. Sakanaka Hideyori, formerly director of the Tokyo Immigration Bureau, became a (rather solitary) advocate for immigration in the early 2000s. Describing the background of the problem, he says, 'Japan is an island country and we didn't let foreigners enter for over 1000 years, so we haven't had great experiences living with other ethnic groups.'[24] His history is a bit off, but the concept is not. Sakanaka joins many others in suggesting that, unless Japan seeks to rebuild itself as a rapidly shrinking society, down to about 80 million from the current 125 million, only a tidal restraint of mass immigration, what he calls the "big option", can withstand the coming economic *tsunami*:

> ... the country would need to accept over 20 million immigrants during the next 50 years. Before welcoming such an unprecedented influx, Japan would need to build a national consensus that new arrivals should be welcomed as 'friends' and contributors to Japanese society. Japan would have to transform itself into a land of opportunity, building an open, fair society which guaranteed equal opportunity, judged people on their merits, and allowed everyone to improve their social status regardless of origin or ethnicity.[25]

But such an initiative would devastate the myths the Japanese have been telling themselves, in their media and elsewhere, for generations. Sakanaka demonstrated a gift for understatement in a Japan Times interview when he said, 'I can't exactly say that the plan I've been advocating over the past three years has generated much enthusiasm.'[26]

Broad-based immigration would create the third episode, in a two-century period, in which Japan has been compelled to deal with the foreign on a substantial scale, the first being the mid nineteenth century era that the myth of Tojin Okichi marks the beginning of, the second being 1945 and on. Both of the previous periods were marked by a speed and scope of change that schoolteacher Endo and

Figure 13: Headline "Tokyo Becoming a Chinatown", subhead: "Impact: The Era of 730,000 Resident Chinese" (*Sunday Mainichi*, 22 July 2018)

Figure 14: Headline: "Japan's Chinese – The Full Story", subheads: "The Unknown Truth about Chinese in Japan" and "The Era of One Million [Chinese in Japan] Is Upon Us!" (Weekly Diamond, 7 July 2018, cover)

millions of others decried as 'far too quickly, and too much.' Both periods also featured the collapse of governments.

And the Japanese well know that a substantial increase in immigration means a substantial increase largely from China. Government figures suggest that foreign residents in Japan who are PRC citizens, 730,000 or so, represent about a third of all foreign residents from Asia, more than a quarter of foreign residents overall. (The next largest group are Korean citizens, about 90 percent from the south.) The Japanese polity have a millennia-long love-hate relationship with the mainland, but have rarely been indifferent, and are certainly not indifferent now, as two recent sensationalist stories in major Japanese media suggest. (Figures 13 and 14)

The resident population of Chinese in Japan would have to nearly double to reach even one percent of the total population. By comparison, resident Chinese in Korea exceed one million, in a country with 40 percent of Japan's overall population.[27]

The ironies pile up – more immigration from China would not only help to address the increasingly dire labour shortage in Japan, but also be to Japan's strategic advantage with its colossal neighbour. More mainland Chinese in Japan would experience a truly developed and civilised country, thereby subjecting their homeland to the incremental sunlight required for incremental disinfection, and also helping to quell the mainland media myths about Japanese militarism. So the more anti-foreign elements of the Japanese populace, which tend to align with those who resist acknowledging wartime atrocities, are fostering the development of precisely the type of China that they claim to fear. Seems similar to a phenomenon of the early twentieth century and Cold War era, when the statements and actions of those who vehemently proclaimed themselves anti-communist contributed substantially to the development of Communism.

The dramas protest too much, methinks

Immigration in Japan, or the lack thereof, may be the most indicative coal mine canary for the country's future – Japanese citizens will have to overcome some of their most cherished myths if the country is to maintain anything like its current economic situation and stature.

The popularity of anti-Japanese dramas on mainland TV, and the broader phenomenon of anti-Japanese propaganda, serve a similar caged-bird function in the People's Republic. The degree to which these persist reflects the degree to which the Party (supply side) and the people (demand side) have not overcome Schell's institutionalised inferiority complex, and failure to overcome will continue to degrade both the country's internal development and its foreign relations. In response to Perry Link in the 2014 New York Review exchange cited above, Schell outlines the risk:

> And here there is a dangerous combination brewing. When a certain quotient of success leads to pride, arrogance, and nationalism, and when these impulses merge with a sense of historical victimization, insecurity, and the indignity of being condescended to in a quest for global respect, as Link suggests, China could easily become more defensive, pugnacious, and truculent as a rival.[28]

There's an additional danger – as the hyperbolic or outright fanciful media myth-telling has continued in both cultures for so long, the cognitive dissonance that many in China and Japan would face were they to surrender their fact-challenged beliefs has become a daunting inertial force. Social psychologist Leon Festinger pioneered the theory of cognitive dissonance and, through study of a doomsday cult, demonstrated that denial of evidence is a well-worn path for those who hope to resolve such dissonance. In *When Prophecy Fails*,[29] Festinger describes how the doomsday cult, faced with the failure of their predictions to come to pass, created an additional delusional assertion to explain away reality – the relevance for understanding China's *Yihetuan*, for example, should be obvious.

Media myth-telling is a chicken-egg phenomenon. It both grows from popular misconceptions and fuels them by turn. Both China and Japan face daunting challenges, of different types, that their media myths are either deflecting their attention from (China) or wildly misrepresenting (Japan). Worse, these myths are to cognitive dissonance as drugs are to an addict. The degree to which Japan and China can use evidence-based decision-making to overcome their various cherished myths, the only healthy path to reducing cognitive dissonance, is the degree to which we may increase our optimism about the coming few decades in East Asia. But historically, societies do not regularly take such an approach to cognitive dissonance reduction, until reality intrudes, often through wars and such.

Appendix: women and the *sumo* ring

Sumo organisers in Japan still bar women from the ring, a legacy of a time when menstruation was considered an impurity. Sumo has the tradition of being quasi-religious – the ceremonies surrounding each bout are largely Shinto-related rituals of, in part, purification.

In 2000, Ota Fusae, Japan's first female governor (Osaka municipality), attempted to take the traditional governor's place in the ring on the final day of the tournament, to recognise the tournament winner. The Japan Sumo Association barred her from doing so.

In April 2018, a small-town mayor had a stroke in the ring of a local *sumo* hall. Some female paramedics in attendance rushed to help the mayor, but were implored by the match officials to leave the ring, who later scattered salt around the ring in the traditional act of ritual purification, actions that led to a national on-line discussion and an apology from the Japan Sumo Association. For a description of the incident and related issues of women and Japanese society, see Fifield, Anna, A Japanese woman tried to save a man's life in the sumo ring, but was ordered away for being 'unclean,' *Washington Post*, 5 April 2018.

ABOUT THE AUTHOR

John Darwin Van Fleet is broadly published on East Asian history and society. In 2015, he published *Tales of Old Tokyo*, a scrapbook tour of the city's history from 1853 to 1964. His second book, *Squabbling Siblings – China and Japan from Antiquity to 2020*, is forthcoming in spring 2019. This essay will appear as one chapter.

E-mail: john.vf@sjtu.edu.cn

With the exception of the figure projecting Japanese demographics in the coming few decades, all graphics are, to the best of my knowledge, in the public domain.

―◇◇―

Endnotes

1 G. B. Sansom, *Japan: A Short Cultural History* (Stanford: Stanford University Press, 1931), p. 468.

2 Yukichi Fukuzawa, *The Autobiography of Yukichi Fukkuzawa*, trans. Eiichi Kiyooka, (New York: Columbia University Press, 1899, trans. 1966), p. 227.

3 James Murdoch, *A History of Japan, Volume III, The Tokugawa Epoch* (London: Kegan Paul, Trench, Trubner & Co., Ltd., 1926), p. 702.

4 Rei Kimura, *Butterfly in the Wind* (Chicago: Olive Press, 2000)

5 Robert Edwin Herzstein, *Henry R. Luce, Time, and the American Crusade in Asia* (Cambridge: Cambridge University Press, 2005), p. 1.

6 Alan Brinkley, (2010), *The Publisher* (New York: Knopf Doubleday, 2010), p. 239.

7 Discovery Networks International (2011), *The Rise and Fall of the Japanese Empire*.

8 Diana Preston, *The Boxer Rebellion* (New York: Berkley Books, 1999), p. 24.

9 North-China Herald, 9 October 1899, quoted in Xiang, Lanxin, *The Origins of the Boxer War: A Multinational Study* (London: RoutledgeCurzon, 2003), p. 112.

10 Philip P. Pan, '*Leading Publication Shut Down In China*, Washington Post Foreign Service, 25 January 2006.

11 Quoted from Richard McGregor, *Asia's Reckoning: China, Japan, and the Fate of U.S. Power in the Pacific Century* (New York: Penguin Publishing Group, 2016), p. 28.

12 'Kungfu master's grandson loses defamation lawsuit against Jet Li film,' Xinhua, 28 December 2006, http://en.people.cn/200612/28/eng20061228_336416.html.

13 Herbert Bix, *Hirohito and the Making of Modern Japan* (New York: HarperCollins, 2000), p. 538.

14 Ernest Kao, 'State broadcaster CCTV slams anti-Japanese war dramas', *South China Morning Post*, 11 April 2013, http://www.scmp.com/news/china/article/1212279/state-broadcaster-cctv-slams-anti-japanese-war-dramas.

15 Miles Yu, 'China's bizarre anti-Japanese TV and movie kitsch backfires', *Washington Times*, 21 May 2015, https://www.washingtontimes.com/news/2015/may/21/inside-china-anti-japanese-tv-propaganda-dramas-ba/.

16 McGregor, *Asia's Reckoning*, p. 327-328.

17 Orville Schell, 'China: Pride, Protest and the Olympic Games,' *Newsweek*, 25 July 2008, http://www.newsweek.com/china-pride-protest-and-olympic-games-93191.

18 Perry Link, 'China Strikes Back': An Exchange', *New York Review of Books*, 20 November 2014, http://www.nybooks.com/articles/2014/11/20/china-strikes-back-exchange/.

19 McGregor, *Asia's Reckoning*, p. 298.

20 Robin Harding, 'Japan suffers record decline in population', *Financial Times*, 5 July 2017, https://www.ft.com/content/62f066cc-615c-11e7-91a7-502f7ee26895.

21 Mark Schreiber, 'Today's web of lies and disinformation: It's a lot to stomach,' *Japan Times*, 10 June 2017, https://www.japantimes.co.jp/news/2017/06/10/national/media-national/todays-web-lies-disinformation-lot-stomach/#.W0y8arh9iUl.

22 Emiko Jozuka and Junko Ogura, 'Can Japan survive without immigrants?' *CNN*, 2 August 2017, https://edition.cnn.com/2017/08/01/asia/japan-migrants-immigration/index.html.

23 Jonathan Soble, 'Japan stands by immigration controls despite shrinking population', *Financial Times*, 2 June 2014, https://www.ft.com/content/32788ff0-ea00-11e3-99ed-00144feabdc0.

24 Matthew Carney, 'Japan - populate or perish: fmr head of Tokyo immigration,' *AM with Sabrina Lane*, Australian Broadcasting Corp., 16 February 2015, http://www.abc.net.au/am/content/2015/s4180383.htm.

25 Hideyori Sakanaka, 'The Future of Japan's Immigration Policy: A

Battle Diary', *The Asia Pacific Journal*, Vol 5, Issue 4, 2 April 2007.

26 Michael Hoffman, Michael, 'Only Immigrants Can Save Japan', *Japan Times*, 28 October 2012.

27 Hyun-Jin Ock, 'Korea Takes Aim at Illegal Immigration', *Korea Herald*, 4 April 2016, http://www.koreaherald.com/view.php?ud=20160404000876; http://www.immigration.go.kr/doc_html/attach/imm/f2016//20160830263386_1_1.hwp.files/Sections1.html (Korean)

28 Orville Schell, 'China Strikes Back': An Exchange', *New York Review of Books*, 20 November 2014.

29 Leon Festinger, Henry Riecken, and Stanley Schachter, *When Prophecy Fails* (Minneapolis: University of Minnesota Press, 1956).

POLITICAL POWER AND MEMORY IN THE HAN DYNASTY:

The Career Of Huo Guang Re-Considered

BY J. BENJAMIN ASKEW

ABSTRACT

This article examines the career of Huo Guang (霍光; d. 68 BCE), a government official in the latter part of the Former Han dynasty, in order to illustrate three features of the historical record. Firstly, it seeks to re-evaluate Huo's career and suggests that far from being a loyal minister as he is usually portrayed in the historical literature, he was in fact a self-serving autocrat who ruled China through a series of puppet emperors. Secondly, it attempts to describe the problems inherent in the traditional Chinese system of government that allowed the rise of ruler such as Huo. Finally, this article tries to illuminate how the ideological assumptions of China's Confucian historical tradition colour the ways in which traditional historians have described the past, by illustrating there are several levels of understanding in the existing literature.

When the First Emperor of the Qin dynasty, Qin Shihuang (秦始皇,259-210 BCE) came to power as the first unifier of all of China, he created a political system that would evolve and change by providing the basic template for China's government for the next two thousand years. The power of the emperor after the Qin dynasty was greatly strengthened by replacing powerful local aristocrats of the Zhou dynasty with salaried civil servants recruited through recommendation and then examination.[1] This model survived even though it conflicted, in many ways, with the idealised feudal system promoted by Confucianism.[2] The key to the relatively strong powers of the Chinese emperors was rooted in the dominance of the bureaucracy by officials with no special family connections. As bureaucrats whose careers depended on the emperor, they would find it difficult to effectively challenge the emperor. Despite this there are isolated exceptions to this rule. In the middle of the first century BCE the Han government had been controlled by a powerful official called Huo Guang (霍光; d. 68 BCE), a medium-ranked official in charge of cavalry remounts for the Han Army, who not only managed to dominate China, but also managed to overthrow an emperor.

In China's very long imperial history, Huo's career and ability to exploit power is such an unusual occurrence that it needs explanation. In the approximately two millennia after Qin Shihuang established the imperial system, Chinese emperors were rarely removed from office. It was especially uncommon for an emperor to be removed by means other than massive peasant uprisings, a military *coup* or a foreign invasion, which were very rare events themselves. This article will attempt to explain three questions: how it was possible for a low ranking official like Huo to dominate the palace, how the Chinese bureaucracy actually worked in practice and also how subsequent generations of Chinese historians have been forced by their ideological assumptions to treat his actions generously.

On 5 July 74 BCE the emperor of China, Liu Fuling (劉弗陵, 94–74 BCE), posthumously known as Zhaodi (昭帝), passed away. Emperor Zhao was still young and had not produced an heir. The death of any emperor without a clear heir presented an obvious and serious problem. The solution put forward by a group of officials, led by Huo Guang, was to invite Liu He (劉賀, d. 59 BCE), the King of Changyi (昌邑王) and a nephew of Zhaodi, to take the throne. What followed was a brief period of 27 days during which Liu He, then aged twenty years old, was accused of violating the ritual norms of the Han Empire. The main allegation was that he was physically intimate with the women of the Imperial Palace at a time when he should have been observing the mourning rites for the previous emperor. The complaint also included claims that he had continued to hunt, had taken valuable objects from the imperial stores and promoted many of his followers from his own kingdom. Due to this violation of the then social norms of China, he was deposed and deprived of his title.[3] It is worth noting that while some of these were not serious issues and would have been ignored in normal times; others were clearly within the emperor's prerogative such as the appointment of officials he trusted and some of them were actually central to the emperor's role such as producing an heir.[4] Although Liu He himself was merely exiled, his supporters were treated more ruthlessly. According to Ban Gu:

> As his officials had not guided Liu He towards propriety, but had entrapped him in evil, Huo Guang had over two hundred of them put to death. As they were being

taken to be executed, they cried out in the middle of the marketplace, 'By not acting decisively, chaos has resulted.'[5]

Regardless of how serious Liu He's ritual violations were, in his old age, he was asked about how he had come to be deposed. He did not cite his moral wrong doings but mentioned the simple fact that he had not taken control of the army.[6] If he had acted decisively, he may well have remained in power as Huo's authority was not uncontested. When Huo attempted to take control of the Imperial Seals after the death of Zhaodi, he was resisted by at least some of the court officials. The official in charge of the Seals was not willing to give them to Huo. Huo attempted to grab them. Grasping his sword firmly, the official said 'You can have my head, but you cannot have the Seals.'[7]

Although the historical record contains no definitive description of how Huo's power was established, it was to grow to such an extent that he was said to have made everyone 'within the Four Seas quake with fear.'[8] In Chinese history, Liu He was exceptional in that he appears to have been displaced solely at the instigation of a group of civilian officials at a time when there was no financial or military crisis.

Even though the Chinese political tradition was dominated by discussions of loyalty, in reality, officials were never especially committed to the survival of a specific emperor or even the dynasty. Their prominence came from their professional competence so that if a ruler or even the dynasty changed, they could expect to continue working for the new regime.[9] Thus, China's officials stood by as the Qin Empire collapsed.[10] That professional competence was not usually in military affairs and therefore the civil officials usually lacked an institutional basis for removing an emperor. That an emperor could be removed from office by a group of low ranking officials was such an unusual event because of the bureaucratic nature of the Han government.

With no institutional counter to the officials, in every dynasty, Chinese emperors faced some serious challenges in using this system in order to rule effectively. They were invariably raised within the Imperial Palace and rarely ventured out. This meant that they rarely had any childhood friends who knew them before they were emperors.[11] Needless to say they could only partially rely on their immediate families. An emperor's closest relatives often stood to gain if an accident happened to the emperor. For most of China's imperial periods, the emperors usually relied on their eunuchs as people strongly attached to the person of the emperor, without families of their own.[12] As S. E. Finer said, of all the emperor's servants, eunuchs 'were likely to be the most subservient, the most faithful, and, because of their proximity to the emperor, the most intimate.'[13] Their rise seemed to have come with the rise in the number of palace women reserved for the emperor, and at this period they had not yet come to prominence. Liu Che (劉徹), posthumously known Wudi (漢武帝, r. 141–87 BCE) was the first emperor to maintain substantial numbers of palace women, although he did not appear to have greatly trusted the eunuchs who guarded them.[14] No eunuch played a significant role in this period. Eunuchs in the Han dynasty did not have the education or the social capital to be commonly accepted as bureaucrats. In this period, their employment in the civil service was limited and often greatly resented. As S. E. Finer states:

> The 2,000 years of Imperial China witnessed a perpetual see-saw between the power of the emperor to pursue his own policy through his own personal instrumentalities, and the power of his relatives and/or the palace officials and central bureaucracy to pursue their own. At times the emperor is an active ruler, at others it is his entourage or officialdom that rules.'[15]

The solution found in the Former Han was for the emperor to rely on the family of his main empress. The emperor's brothers-in-law had an interest in the survival of the emperor and his children in a way that his brothers did not. This simply subjected the emperor to control by his in-laws, a feature of Chinese history apparent to the end of the imperial system. In fact the former Han was eventually overthrown by Wang Mang (王莽, c. 45 BCE–23 CE), whose family had dominated the Court through marriage for three generations.

The explanation for how someone of low rank like Huo Guang could take control over the Han government and dethrone the Emperor, was likely due to the state of the government at the time. In turn this, went back to chaos and de-moralisation under the previous emperor. The Emperor Wu was born in 156 BCE and he was on the throne since 141 BCE and would only die in 87 BCE. Altogether he reigned for just over 54 years, the second longest reign of any

Chinese emperor. By 92 BCE, he appears to have become increasingly suspicious of those around him. He ordered soldiers to search the grounds of a park in the capital which turned up several dolls that were suspected of use in witchcraft. This promoted a series of trials of prominent political figures at court. The first people to be put on trial in 91 BCE were two of Wudi's leading officials, Gongsun He (公孫賀, d. c. 91 BCE), who was the Prime Minister at the time, and his son Gongsun Jingsheng (公孫敬聲, d. c. 91 BCE) who had succeeded his father as Superintendent of Transport, one of the Nine Ministers of the central government. The situation was complicated by the fact that Gongsun He's wife, Wei Junru (衛君孺), who was also arrested, was the sister of the Emperor Wu's leading spouse, the Empress Wei.

The emperor followed this purge by appointing a provincial official Jiang Chong

(江充, d. 91 BCE), to investigate. Jiang relied on shamans from Inner Asia and torture to conduct the inquiry.[16] This rapidly spread out of control with tens of thousands of people in the capital being executed for 'immorality.' The investigation also led Jiang directly to the heir apparent, Liu Ju (劉據, 128–91 BCE) and his mother, the Empress Wei Zifu (衛子夫, d. 91 BCE).[17] Although it is not clear what happened next, faced with the threat of this investigation, the Crown Prince seemed to have tried to make a bid for power by subverting the army in the capital. In the course of this attempted coup, Jiang was seized and executed for allegedly attempting a coup himself and his shamans were burnt to death in public.[18] The political class in Chang'an had faced a literal witch hunt, in which evidence was produced by magical means, with a subsequent mass execution and an attempted *coup* by the heir apparent. The most likely effect of this was a plunge in the morale of the surviving government officials.

The problem for the dynasty represented by this unrest went even deeper. The Empress Wei herself had experienced a meteoric rise in her fortunes. She had been born an illegitimate serf and had been a dancing girl before catching the eye of the emperor and becoming his favourite wife. With her rise, her family also rose to important government offices. Her brother Wei Qing (衛青, d. 106 BCE) and her nephew Huo Qubing (霍去病, 140–117 BCE, the illegitimate son of her sister Wei Shaoer, 衛少兒) were two of China's leading military commanders.[19] Her brother-in-law Gongsun He was China's Prime Minister. By the time of these trials, the emperor had started to favour other concubines, including the Lady Li (李夫人), sister to another of Wudi's generals, Li Guangli (李廣利, d. 88 BCE). The slow decline in the Empress's position became apparent with the birth of a son, Liu Fuling, by the Lady Zhao in 94 BCE.[20]

It is in this context of rivalry for dynastic succession that these accusations of witchcraft were made. If the dolls that had been discovered on the grounds of the palace of Empress Wei's son, the Crown Prince Ju, had been used for magical purposes against the emperor himself, they had precedent. In 130 BCE, Wudi's previous empress, the Lady Chen (陳, d. c. 110 BCE),[21] had been caught using witchcraft in an attempt to retain the affections of the emperor against no other than his new favourite, the future Empress Wei.[22] In that incident, over three hundred people were sentenced to death, destroying whatever basis of power the Chen family had in the capital. In light of experience, it would have been extremely foolish for anyone to have engaged in further witchcraft against the emperor and there are reasonable grounds for suspecting that it was an attempt to frame the Crown Prince. If so, it was highly successful, as the Emperor Wu had the entire Wei family arrested. The Lady Wei and her son, Prince Ju, were allowed to commit suicide. In 91 BCE, all the other members of her family, including her in-laws Gongsun He and Gongsun Jingsheng, down to the last infant, were executed. This purge did not end the bloodshed since the following year, the last prominent commander of the Han Armies, Li Guangli, brother of Wudi's other favourite, the Lady Li, surrendered to the Xiongnu tribes on China's northern border. This caused Wudi to order his surviving brothers and his son executed as well.[23] In the few years left to him on the throne, Wudi would execute two more Imperial Counsellors (Bao Shengzhi, 暴胜之 and Shangqiu Cheng, 商丘成) as well as his Chancellor (Liu Quli, 劉屈氂).[24] Thus in his last years, Wudi had executed almost all of his highest government officials with the result that at his death, many important posts were unfilled. Thus, two of the key pillars of the emperor's support – his officials and his in-laws – had been removed from the centre of power by the time Wudi died. This vacuum in the heart of the Han government seems to have been key to Huo Guang's rise to power.

Four years after the purge of the Wei family, in 87 BCE, Emperor Wu became ill. According to the *Han Shu* and other traditional records, the dying emperor appointed three low ranking officials to take power as regents for his infant son Liu Fuling. Two days later, the emperor died. At the age of eight, Liu Fuling took power as Emperor Zhao. The three officials named were Huo Guang, Jin Midi (金日磾 134–86 BCE), a Xiongnu slave who had risen from a position in the Imperial Stables, and Shangguan Jie (上官桀, d. 80 BCE).[25] These three men were linked by ties of marriage. Jin Midi was married to one of Huo Guang's daughters. Another of Huo's daughters was married to Shangguan Jie's son, Shangguan An, (上官安, d. 80 BCE). A daughter from this marriage, grand-daughter to both Huo Guang and Shangguan Jie, but formally a member of the Shangguan family, was later married to Emperor Zhao. Another friend of the group, Sang Hongyang (桑弘羊, c. 152–80 BCE), was appointed Imperial Counsellor while a reputed non-entity, Tian Qianqiu (田千秋), was appointed Chancellor.

This was a rather unusual arrangement as the Emperor Zhao had several older brothers who could have been appointed emperor. The official history simply records that towards the end of Wudi's life, the Crown Prince had come to a bad end, and two of his brothers Liu Dan (旦), Prince of Yan (燕) and Liu Xu (胥), Prince of Guangling (廣陵) had become arrogant.[26] This does not seem a particular good reason to exclude them from the throne given that the alternative was a child. The Han dynasty had already had the unfortunate experience of the Empress Lü (呂后 241–180 BCE) who had dominated China through a series of infant emperors. An infant would not have any choice but to rely on the advice and recommendations of his officials and so another infant would have been a dangerous choice for the Emperor Wu. There is evidence to suggest that, Wudi did not choose these three men as regents. An official who claimed to be eyewitness to Wudi's death denied that the emperor had done so. The *Han Shu* records:

> At that time, [Guard Commander] Wang Mang (王莽) had a son called Hu (忽) who served in the Palace, who openly said 'When the emperor died, I was always nearby. How can it be that the emperor's dying instructions were to enfeoff these three? Everyone can believe their own ears.' Huo Guang heard this, he put pressure on Wang Mang. Wang Mang poisoned his son.[27]

The very fact that Huo Guang reacted so strongly to this rash young man suggests a guilty conscience. If his position in the Court was firmly established and backed by precedent, law and the emperor's known wishes, it would have been unlikely that he needed to respond so brutally to idle gossip. As with the unnamed official who refused to hand over the seals of office, if Huo's position was lawful, these challenges would not have happened.[28] There is no good reason to think that Wudi wanted to establish a regency under these three men. That they held such junior posts and were so closely related to each other makes them an unlikely choice for regents. Despite this, it is the uniform opinion in the traditional, as well as the modern, Chinese literature that Wudi did appoint these three men. Most significantly, after all the purges, there were few people left who could challenge them.

Amicable relations between Huo Guang and the rest of the imperial family on the one hand, and with Shangguan Jie on the other, did not last long. In 86 BCE, Liu Dan, son of the Lady Li, and King of Yen since 117 BCE, allegedly plotted with two fellow clansmen, Liu Zhang (劉長) and Liu Ze (劉澤), to overthrow the Emperor Zhao. When discovered, Liu Dan is said to have managed to avoid responsibility and so escaped punishment.[29] On 29 September of that year, Jin Midi died, presumably of natural causes, leaving just two regents. A triangle may be a fairly stable political arrangement, but a partnership is not. In 80 BCE, Liu Dan was alleged to have plotted again. This plot was not particularly sophisticated as Liu Dan is said to have sent a letter to the Emperor Zhao accusing Huo of misrule. This would not normally be considered a plot at all. The young emperor wasted no time in telling Huo and this time a whole range of important figures were arrested including Shangguan Jie, his son Shangguan An, the emperor's sister the Princess Eyi and Sang Hongyang.[30] As there is no actual evidence of wrong doings by any of these figures, this appears to have been an excuse for Huo to remove any competitor to his position. Huo Guang, in firm control of the capital, had the Shangguans executed while Liu Dan and the Princess Eyi were forced to commit suicide. That is, a man who had been a former middle-ranking bureaucrat of no great distinction had the emperor's brother, his sister, his father-in-law and his grandfather-in-law killed on the basis of allegations that they had plotted to remove Huo from power.

After the death of Shangguan Jie, Huo Guang held undisputed power in Chang'an. There was only one person who could threaten his control over the government and that was the emperor. There is no record that Zhaodi openly challenged Huo but the *Han Shu* state:

> Rulers receive the Mandate of Heaven, they act as father and mother to the people, how can they not do this? What can Heaven not see? In Wudi's time, there were several selections of good women totalling several thousand people, filling the Imperial Palace. Neglecting the Empire, Zhaodi was young and weak; [leaving] Huo Guang solely responsible for [government] affairs; he did not understand ritual or propriety; he recklessly used gold, money and precious objects, wild animals, fish, turtles, cows, horses, tigers and leopards and birds, up to 190 different types, when he sacrificed to Wudi; women from the Imperial Palace were left in the Tombs;[31] there were grave violations of propriety; and Wudi's intentions were ignored. Zhaodi died and Huo Guang did it again.[32]

This passage suggests that Huo's policies were not popular with all of the Court. As Zhaodi grew up into adulthood, it is likely that he would have become more assertive so his death had come not a moment too soon.[33] However the death of the Emperor left the obvious problem of succession, given how few candidates acceptable to Huo were left.

The official history records that more than a month passed without any obvious candidate being found for the throne, before a former prison official named Bing Ji (丙吉, d. 55 BCE) remembered that eighteen years previously, when the Emperor Wu purged the Empress Wei and her family, Bing had closed the prison gates and refused to allow the innocent great-grandson of Wudi be put to death. Bing then cared for the sick infant, arranging for a wet nurse, as well as food, clothing and medicine out of his own funds.[34] By the time Zhaodi died, Bing was a client of Huo Guang and so was able to recommend the boy, known as Liu Bingyi (劉病已, 91–49 BCE) as a candidate for Emperor. Huo Guang lost no time in calling Bingyi to the capital and appointing him the next Emperor so that he would be known posthumously as Xuandi.[35]

With Xuandi's enthronement, one of the most unusual shifts of power in Chinese history had taken place. Although this story is repeated in all the surviving records, there is no particular reason to give it any credit. No one at the time questioned Liu Bingyi's origins. The very lack of any debate about the likelihood of Bingyi being a member of the Liu family makes it even more likely that he was not in fact rescued as a baby.[36] What is especially unusual about this story is that before he died, Emperor Wu had been informed that his direct orders had been flouted by Bing and his great-grandson had survived.[37] In the *Han Shu*, Wudi is said to have described Bing as heaven-sent for saving his great-grandson.[38] This gratitude was clearly limited as for the remaining years of his life, Wudi did not order his great-grandson to be brought back to the palace and raised at court. Nor did Zhaodi do so during the fourteen years he was Emperor. For eighteen years after the rest of his maternal family had been executed, Liu Bingyi was simply ignored by the rest of the Liu family. Even though the public security risk of an heir to the throne living outside the influence of the Imperial family is obvious, nothing was done to provide for his education or upbringing. It also appears that for eighteen years Bingyi did not think to mention to anyone that a member of the Liu family was living in the countryside. This is highly implausible.[39]

There are signs that the official historians knew something was unusual about Liu Bingyi. He was also described as being of an unusual physical appearance with hair on the soles of his feet. Prior to becoming Emperor, he had married a woman called Xu Pingjun (許平君, d. 71 BCE), a daughter of Xu Guanghan (許廣漢), a disgraced, and ostracized convict, over the objections of the woman's mother.[40] This suggests a very low social origin, as does the fact that he could not even afford to pay the bride price. There is no logical explanation why other women were not keen to marry this supposedly off-shoot member of the imperial family. Nor does the Liu family appear to have been involved in arranging or conducting the marriage for Bingyi which was also unusual.

If Bingyi was not a member of the Liu family, then the obvious question is who was he? It is likely that, just like his father-in-law, Bingyi was of very low social status, perhaps a slave, and given his unusual amount of body hair, perhaps even of foreign origin.[41] As implausible as the idea may sound, it is not as inherently unlikely as the story recorded in the official history.

Further circumstantial evidence is provided by the fact that for the rest of Huo's life, Xuandi did not ever challenge Huo's position at

Court. Huo and his family continued to dominate Han politics until Huo's death in 68 BCE. The emperor showed no signs of rebelling against his control at all. He even went so far as to rebuke his son for pointed criticisms of Huo's administration. One scholar, Li Yuandeng, even asserted that Xuandi's policies were Huo Guang's policies[42] When Huo died, Xuandi personally attended Huo's funeral, which was conducted in a grand style usually reserved for the imperial family.[43]

Shortly after Huo's death, Xuandi began to indicate he held a different view of the Huo family. He began to appoint some of Huo's powerful supporters, such as his sons-in-law to posts in the provinces.[44] Bing Ji, the prison official who had supposedly saved his life as an infant, was appointed to be Senior Tutor to the heir apparent and Imperial Counsellor in 67 BCE.[45] Next year, a friend of Bing's, Wei Xiang, started to submit memorials to the throne calling for the influence of the Huo family to be limited. Two years passed after Huo Guang's death before Xuandi felt strong enough to act. In 66 BCE, he had the entire Huo family arrested and executed all except for his wife, who was kept under house arrest before being allowed to commit suicide eight years later in 54 BCE.[46] The formal justification for this was the poisoning of Xuandi's Empress Xu several years earlier in 71 BCE, not by Huo Guang himself, but allegedly by his wife and without his knowledge.[47]

This long, complicated and involved process is hard to explain if Huo's loyalty to the Liu family was assumed and it led to some unusual conclusions. The Song dynasty historian Sima Guang even took Xuandi to task for his execution of Huo's entire family, accusing the emperor of ingratitude.[48] Modern scholarship tends to follow Sima Guang's lead and assign blame to Xuandi's supposedly difficult and unpleasant personality.[49] This conclusion has remained central to the traditional historical evaluation of Huo. In the classical literature, in so far as any blame was assigned to Huo Guang, it was for not properly educating his sons.[50] It is much more persuasive that the emperor's years of living in fear drove him to take revenge on Huo Guang's family so that finally he could rule.

The story of Xuandi is so implausible that it cannot be accepted uncritically and hence there is no reason to consider that Xuandi was a member of the Imperial Liu family. All over the world it was fairly common for imposters to attempt to take power, but it was very rare for them to succeed. This does not mean that it did not happen.[51] In the case of Xuandi, it would appear that China had an example of an imposter who successfully passed himself off as emperor. It is not hard to understand how this could have happened. The origins of Huo's power lay in the vacuum at the top of the Han government, which together with a strong degree of ruthlessness on the part of Huo and a large number of daughters he could marry to important people, allowed Huo to take control. Those sons-in-law often held major military commands within the capital. Thus, Huo Guang did not control the government 'by virtue of his title of [Da Sima]' but rather held the title because he controlled the government.[52] In fact, Huo largely invented the shape of late Western Han politics which revolved around the control of an infant emperor by his in-laws, who held nominal military titles despite rarely commanding any armies.[53] That this innovation began with Huo himself is likely because Huo's need for military recognition was probably less political or constitutional than personal. Huo was the half-brother of the much more famous and distinguished military commander Huo Qubing. Even though Huo Guang was originally a minor official in the Bureau of Remounts, who appears to have gotten his job only through the influence of his famous older brother, and who never served in the military, much less commanded any armies or campaigned on the steppe, he did feel the need to award himself a series of grandiose military titles greater than those of his brother.[54]

There are three features of the Han dynasty's political tradition that explain why the traditional histories ignore the problem with Huo Guang's career and the historical record that described it. The first flows from the purpose of history in traditional China. The role of the historian in China began with astronomers recording the omens that would signify the will of the ancestors and Sima Qian continued this tradition by assuming that history reflected the moral order of the universe. In theory Chinese dynasties came to power because the founding emperors were believed to be the most moral candidates. This is unlikely to have occurred often in Chinese history and instead Chinese historians endorsed the victors of the civil war. It is not exactly a circular argument where the objective test of Heaven's favour was to win power.[55] Rather, it is the assumption that because victory *should* go to the most righteous, the winner *must have been* the most moral candidate. Mencius said:

It was by benevolence that the three dynasties gained the throne, and by not being benevolent that they lost it…. If the sovereign be not benevolent, he cannot preserve the throne from passing from him. If the Head of a State be not benevolent, he cannot preserve his rule.[56]

Mencius specifically denied that the end of the Xia and Shang dynasties involved regicide as the last emperors of both dynasties had behaved so immorally that they had lost the right to rule.[57] For Huo, there is a direct parallel with Mencius' discussion of the legendary emperors Yao and Shun. Mencius said:

The Emperor can recommend a person to Heaven, but he cannot make Heaven give that man the Empire…. Yao recommended Shun to Heaven and Heaven accepted him…. [Yao] had [Shun] preside over the sacrifices, and the [spirits] enjoyed them. This means Heaven accepted him. He had him preside over the conduct of affairs, and the affairs were well managed, and the people felt satisfied. This means that the people accepted him. It was Heaven that gave the empire to him. It was the people that gave the empire to him.[58]

To someone raised in the Mencian tradition, Huo Guang could not make Zhaodi or Xuandi Emperor; only Heaven could. If Huo remained in power, ruling through puppet emperors, then those emperors must have retained Heavenly favour. No matter how Huo Guang behaved, as long as no evil omens appeared and disaster did not strike China, it must follow that he was accepted by Heaven. As Heaven had accepted these Emperors, to China's traditional historians it must follow, therefore, that Huo was loyal and Xuandi was the great-grandson of Wudi.

The key for Huo to continue was to carry on the pretence that he was a loyal minister. Unlike Wang Mang, Huo Guang ruled without many incidents because he did not upset the ritual arrangements of the Han dynasty. That is not to say that all the rituals were carried out properly. As Michael Loewe notes, there was a long break in the worship of Huangdi starting from Zhaodi ascending to the throne and continuing for twelve years of Xuandi's reign (that is, for six years after

Huo Guang died).[59] However, Huo did not overtly over-throw the Liu family nor introduce the worship of another set of ancestors into the Imperial Ancestral Temples. He may have reduced the emperor to a figurehead, but that figurehead remained at the ceremonial heart of the empire. Even though this period saw massive violations of Confucian norms, (especially by Huo Guang himself, who had, after all, somehow got his grand-daughter to help him condemn her father and paternal grandfather to death) as long as the roles of loyal minister and dutiful emperor correctly performed, everyone else was reasonably content. By allowing the correct rituals to be carried out, Huo not only managed to remain at the centre of Han politics, but he also managed to maintain a good reputation in the historical accounts. Facts that appear to contradict this narrative could be explained away as faults of his wife or his sons or otherwise ignored.

The second feature is the basis on which Chinese historians judge officials as 'good'. In the Chinese historical tradition, what made an official 'good' or not clearly revolved around loyalty and the rituals rather than economic competence or a good record on civil liberties. Even when the historical records seem to call out for Huo to be criticised, they almost never do. For instance, the *Han Shu* records that under Zhaodi, when Huo Guang was actually in charge of the government, expenditure by the government had grown out of control, with so many people dying of hunger that they were buried in mass graves, or eaten by dogs and pigs, with cases of cannibalism being recorded. At the same time, the imperial stables were said to contain horses that ate so much grain people worried about them being too fat.[60] Yet, no criticism is levelled at Huo himself.

The third feature is that it does appear that Chinese historians knew there was something unusual about Huo's reign. That something appeared to be wrong with this period is never openly stated in the sources, but it is repeatedly implied. The traditional historical accounts record many signs of something being wrong with the social order, but do not assign these faults to Xuandi's reign but to Zhaodi's. An example of this is the record of the other possible heir, Liu Dan, the Prince of Yan, questioning Zhaodi's parentage. As Zhaodi was a child who had grown up in the palace and had surviving relatives, not least his older sister, there was no reason to think that he was not who he said he was. Xuandi, on the other hand, had not one single surviving relative to attest to his origins, nor could anyone provide credible proof of his imperial background except the word of Bing Ji, who was dependent on Huo Guang. It is more likely that people were questioning Xuandi's parentage, but that the *Han Shu* could not record it given his descendants ruled to the end of the Former Han dynasty. In another omen, in the summer of 82 BCE, during the reign of Zhaodi, a man is supposed to have turned up at the palace gates claiming to be a long-lost heir of the Wei family. This is a remarkably short entry that provides no context or explanation stating only, 'In the summer, a man named Zhang Yannian (張延年) appeared at the Northern Tower [of the Imperial Palace] claiming to be Crown Prince Wei, he was denounced and executed.'[61] Although seemingly irrelevant, the compilers of the *Han Shu* thought it worth recording. Omens had a central place in the political ideology of the early Empire. As Confucius himself said, '[w]hen a nation or a family is about to perish, there are sure to be unlucky omens.'[62] The likely explanation is that the compilers recognised there was something unusual about this period, but it was not able to be spoken about openly. The only safe way this could be mentioned was to assign these events to the reign of Zhaodi who died childless and not to Xuandi who was the father of the remaining Emperors of the Former Han dynasty.

Although the compilers of the Han histories had ample evidence that there was something unusual in the story of Huo Guang and the emperors he served, they recorded it without drawing what seemed obvious conclusions. Even so, every now and then, there is evidence that Chinese historians have been well aware of another interpretation of Huo's life. When Wang Mang overthrew the Former Han dynasty he began by building a temple to Huo Guang, among others. Huo was clearly a useful historical precedent for him, through which he could signal his intentions and claim legitimacy. That signal could only be effective if everyone understood the true nature of Huo's power. The Emperor Shao (少帝, 406–424 CE) of the Liu Song dynasty (劉宋) accused his officials of wanting to act like Huo Guang. Shortly afterwards they did in fact remove him from power and enthroned his brother. The compilers of the *History of the Later Han dynasty* quote a letter which lists Huo with three other officials who had changed their loyalties.[63] That these instances were praised in the letter does not change the fact that what they did was morally ambiguous.

A generation later, under Xiandi's son, Emperor Yang, a court official named Yi Feng (翼奉), understood the lesson of Huo Guang's domination and so took the emperor to task for over-reliance on relatives of his wife and mother to provide officials. The *Han Shu* records that Yi said:

> In the ancient Royal courts, there had to be officials with the Imperial surname because of the intimacy of the family, as well as officials of other surnames to show the Emperor's wisdom. That is why a Sage King could rule the entire world. Those of the same surname would be close and so could be promoted easily. Those of a different surname were distant and so they would have difficulty [getting promoted]. The way to have a balance would be to have one official of the Imperial surname for every five with a different surname. Now you have no officials with the same surname. The Court is filled by the factions of the Consort families. They not only hold high positions, they are also extravagant. What will happen can be predicted from what happened with the Lü, Huo and Shangguan families. This is not the way to love the people, nor is it a way to leave your descendants a long-lasting government.[64]

The lesson of over-reliance on his in-laws was obvious and a possible solution was offered. The emperor does not seem to have listened, perhaps because reliance on his own relatives may have seemed a greater risk than relying on his wives' families.

The career of Huo Guang is an interesting example of the difference between the facts stated in an official public discourse and the common interpretation of those facts. Huo exploited the vacuum caused by Wudi's purges to rise from a minor bureaucratic post to dominate China to the extent that he could depose an emperor. By continually posing as a loyal official to the emperor, he was able to rule China as he pleased while committing numerous fundamental violations of Confucian moral norms. That normative pose was powerful enough to allow him to receive a favourable historical judgement for posterity. Historians have accepted Huo as a loyal minster even though there is ample reason to think otherwise and many hints that a different view of him was widely understood. Although it is not often stated clearly in the historical record, government officials clearly did pursue their own interests in direct opposition to the Emperors they claimed to serve. Chinese emperors, isolated in their 'Forbidden Cities,' had no one else to rely on apart from eunuchs and their relatives by marriage. This remained a fundamental feature of the post-Qin Imperial system, which remained until 1911.

ABOUT THE AUTHOR

Joseph Benjamin Askew studied at the University of Adelaide before completing his post-graduate studies at Monash University. In 2004 he was employed with the British Library before moving to the University of Oxford. Since 2007 he has been a Lecturer in Modern Chinese History at the University of Nottingham Ningbo China. E-mail: Joseph.askew@nottingham.edu.cn

Endnotes

1 S. E. Finer, *The History of Government from the Earliest Times* (Oxford: Oxford University Press, 1997, 2003), p. 470.

2 For a discussion of the Zhou dynasty system idealized by both Confucius and Mencius see Yu-lan Fung, *A History of Chinese Philosophy, Volume I, The period of the Philosophers (from the beginnings to circa 100 B.C.)*, trans. Derk Bodde (Princeton University Press, 1983), pp. 108-111

3 Michael Loewe, 'The Former Han Dynasty' in *The Cambridge History of China, The Ch'in and Han Empires, 221 B.C. – A.D. 220* (Cambridge University Press, 1995), p. 184; Michael Loewe, *The Government of the Qin and Han Empires, 221 BCE – 220 CE* (Indianapolis: Hackett Publishing, 2006), pp. 96-7.

4 It is perhaps unlikely many 20 year-olds would have observed the full three years of mourning before attempting to produce an heir with a palace full of young women. It is not often asked how seriously the proper mourning period was observed in traditional China.

5 Ban Gu 班固 et al. *History of the Han Dynasty* 漢書(Beijing 北京: Zhonghua Publishing Company 中华书局, First Published in 1962, Reprinted in 2009), *chuan* 68, p. 2946. This 'about 200' is the same number of officials, servants and slaves Liu He is said to have brought to Chang'an with him. Presumably Huo Guang had Liu He's entire retinue executed. This seems to be the assumption of the modern Chinese literature. See Liu Zeyong, 刘则永, 中兴名臣霍光, 文史知识, no.7, (1999), p. 100. It is likely that By 'not acting

decisively' Ban Gu was implying that they did not take firm control of the government.

6 Ban Gu et al. *History of the Han Dynasty, chuan* 63, pp. 2769-2770

7 Ibid., *chuan* 68, p. 2933

8 Carney T. Fisher, *The Chosen One: Succession and Adoption in the Court of Ming Shizong* (Boston: Allen and Unwin, 1990), p. 9.

9 Although the Soviet Union tried to promote workers, until the 1950s there must have been thousands of East German officials who had worked for the German Emperor, the Weimar Republic, the Nazis and then the Communists, such as the former Prussian cavalry officer and commander of the tank forces of the East German Volksarmee Arno Ernst Max von Lenski. Perhaps the best example of an 'amoral' technocrat is Wernher von Braun, made famous by Tom Lehrer's satirical song.

10 When the Han dynasty was created, Liu Bang handed out roughly half the territory to his relatives or his generals as personal fiefs. By the time of Wudi, most of these had been taken back under central control and so the Emperor's relatives did not command territory and armies. The distinction is likely to have been important in the difference between the success of the Empress Lü and Wang Mang.

11 The presence of childhood friends was normal in most other countries and they often took positions at court. Usually Chinese Emperors did not have the source of loyal ministers in West – Churchmen. Under rulers who lacked Confucian legitimacy, especially women such as Wu Zetian and non-Han dynasties, Buddhist monks served as officials and advisors.

12 Finer defends eunuchs against the traditional contempt found in most historical records at some length. See Finer, *The History of Government from the Earliest Times,* pp. 300-301, pp. 492-495, pp. 641-643, pp. 704-705, pp. 786-792.

13 Ibid., pp. 492-493.

14 The *Han Shu* says that in Wudi's time the number of palace women was measured in the thousands. While he certainly created some famous eunuchs, he does not seem to have employed many.

15 Finer, *The History of Government from the Earliest Times*, p. 480.

16 Michael Loewe, *Crisis and Conflict in Han China* (Abingdon: Routledge: 2005), p. 41, p. 86. Ban Gu et al. *History of the Han Dynasty, chuan* 45, p. 2178, *HS* 2009, *chuan* 63, pp. 2742-2744. Compare with Ban Gu et al. *History of the Han Dynasty*, pp.

208-209. It would have been impossible to dispute evidence that is produced by a shaman through the interpretation of her own dream. Such procedures would not result in good morale among officials.

17 See Loewe, *Crisis and Conflict in Han China*, p. 40. As Jiang had, in the previous year, arrested, tried and executed one of the Emperor's nephews for incest and immorality, it seems a reasonable supposition that Wudi intended this investigation to be of his immediate family.

18 Ibid., pp. 40-46.

19 Michael Loewe refers to Huo Guang being part of the Empress Wei's faction and being 'related by marriage', see Loewe 1995, p. 107. In fact, they were not related by marriage as Huo Qubing's father did not marry his mother. Huo Qubing grew up in the Wei household, not among the Huo family. The fact that Huo Guang was not purged with the rest of the Wei family suggests that the Emperor did not consider him related to them. In the *Han Shu*, Ban Gu put Huo Qubing's biography with his mother's other son Wei Qing, not his father's other son Huo Guang.

20 The *Han Shu*, *chuan* 7, p. 217 stresses the unusual fortune of the Lady Zhao. Although the reasons for doing so are never made clear and omens around imperial births are fairly common, Wudi was over 60 years-old when this son was born after a fourteen-month pregnancy.

21 Remarkably little is known about the Lady Chen, including her date of birth and real name. She is usually known only by her baby name 阿嬌.

22 Loewe, *Crisis and Conflict in Han China*, p. 88. See also Ban Gu et al. *History of the Han Dynasty*, *chuan* 97a, p. 3948.

23 Loewe, *Crisis and Conflict in Han China*, p. 45.

24 Michael. Loewe 'The Former Han Dynasty' in Denis Twitchett and Michael Loewe (eds.), *The Cambridge History of China, The Ch'in and Han Empires, 221 B.C. – A.D. 220* (Cambridge: Cambridge University Press, first published 1986, reprinted 1995), p. 178.

25 Ban Gu et al. *History of the Han Dynasty*, *chuan* 68, p. 217.

26 Ban Gu et al. *History of the Han Dynasty*, *chuan* 7, p. 217.

27 Ban Gu et al. *History of the Han Dynasty*, *chuan* 68, p. 2933. Although his name has the same pinyin, this Wang Mang is a different Wang Mang to the one mentioned elsewhere who founded the short-

lived Xin dynasty in 9 CE.

28 For the Seals Incident, see above and ibid., p. 2933.

29 Loewe, *Crisis and Conflict in Han China*, p. 57.

30 Liu Zeyong, 刘则永 'Famous Officials during China's rise: Huo Guang, 中兴名臣霍光,*Knowledge of Literature and History* 文史知识,*chuan* 7, (1999), p. 100.

31 There is no clear or definitive meaning to the verb used in this passage but it seems to imply that these women were sacrificed.

32 Ban Gu *et al. History of the Han Dynasty, chuan* 72, pp. 3070-3071.

33 There could have been a small but reasonable suspicion of murder given the convenience of his death. This criticism comes from the reign of Yuandi, the next Emperor and the son of Xuandi. It is a very unusual reference to wrong-doings in an emperor who is usually praised for his good behaviour. He was a child of eight when he became Emperor. Chinese historians, following Chinese officials, usually praise child emperors perhaps because they often do what they are told by their officials.

34 Ban Gu et al. *History of the Han Dynasty, chuan* 74, p. 3142.

35 Ibid., p. 3143.

36 The modern scholarship is remarkably uncritical of this account. For an example see Liu, 'Famous Officials during China's rise: Huo Guang', p. 101. It is not uncommon for historical records to fail to discuss unusual events. The lack of any discussion of Liu Bingyi's claims is unexpected given how important his origins were.

37 Ban Gu et al. *History of the Han Dynasty, chuan* 74, p. 3142.

38 Ibid., Wudi's comment is likely to be a retrospective rehabilitation of what Bing Ji did. After all, he directly defied the Emperor's order. At some point it is likely that this became embarrassing and so the historical record was altered to make it appear acceptable.

39 There is only one other obvious case that is similar to this. The Ming Emperor Chenghua (成华, r. 1464-1487) married his wet-nurse, the Lady Wan (萬貞兒). The Lady Wan is said to have killed all the Emperor's children or forced their mothers to abort. One child, born to a lowly slave girl, was, supposedly, hidden by the Emperor's former Empress, the Lady Wu, raised in secret and so survived. The difference here is that this child was hidden for just five years and raised entirely within the palace under the supervision of his family. See John King Fairbank, Denis Crispin Twitchett and Frederick W. Mote (eds.), *Cambridge History of China: Volume 7, The Ming*

Dynasty, 1368-1644. Part I (Cambridge: Cambridge University Press, First Published 1988, Reprinted 2004), pp. 346-348

40 The *Han Shu* reports, without apparent irony, that an official called Zhang Anshi had prevented his older brother from marrying his daughter to Liu Bingyi because it would have been too great an honour for the Zhang family. So, he arranged this marriage to the daughter of a castrated convicted thief instead. This does not seem plausible. See also Loewe, *Crisis and Conflict in Han China*, p. 124.

41 This would not be all that unusual for the period, given the rise of Jin Midi, a Xiongnu slave and that the Princess Eyi, sister to the Emperor, had a lover called Ding Wairen (丁外人) which suggests foreign origin.

42 '宣帝之政治，即霍光之政治'. Liu, 'Famous Officials during China's rise: Huo Guang', p. 98, quoting Li Yuandeng李源澄, 泰漢史, 第6.

43 Loewe, 'The Former Han Dynasty', p. 186.

44 Loewe, *Crisis and Conflict in Han China*, p. 135, n. 61.

45 For actually saving Xuandi as a child, Bing had been rewarded extremely ignobly with a minor noble title equivalent to a knighthood in that it was not hereditary and carried no stipend. His proper reward only came after Huo's death. See Loewe. *Crisis and Conflict in Han China*, p. 122, p. 136, p. 147.

46 This Empress was in the unusual position of being the adopted daughter-in-law to her sister's daughter. There was some violence from the Huo family, but it appears to have been after the purge. For instance, one of Huo's sons-in-law was accused of trying to kill Xuandi. *HS*, 88:3600. '是时，霍氏外孙代郡太守任宣坐谋反诛，宣子章为公车丞，亡在渭城界中，夜玄服入庙，居郎间，执戟立庙门，待上至，欲为逆。'

47 Loewe, 'The Former Han Dynasty', p. 186.

48 Sima Guang司馬光', *Comprehensive Mirror to Aid in Government* 资治通鉴(Beijing 北京: Zhonghua Publishing Company 中华书局, 2007), 卷第二十五【汉纪十七】, pp. 287-289.

49 For instance, see Song Chao宋超, '霍氏之祸，萌于骖乘" 发微 – 宣帝与霍氏家族关系探讨；史学月刊, Song Chao宋超, 'Exploration on the Relations between Xuan Di and Huo Family 霍氏之祸，萌于骖乘 发微–宣帝与霍氏家族关系探讨. *Historical Studies Monthly* 史学月刊. 5, 2000, pp. 26-36.

50 For instance, the *Song Shu* contains a fairly rare record of a joke

where someone recommends reading about Huo's life. See Tuo Tuo脱脱,*et al. History of the Song Dynasty* 宋史。(Beijing 北京: Zhonghua Publishing Company 中华书局, 2000), 列傳四十，寇准傳，pp. 7776-7777. This makes the standard criticism of Huo that he was rude and uneducated. The *Ming Shilu* contains praise for Huo's achievements but condemns him for being too attached to his wife and failing to raise his children properly. See *MSL*, 大明太祖高皇帝實錄，卷之一百四十。

51 Herodotus has preserved an account of the rise of Darius, the emperor of Persia that simply cannot be true and is widely disbelieved in the modern literature. See Herodotus, *The Histories* Book 3, pp. 61-79, trans. Robin Waterfield, (Oxford University Press 2008), 195-204. Darius seems to have thought other people might have doubted his version as he left dozens of inscriptions proclaiming his right to be Emperor, including the famous rock carving at Behistun. See also Finer *Government*, pp. 289-290.

52 Loewe, *Crisis and Conflict in Han China,* p. 258. Loewe (2005, p. 134) elsewhere recognises that this title was purely honorary.

53 It is worth noting that Huo's power came before he married his daughter to the Emperor. That is, his daughter married the Emperor because he was powerful, rather than Huo being powerful because his daughter was married to the Emperor.

54 The title of Marshall of State (大司馬) was first awarded to Huo Guang's half-brother Huo Qubing and his uncle Wei Qing. Huo's appropriation of this title seems to have worked. The Song-era *New History of the Tang*, by Ouyang Xiu and Song Qi included Huo Guang with the famous military commanders Xiao He Zhang Liang and Huo Qubing. See Ouyang Xiu 歐陽修 and Song Qi 宋祁. *The New History of the Tang* 新唐書 (Beijing: Zhonghua Publishing Company 中华书局，2000), 列傳第六十五卷一百四十，崔苗二裴呂, pp. 3653-3654. '漢興，蕭何、張良、霍去病、霍光以文武大略，佐漢致太平，一名不盡其善，乃有文終、文成、景桓、宣成之諡。'

55 Finer, *The History of Government from the Earliest Times*, p. 456.

56 Mencius, "The Works of Mencius", *The Chinese Classics*, Volumes I & II, trans. James Legge, (Taipei, SMC Publishing, 2001), Book IV, Part I, Chapter VI, 1-3, pp. 293-294.

57 Mencius 1B:8 in Chan Wing-tsit, *A Source Book in Chinese Philosophy*, (Princeton University Press, 1962), 62. Mencius 2001,

Book I, Part II, Chapter VIII, 3, p. 167.

58 Mencius 5A:5 in Chan, *A Source Book in Chinese Philosophy*, pp. 77-78. Mencius 2001, Book 5, Part I, Chapter V, 1-6, pp. 354-356.

59 Loewe, *Crisis and Conflict in Han China*, pp. 169-70.

60 Ban Gu et al. *History of the Han Dynasty, chuan* 72, p. 3070.

61 Ban Gu et al. *History of the Han Dynasty, chuan* 7, p. 222, '夏陽男子張延年詣北闕，自稱衛太子，誣罔，要斬'. Loewe, *The Government of the Qin and Han Empires* pp. 70-71.

62 Chan, *A Source Book in Chinese Philosophy*, p. 246.

63 Fan Ye 范曄 *et al. History of the Later Han Dynasty* 後漢書(Beijing 北京: Zhonghua Publishing Company 中华书局, First Published in 1965, Re-printed in 2014), 17, pp. 642-643 卷十七第七馮岑賈列傳，'昔微子去殷而入周，項伯畔楚而歸漢，周勃迎代王而黜少帝，霍光尊孝宣而廢昌邑。彼皆畏天知命，睹存亡之符，見廢興之事，故能成功於一時，垂業於萬世也' Weizi（微子）was the brother of the last King of the Shang dynasty who accepted the fief of Song (宋) under the Zhou dynasty. Zhou Bo (周勃, d. 169 BCE) was an elderly general who rebelled against the Empress Lü's puppet emperor, Houshao, and placed the Prince of Dai on the throne as Wendi. Xiang Bo (項伯, d. 192 BCE) was a noble from Chu who prevented his nephew killing the first Emperor of the Han dynasty Liu Bang.

64 Ban Gu et al. *History of the Han Dynasty, chuan* 75, pp. 3173-3174. Although it is not openly stated, Huo Guang is compared with the Empress Lü and so showing, again, there was another level of understanding of Huo's record at the time.

Section 2:
Considering the Present

Section 2
Considering the Insect

DRAGON MARBLE RELIEFS FROM THE IMPERIAL PALACES, TEMPLES AND MAUSOLEUMS IN MING AND QING DYNASTY

BY JIMMY NUO ZANG

ABSTRACT

The purpose of this article is to identify and date the marble carved dragon artefacts found in the imperial palaces and mausoleums around the city of Beijing. Dragon marble reliefs from the early Ming dynasty to the end of the Qing dynasty have been photographed, studied and analysed. Research has focussed on existing dragon marble reliefs located in the Forbidden City, the Temple of Heaven, the Ming Tombs and the Eastern and Western Qing Tombs. In general terms, the dragon form and style evolved from a bold and powerful formation of the early Ming dynasty to a slender, powerless and snake-liked formation of the late Qing dynasty over a period of five centuries. The most significant challenge encountered in this research was the identification of artefacts that were either original or represented a later carved replacement, due to the fact that certain buildings in those locations have been either modified, repaired or completely re-constructed following catastrophic fires or other purposes. Therefore, analysis and comparison of both existing relics and the relevant historical records of the Forbidden City, the Temple of Heaven, the Ming Tombs and the Eastern and Western Qing Tombs was undertaken. Artefacts where date of origin is indisputable were used to compare with carvings where dating is uncertain. Based on the author's research, a conclusion has been reached that, dragon reliefs carved in a particular reign may comprise more than one design scheme that ranges from the middle Ming to the end of Qing dynasty: the one that imitated an early period and then one with its typical style of the period. The existence of imitated artefacts is due to the fact that a similar design scheme was adopted in order to maintain a consistent appearance of the overall building when it was repaired or altered during a later reign. However, imitated (later-copied) examples can still be distinguished from the original by the features of the dragon details and the cloud formation design. Furthermore, the high-relief carving technique was transformed to a low-relief carving technique from early Ming to late Qing dynasty, with the only exception being the Yongzheng reign of the Qing dynasty.

The dragon motif

The dragon is the most important symbol of Chinese imperial authority. The five clawed Lung Dragon was utilized as the personal emblem of the emperor across virtually all dynasties.[1] The Imperial Throne is referred to as the 'Dragon Throne', thus giving further evidence of the importance of dragon iconography in Chinese culture. Dragon designs feature extensively in the marble reliefs and carvings, on the ornamental tops of newels, walkways, columns and archways of imperial palaces, temples and imperial mausoleums, such as at the Forbidden City, the Temple of Heaven and the Royal Tombs of Ming and Qing dynasty in Beijing.

The marble stone

The marble used for most of the imperial carvings from the Ming and Qing dynasty was excavated in Da Shi Wo (大石窝), Fangshan District of Beijing, approximately 70 kilometers from the city. This particular marble, also known as 'Han White Jade' (汉白玉), was exclusively reserved for imperial usage. During the Ming and Qing dynasties, palaces and tombs were visual evidence of imperial sovereignty. High ranking officials were therefore specifically assigned to the supervision of the extraction of the precious marble.[2] The marble was discovered buried in a pond called Baiyutang (白玉塘) in the production area, and the extraction work was therefore extremely labour-intensive, particularly as the water in the pond had to be drained before the marble could be removed.[3] Production costs were therefore very high and as a result, no one could afford using such an expensive building material except the imperial family. This special white marble was relatively soft with a snow-white colour. It was the best form of marble for carving in China during the Ming and Qing dynasty.[4]

The marble carving techniques

The marble carving techniques including three-dimensional carving, high/low relief carving, line engraving and skeleton carving.[5] The carved artefacts discussed in this article were executed by the high/low relief carving technique. The process of relief carving involves removing the marble from a flat or curved surface, in such a way that an object appears to rise out of the marble surface.

THE FORBIDDEN CITY故宫

The Forbidden City is a palace complex situated in central Beijing. The buildings comprised the former Chinese Imperial Palace from 1420 in the Ming dynasty (Yongle emperor r.1402-1424), when the Imperial Capital moved from Nanjing to Beijing, to the end of the Qing dynasty in 1911 (Xuantong emperor r. 1908-1911).[6] Today, it is the home of the Palace Museum. Constructed between 1406 to1420, the complex covers 780,000 square meters.[7] The Forbidden City was declared a World Heritage Site in 1987 and is listed by UNESCO as the largest collection of preserved ancient wooden structures in the world.[8]

Before undertaking an analysis of the dragon reliefs and carvings from the Forbidden City, a thorough understanding of the site's development history is of great relevance because not all of the existing marble relics in the Forbidden City represent the period when the building was originally constructed. For instance, certain aspects of the architectures within the Forbidden City has been modified, or re-constructed, at specific times in its history due to fire damage that required major renovation of the structure. Therefore, the date that the architectural compound was initially completed does not necessarily correspond to the dating of the existing marble relics found in situ today.

In order to have an accurate periodisation, a historical record check of the architecture is necessary before being able to conclude of date of construction for such marble carvings. A comparison of the patterns of various dragon reliefs and carvings is another way to cross-verify or date a piece. The dragon patterns evolved over time and dating can be concluded from the aspects of the dragon's features and the cloud formations. The dragon form evolved from a primitive and powerful body with large and strong claws of the early Ming dynasty to a bloated, powerless with small and skinny claws during the late Qing dynasty. Furthermore, based on the author's direct inspection, newly-carved architectural marble components also can be identified and these artefacts would have been carved during the maintenance and repair work anywhere during the Republic period (1911-1949) up until today. This is not only the case in the Forbidden City; similar newly-carved artefacts have also been observed in the Temple of Heaven and the Imperial Tombs of Ming and Qing dynasty.

The Ornamental Columns 华表

The Ornamental Columns were constructed in pairs, one in front of the Gate of Heavenly Peace (tiananmen), and the other pair at the back. These Ornamental Columns have also been installed in the four corners of the 'Monument of Merits' at the Imperial Tombs and it is part of the traditional form of the architecture. These columns are usually made of the best grade of marble material, which is the Han white jade. The lower grade of marble, the greenish white marble, was used to make traditional sumeru-styled architectural pedestal (须弥座) beneath the palace architecture.[9] On the marble newels, around the Ornamental Columns, a rising dragon was engraved on the tubular surface and a pair of walking dragons were engraved on the base section of the marble newel. The Ornamental Columns were surrounded by marble newels which were engraved with dragon reliefs. The columns in front of the Gate of Heavenly Peace were built during the Yongle period (1402-1424 - Ming Dynasty).[10] Although parts of the newel pillars were damaged by the Eight-Nation Allied Army following the Boxer Rebellion in 1900 (late Qing period),[11] the majority of the reliefs and carvings survived the war. The dragon reliefs on the marble newels are typical of Yongle period. The dragon form from this period has its own distinct characteristics. Firstly, the long hair of the dragon curled upwards; secondly, the dragon's mouth is considerable thicker and longer in front of the nose, especially the upper lip; thirdly, the body and legs are in a strong live form and there is almost no hair at the end of the tail; lastly, the *ruyi* shaped cloud (如意云) form has narrow and curved tails in different directions. After

Figure 1: Walking Dragon Relief on the Base Section of the Newels from Yongle Reign of the Ming Dynasty. Photo by Jimmy Zang.

the Yongle period, the dragon's body became slimmer and less strong in form. The cloud formation also changed markedly in the Qing dynasty (1644-1911). The dragon patterns have evolved for thousands of years in China and each period represents its unique character. This author believes this evolution of pattern reflects the inheritance, aesthetic standard and cognitive process of the descendants.

Hall of imperial peace钦安殿

The Hall of Imperial Peace was built above a traditional sumeru-styled architectural pedestal (须弥座), which was surrounded by the ornamental tops of the newels with carved dragon reliefs during the Yongle period of the Ming dynasty.[12] According to the author's research of historical records, several additional surrounding walls were added adjacent to the hall in the 14th year of the Jiajing reign (1535) and three attached rooms were built as an extension to the existing hall during the Qianlong period (1735-1796) but for some reason were dismantled at a later date.[13]

Figure 2: The Ornamental Top of the newel (left) and the Walking Dragon Relief on the Marble newel (right), both are from Yongle reign of the Ming dynasty.
Photo by Jimmy Zang.

The ornamental tops and newels (Figure 2) are decorated with carved dragon reliefs. These dragon reliefs are dated to the Yongle period and are found at the Hall of Imperial Peace.[14] They are considered one of the best marble carving art in the Forbidden City.[15] Both the dragon and cloud formations are very similar to the ones found on the Ornamental Columns (Figure 1) in front of the Gate of Heavenly Peace.

The three main halls of state 故宫三大殿

Since the initial completion of the Forbidden City in 1420, three fire related accidents have destroyed several of the halls in the years 1421, 1557 and 1597.[16] Reconstruction work continued throughout the Ming and Qing dynasties. According to the author's research, the main causes for the fires are due, but not limited, to the following five factors:[17]

1. The main construction material of the halls was bricks and wood;
2. Fire caused by lightning strikes due to the height of the halls;
3. Misuse of fire, particularly during winter;
4. Fires related to arson;
5. Deficiency of firewalls.

The wooden structure of the halls, of course could not survive a fire-related accident. However, readers may be curious about the fate of the marble newels and imperial walkways. This assumption can be verified by a fire accident at Qingquan Temple of Hebei province on 13 December 1980, where more than 30 pieces of stone carving works were destroyed after the fire.[18] This has been cross-verified by the author in accordance with the existing marble relics from the current Hall of Supreme Harmony, Hall of Central Harmony and Hall

Figure 3: The Ornamental Top of the Newel, Kangxi reign of Qing dynasty (left) and the Imperial Walkway, Qianlong reign of the Qing dynasty (right).
Photo by Jimmy Zang.

of Preserving Harmony as the majority of the marble relics found in these three halls are considered to have been engraved in the Qing dynasty, based on the design of the reliefs and carving works.

After comparing the dragon patterns which feature on the marble newels of these three halls, the author believes that the majority of the dragon reliefs were engraved in Kangxi and Qianlong period of the Qing dynasty (1661-1722 and 1736-1795). The ornamental top illustrated (Figure 3 left) is typical of the Kangxi period, which functioned as a transitional period from Ming to Qing dynasties. The overall design pattern is still similar to the late Ming style, especially the cloud formation with *ruyi* shape, but the dragon form is inclined to the Qing style, particularly with the less powerful body and claws. The dragon reliefs on the imperial walkway are of the same Qianlong style that could be cross-verified by similar designs found in Yuling Tomb (for Qianlong Emperor) of the Eastern Qing Tombs. During this period, the dragon's hair was often curled and angled backwards with lined cloud formations (Figure 3 right).

Pavilion of literary profundity 文渊阁

The Pavilion of Literary Profundity was dedicated to the storage of court books. The architecture was modelled after Tianyi Pavilion (天一阁) of Ningbo, Zhejiang Province. The Qianlong emperor ordered the building of the imperial library within the Forbidden City in 1774. The pavilion was built in 1776 and the name 'Pavilion of Literary Profundity' was given personally by the Qianlong Emperor. The Complete Library of the Four Branches of Books (四库全书) was housed in the pavilion immediately after its completion.[19] A pond was also created in front of the pavilion, which functioned as a precaution in case of fire and the library was surrounded by marble newels with dragon-carved ornamental on the top. After a review of the relevant historical records, no record of fire accident or amendment to the building could be found. The present marble newels (Figure 4) therefore are considered to be of the same period as the completion of the building. Comparing the dragon form of the Ming style with the one of the Qianlong period, the more recent example has lost some of the power in its shape, and the claws are found to be less visible and of an emaciated form. Furthermore, a lower relief carving method had been utilized during the Qing dynasty. The cloud formations, among the coiled dragons, carved during this period also has certain

Figure 4: The Ornamental Top of the Newel, Qianlong reign of the Qing dynasty. Photo by Jimmy Zang.

unique characteristics. The claw of the dragon has reduced in size, long spikes were added at the end of the dragon tail and the dragon nose was considerably enlarged. Unlike individual *ruyi* shaped cloud patterns from Ming dynasty, this connected cloud formation is widely found in imperial architecture created during the Qianlong reign. An example of this is the Palace of Compassion and Tranquility (慈宁宫) within the Forbidden City, which was initially built in 1536 and rebuilt in 1769 (34th year of the Qianlong reign).[20] However, based on the author's research, there are further variations of dragon style and cloud formation during Qianlong reign, and this will be discussed later in this article.

THE TEMPLE OF HEAVEN 天坛

The Temple of Heaven is an imperial complex of religious buildings situated in the southeastern part of central Beijing. The complex was visited by the Emperors of the Ming and Qing dynasties for annual ceremonies of rituals and prayers to the Heaven for good harvest. The temple complex was constructed between 1406 and 1420 during the reign of the Yongle emperor. The complex was extended, and renamed the 'Temple of Heaven' during the reign of the Jiajing Emperor (1521-1567).[21] The Temple of Heaven was designated as a UNESCO World Heritage site in 1998.[22]

THE IMPERIAL HALL OF HEAVEN皇乾殿

The Imperial Hall of Heaven was known as 'the Heavenly Warehouse' at the Altar of Prayer for Grains. The tablet of 'The God of Heaven' and the tablets of the emperor's ancestors were displayed and worshipped during the ceremony held in the Hall of Prayer for Good Harvests where they were stored. The Imperial Hall of Heaven was first built in 1545 (the 24th year of the Jiajing reign), and the hall placard bears an inscription in the handwriting of Emperor Jiajing of the Ming dynasty.[23]

Three types of ornamental tops from the marble newels (Figure 5) in the Imperial Hall of Heaven were identified for study by the author. The left ornamental top (Figure 5) has identical features of Yongle style from the Ming dynasty. The dragon has a lithe and strong body coiled among *ruyi* shaped clouds. Furthermore, the dragon relief occupied the upper half of the ornamental top. The middle ornamental top, in the author's opinion, should be dated to Jiajing reign of the Ming dynasty. It possesses a typical dragon form similar to the dragon reliefs on the walkway in the Hall of Prayer for Good

Figure 5: Yongle reign of the Ming dynasty (left), Jiajing reign of the Ming dynasty (middle) and Qianlong reign of the Qing dynasty (right). Photo by Jimmy Zang.

Harvest (Figure 6 Right) and the Marble Archway (Figure 8 Upper-left) at the Ming Tombs. The dragon's head is proportionally larger compared to the ones made during the Yongle reign. Furthermore, its cloud formation differs from the typical Yongle style (Figure 2 Left and Figure 5 Left), particularly in the gap between each layer of the *ruyi* cloud. Its cloud formation is similar to the ornamental top, with the phoenix relief (Figure 9 Upper-middle), at the Xiaoling Tomb of the Imperial Eastern Qing Tombs, which has been identified by scholars as having been created in Jiajing period.[24] The assessment of the right ornamental top (Figure 5) is based upon the author's opinion as a later copy from the Qianlong reign of the Qing dynasty. Regarding the aspect of the cloud formation, the last layer of the *ruyi* cloud is not as big as the ones made during the Ming dynasty. The dragon arms and claws are also much slimmer. The nose of the dragon has become noticeably bigger whilst the hair has become shorter and has lost the impression of flowing. This conclusion can be cross-verified by comparing the ornamental tops (Figure 7 Right) at the Imperial Vault of Heaven, which was rebuilt in the Qianlong reign. The dragon style and cloud formation are of the same pattern.

THE HALL OF PRAYER FOR GOOD HARVEST祈年殿

The Hall of Prayer for Good Harvests was first built in the year 1420 (the 18th year of Yongle reign of the Ming dynasty) and is named as The Hall of Great Prayer (大祈殿). This hall was dismantled in 1540 (the 19th year of Jiajing reign) and rebuilt in 1545 (the 24th year of Jiajing reign) with the reconstruction transforming the rectangular hall into a magnificent triple-gabled circular building. The building was renamed the 'Hall of Great Enjoyment' by the Jiajing Emperor after its completion, and the triple gables were roofed with blue, yellow and green-glazed tiles to reflect the harmony among the Heaven, Earth and Creations. The Hall of Great Enjoyment was based on three levels of marble stone pedestals with carved newels around it. The Hall was further amended in Qianlong reign by applying a blue-glazed roof tiles to replace the former triple gables. Furthermore, the building was renamed 'The Hall of Prayer for Good Harvests.' The building burned down due to fire caused by a lightning in 1889. The current building was rebuilt several years later.[25] Although, as documented in an earlier section of this article, the author assumes that the marble carvings and reliefs did not survive in their entirety after a fire accident. The

Figure 6: The Ornamental Top of the Newels (left) and the Imperial Walkway (right), Both from Jiajing Reign of the Ming Dynasty.
Photo by Jimmy Zang.

author has compared and examined the patterns of the present marble newels with the ones from the Yongling Tomb. The author believes the majority of the current ones are from the Jiajing reign when the reconstruction work was completed in 1545. The considerable distance between the building and marble newels could be the reason that the majority of the carved marble survived the fire and the author assumes the reconstruction work after the fire in 1889 did not involve the reproduction of the marble newels.

From the author's observations and comparison of examples, both the ornamental tops of the newels and the imperial walkway (Figure 6) appear to have been created in the Jiajing reign of the Ming dynasty. This typical design combining the dragon motif, cloud and fretwork background has never been found in any previous period. Based on the author's study, this particular fretwork background appeared in Jiajing reign and continued to be used in Wanli reign of Ming dynasty (1572-1620). This fretwork design has also been found in the Changling and Dingling Imperial Ming Tombs. The author also believes this cloud design with tails pointing at different directions (四合如意云) is of typical style used from the middle Ming till the early Qing dynasty. A similar styled imperial walkway (Figure 7 Left) was also found at the Imperial Vault of Heaven, but it seems to be a later copy from the middle Qing dynasty. The difference can be identified by the cloud formation and the shape of the dragon. Unlike the Ming cloud design

(Figure 6 Right) with tails pointing at different directions, one of the Qing cloud formation (Figure 7 Left) has changed to a continuously floating type. The hair of the dragon has changed from forward curled above the head like a torch light (Figure 6 Right) to backward curled type (Figure 7 Left). Furthermore, the spike-shaped dragon tail (Figure 7 Left) was adopted in Qing dynasty and this particular design had never existed in the Ming dynasty.

The imperial vault of heaven 皇穹宇

The Imperial Vault of Heaven was built in 1530 (the 9th year of Jiajing reign of the Ming dynasty). It is of a round shape with a double-gable and named the 'Hall of Appeasing Gods' (泰神殿). It was the main hall of the Celestial Treasure House of the Circular Mound Altar, housing the Gods' tablets to be used at the ceremony of worshipping Heaven. It was renamed the 'Imperial Vault of Heaven' in 1538 (the 17th year of Jiajing reign of the Ming dynasty) and rebuilt into its present shape in 1752 (the 17th year of Qianlong reign of the Qing dynasty).[26]

From a general perspective, the imperial walkway with dragon reliefs (Figure 7 Left) at the Imperial Vault of Heaven is very similar to the one found at Hall of Prayer for Good Harvests (Figure 6 Right). These marble walkways contain the same elements of dragon, cloud and fretwork background. However, on examination, the cloud formation of the imperial walkway with dragon reliefs (Figure 7 Left)

Figure 7: The Imperial Walkway (left) and The Ornamental Top of the Newel (right), Both from Qianlong reign of the Qing dynasty.
Photo by Jimmy Zang.

at the Imperial Vault of Heaven appears to share a similar pattern to the imperial walkway (Figure 3 Right) in the Forbidden City. Furthermore, the dragons engraved on both of the imperial walkways share the same characteristics regarding body type, hair style, tail and claws. By reviewing the history of this building, it was rebuilt into its present state in the 17th year of the Qianlong reign of the Qing dynasty.[27] The author concludes that the dragon-engraved walkway (Figure 7 Left) found at the Imperial Vault of Heaven is from the Qianlong reign of the Qing dynasty. Similar designs are not found elsewhere that are from the Qianlong reign and the author believes the design was directly copied from the pattern on the Imperial Walkway (Figure 6 Right) at the Hall of Prayer for Good Harvests to make the design consistent with that of the Temple of Heaven. The ornamental top (Figure 7 Right) at the Imperial Vault of Heaven is of the same style as the one at the Imperial Hall of Heaven (Figure 5 Right) and therefore, also dates to the Qianlong reign.

THE CIRCULAR MOUND ALTAR圜丘

The Circular Mound Altar was constructed in 1530 (the 9th year of Jiajing reign of the Ming dynasty). The altar served as a place for holding the ceremony of worshipping the heaven at the winter solstice each year, and was popularly known as the 'Heaven Worshipping Terrace.' The round terrace was first covered with blue-glazed slabs and balustrades. These were later changed to green stone slabs surrounded by marble newels with ornamental tops and dragon motifs when the altar was enlarged in 1749 (the 14th year of Qianlong reign).[28] Based on the author's observations, the ornamental tops with dragon relief had a serious weathering impact and most of the engraved dragon reliefs are hardly recognizable.[29] The dragon motif found on the ornamental tops of the existing marble newels in the Circular Mound Altar are of the same design style compared with the ones at the Imperial Hall of Heaven (Figure 5 Right) and at the Imperial Vault of Heaven (Figure 7 Right). The author therefore concludes the marble reliefs at the Circular Mound Altar were of the Qianlong reign of the Qing dynasty.

THE DRESSING TERRACE具服台

The 'Dressing Terrace' was positioned to the south of the Hall of Prayer for Good Harvests and was surrounded by marble newels with ornamental dragon-carved tops. Before the ceremony of Worshipping

Heaven commenced, a yellow brocaded canopy was erected for the emperor's use. The Dressing Terrace functioned as a temporary changing room for the emperor before he left for the Imperial Palace. Hence, the Dressing Terrace was also well-known as the 'Clothes-Changing Terrace.' From existing records, the author could not find information when the Dressing Terrace was built, however the Palace above the Dressing Terrace was dismantled in 1543 (the 22nd year of Jiajing reign of the Ming dynasty).[30] By identifying and comparing the dragon reliefs on the ornamental tops of the marble newels around the platform to similar styles found in the Hall of Imperial Peace (Figure 2 Left), the Imperial Hall of Heaven (Figure 5 Left) the author concludes the Dressing Terrace was built, together with the Hall of Prayer for Good Harvests, in the Yongle reign of the Ming dynasty. Since the Dressing Terrace only functioned as the temporary 'Changing Room' for the emperor, it may explain why it has not been altered since it was built.

THE BEAMLESS HALL OF THE FASTING PALACE斋宫

The 'Beamless Hall', which is the main hall of the Fasting Palace, was built in 1420 (the 18th year of Yongle reign of the Ming dynasty). The name is derived from the fact that the hall is supported by a brick dome without any beams. The emperor held ceremonial rituals here on his arrival and prior to his departure.[31] Based on the author's observations, the majority of the marble newels surrounding the hall are still in their original condition but with a degree of weathering impact. It is similar to the case at the Circular Mound Altar, some of the dragon reliefs on the ornamental tops are hardly recognizable. The author assumes the dragon reliefs found in the Beamless Hall are of the same type compared with the ones in the Hall of Imperial Peace (Figure 2 Left), Imperial Hall of Heaven (Figure 5 Left) and the Dressing Terrace.

THE MING TOMBS明十三陵

The Ming Tombs are a collection of mausoleums built by the emperors of the Ming dynasty. The majority of the Ming tombs are located in a cluster near Beijing and are collectively known as the 'Thirteen Tombs of the Ming Dynasty' (明十三陵). They are within the suburban Changping District of Beijing, around 42 kilometres northwest of Beijing city centre. After the construction of the Imperial

Palace (Forbidden City) in 1420, the Yongle Emperor selected his burial site and created his own mausoleum. Subsequent emperors placed their tombs in close proximity to the tomb of Yongle emperor within the same valley.[32] There were 17 emperors of the Ming dynasty and the reader may wonder why there are only 13 imperial tombs in Beijing. From the Yongle Emperor onwards, Ming emperors were buried in the same area as Tianshou Mountain. The XiaolingTomb (明孝陵) of the first Ming emperor, the Hongwu emperor, is located near Nanjing where he was crowned and was the location of the initial Ming capital.[33] The second emperor, the Jianwen emperor (建文帝), was overthrown by the Yongle emperor and disappeared during the Jingnan Campaign (靖难之役) and is therefore without a known tomb.[34] The 'temporary' emperor - Jingtai emperor (景泰帝), was also not buried here, as the Tianshun emperor (天顺帝) had denied him an imperial burial, instead, he was buried west of Beijing.[35] The last Ming emperor buried at this location was the Chongzhen emperor (崇祯帝), who committed suicide by hanging himself on 25 April 1644. He was buried in his concubine Tian's tomb, which was later declared as an imperial mausoleum (Siling Tomb思陵) by the emperor of the short-lived Shun dynasty in 1644, Li Zicheng, but is on a much smaller scale compared to the other imperial tombs built for the Ming emperors.[36] The Ming Tombs were listed as a UNESCO World Heritage Site in August 2003. They were listed along with other tombs under the 'Imperial Tombs of the Ming and Qing Dynasties' designation.[37]

THE MARBLE ARCHWAY石牌坊

The 'Marble Archway' was built in 1540 (the 19th year of Jiajing reign of the Ming dynasty). It was originally a memorial archway, built under the edict of Jiajing emperor, to commemorate the merits and achievements of his imperial ancestors. The Ming officials were required to exit their carriage and then proceed by horseback as a mark of respect to the ancestors.[38]

The archway is comprised of five individual arches with six square pillars and eleven gables. The widest arch is installed in the centre and the side arches are of decreasing size. The carved pillar bases are decorated with 'dual-lions with ball'(双狮滚绣球), cloud dragon (Figure 8 Upper-left) and grass dragon(草龙).[39] The lying *kylins* are engraved on top of the pillar base and facing to the centre arch. The

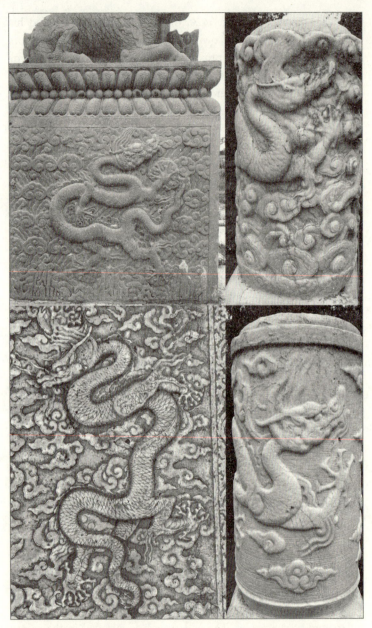

Figure 8: The Marble Archway, Jiajing reign of the Ming dynasty (upper-left), The Ornamental Top of the newel at Changling Tomb, Yongle reign of the Ming dynasty (upper-right), The Imperial Walkway at Changling Tomb, Xuande reign of the Ming dynasty (bottom-left) and The Ornamental Top of the newel at Dingling Tomb, Wanli reign of the Ming dynasty (bottom-right).
Photo by Jimmy Zang.

two forms of dragon are the grass dragon and cloud dragon, engraved on the pillar base, and the coiled body with head raised and the tail over the mountain and waves of the base and a dragon with a coiled body and a tail raised to the upper clouds and head towards the lower mountain and waves. Based on the author's observations at a number of imperial palaces and mausoleums, this marble archway set the standard for marble carving art in the mid Ming dynasty.

It is appropriate to take a close inspection of one of the dragon-carved relief (Figure 8 Upper-left) found on the marble pillar base. The content of the carving is comprised of three main elements: the dragon, cloud formations and the mountain surrounded by sea waves.[40] This is a typical carving relief design from the middle of the Ming dynasty (Jiajing reign). The image depicts a coiled dragon flying above the mountain and waves with a full background of cloud formations. During the middle of the Ming period, cloud formations had become a relatively 'fixed format' with similar *ruyi* shaped clouds arranged in layers. This particular form of lined-clouds has not been attributed to the early years of the Ming Dynasty. With regard to the dragon's body in the mid Ming period, the head is proportionally bigger in size, with shorter curled-up hair, compared with earlier examples. The dragon motif carved on this marble pillar base shares the same design in style compared with the ornamental top (Figure 5 Middle) found at the Imperial Hall of Heaven.

CHANGLING TOMB 长陵

Changling is the tomb of Emperor ZhuDi (1360-1424), the third emperor of the Ming Dynasty.[41] Construction of the Changling tomb began in and 1409 (the 7th year of Yongle reign) and was completed in 1427 (the 2nd year of Xuande reign of the Ming dynasty).[42] It is the largest and the most completely preserved of the 13 Ming tombs in the vicinity of Tianshou Mountain. The Changling Tomb is also notable for its well preserved Ling'en Hall (Hall of Eminent Favor 祾恩殿), which was constructed of a rare hardwood known as 'Phoebe nanmu'[43] The name of the Ling'en Hall, and Ling'en Gate, were given by the Jiajiing Emperor in 1538 (the 17th year of Jiajing reign) and both were built on marble pedestals with imperial walkways and surrounding marble newels with dragon-relieved ornamental tops.[44] The ornamental top of the marble newels (Figure 8 upper-right) found at the Ling'en Hall is a typical design from the Yongle reign. It processes the key features of the dragon design and cloud formation of that period. Other examples from the same period can be found at the Hall of Imperial Peace (Figure 2 Left) in the Forbidden City and the Imperial Hall of Heaven (Figure 5 Left) at the Temple of Heaven. Apart from these Yongle-dated ornamental tops, the author believes there are later produced examples from Jiajing reign of the Ming dynasty and additionally also from the early Republic period (1912-1930) or of an even later period which have been identified by the author.[45] The identification process involves a comparison of the existing marble reliefs found in the Changling Tomb together with examples found in the Forbidden City, the Temple of Heaven and the other Royal tombs from the Ming and Qing dynasty. This conclusion has been cross-verified with the historical maintenance record from the official publications for the Ming Tombs.[46] According to this record, the Changling Tomb was under repair and renovation during the following periods: in 1485 (the 20th year of Chenghua reign) due to earthquake damage; in the years 1490, 1498 and 1499 (the 3rd, 11th, and 12th year of Hongzhi reign); between 1536 to 1543 (the 15th to the 22th year of Jiajing reign); further repair work was undertaken in 1935 (the 24th year of the Republic period) and finally in 1955. The identification of the relevant dragon reliefs on the ornamental top of the marble newels were difficult to identify due to the complexity of the repair records of the Changling Tomb. The author assumes that relics from the Chenghua and Hongzhi reign of the Ming dynasty could also exist but this cannot be identified until a confirmed study of such relics is undertaken by future scholars. The Imperial Walkway (Figure 8 bottom-left) in the Changling Tomb are not from the Yongle reign based on the author's observation and comparison with other examples. Observation indicate that, dragon reliefs have slightly different patterns in design from two to three-dimensional effects. The imperial walkways, and the base section of the marble newels for instance illustrate dragon relief in a two-dimensional form. In contrast, dragon reliefs found at the Ornamental Columns, and top of the marble newels, are in a three-dimensional form. The dragon reliefs found at the Imperial Walkway (Figure 8 bottom-left) in the Changling Tomb are slightly different compared to the artefacts made in the Yongle reign. For example, such as the dragon reliefs on the base of the Ornamental Columns (Figure 1) in the Forbidden City and the Imperial Walkway in the Imperial Ancestral Temple. This finding has been primarily based on the design of the mouth of the dragon. The Yongle-styled dragon always has thick lips in front of the nose, which was lacking in the dragon relief on the Imperial Walkway at the Changling Tomb. A dragon relief, of a confirmed source from Xuande reign of the Ming dynasty has yet to be identified due to the scarcity of stone carving works created during this particular period. However, the discovery of a carved dragon relief on a lacquered table from the Victoria & Albert Museum in London, UK has led the author to believe that the dragon relief found in the Imperial Walkway (Figure 8 bottom-left) was of the Xuande period of the Ming dynasty.[47]

DINGLING TOMB定陵

Dingling is the tomb of Emperor Zhuyijun (1563-1620), the thirteenth emperor of the Ming Dynasty. He was also known as Wanli emperor and ruled from 1572 to 1620. The Dingling Tomb was built between 1584 and 1590 and occupies a surface area of 180,000 square metres.[48] In 1959, the Dingling Museum was established at the original site and opened to the public.[49] Repair and maintenance was undertaken during the years 1785 to 1787 (the 50th to 52nd year of Qianlong reign of the Qing dynasty). The Ling'en Gate and Ling'en Hall were reduced in size but these buildings were burned down again during the Republic period.[50] The Ornamental Top of the Newel (Figure 8 Bottom-right) found at the ruins of Ling'en Hall is of the Wanli reign of the Ming dynasty. Apart from the illustrated example, the author also observed another type of design, an open-mouthed dragon with a similar fretwork background and cloud formation. By comparison and analysis, the author believes these two variations are from the same period. Ornamental tops of this period share a similar design compared with the ones from Jiajing reign of the Ming dynasty (Figure 6 Left). Based on the author's observations, the only difference is the hair style. Dragon relief from Jiajing reign had hair that curled together, whilst the ones from the Wanli reign had curled hair that was divided into three strands.

THE EASTERN QING TOMBS清东陵

The Eastern Qing tombs are an imperial mausoleum complex of the Qing dynasty located in Zunhua, Hebei Province, around 125 kilometres northeast of Beijing city. The Eastern Qing tombs occupies 2500 square kilometre and they are the largest and most complete

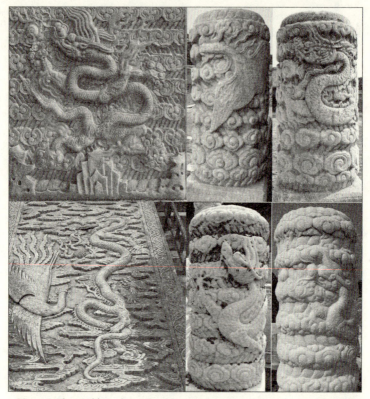

Figure 9: The Marble Archway, Kangxi reign of the Qing dynasty (upper-left), The Ornamental Top of the newel at Xiaoling Tomb, Jiajing reign of the Ming dynasty (upper-middle), The Ornamental Top of the newel at Xiaoling Tomb, Shunzhi reign of the Qing dynasty (upper-right), The Imperial Walkway at Yuling Tomb, Qianlong reign of the Qing dynasty (bottom-left), The Ornamental Top of the newel at Yuling Tomb, Qianlong reign of the Qing dynasty (bottom-middle), The Ornamental Top of the newel at Ding Dong (bottom-right).
Photo by Jimmy Zang.

mausoleum complex in the world.[51] There are many stone carving artefacts in the Eastern Qing Tombs, which contain in-depth cultural connotation and substantial historic information.[52]

Xiaoling tomb孝陵

At the centre of the Eastern Qing Tombs lies the Xiaoling Tomb of the Shunzhi emperor (1638–1661), who became the first Qing emperor to rule over China (1644). The Shunzhi emperor was also the first emperor to be buried in this area. Due to the intensive war with the Ming resistance during the early Qing period, the Shunzhi emperor did not build his tomb while he was young. The Xiaoling Tomb was built after the death of Shunzhi emperor (1661) and the construction started in 1663 (the 2nd year of Kangxi reign of the Qing dynasty).[53]

The Marble Archway at the Xiaoling Tomb was modelled on the one at the Ming Tombs. The architecture and relief design found on the Marble Archway at Xiaoling Tomb represented an example of the fusion of the architectural style of the Han and Manchu civilizations. By examining the dragon relief (Figure 9 Upper-left) on the Marble Archway, the author can verify that all design elements were consistent with the examples (Figure 8 Upper-left) at the Ming Tombs. The carved dragon relief (Figure 9 Upper-left) at the base support of the archway at the Xiaoling tomb is comprised of a dragon with a proportionally larger head and smaller claws with shorter arms and legs. The coiled body of the dragon is shorter in length comparing with the example (Figure 8 Upper-left) in the archway of the Changling tomb. Furthermore, the cloud formation is not as wide and full as compared with the same-styled artefacts from the Ming dynasty (Figure 8 Upper-left).

In 1661, the Shunzhi emperor died of smallpox. Unlike the majority of emperors from the Ming dynasty, Shunzhi died at a young age and therefore had not constructed his tomb before his death, so there was an urgent need for a tomb to be constructed quickly. Consequently, Ching Fu Temple (清馥殿) and the associated Jin Fang Pavilion (锦芳亭) were dismantled and re-constructed for the Long'en Hall (隆恩殿) of the Xiaoling Tomb.[54] The Ching Fu Temple was built in 1531 (the 10th year of Jiajing reign of the Ming dynasty), the Jin Fang Pavilion was built one year later. Furthermore, the ceiling's decorative panels at the Long'en Hall of the Xiaoling Tomb were also decorated with 'Golden lotus with water grass' (金莲水草) imagery and carried the mark of the Ching Fu Hall.[55] The ornamental tops (Figure 9 Upper-middle and Upper-right) are from the Long'en Hall, these two artefacts were selected by the author for study. Based on the author's observations, only three ornamental tops with the dragon motif (Figure 9 Upper-right) were identified at the Long'en Hall, and the remaining ornamental tops were all decorated with a phoenix relief (Figure 9 Upper-middle). By comparing the ornamental tops with a phoenix relief with the ornamental top (Figure 5 Middle) at the Imperial Hall of Heaven and the Imperial Walkway of double phoenixes at the Hall of Prayer for Good Harvests, the author believes the ornamental tops (Figure 9 Upper-middle) at the Long'en Hall were carved in the Jiajing reign of the Ming dynasty at the Ching Fu Temple. With reference to the dragon relief, the author believes the three ornamental tops (Figure 9 Upper-right) found at the Long'en Hall were carved in the early years of the Kangxi reign (1661-1700) of the Qing dynasty. Although the cloud formation found on these three ornamental tops are of the same design compared with the ornamental tops with phoenix relief at the same location, the dragon formation differs from the ones from the Jiajing reign (Figure 5 Middle). The dragon formation shared the same design as the one outlined on the column base (Figure 9 Upper-left) at the Marble Archway and newel base at the Ornamental Columns (华表) of the Xiaoling Tomb.

Jingling tomb 景陵

Jingling is the tomb of the Kangxi Emperor, and was built from 1676 (the 15th year of Kangxi reign of the Qing dynasty).[56] According to historical records, there were two fire accidents at Jingling Tomb in 1905 (the 31th year of Guangxu reign of the Qing dynasty) and 1952. The Long'en Hall was completely destroyed by fire in 1905 and was rebuilt in the Xuantong reign of the Qing dynasty (1908-1912).[57] Based on the author's observation, the dragon reliefs on both the ornamental tops of the newels and Imperial Walkway at the Long'en Hall of the Jingling Tomb, were carved in the very late Qing period. Similar-styled dragon relief can be found on the ornamental tops (Figure 9 Bottom-right) of the newels at the Ding Dongling Tomb (Cixiling Tomb).

Yuling tomb 裕陵

Yuling, the tomb of the Qianlong Emperor (the fourth emperor of the Qing dynasty), is the most eye-catching of all imperial mausoleums in the Eastern Qing Tomb.[58] The Qianlong Emperor, who died in 1799, selected the site of his mausoleum in 1742 and construction began the following year. Construction was completed in 1752, but the mausoleum was further expanded between 1755 and 1762.[59] The design of the Imperial Walkway at the Yuling Tomb was very similar to the one at the Forbidden City (Figure 03Right) and the New Summer Palace (颐和园), where many of the buildings were also constructed during the Qianlong reign. The dragon relief found on the ornamental tops of the newels (Figure 9 Bottom-middle) at the Yuling Tomb represents another distinctive design found in this particular period. The cloud formation is in five to seven layers with *ruyi* shaped clouds of the same size. Together with the dragon relief found on the ornamental top of the newel (Figure 4) at the Pavilion of Literary Profundity, these two types of dragon design, in the author's opinion, were specifically created during the middle to late period of Qianlong reign. There are other design versions, such as the ones found at the Imperial Hall of Heaven (Figure 5 right) and the Imperial Vault of Heaven (Figure 7 right). In the author's opinion, these artefacts were carved in the early period of the Qianlong reign as they imitate the designs of the Ming dynasty.

DING DONGLING TOMB (CIXILING)定东陵(慈禧陵)

In 1873, the tomb of Empress Dowager Cixi - Ding Dongling, began building at Putuoyu. The tomb was completed in 1879. The tomb was further expanded between 1895 and 1908.[60] The Long'en Hall was constructed from mahogany timbers and surrounded by carved marble newels, from which, carvings of dragons and phoenixes, flowing water and clouds were adorned. General regulations established in the previous reigns of the Ming and Qing dynasties determined that the ornamental tops with dragon and phoenix were carved on the marble newels, and normally one phoenix newel was placed beside each dragon newel as a sequence. In the Long'en Hall of Ding Dongling Tomb, however, only phoenix reliefs were carved on the ornamental tops. Instead of a traditional Begonia-outlined (海棠池) pillar base beneath the ornamental top, a rising dragon relief was carved on it. Therefore, the expression of 'phoenix above dragon' was created. This is a unique characteristic of the Ding Dongling Tomb and it could be an indication that once the Tongzhi and Guangxu Emperor were held hostage to the Empress Dowager Cixi.[61] In the author's opinion, the dragon relief on the ornamental top of the newel (Figure 9 Bottom-right) at the Three-arch Bridge is a typical design relating to the Tongzhi - Guangxu reigns of Qing dynasty (1861-1908). This dragon relief is assumed to be of the same period as found on the pillar base of the marble newels in the Long'en Hall. By the author's observation, in the late Qing dynasty, the dragon relief on the ornamental top was considerably reduced in size, the nose became considerably bigger and almost occupied one-fourth of the head. The hair of the dragon was much shorter comparing with the previous reigns and the *ruyi* shaped clouds were carved in the same size and joined together.

Figure 10: The Marble Archway, Yongzheng-Qianlong reign of the Qing dynasty (upper-left), The Ornamental Top of the newel at Tailing Tomb, Yongzheng reign of the Qing dynasty (upper-middle), The Ornamental Top of the newel at Changling Tomb, Jiaqing reign of the Qing dynasty (upper-right), The Imperial Walkway at Muling Tomb, Daoguang Reign of the Qing dynasty (bottom-left), The Ornamental Top of the newel at Muling Tomb, Daoguang reign of the Qing dynasty (bottom-middle), The Ornamental Top of the newel at Chongling Tomb, Xuantong reign of the Qing dynasty – Republic Period (bottom-right).
Photo by Jimmy Zang.

THE WESTERN QING TOMBS 清西陵

The Western Qing tombs occupies approximately 100 square kilometres and are located some 140 kilometres southwest of Beijing in Yi County, Hebei Province. They constitute a necropolis that incorporates four imperial mausoleums of four emperors of the Qing dynasty plus their empresses, imperial concubines, princes and princesses, as well as other royal servants.[62]

TAILING TOMB 泰陵

Tailing Tomb is the mausoleum of Yongzheng emperor and was constructed between 1730 and 1737. It was the earliest, the largest and most complete of the Western Qing Tombs.[63] The Yongzheng emperor ruled China from 1723 to 1735 and this reign was in the middle of the so-called 'Golden Age of the Three Emperors' (康乾盛世).[64] The Marble Archway found at the Tailing Tomb was also modelled after the Marble Archway from the Ming Tombs. However, instead of a single archway, Yongzheng emperor decided to build three arches, one in front of the Red Gate (大红门) and the other two on each side. The layout of three arches is unique of its kind, together with the Red Gate, this group of architecture formed a layout of a courtyard.[65] Based on author's observations, the existing Marble Archway is assumed of the Yongzheng reign and there is no historical records of alteration or repair works to be found. Through analysing the dragon motif on the archway (Figure 10 Upper-left), it is evident that a completely new design has been adopted with reference to the cloud formation. Instead of a design with individual *ruyi* shaped clouds, as the ones appeared on the Archway of the Ming Tombs (Figure 8 Upper-left) and the Xiaoling Tomb (Figure 9 Upper-left), a continuously connected cloud formation was created to produce a sense of continuity. The author believes this particular cloud formation functioned as a 'bridge design' for the transition period between Kangxi and Qianlong reigns. With reference to the dragon's appearance, the head is further enlarged with a much larger nose and mouth, the hair does not curl to the upper-front as usually found in the previous Qing and Ming dynasties but points in the opposite direction to the nose. The sequence of change regarding the dragon motif during the reigns of Kangxi, Yongzheng and Qianlong can be easily observed by comparing the designs on the three carved column bases (Figure 9 Upper-left, Figure 10 Upper-left and Figure 9 Bottom-left).The carving techniques used for the ornamental top of the newel (Figure 10 Upper-middle) in Yongzheng period, particularly for the cloud section, has a higher relief in comparison with Ming and the later part of the Qing dynasty. The dragon motif on the ornamental top is smaller in size compared with the one made in the previous Kangxi reign (Figure 9 Upper-right). The dragon appearance is in line with the one found on the Marble Archway (Figure 10 Upper-left), and thus, in the opinion of the author, of the same period.

CHANGLING TOMB 昌陵

Changling Tomb is the mausoleum of the Jiaqing emperor and was constructed between 1796 and 1803. The Jiaqing reign represented the transition period of Qing dynasty, from powerful and prosperous to decaying.[66] In the author's opinion, the art of marble carving also marked a turning point in Jiaqing reign, the craftsmanship and aesthetic style started to decline. This can be confirmed by studying the carved marble reliefs in the mausoleums after Qianlong emperor. Observation of the ornamental top of the newel (Figure 10 Upper-right) at the Three-arch Bridge (三孔桥) of the Changling Tomb, reveal the dragon and cloud patterns were executed with low-relief carving technique. Although white marble is relatively easy to carve compared to a variety of other stones, tremendous time can be saved by adopting a low-relief approach. By comparison of the carved reliefs on the ornamental tops at the Changling (Figure 10 Upper-right) and Tailing Tomb (Figure 10 Upper-middle), the relief of the latter is approximately three times deeper.

MULING TOMB 慕陵

The Muling Tomb is the mausoleum of the Daoguang emperor and was constructed between 1832 and 1836. Muling Tomb is the smallest among all mausoleums from Eastern and Western Qing Tombs. Daoguang emperor did not follow the Qing regulations regarding imperial mausoleum construction.[67] Instead, he simplified the overall layout and reduced the size of the Long'en Hall and additionally the Monumental Columns and Divine Merit Stele Pavilion (圣德神功碑亭) were cancelled.[68] The dragon relief (Figure 10 Bottom-left) shown in the Imperial Walkway of the Long'en Hall is of the period of the Daoguang reign. The cloud formation of the marble relief shows a continuous design with the enlarged *ruyi* shaped clouds. After the Jiaqing reign of the Qing dynasty, the shape of the dragon's claws has changed significantly. Before the Jiaqing reign, the five toes of a dragon claw were stretched out equally but after the Jiaqing reign, one toe was carved almost in the opposite direction of the other four. This can be easily identified on the marble reliefs in the Muling Tomb and the mausoleums built after that. Furthermore, the curve of the coiled dragon body is not smoothly executed but portrays a feeling of stiffness. The ornamental top (Figure 10 Bottom-middle) of the Daoguang reign was identified on the marble newels at the Three-arch Bridge. The number of the cloud layers on the ornamental top has been reduced from six to five compared with the dragon relief (Figure 10 Upper-right) at the Changling Tomb made for the Daoguang emperor's father. The dragon body on these two ornamental tops has no significant differences, but the nose of the dragon is unproportionally enlarged on the ornamental top of Muling Tomb compared with the one carved in the previous reign.

CONCLUSION

After identification, review and comparison on the existing dragon marble reliefs located in the Forbidden City, the Temple of Heaven, the Ming Tombs and the Eastern and Western Qing Tombs, the author concludes that the dragon style evolved from a bold formation (curved shorter body, eagle-liked claws and torch-like curled hair) of the early Ming dynasty to a slender formation (curved longer and slimmer body, small claws and shorter/less curled hair) of the late Qing dynasty. The cloud formation evolved from the irregularly shaped *ruyi* style of the early Ming dynasty to a consistent shaped *ruyi* style in smaller size of the late Qing dynasty. Over the period of five centuries, the carving technique was transformed from a high relief to a low relief craftsmanship with the only exception of the Yongzheng reign of the Qing dynasty. Later carved replacement is another issue arises in this article, as the original marble carving works could be replaced by later carved ones during repair work or reconstruction of the architecture. The author believes the existence of imitated artefacts is due to the fact that a similar design scheme was adopted. In the author's opinion, later carved replacement can still be identified by a complete examination of the dragon form, cloud formation and carving techniques. Weathering issue is another measurement to roughly grouping the examples, as theoretically speaking, the longer that a carved marble artefact is exposed in the open air, the less visible carving content that a carved marble artefact remains, due to the break down process by the earth's atmosphere, water and biological organisms.

ABOUT THE AUTHOR

Jimmy Nuo Zang is a native Beijinger and a member of the Lions Club International. He has been collecting ancient Chinese art since 2006 in the area of court textile, stone carving, cloisonné and glazed architectural components. His book *The Imperial Court Insignia* was published by Huaxia Publishing House in 2016.

Email: j.zang@visiontroupe.com

Endnotes

1 Nengfu Huang and Juanjuan Chen, *Chinese Dragon Patterns* (Taipei: South Sky Press Ltd, 1989), p. 27.

2 Record of Jiajing Emperor. Beijing, China: 1522-1566, dossier 498.

3 Menglin Wu and Jingyi Liu, 'The Stone Excavations for the Ming Palaces and Tombs in Dashiwo of the Fangshan District', *Journal of the Forbidden City Academic Committee* 1, no.10, 1996, pp. 253-255.

4 Lijuan Bai, *Stone Carving Works in the Forbidden City Architecture* (Beijing: China Industrial Construction Publishing House, 2011), p. 7.

5 Ying Wu, *Stone Carving in Ancient China* (Beijing: China Commercial Publishing House, 2017), pp. 10-11.

6 Suqin Zhou, *The Forbidden City Architecture* (Beijing: The Forbidden City Publishing House, 2014), p. 3.

7 Ibid.

8 'World Heritage List, Imperial Palaces of the Ming and Qing Dynasties in Beijing and Shenyang', *World Heritage Convention* UNESCO, http://whc.unesco.org/en/list/439/ (accessed July 4, 2018).

9 Lijuan Bai, *Stone Carving Works in the Forbidden City Architecture*, p. 7.

10 Shoudong Wang, 'History of the Ornamental Columns', *Journal of Dezhou University* 22, no.1, 2006, p. 67.

11 Yuan Lu, 'The Ornamental Columns in front of the Tiananmen Square', *China Archives News* (Beijing), 9 September 2005.

12 Zilin Wang, A Summary of Literatures Related to the Hall of Imperial Peace,' *Journal of the Forbidden City Studies*, no.5, 2014, p. 238.

13 'Hall of Imperial Peace', The Palace Museum, http://www.dpm.org.cn/explore/building/236494.html (accessed 4 July 2018).

14 Nengfu Huang, *Ancient China Decorative Patterns* (Beijing: China Tourism Publishing House, 1999), p. 157.

15 'Hall of Imperial Peace', The Palace Museum.

16 Suqin Zhou, *The Forbidden City Architecture*, pp. 190-191.

17 Mingzhen Wang, 'The Historical Accidents and Fire Precaution Measures in the Forbidden City', *Journal of Security Today*, no. 11, 2008, pp. 64-65.

18 'Fire Accidents in the Old Architecture Buildings in Mainland China',

Cultural Expo Online, http://wenbozaixian.com/WenboCircle/Onlineview/id/614 (accessed July 4, 2018).

19 Si Xiang, 'The Pavilion of Literary Profundity and the Complete Library of Four Branches of Books', *Everbright Daily* (Beijing), 29 April 2015.

20 Hongwu Liu, 'The Construction and History of the Palace of Compassion and Tranquility,' *Journal of the Forbidden City Academic Committee*, no.5, 2007, pp. 364-366.

21 Ying Qian, *Altars and Temples, Beijing Architectural Heritage Series* (Beijing: Beijing Publishing Group, 2010), 4-5.

22 'World Heritage List, Temple of Heaven (China),' *World Heritage Convention* UNESCO, http://whc.unesco.org/en/list/881/ (accessed July 4, 2018).

23 Record of Jiajing Emperor, Beijing, China: 1522-1566, dossier 300.

24 Shanpu Yu, 'Ming Palace Was Dismantled for Building the Xiaoling Tomb', *Forbidden City Journal*, no. 03, 1992, pp. 46-48.

25 Ying Qian, *Altars and Temples, Beijing Architectural Heritage*, p. 4-5.

26 Peng Cao and Qiheng Wang, 'Illustration for the Construction History of Building Group of the Hall of Prayer for a Good Harvest of the Temple of Heaven in Beijing', *Journal of New Architecture*, no. 2, 2010, pp. 116-117.

27 Ibid.

28 'World Heritage List, Temple of Heaven (China).

29 Weathering is the breaking down of rocks, marbles, soil, and minerals as well as wood and artificial materials through contact with the Earth's atmosphere, water, and biological organisms. Weathering occurs in situ (on site), that is, in the same place, with little or no movement.

30 Record of Jiajing Emperor, Beijing, China: 1522-1566, dossier 279.

31 Ying Qian, *Altars and Temples, Beijing Architectural Heritage*, p. 36.

32 Yang Yu, *Mausoleums and Tombs, Beijing Architectural Heritage Series* (Beijing: Beijing Publishing Group, 2010), pp. 26-27.

33 Wenxuan Su, 'Xiaoling Tomb', *Journal of Cultural Relics*, no. 8, 1976, p. 88.

34 Deyang Kong, 'The Utilization of Celestial Disaster During the Jingnan Campaign by Zhudi', *Forbidden City Journal*, no. 10, 2010, pp. 80-81.

35 Yang Yu, *Altars and Temples, Beijing Architectural Heritage*, p. 108-109.

36 Hansheng Hu, 'Siling Tomb of the Ming Dynasty', *Forbidden City Journal*, no. 3, 1992, p. 9.

37 'The Imperial Tombs of the Ming and Qing Dynasties', *World Heritage Convention* UNESCO, http://whc.unesco.org/en/list/1004/ (accessed July 4, 2018).

38 Yang Yu, *Mausoleums and Tombs, Beijing Architectural Heritage Series*, p. 36.

39 'Grass Dragon' is one type of dragon form with curved grass-shaped tail. The 'Grass Dragon' motif is considered less important comparing with the traditional dragon and occasionally decorated together with the dragon, kylin and lion motifs.

40 'Mountain with sea waves (海水江崖纹)' is frequently found in the design for imperial purpose. The curved stripes are lined at the bottom of the image to represent water, while a grand mountain motif is raised above the water. The combined design has a meaning of longevity and prosperity, often referred to the eternity of imperial sovereignty.

41 Yang Yu, *Altars and Temples, Beijing Architectural Heritage*, p. 52.

42 Ibid.

43 Chunqiu Zhang, 'The Construction of the Ming Changling Tomb and Its Artistic Features', *Journal of the Academic Symposium on the 600th Anniversary of the Ming Changling Tomb*, no. 5, 2009, p. 592.

44 Ibid.

45 Apart from the comparison of patterns, the author believes the weathering impact (风化程度) could be used as another source to compare carved marble reliefs for rough dating. For instance, the weather impact on a marble relief from Qing dynasty is more noticeable comparing with another example after the Republic period.

46 'The Memorabilia of the Royal Ming Tombs', The Administration Committee of the Royal Ming Tombs, http://www.mingtombs. com/ (accessed 4 July 2018)

47 This table is arguably the most important piece of Chinese lacquer furniture. It was made during the reign period (1425-1436) of the Xuande Emperor in a workshop in Beijing under direct imperial control. It is unique because no other carved lacquer furniture of this size from the early fifteenth century has survived - not even in the Palace Museum in Beijing. The workmanship is superb. There is no similar object in existence, probably because it was too labour-

intensive even for the court to mass produce. http://collections. vam.ac.uk/item/O75869/table-unknown/ (accessed July 4, 2018).

48 Yang Yu, *Altars and Temples, Beijing Architectural Heritage*, p. 72.

49 Ibid.

50 Hansheng Hu, 'Textual Research on Renovation Works of Royal Ming Tombs during Qianlong Period', *Architecture History and Theory* 5, no. 6, 1994, p. 35.

51 Haisheng Ren, 'The Largest Mausoleum in the World-The Eastern Qing Tombs', *Journal of Tangshan Normal University*, no. 02, 1995, p. 2.

52 Qinglin Yin, 'A Discussion of the Cultural Inclusion of the Marble Carving Art in the Eastern Qing Tombs', *Journal of the Academic Committee of the Forbidden City* 2, no. 11, 1997, pp. 194-195.

53 Haiyan Wang, 'Rise and Decline of the Qing Dynasty through the Construction and Maintenance of the Eastern Qing Tombs', *Journal of Manchu Minority Research*, no. 9, 2009, pp. 47-48.

54 Shanpu Yu, 'Ming Palace Material Used in Qing Xiaoling Tomb', *Forbidden City Journal*, no. 10, 1996, p. 46.

55 Ibid.

56 Haiyan Wang, 'Rise and Decline of the Qing Dynasty through the Construction and Maintenance of the Eastern Qing Tombs', *Journal of Manchu Minority Research*, no. 9, 2009, p. 50.

57 Guangyuan Xu, 'The Fire Acicident in the Long'en Hall at Jingling Tomb', *Forbidden City Journal*, no. 4, 1985, p. 38.

58 Yin Li, 'The Eastern Qing Tombs-the Yuling Tomb', *Journal of China Place Name*, no. 1, 2005, p. 47.

59 The State Administration of Cultural Heritage of the People's Republic of China, 'Imperial Tombs of the Ming and Qing Dynasties, WHC Nomination Documentation', http://whc.unesco. org/uploads/nominations/1004ter.pdf (accessed July 4, 2018).

60 Ibid.

61 Lianping Gui, 'Decrypting the Eastern Qing Tombs', *Journal of Archives World*, no. 9, 2005, p.18.

62 Jinsheng Yuan, 'The Stone Carving Art at Western Qing Tombs', *Stone Journal*, no. 9, 2012, p. 42.

63 Ibid.

64 Ibid.

65 Ibid.

66 Ibid.

67 Enyi Du, 'The History of Daoguang Emperor's Muling Tomb', *Journal of Literature and History*, no. 4. 2017, p. 25.
68 Ibid.

HAWKERS IN HONG KONG:
The Informal Sector In A Contemporary City
BY PARUL REWAL

ABSTRACT

Any visit to Hong Kong, even today, is incomplete without a trip to the Ladies' Market, the Night Market in Kowloon or the Street Market in Stanley. Strolling through the hawker occupied streets in Wanchai, Central or Sheungwan, past stalls selling everything from clothes, bags, accessories to dried foods, live seafood, including fish that occasionally jump out at the unwary passerby, imparts a real flavour of the city's cultural identity at street level, just as much as its high-rise skyline projects its image as one of the most prominent financial centres in the global network. While the life and character of these street markets resonates with various urban discourses around how informal economic activity in public spaces make cities lively, robust, even safer due to 'more eyes on the street' and bring an element of the carnivalesque to the otherwise monotonous cityscapes, hawkers have not been at the centre of any conscious policymaking, except one of regulation, licensing and eviction. As early as the nineteenth century, one comes across records of how hawkers were treated as a nuisance by the authorities, to be regulated and contained as much as possible. This paper examines how hawkers in the city of Hong Kong have been closely intertwined with the political economy of the city - from the city of Victoria, the first urban settlement in Hong Kong after it became a British crown colony in 1842, through the cross migration across the borders with China during the Japanese occupation and post Second World War, right up to Hong Kong's development into its contemporary manifestation as a global financial hub. This article uses various historic accounts of the hawking trade in the city and examines the government's policies and attitude regarding hawkers over the years.

INTRODUCTION

Hawkers in cities fit into the category of the Urban Informal Sector, which is broadly defined by the Global Development Research Centre (GDRC) to include all economic activities which are not officially regulated and which operate outside the incentive system offered by the state and its institutions.[1] The International Labour Organisation (ILO) brought the term Informal Sector into international usage in 1972 in its Kenya Mission Report, defining it as a way of doing things characterized by ease of entry; reliance on indigenous resources; family ownership; small scale operations; labor intensive and adaptive technology; skills acquired outside of formal education; and operating in unregulated and competitive markets. Thus, petty traders, street hawkers and shoeshine boys operating on the streets of big towns and cities, all came under the informal sector, a category which, as the ILO went on to note 'is largely ignored, rarely supported, often regulated and sometimes actively discouraged by the Government'.[2]

In the current phase of globalisation, as most cities tend towards a homogenous model of development where traditional is being replaced with modern, small scale with big scale, and disorganised with organised, as per the dualistic model of economic development, the informal sector in cities was gradually expected to shrink and eventually disappear.[3] However in most cities, even in advanced economies, the informal sector remains persistent. It is widely recognised that the informal sector contributes immensely to the economy of a country and that it plays a major role in employment creation, production and income generation.[4] Yet hawkers are generally treated as a civic nuisance and more often than not, associated with an illegality discourse as the vendors occupy space where they have no legal rights, create obstruction and congestion in public spaces and are seen to hamper legal businesses.

Hong Kong is a case in point, where from historic and contemporary accounts, we can see how city planning and governance fails to make adequate space for an economic activity that is entrenched in local culture, indispensable for the poor and critical to the liveliness of public spaces in the city. The Hong Kong Hawker Association estimated there were more than 70,000 hawkers in Hong Kong and Kowloon in 1946.[5] Nowadays, only around 6000 legal permits are in place for hawkers to operate in designated areas of the city.[6] According to the Hong Kong government's Food and Environment Hygiene Department, which is responsible for the management and control of hawkers in the city, there were 23,473 convictions of unlicensed hawker or hawker-related offences in 2015.[7] One often hears Hong Kong residents lament about how traditional eateries or *Dai Pai Tongs* (referring to the out-sized food stalls which became popular after the Second World War and flourished in the 1950s and 1960s), have all but disappeared. Only about 25 *Dai Pai Tongs* now remain in the city[8].

THE HISTORY OF HAWKERS IN HONG KONG

The existence of street hawkers in Hong Kong can be traced back over a long period and the earliest record by J. Nacken, a British missionary living in Hong Kong, describes the local hawker's daily life of Victoria in 1873,[9] demonstrating how entrenched street hawking has been with the historic, cultural and visual identity of the city. Nacken provides a charming account of the hawkers and their varied cries as they went about either selling their wares of food, fruit and various articles of daily use, both on land or as they paddled their canoes in the waters. While some sold illicit bottles of *samshu* (local wine) concealed under piles of fruit, others sold the absolute essentials for the poorest, like *mai tau fu* (bean curd) and *han yu* (salt fish), which, as Nacken observes, 'was often the only *sung* on the table' (*Sung* refers to whatever is on the table besides rice). The roads were also occupied by coolies and jin-rickshaw bearers jostling past passers-by, others occupied in buying refuse for recycling, those offering repair services and some selling articles of idolatry such as joss paper, incense sticks, candles and fortune telling. Nacken offers a fine testimonial of the skillful repair services that were on offer by metalsmiths, cobblers, tinkers and tailors; repairing foreign umbrellas, spectacles, clasps and hinges, marking chinaware, sharpening razors and whetting scissors. He describes how the noon meals presented an interesting aspect of street life with tables and benches set out at convenient spots by food vendors under the shade of umbrellas for customers, and in the evenings all the stalls and hawking tables would be illuminated by paper lanterns making the streets look lively and interesting. This conundrum of street activity is further romanticised by Henry Norman who described the streets of Victoria in 1895 as 'far from being beautiful or well managed, but you forget this in the rush of life about you …. [even as] messengers jostle you, rickshaws run over your feet and chair poles dig you in the ribs', contributing to its reputation as 'the colony that just hums all the time'.[10]

From Nacken's accounts, we also know that from as early as 1872, Hong Kong hawkers were subject to licensing and control, issued with wooden tickets that had to be renewed quarterly at the rate of 50 cents, on the back of which was stamped a notice stating that crying out was prohibited in Chung-wān, on Queen's Road and on the *praya* (waterfront). Nacken reported that 1,146 such licenses were issued that year, with about as many more unlicensed hawkers trading their wares.[11] He calculated that if each hawker would call out even once a minute to draw attention to his wares, as was quite common, it would amount to a million cries a day on the island! The cacophony created by the hawkers led to an ordinance being passed in 1872 stating:

> Every person is subject to penalties if they use or utter cries for purpose of buying or selling any articles whatsoever ..... within any district or place not permitted by some regulation of the Governor in Council.[12]

It is interesting to note from Nacken's accounts however, that refuse buyers did not come under this ordinance. These refuse collectors went about buying all kinds of discarded and broken goods from the back of houses, ranging from feathers, bones, metal, glass, rags, empty tins, paper and nails to be sold to Marine stores for recycling purposes, which probably goes to show how this ubiquitous form of garbage collection was considered a necessary and acceptable service by the government. By the mid-1930s, the number of licensed hawkers in Hong Kong had grown to 16,000, with another estimated 5 unlicensed hawkers for every licensed one, largely attributed to the influx of refugees from China escaping the war.[13] Management of hawkers had become a major public administration problem for government officials in Hong Kong by then. During the Japanese occupation of Hong Kong from 1941 to 1945, many of these recent immigrants fled the Colony and returned to their home villages in China, leading to a corresponding decline in street hawking.[14] However, after the Second World War, it is estimated that about 1.285 million refugees entered Hong Kong from China in the period from 1945 to 1949, escaping the communist regime, which effectively doubled the existing population.[15] Hong Kong did not have the ability to deal with the tremendous increase in population it was experiencing, which led to unprecedented social and economic problems. While a component of the immigrants were wealthy entrepreneurs and skilled workers, a vast majority were unskilled and uneducated, and a large number of them became involved with street hawking for a source of income

Figure 1: Images of hawkers in Old Hong Kong,
Source: The Hong Kong Heritage Project, retrieved on 5 April, 2018,
https://www.hongkongheritage.org/pages/about_photo_gallery.aspx.

with lower operating cost. The Japanese occupation had drastically deteriorated the economic conditions in Hong Kong and people did not have much money to spend.[16] Hawkers not only provided daily necessities at affordable prices to lower income working class families, but the trade also became an affordable way to make a basic living for the poor without having to rent a shop or needing to buy a license to operate a business.[17] Around this time, the government became increasingly alarmed at the dramatic rise in street hawking activities, and its 'disorderly effect on the city streets.'[18] The Hong Kong Hawker Association estimates there were more than 70,000 hawkers in Hong Kong and Kowloon in 1946.[19] After the war, a committee appointed by the Governor of Hong Kong to review the 'hawker problem' concluded:

> [Hawkers] should have no place in any ideal state of affairs in a properly regulated modern city of metropolitan status such as Hong Kong, and the ultimate object to be aimed at can only be, in any long-term plan, its total abolition in the urban area, except possibly a limited number of newspaper vendors and the pedlar class.[20]

Until 1949, Hong Kong's economy had centred on its role as an entrepôt, predominantly serving as a trade gateway between the west and China and other Far East nations.[21] Post 1950, due to a curtailment in the Chinese consumer market during the communist revolution, a UN embargo against Chinese goods during the Korean war in 1951, and the sudden availability of cheap and abundant labour, Hong Kong's economy was forced to evolve from trade dependancy to manufacturing; a shift which was completely unplanned and unpremeditated.[22] Alan and Josephine Smart describe, in their introduction in *Petty Capitalists and Globalisation*, how the period up to the 1980s saw a rampant growth of the informal economy in Hong Kong, not just in the form of burgeoning street trading but also in small scale manufacturing, as the population again doubled during this time due to the uncontrolled influx of both legal and illegal immigrants from China. They laid out how the government's laissez-faire approach to industrial regulation at the time resulted in a lack of social welfare and growth of small firms and family run businesses (stemming from the traditional Confucius ethic), which operated in crammed spaces over long working hours, churning out anything that could be produced in a small space, including buttons, artificial flowers, umbrellas, textiles, enamelware, footwear and plastics.[23] As Hong Kong started to pursue an export-led development strategy, manufacturing apparel, toys, electronics, watches and other items geared for export, producers started to follow flexible, adaptive strategies in order to compete with strong global competition, typically operating as small businesses and original equipment manufacturers (OEMs) using imitative technology instead of developing creative or innovative products and processes, and subcontracting the manufacturing of components to small firms to reduce capital costs.[24] Thus, these industries rode on the informal economy and the growth of petty capitalism was reflected in 'sweat shops of epic scales, factories crammed into 300 square foot apartments or smaller public housing units, yet small producers managed to continually increase production till the mid 1980s.'[25] This was an epic account of how the informal sector contributed to the prosperity of the colony while continuing to expand and operate with few safeguards and protection. Needless to say, street vending, too, flourished during this period and in 1981, there were 63,000 full time hawkers (of which only 40,000 held licenses) and the hawking trade is estimated to have contributed $1 billion to the Hong Kong economy in 1983, accounting for 11 per cent of retail sales.[26]

During the period from 1950 to 1980, several hawker policy reviews took place to decide on the course of action to deal with hawkers in the city. A review of the hawker policy in 1957 took into account the vast scale of unemployment following the influx of Chinese immigrants, which the existing industrial and service industries were unable to absorb. The administration was advised to make considerable concessionary changes in policy to:

> accommodate as many small- scale traders as the public seems to demand; to bring in as much orderliness to the dense crowd as is necessary for good trading and the convenience of the public; and to ensure that the streets are cleaned thoroughly.'[27]

Thus, pedlar licenses were issued on an unrestricted basis and simultaneously, a hawker control squad was set up to keep hawkers in the allocated areas and manage unruly operations. In 1959, the administration proposed to build off-street bazaars to accommodate peddler hawkers and fixed-pitch hawkers selling market commodities so as to relieve congestion in the streets near certain markets.[28] A review of hawker policy in 1968 further accepted the legitimacy of hawking as an activity which provided alternative employment to a large section of people and a convenience to the daily life of the public. Yet, the authorities adjourned the issuing of more licenses to hawkers since it felt their numbers should not be allowed to increase further. As T. G. McGee contends, in the first comprehensive study of hawkers published in 1973, this was due to the labour shortages in factories during the time and hawking was seen as an occupation that was diverting potential labour from the industrial sector. Even the Hawker Liaison Committee that was set up to improve communication with hawkers failed to draw responses per him, as not many hawkers were willing to come forth to act as spokesmen to cooperate with the authorities, presumably due to the long history of confrontation with the government.[29] In 1973, the Urban Council decided to designate suitable areas known as Hawker Permitted Places where hawkers would be allowed to trade freely. By 1974, there were almost 50,000 day time stalls in business areas around Hong Kong and Kowloon, with ostensibly '150 stalls for every 10,000 people, with most stalls in high-density, low-income districts.'[30] Furthermore, the large extent of unemployment in 1975 due to the slowdown in the economy, led the government to permit hawkers on a first come, first served basis; however, this system failed as the traditional organised crime gangs, known as the Triad Societies, took control of the allocated areas, only allowing hawkers to operate their businesses when they paid 'protection money.'[31] To overcome this problem, the government proposed installing fixed pitch stalls in these hawker permitted streets to regain control over hawker operation.[32]

In the 1980s, intense competition for space led to a dramatic rise in real estate prices, while the success of the manufacturing sector led to labour shortages and rising labour costs, thus increasing the pressure on the costs of production in Hong Kong.[33] As a consequence of this and Deng Xiaoping's open-door policy, as the People's Republic of China's economic reform started in 1979, Hong Kong's manufacturing sector gradually moved north across the border to Mainland China in the 1980s in order to lower costs and maintain profit margins. As such, Hong Kong's economy again transitioned from manufacturing to more service-based sectors. Scholars have studied how the labor regime in

Hong Kong become even more flexible after deindustrialization began in the 1980s. Residual labour from industrial sector began to choose more flexible and entrepreneurial occupations.[34] Alan Smart relates vivid accounts of how informal economic activity in Hong Kong in the 1970s and 1980s spilled into any available public or private space possible, through encroachment of staircases and airwells, balcony extensions and rooftop squatting.[35] He describes how the streets were constantly subject to spontaneous encroachment, with bags of belongings hanging out of windows, vegetables being washed, plastic flowers being assembled on the street, and illegal street vending being rampant. The situation led to a need for stepping up surveillance and routine patrolling in the city to maintain some form of control or vigilance over public space. According to Smart, this became a source of great entertainment at the street level:

> One of the exciting features of daily life in the 1980s was the instantaneous disappearance of an entire street market when spotters observed the Urban Services Department Hawker Control Squad arriving. As long as bystanders could avoid the hurtling cooked food carts, particularly those bearing vats of boiling oil, the scattering of hawkers like a flock of pigeons was an amusing side-show. although vexing for those who simply wanted to do their shopping.[36]

Smart's account reiterates how the emotional experience of street life contributed to the pulse of the city, despite its possibly hazardous consequences. He further quotes Frank Leeming, who in his insightful description of Hong Kong localities in *Street Studies in Hong Kong* comments, 'Everywhere in this great city, in a limitless range of circumstances, the community has a limitless capacity for life and livelihood, and encroachment as well, wherever it finds security and opportunity.'[37] Yet, the very industriousness appreciated here also created problems of obstruction of thoroughfares due to overzealous hawking activity. The congestion created by hawkers often resulted in conflicts with other road users since they tended to congregate in already busy areas, and repeated pedestrian accidents due to hawker encroachment again brought the hawker issues into the forefront in 1981, leading to confrontation with the government and further licensing and policy related changes.[38]

One of the most important employment trends in the 1990s was the replacement of permanent, full time jobs by temporary and part-time jobs and an increase in the number of people who were employed as contingent workers.[39] This shift to subcontracts is generally referred to as employee casualisation. The shrinking of the market and the foreign investors since the early 1990s had a direct impact on the job market. The 1997 Asian economic crisis intensified and prolonged the decimation of regional markets.[40] In the second quarter of 1998, for instance, the GDP of Hong Kong declined by 5.2 per cent, and the unemployment rate increased by 5.3 per cent.[41] As noted by Smith, employee casualisation tended to be intensified during economic downturn, where employers used more contingent workers to replace full-time permanent workers.[42] Although accurate estimates of the number of contingent workers in Hong Kong is difficult to obtain,[43] there are accounts of extensive casualisation of labour across a wide spectrum of economic activities, especially in the retail sector.[44] The economic difficulties in the wake of the Asian financial crisis, caused the Administration to take a more tolerant approach in its enforcement actions against unlicensed hawking activities in 2001, 'so long as food safety and environmental hygiene would not be compromised.'[45] However, the outbreak of the SARS virus in 2003 again led to a crackdown on hawkers and public markets with a tightening of hawker policy, reflecting yet again how the stance of the government towards hawkers fluctuated repeatedly as per the changing political economy; adopting a tolerant stance to suit its laissez faire approach to employment and welfare provision in times of social or economic upheaval and tightening of regulations when it was seen to interfere with labour shortages in the industrial sector or when the 'nuisance' factor came into prominence.

THE CONTEMPORARY SCENARIO

The last few decades have seen Hong Kong's growth as a global financial hub. In addition, the service industry has transitioned to higher order services, predominantly finance, insurance, real estate and manufacturing-related producer services, accompanied by related services such as retail, wholesale, trade, hospitality and tourism.[46] In 2014, the services sector accounted for 92.7 per cent of Hong Kong's GDP.[47] Sectors with median income levels such as construction and transport, storage and communications have not developed

Figure 2: Hawkers selling phone accessories and ribbons.
Photos by Parul Rewal.

adequately, leading to great income disparities.[48] Wage inequalities within and across the industries has propelled more individuals to become small scale entrepreneurs or flexible, free-lance workers. The hawking trade has also transformed, and in contrast to the hawkers of the 1950s, who were forced to take up hawking as a means of livelihood due to lack of available employment opportunities, many of the current young hawkers are more entrepreneurial and view their businesses as commercial enterprises. The younger generation hawkers are more into clothing, accessories, shoes, luggage and light household goods, selling items not too different from what one might find in stores nearby. One also finds a lot of cheap electronics and phone accessories, nuts and dried foods, potted plants and cut flowers along with traditional artefacts and food items that are also sold extensively. Hawking is seen as a way of remaining competitive in the retail market by sidestepping the high rentals of commercial properties in Hong Kong, which are among the highest in the world. Rental prices have risen by around 60% for private rental spaces and by 86 per cent for Link REIT properties from 2006 to 2014.[49] As such, hawking serves as a means to diversify the economy and break away from the monopoly of supermarkets and chain stores. These big stores are replacing many of the small family run shops in the city, which struggle to survive in this environment of high rentals and the hegemony of private developers in Hong Kong.

Many of the hawker areas are routine tourist destinations, such as the Ladies' Night Market in Mong Kok, the open-air market on Temple Street, Stanley Market, the Jade Market in Yau Ma Tei and the Lanes in Central, all of which draw in throngs of visitors. Some have developed into dedicated specialty bazaars for specific types of goods. Pottinger Street is known for costumes and hair accessories, which everyone makes a bee-line for as Halloween approaches, or to equip themselves for theme parties or attendance at the annual Sevens Competition. Sham Shui Po has a street dedicated to all sorts of electrical and electronic goods ranging from LED lights to power drills, another to fishing equipment. Yen Chow Street stocks sewing accessories with a wide assortment of threads, fabrics, embroidered appliqué patches, lace and bric-a-brac. The flower market on Prince Edward Road is the largest in the city for flowers, potted plants and gardening supplies. These hawker streets are the go-to destination for most people when they want to view a wide range of specific items in one place at competitive prices. So much so, that when the fabric market in Yen Chow Street faced eviction to facilitate the development of a five storey fashion and design centre in the vicinity, fashion design students joined the hawker representatives in protests, fearing it would spell an end to affordable textile sources.[50] The community action resulted in the hawkers being rehoused in a nearby temporary market through priority bidding and discounted rents.

Besides this, one finds street-side repair stalls in various places, with people setting up corner kiosks repairing watches, umbrellas and bags as well as minor clothes alterations. In Sham Shui Po, one can see repairmen with tables laden with mounds of remote controls, old VCR or DVD players, lamps, blenders and other electric kitchen equipment awaiting repairs. Adjacent to an entrance to the Central MTR Station is what is colloquially known as 'Shoe Lane,' where a row of cobblers and key smiths have set up stalls. They carry out all kinds of resoling, repairs and shoe-shine jobs and spare keys can be cut within half an hour while one browses the stores nearby. These repair stalls charge customers a fraction of what corporatised chainstores in malls and metro stations, like what Mr Minit charge. A shoe repair that may cost only 10HKD on Shoe Lane could cost a customer close to 80HKD at a Mr Minit outlet. These street side repair stalls are thus an invaluable environmental asset in the urban area, offering more accessible and economical options for repair and reuse of household and personal

Figure 3: Hawkers selling electrical goods in Sham Shui Po
Photos by Parul Rewal.

Figure 4: Hawkers selling gardening supplies and cut flowers
Photos by Parul Rewal.

items which are past their warranties and would otherwise simply be thrown away. If not for these street side repair shops, the culture and skills of repairing broken goods would slowly but surely vanish, further perpetuating the unsustainable patterns of production and consumption cycles that most cities are caught in.

During Chinese New Year, Lantern Festival, Halloween or Christmas, one finds the hawker streets swathed in festival paraphernalia, a large contributor to the festive appearance of the city. Also conspicuous is the appearance of temporary vendors (mostly illegal) who are eagerly awaited every year for their fare of traditional goodies and food items only found seasonally. Customers line up for their personal favourites for long periods, a testament to how precious these hawker experiences are to locals at large. So much so, that over Chinese New Year in 2016, riots broke out in Mongkok, one of Hong Kong's busiest districts, as public protests against the hawker control squads cracking down on illegal food hawkers escalated into violence. These traditional food hawkers had enjoyed a decades long tradition of being on these streets over the first few days of the lunar new year festivities with much more tolerance. The street clashes earned the nickname 'Fishball Revolution' after a popular Cantonese snack, indicating wide public sympathy for the hawkers and several grassroots activist groups such as 'Hong Kong Indigenous,' and 'Scholarism' strongly supported the cause of the Hong Kong hawkers, who they believe are an integral part of the indigenous culture and are under threat of eradication.[51]

Hawker stalls crammed with goods overflowing onto the street make a chaotic yet visually stimulating experience in the city. Hawker areas are undoubtedly crowded and messy and often difficult to manoeuvre through, and while some people may choose to avoid them when in a rush to get somewhere, they still draw people in for a browse even when they have no specific intention of buying anything. There is a certain sense of exhilaration in taking in the visual sights or at finding the odd bargain. Urbanists often refer to this phenomenon of 'urban place-making' as one of the desirable ideas about cities and the use of public space to create lively neighbourhoods. Jonathan Raban in *Soft City* discusses harnessing the emotional experience of places to create better urban space.[52] Adrian Franklin in *City Life* reiterates the need for cities to be a bit 'edgy' to be interesting.[53] Franklin discusses the importance of human tolerance for the carnivalesque in city life when

Figure 5: Cobblers and Locksmiths in Central.
Photos by Parul Rewal.

Figure 6: Electrical repair and used good stalls in Sham Shui Po. Photos by Parul Rewal.

Figure 7: Festival paraphernalia and artefacts lined hawker streets entice passers-by. Photos by Parul Rewal.

manifested as freedom of expression. In the constant bid for attaining orderliness and glamour in cities, what mostly gets overlooked is the fact that the disorderly and chaotic parts of the city also hold the capacity to enrapture people in their folds. Such elements need to be incorporated rather than shunned or eradicated though policy and planning.

GOVERNMENTAL REGULATIONS

It is evident that the government's general policy regarding hawker management over the years has been focused primarily on containment and regularisation (or 'formalisation') of hawkers. The official stance of the government since the 1970s has been that there should be no increase in the number of hawker licenses issued and that on-street licensed hawkers should be gradually relocated to off-street public markets.[54] This reflects the government's underlying view that street hawkers do not have a place in its long term vision of modern Hong Kong, now positioned to become 'Asia's World City.' Examination of the government's website and legislative council papers regarding hawker policies reveal how minutely the rules for the hawking trade are controlled. Today, in Hong Kong, hawkers can be classified into two types: Fixed Pitch Hawkers (selling mainly dried-goods and some cooked-food stalls) and the Itinerant (mobile) Hawkers who push carts. The number of fixed-pitch and itinerant hawker licences have been steady at 5,127 and 191 respectively in the urban area and 214 and 208 respectively in the New Territories. There are currently 43 allocated locations for fixed pitch hawkers and 18 locations for hawker markets in Hong Kong.[55] Fixed pitch hawkers are allowed to sell up to 12 commodities, mostly convenience goods, while itinerant hawkers are permitted to sell a maximum of 4 items endorsed on their license.[56] So, not only does the government controls where the licensed hawkers can sell their wares, it also controls what they are allowed to sell.

In 2000, the responsibility of management of hawkers shifted to the Hong Kong Food and Environment Hygiene Department (FEHD), after the dissolution of the Urban Council and the Regional Council (the two municipal councils of Hong Kong) in 1999, soon after Hong Kong's handover to the People's Republic of China.[57] This firmly framed hawker management purely under the public health and safety regulatory framework, predominantly geared to 'reduce street obstruction, prevent environmental nuisance to nearby residents and contain hygiene and fire risks in hawker occupied areas.' The FEHD has, since, been trying to periodically buy back hawker licenses in order to further reduce the number of hawkers. A five-year Voluntary Surrender Scheme was introduced in 2002 to encourage *Dai Pai Tong* hawkers and itinerant hawkers to give up their licenses, since they were viewed to be most likely to cause environmental hygiene problems, noise, congestion of public passageways and fire risks,.[58] Under this scheme, these hawkers were to be compensated with a one-off ex-gratia payment of HKD 60,000 (for *Dai Pai Tongs*) and HKD 30,000 (for Itinerant hawkers), a vacant stall rental in public markets under concessionary terms, or they could become (non-cooked food) fixed pitch hawkers in exchange for surrendering their licenses. The scheme directed at itinerant hawkers was extended unto 2012, resulting in more than 500 itinerant hawkers surrendering their licenses in the Urban Areas and the New Territories.[59] Such eradication-centred policies have led to a sharp decrease in the number of licensed hawkers from 20,000 in the late 1980s to only around 6,300 currently. By 2009, there were only 29 *Dai Pai Tongs* remaining in the territory.[60]

In 2008-2009, The Food and Health Bureau (FHB) and the Food and Environmental Hygiene Department (FEHD) jointly reviewed the policy on hawker licensing in consultation with District Councils, Hawker Associations and relevant stakeholders. In view of the fact that no new hawker licenses had been issued since 1970, and succession and transfer of these licenses was strictly regulated, leading to an overall decline in numbers, it was decided to relax hawker licensing regulations leading to the issuance of 61 new Itinerant Ice-Cream Vendors and 218 new Fixed Pitch Hawker Licenses from July 2009 to April 2012.[61] Since then, the government has kept the number of fixed pitches unchanged.

License conditions are strictly controlled and regulated by the FEHD. A hawker license is not accessible to any person who is below 18 years of age or who already has a valid hawker license. The Hong Kong government also introduced a one-family-one-license policy which not only disallows multiple holding of hawker licenses in one single family but also requires that licensed hawkers and their immediate family members cannot hold other commercial tenancies. License fees are levied on an annual basis and range from HK$1,000 to HK$3,000 depending on the size, location and type of stall. The size and structure of the fixed pitch stall ranges from 1.1sq.m. to 2.2 square

Figure 8: New Fixed Pitch Stalls being installed in Wan Chai in 2016.
Source: Author

metres with majority of stalls not exceeding 1.1 square metres with a dimension of 900x1200mm.[62]

The conditions of operating stalls and succession and transfer of licenses are strictly stipulated. License holders are required to attend to their stalls in person during operating hours but may hire an assistant who must be registered with FEHD. Licenses cannot be traded freely in the market. In case of death, old age or ill-health of a licensee or voluntary surrender, only an immediate family member such as spouse, parent or child can take over the license to operate the stall.[63] However, in reality it is often the case that the 'assistant' is. the owner of the stall through a mutual understanding between the two parties, since legal transfer of licenses is disallowed.

In recent years, the conditions of succession and transfer of fixed pitch licenses have been slightly relaxed. In cases of voluntary surrender of license, the vacant pitches can be transferred to new candidates, with priority being given either to the registered assistant of the original owner or to allow adjacent licensees to use the vacant pitches to widen their operating areas if they are willing to pay the stipulated fees.[64] With the intention of enhancing the vitality of hawker areas and to minimise illegal occupation of vacant stalls, the administration prefers to give priority to fixed pitch hawkers at the front row to take up the use of the adjacent vacant fixed pitch at the back row, thus promoting better utilization of the pitches with less attractive locations.[65]

The FEHD runs about a 100 public markets including 25 cooked food markets, which are usually two storied air-conditioned buildings in various areas of the city, and has also incorporated retailing provisions including cooked food kiosks in public housing estates.[66] It aims to relocate hawkers to these public markets, where the stalls are openly auctioned for a 3 year rental lease with monthly rents ranging from about 1,100 -11000 HKD depending on location and the type of goods allowed to be sold, with additional electricity, AC and maintenance charges.[67] But due to the shortfall in numbers, high rents, generally poor location and design of these markets, they have not been entirely successful. There is a high rate of vacancy in the public markets and hawkers continue to provide stiff competition by positioning themselves at the most convenient spots on the streets to suit market demand.

Hawker monitoring and control

In order to monitor and control the hawking operations in the city, the Food and Environmental Hygiene Department of the Hong Kong government has deployed 191 squads of Hawker Control Teams (HCT) - 125 squads in Hong Kong and Kowloon and 66 squads in the New Territories - both at district and division levels.[68] The squads comprise of trained staff who are equipped with portable radios and vehicles to control hawking activities. They are in charge of management of licensed hawkers to ensure they operate their stalls

Figure 9: Hawkers selling food items in Wan Chai just outside one of the Public wet markets.
Photos by Parul Rewal.

as per the conditions of their license, minimise street obstruction and nuisance, as well as control and eviction of unlicensed hawkers. They also regulate the operation of itinerant hawkers whenever they are found hawking in the streets, taking enforcement action to deal with irregularities, which in itself resulted in 5,622 convictions in 2015.[69]

The government has also identified a list of 45 'hawker black spots' - locations where no prior warning would be given by HCT staff before taking prosecution action against hawking and related offences.[70] To combat unlicensed hawking, the Hawker Control Teams conduct sector patrols and raids at hawker black spots, some even working overnight shifts to apprehend unlicensed hawking activities during the late-night and early-morning hours. Enforcement action is extremely stringent against unlicensed hawkers selling prohibited/restricted food or cooked food. In cases of unlicensed hawkers selling dry goods which cause no public health concerns, but which may be causing obstructions in major thoroughfares and areas of high pedestrian flow such as heavily used footbridges, entrances and exits of MTR and rail lines, ferry concourse and bus termini, tourist spots and pedestrian precincts or in case complaints are registered, the HCT staff are instructed to first issue verbal warnings and if not heeded, to resort to the normal course of enforcement and seizure action.[71]

There were a total of 23,473 convictions of unlicensed hawker or hawker-related offences in 2015, 17,803 in 2016 and another 6,270 in 2017.[72] Compared to almost 6,000 unlicensed hawkers in 1995, the number of unlicensed hawkers as per FEHD records was only around 1,500 at the end of December 2017.[73] Hong Kong government's annual budget in 2016-17 allocated an estimated financial provision of 1,896 million HKD for Market management and Hawker Control, which was a 12 per cent increase from the previous year estimates, and almost 30 per cent of the entire budget estimate for the Food and Environmental Hygiene Department.[74] These amounts include estimates for approximately 116,700 raids by Hawker Control Teams over the year and 2100 trained personnel, giving an indication of the extent of governmental financial resources and man-power spent on monitoring and regulating hawking activity in the city. However, despite all this enforcement action, the number of illegal hawkers has not visibly declined much since 2012, as per the research office of the LegCo Secretariat.[75]

RECENT POLICY REDRESSALS

In recent years, the government has tried to revamp its approach to hawkers to keep in sync with popular sentiments regarding the hawking trade as a part of the city's cultural heritage. The department sought to address the lack of a comprehensive hawker related policy by setting up a sub-committee that met between 2013 and 2015 to advise on how to deal with hawkers in the city.[76] Studying overseas models of hawker management in Singapore, Taiwan, Australia and Thailand, the sub-committee expressed its grave concerns over the existing policy of the Hong Kong administration being one of only regulation and control, and suggested a more flexible approach by the government aimed at development of the hawking trade. They urged the government to recognise it as an integral element that contributed to Hong Kong's sustainability, diversity of its economy, social capacity building and liveability, and not only suggested issuing more hawker licenses but also identifying more venues suitable for hawking during urban renewal and town planning. The sub-committee suggested promoting culture and handicrafts through more open-air hawker bazaars and night markets, based on more bottom-up, district led proposals. They also proposed reviving the traditional *dai pai tongs* and turning vacant off-street hawker markets into cooked food centres. The idea of allowing a certain number of wooden food carts and food trucks to offer more lunch options to young office employees at strategic locations in the city was also raised, urging accompanying measures to avoid their monopolisation by large consortia. The role of the district councils in Hong Kong have been sought to be strengthened in managing, regulating and organising hawker licensing and hawker bazaars. It was proposed that they should be responsible for proposing new hawker locations in consultation with the communities, sorting conflicts that may arise between hawkers and the public and to ensure hawker policy can meet the diverse needs and demands of the community in each district and the whole development of the city.[77]

There have been a few instances of public consultations by FEHD regarding hawker areas in recent years. Public consultations were sought on fire safety management in hawker areas, following two serious incidents of fire break-outs on Fa Yuen Street in Mongkok in 2010 and 2011, with several medium and long-term options floated, including cancellation of licenses, re-siting of hazardous stalls, upgrading the stalls with fire resistant materials and installation of sprinkler systems. Based on the consultations, in which cancellation of licenses was vehemently opposed by district councils and hawker associations, a five-year assistance scheme was launched in March 2013, for which a fund of 230 million HKD was sanctioned. This was aimed to relocate 500 stalls identified to be causing obstruction (such as blocking building stairwells, entrances and discharge points and emergency vehicular movement), to upgrade stalls to fire resistant material, and suspend licenses of repeat offenders who fail to comply with fire safety regulations, such as stall location, material specifications and overnight storage of goods.[78] Of the targeted 4,300 hawkers, about 60 per cent applied for grants for relocation or in-situ upgradation by December 2016[79], while around 860 hawkers (about 20% of the total number) ended up surrendering their licenses, again contributing towards a decline in numbers.[80]

Thus, despite the policy reviews intended at developing a more wholistic approach to hawkers, the evident outcomes continue to be ones of containment, with limited influence in effecting any distinct improvement in the operating environment for hawkers. Nor has there been much visible publicity to disperse information about more flexible hawker policies. What also remains conspicuous in its absence, in the proposals accepted by the government, is the inclusion of any distinct measures aimed to develop and promote the hawking trade, such as enhancing the physical environment and accessibility of hawker occupied areas through urban design as part of wider public space up-gradations, providing infrastructure for lighting and electricity especially for the night markets, or increasing the hawkers' permitted pitch areas to more realistically feasible sizes to eliminate the need for extensions and encroachment. There has been no effort to refer to the extensive research on the informal sector conducted globally that points to wider institutional measures essential to provide a more favourable policy environment and terms of trade for informal economic activity, such as: provision of training for hawkers in environmental hygiene and food safety; availability of business coaching and skill upgradation opportunities; access to credit to improve their financial viability; or provision of safeguards for hawkers in case of accidents, ill health or untimely death.[81] Hong Kong is known to be one of the densest cities in the world, and in a city where space is at one of the highest premiums in the world, the inclusion of more allocated spaces for hawker markets in town planning and urban redevelopment schemes will invariably be a challenge. The 2030 Planning Vision and Strategy report for Hong Kong's development makes no reference to hawkers in its vision for 'reinventing public spaces' despite its aim to 'to celebrate diversity and vibrancy ... [and] to celebrate the uniqueness, identity and sense of place of Hong Kong.'[82] This raises doubts about the efficacy of Hong Kong's hawker management policies in making hawking sustainable in the future without their inclusion in a comprehensive vision for the city, backed by strong political will, adequate financial resources and inter-department cooperation.

On the other hand, some innovative solutions have come from the private sector to modernise the hawking trade. A private financial services group rolled out the Alipay HK electronic payment platform to 43 hawkers in Kwun Tong District around the end of 2017, thus spearheading cashless transactions among hawkers and simultaneously improving hygiene at wet markets by preventing hawkers from handling money and food at the same time.[83]

There has been a rise of private think tanks and organisations such as Civic Exchange, that conduct policy related research on issues including hawker management and the vibrancy of streets in Hong Kong to promote better urban well-being.[84] These are hopeful signs for the future that private stakeholders may be able to provide further innovative and synergetic ways to contribute to the upgradation and sustainability of street hawkers in the city, thereby reducing the sole burden on the government for their control and management. But in order to pave the way for private stakeholder action, it seems vital to remove the illegality framework with which hawkers are associated, and to embrace this informal economic activity as part of a wholistic urban vision to help develop and modernise in pace with the city.

CONCLUSION

It is apparent from Hong Kong hawkers' long and turbulent history, as well as from the statistics over the years, that hawking is an intrinsic 'lower circuit' economic activity, closely intertwined with Hong Kong's identity and development. It is also clear that many more people are involved in making a livelihood through hawking than the number of licenses permitted under current government policy. A distinct demand exists in the market for hawkers' goods and services, as is shown by their persistence. Moreover, hawker streets in Hong Kong are part of an important cultural inheritance which continue to bring richness and vibrancy to the urban fabric.

Hawkers form a bridge between traditional forms of transaction and the contemporary city. They make available more affordable and socially inclusive alternatives to retail spaces; providing useful services that are invariably becoming scarce and expensive in most advanced economies. Hawkers successfully identify voids in the supply and demand chains to fill as they position themselves strategically at vantage locations in the city, while licensed operators try in futility to contain their overflowing supplies within the fixed pitch stalls sanctioned by the government, often turning streets into constant spaces of negotiation between vendors, shoppers and passersby. Yet one can see how the hawker culture is cherished by the public at large who, in many instances, have risen in protest to stand side by side with hawkers when faced with eviction or relocation.

Despite its long historical and cultural presence, hawking activities in Hong Kong continue to struggle under stringent regulations, often bringing it into very close proximity of an illegality discourse. The number of licenses issued has been tightly controlled and transfer and succession policies make it very difficult for new entrants interested in joining the trade. Several recent hawker policy reviews by the government, in consultation with District Councils, hawker associations and urban academics, have acknowledged all the value-added characteristics of the hawking trade. Yet, it remains to be seen whether future policies will implement wider institutional measures to improve the operating environment and business sustainability of Hong Kong hawkers. Sensitive and strategic planning is needed to successfully integrate hawker culture into a cohesive vision for the future development of Hong Kong.

ABOUT THE AUTHOR

Parul Rewal is an architect who has been living and working internationally in India, South Africa, Singapore and the UK. She holds a MA degree in Urban Management and has been engaged in research related to urban governance, housing affordability and the urban informal sector. She currently lives in Shanghai and is a Council Member of the Royal Asiatic Society China.

E-mail: parulrewal@gmail.com

Endnotes

1 'Research programme on the Informal sector', Global Development Research Centre (GDRC), http://www.gdrc.org/informal/about-informal.html (accessed October 2015).

2 International Labour Office (ILO), '*Employment. Income and Equality: A Strategy for Increasing Productivity in Kenya,*' Report of an inter-agency team financed by the UNDP and organised

by the ILO (Geneva), 1972, 6, http://www.ilo.org/public/libdoc/ilo/1972/72B09_608_engl.pdf (accessed May 2016).

3 Martha A Chen, 'The Informal economy- Definitions,Theories and Policies', WEIGO Working Papers, no.1, August 2012, 1, http://www.wiego.org/sites/default/files/publications/files/Chen_WIEGO_WP1.pdf

4 See for example International Labour Office (ILO), *Key Indicators of the Labour Market* (Geneva: ILO, 2000); J. Charmes, '*The Contribution of Informal Sector to GDP in Developing Countries: Assessment, Estimates, Methods, Orientations for the Future,*' Paper presented at the Fourth Meeting of the Expert Group on Informal Sector Statistics (Delhi Group), Geneva, 2000, pp. 28-30; Joann Vanek, Martha Alter Chen and Ralf Hussmanns, 'Statistics on the Informal Economy: Definitions, Findings and Challenges.' WIEGO Working Paper No. 2, Cambridge, MA: WIEGO, 2014, pp. 9-12.

5 Suzanne Satalin and Adam Renton, 'A Closing-time: How Hong Kong's Hawkers face a struggle to live', *South China Morning Post* (Hong Kong). 3 March 2015, http://multimedia.scmp.com/hawkers/5

6 Hong Kong - The Facts, Food Safety and Environmental Hygiene, FEHD, GovHK, 2018, http://www.fehd.gov.hk/english/publications/facts_sheet/fact_sheets.pdf

7 'Hawker Overview', Food and Environmental Hygiene Department (FEHD), The Government of the Hong Kong Special Administrative Region. http://www.fehd.gov.hk/english/pleasant_environment/hawker/overview.html

8 'Issues related to Hawkers and Hawking/, LegCo Panel, LC Paper No. CB(4)566/13-14(01), April 2014, http://www.legco.gov.hk/yr13-14/english/panels/fseh/fseh_hp/papers/fseh_hp0415cb4-566-1-e.pdf

9 J. Nacken, 'Chinese Street Cries in Hong Kong', *Journal of the Hong Kong Branch of the Royal Asiatic Society*, vol. 8, 1968, pp. 128- 134, http://hkjo.lib.hku.hk/archive/files/4a3f76eb3b0ec5f0492edb2389d1e0a8.pdf

10 Henry Norman, *The People and Politics of the Far East* (New York: Charles Scribner's Sons, 1895).

11 Nacken, 'Chinese Street Cries in Hong Kong', p. 129.

12 Ibid., p. 128.

13 David Faure (ed.), *Society- A Documentary History of Hong Kong* (Hong Kong: Hong Kong University press, 1997), p. 201.

14 Josephine Smart, 'The Squatter Economy of Street Hawkers in Hong Kong', *Centre of Asian Studies occasional papers and monographs*, no. 81, University of Hong Kong, 1989,

15 David Podmore, 'The Population of Hong Kong' in Keith Hopkins (ed.), *Hong Kong: The Industrial Colony* (Hong Kong: Oxford University Press, 1971), pp. 21-54.

16 See for example: 'The Second World War and the Japanese Occupation' in David Faure (ed.), *Society- A Documentary History of Hong Kong*", pp. 209-232.

17 Terence Gary McGee, 'Hawkers in Hong Kong: A Study of Planning and Policy in a third World City', *Centre of Asian Studies Occasional Papers and Monographs*, no.17, University of Hong Kong, 1973, pp. 37-38.

18 F. S. Sit, in a speech delivered to the Hawkers Forum on 4 November 1984, as quoted by Hoi Leung Man, 'Hawkers and Urban Planning in Hong Kong, an Evaluation', Thesis, Centre for Urban Studies and Urban Planning, University of Hong Kong, 1985, MSS-711.4095125.M266

19 Suzanne Satalin and Adam Renton, "A Closing-time: How Hong Kong's Hawkers face a struggle to live", *South China Morning Post* (Hong Kong), 3 March 2015, http://multimedia.scmp.com/hawkers/ .

20 'Report of Committee on Hawking', LegCo sessional papers no.1, Hong Kong Government Printer, Hong Kong, 1, as quoted by Hoi Leung Man, 'Hawkers and Urban Planning in Hong Kong, an Evaluation.'

21 See Jeffrey Henderson, 'Pacific Rim cities in the world economy', in Michael Peter Smith (ed.), *Comparative urban and community research*, vol. 2, (New Brunswick: Transactions Publishers, 1989); R. Hsia and L. Chau, *Industrialization, employment and income distribution: A case study of Hong Kong* (London: Croom Helm, 1969); Alexander Youngson, *Hong Kong economic growth and policy* (Hong Kong: Oxford University Press, 1982).

22 Amy K. Glasmeier, 'Flexibility and Adjustment: The Hong Kong Watch Industry and Global Change', *Growth and Change*, vol 2, Centre for Business and Economic Research, University of Kentucky, (1994), p. 225.

23 Alan Smart and Josephine Smart, 'Introduction' in Alan Smart and Josephine Smart (ed.), *Petty Capitalists and Globalization:*

Flexibility, Entrepreneurship and Economic Development, (Albany, New York: State University of New York Press, 2012), pp. 1-22.

24 Tony Fu-lai Yu, *Entrepreneurship and Economic Development in Hong Kong* (London: Routledge,1997), p. 29.

25 Alan Smart and Josephine Smart, "Introduction", p. 15.

26 Josephine Smart, *The Political Economy of Street Hawking in Hong Kong*, (Hong Kong: Centre of Asian Studies, 1989)

27 'Hawkers, A report with Policy recommendations', Urban Council, Government of Hong Kong, 1957, 1, as quoted by Hoi Leung. Man, 'Hawkers and Urban Planning in Hong Kong, an Evaluation.'

28 'Issues Related to Hawkers and Hawking', p. 1.

29 McGee, 'Hawkers in Hong Kong: A Study of Planning and Policy in a third World City', p. 62.

30 Suzanne Satalin and Adam Renton, 'A Closing-time: How Hong Kong's Hawkers face a struggle to live', *South China Morning Post* (Hong Kong), 3 March 2015, http://multimedia.scmp.com/hawkers/

31 W. P. Morgan, 'Internal Organisation of Triad Societies in Hong Kong', Kingley Bolton and Christopher Hutton (eds.), *Triad Societies* (London, Routledge, 2000), p. 90.

32 Hoi Leung Man, 'Hawkers and Urban Planning in Hong Kong, an Evaluation.'

33 Amy K. Glasmeier, 'Flexibility and Adjustment: The Hong Kong Watch Industry and Global Change', *Growth and Change*, vol 2, Centre for Business and Economic Research, University of Kentucky, 1994, p. 230.

34 See Stephen W. K. Chiu and Y. So Alvin, 'Flexible Production and Industrial Restructuring in Hong Kong: From Boom to Bust?' in Raul Fernandez et al. (eds.), *Labor Versus Empire: Race, Gender, Migration* (London & New York: Routledge, 2004), pp. 197-213; Stephen W. K. Chiu, Yeuk-mui Tam and Y. So Alvin, 'Employment in Hong Kong: Trends and Patterns in Comparative Perspective,; *Asian Survey*, 48(4), 2007, pp. 673–702.

35 Alan Smart, *The Shek Kip Mei Myth, Squatters, Fires and Colonial Rule in Hong Kong, 1950-1963* (Hong Kong University Press, 2006), p. 51.

36 Ibid., pp. 51-52.

37 Frank Leeming, *Studies in Hong Kong: Localities in a Chinese City* (Oxford: Oxford University Press, 1977), p. 161.

38 Hoi Leung Man, 'Hawkers and Urban Planning in Hong Kong, an Evaluation.'

39 See Polly Callaghan and Heidi Hartmann, 'Contingent Work, A Chart Book on Part-time and Temporary Employment'" Washington, DC: Institution Women' policy Resources and Economic Policy Institute, 1991.

40 Michael Curtin, 'Industry on Fire: The Cultural Economy of Hong Kong Media,' *Post Script* 19(1), 1999, pp. 28-52.

41 Catherine Schenk, 'Economic History of Hong Kong' in Robert Whaples (ed.), *EH.Net Encyclopedia*, updated on March 16, 2008, http://eh.net/encyclopedia/economic-history-of-hong-kong

42 Vicki Smith, 'Institutionalizing Flexibility in a Service Firm: Multiple Contigencies and Hidden Hierarchies', *Work Occupation*, 1997, 21(3), pp. 284-307.

43 Chris Tilly, 'Resource for the Continuing Growth of Part-time Employment', *Monthly Labor Review*, 114(3), 1991, pp. 10-18.

44 See for example, Mei Ling and May Wong, 'Employee casualisation in department stores in Hong Kong', *Hong Kong institute of Business Studies, Lingnan University*, Working paper series 038-990, 2000.

45 'Issues Related to Hawkers and Hawking', p. 5.

46 Zhigang Tao and Y. C. Richard Wong , 'Hong Kong: From an Industrialised City to a Centre of Manufacturing-related Services', *Urban Studies* ,vol 39, issue 12, 2002, pp. 2345 – 2358.

47 'Commerce and Industry', Research Office, Legco Secretariat, Statistical Highlights, Paper no. ISSH01/16-17, 24 October 2016, https://www.legco.gov.hk/research-publications/english/1617issh01-hong-kongs-economic-structure-20161024-e.pdf

48 R. Hsia and L. Chau, *Industrialization, employment and income distribution: A case study of Hong Kong* (London: Croom Helm, 1969).

49 'Private Retail- Average Rents and Prices from 1989', GovHK, Rating and Evaluation Department, http://www.rvd.gov.hk/mobile/en/property_market_statistics/index.html

50 Joyee Chan, '40 years of fashion finished: demolition of Hong Kong's famed Yen Chow Street a Bazaar dismays designers', *South China Morning Post*, 7 December 2015, https://www.scmp.com/lifestyle/fashion-luxury/article/1886774/social-fabric-hong-kong-textile-bazaars-demolition-dismays

51 Tony Cheung and Ernest Kao, 'Mong Kok riot: 38 charged and to

appear in court as Hong Kong asks how New Year's night turned to violence', *South China Morning Post* (Hong Kong), 11 February 2016, https://www.scmp.com/news/hong-kong/law-crime/article/1911354/mong-kok-riot-38-charged-and-appear-court-hong-kong-asks.

52 Jonathan Raban, *Soft city: What cities do to us, and how they change the way we live, think and feel* (London:Hamish Hamilton, 1974).

53 Alex Franklin, *City Life* (London: Sage Publications, 2010).

54 'Issues Related to Hawkers and Hawking', p. 2.

55 Ibid., 3.

56 'Report of Sub-Committee on Hawker Policy', *LegCo Panel on Food Safety and Environmental Hygiene*, LC Paper No. CB(4)1497/14-15, July 2015, http://www.legco.gov.hk/yr14-15/english/panels/fseh/fseh_hp/reports/fseh_hpcb4-1497-e.pdf

57 'Issues Related to Hawkers and Hawking', p. 5.

58 'Review on Hawker Licensing Policy, 2009', *Advisory Council on Food and Environmental Hygiene*, AFCEH Paper 92, January 2009, http://www.fhb.gov.hk/download/committees/board/doc/2009/paper20090115_92.pdf

59 "Issues Related to Hawkers and Hawking", p. 8.

60 'Review on Hawker Licensing Policy, 2009.'

61 'Hawker Control', Food and Environmental Hygiene Department, The Government of the Hong Kong Special Administrative Region, Retrieved in May 2016, http://www.fehd.gov.hk/english/pleasant_environment/hawker/overview.html

62 "Issues Related to Hawkers and Hawking", p. 8.

63 'Review on Hawker Licensing Policy, 2009.'

64 Ibid.

65 Ibid.

66 'Public Markets', FEHD GovHK, http://www.fehd.gov.hk/english/pleasant_environment/tidy_market/overview.html

67 'Open Auction of Vacant Market Stalls', FEHD GovHK, Retrieved in March 2018, http://www.fehd.gov.hk/english/pleasant_environment/tidy_market/201805_hk_auction.html

68 'Hawker Control', FEHD GovHK, Retrieved on 6 July 2016, http://www.fehd.gov.hk/english/pleasant_environment/hawker/blackspot.html

69 Ibid.

70 Ibid.

71 Ibid.

72 'Control of Licensed and Unlicensed Hawkers', FEHD GovHK, Last updated 20 February 2018, http://www.fehd.gov.hk/english/pleasant_environment/hawker/control.html

73 Ibid.

74 GovHK 2016-17 Budget Estimates, Head 49- FEHD, p 245: https://www.budget.gov.hk/2016/eng/pdf/head049.pdf

75 'Hawker control in Hong Kong', Research Office of LegCo Secretariat, GovHK, Statistical Highlights, paper no ISSH05/17-18, Updated 1 December 2017, https://www.legco.gov.hk/research-publications/english/1718issh05-hawker-control-in-hong-kong-20171201-e.pdf

76 'Proposals on Hawker Management', *Legco Panel on Food Safety and Environmental Hygiene, Sub-Committee on Hawker Management,* LC Paper No. CB(4)561/14-15(01), February 2015, http://www.legco.gov.hk/yr14-15/english/panels/fseh/fseh_hp/papers/fseh_hp20150302cb4-561-1-e.pdf

77 'Report of Sub-Committee on Hawker Policy', *LegCo Panel on Food Safety and Environmental Hygiene,* LC Paper No. CB(4)1497/14-15, July 2015, http://www.legco.gov.hk/yr14-15/english/panels/fseh/fseh_hp/reports/fseh_hpcb4-1497-e.pdf

78 'Public Consultation on the management of Fixed Pitch Hawkers', FEHD GovHK, February 2012, https://www.gov.hk/en/residents/government/publication/consultation/docs/2012/Fixed_Pitch_Hawkers.pdf

79 'Chapter IV- Environmental Hygiene', Annual Report 2016, FEHD GovHK, Last Revised 28 November 2017, http://www.fehd.gov.hk/english/publications/annualrpt/2016/4.html

80 Ko Wing Man, 'LCQ21:Fixed Pitch Hawker Licenses', Press Release by GovHK, 22 March 2017, Annex 2, http://www.info.gov.hk/gia/general/201703/22/P2017032200720.htm

81 See for example- Hernando de Soto, *The mystery of capital: Why capitalism triumphs in the West and fails everywhere else* (New York: Basic Books, 2000); Marjo Riita Liimatainen, *Training and skills acquisition in the informal sector: a literature review,* International Labour Organization, 2002; Martha Alter Chen, "The Informal Sector: Definitions, Theories and Policies", WEIGO Working Paper, No. 1, 2012, pp. 17-19.

82 Hong Kong SAR Government, *Hong Kong 2030 +:Towards a*

Planning Vision and Strategy transcending 2030 (Hong Kong: Development Bureau and Planning Department, 2007), p. 32.

83 Zen Soo, 'Hong Kong's hawkers and fishmongers to spearhead city's cashless push with Alipay roll out'" *South China Morning Post*, 23 October 2017, http://www.scmp.com/tech/innovation/article/2116622/hong-kongs-hawkers-and-fishmongers-spearhead-citys-cashless-push

84 See for example, Civic Exchange, http://civic-exchange.org.

ANALYSIS OF MEXICAN FOREIGN POLICY. THE CASE OF THE DIVERSIFICATION OF FOREIGN RELATIONS:
A LOOK AT THE RELATIONSHIP WITH THE PEOPLE'S REPUBLIC OF CHINA

BY EDITH YAZMIN MONTES INCIN

ABSTRACT

In the discourse of Mexican foreign policy, diversification is a constant theme and is interpreted as a positive goal. For decades, the government has established a wide network of diplomatic offices as part of regional and multilateral mechanisms and forums on promoting international relations matter by signing agreements and treaties with other countries. In the economic sphere, efforts to establish trade ties have been concentrated on interactions with the United States. However, this relationship is becoming increasingly problematic. Currently, in the face of the protectionist tendencies by the Donald Trump administration in the United States, the discourse on the diversification of foreign relations has been strengthened in Mexico. Much attention is being given to Mexico's relationship with the People's Republic of China (PRC) due to China's powerful position in the world economy. China has always been considered one of the most important strategic partners in Mexico's foreign relations. The main objective of this article is to evaluate the political and economic relations between Mexico and China during the twenty-first century and determine the scope and limits of this relationship to suggest some recommendations for improving Mexico-China relationship.

INTRODUCTION

The diversification of foreign relations has been present since the advent of Mexico's independence that ensues to this day. Although Mexico has 156 representations (embassies and consulates) in the world and has signed multiple bilateral and multilateral treaties and participates actively in regional and multilateral forums on various issues on the international agenda, Mexican economic relations are highly concentrated with the United States. From 2000 to 2017, 80 per cent of total Mexican exports went to the United States, while 46 per cent of imports came from this country and from 1999 to 2017, the 49 per cent of total foreign direct investment to Mexico came from the United States.[1] Mexico has twelve Free Trade Agreements with forty-six countries and thirty-two agreements for the promotion and protection of investments with thirty-three countries. In addition, it is a part of organization such as the World Trade Organization (WTO), the Asia-Pacific Economic Cooperation Forum (APEC), and the Organization for Economic Cooperation and Development (OCDE), among others.[2]

There is a need for Mexico to deepen ties with the United States, but at the same time diversify foreign relations, especially in light of the current situation with the President of the United States, Donald Trump. Recently the discourse of diversification of foreign relations has gained strength in Mexico. For example, at the end of January 2017, the President of Mexico, Enrique Peña announced that Mexico would seek to diversify and strengthen its commercial ties with Asia, Europe and Africa as the main objective in terms of foreign policy.[3] In view of the imminent protectionist tendency that the United States' government has proclaimed, Mexico should diversify its relations and seek to balance its economic relations with other countries, especially with those that have a prominent role in the world economy, such as the People's Republic of China (hereinafter China).

Is this possible? The purpose of this paper is to try to answer this question in three parts. Firstly, I will review the antecedents of Mexico's relationship with China that lasted until the end of the twentieth century. Secondly, I will give an overview of Mexico's external relations with China during the period of 2000-2017 to identify the main successes and failures. The last part will be about the opportunities and challenges that both countries face, given the protectionist tendency of the United States and the change of government in Mexico that will occur in July 2018. Please note that the analysis of this relationship is made from a Mexican perspective and that the criticisms and suggestions are focused on what should be done by the makers of Mexican foreign policy.

ANTECEDENTS OF THE RELATIONS OF MEXICO WITH CHINA: BETWEEN TENSIONS AND APPROACHES

One of the first antecedents in the relations between Mexico and China was developed in commercial terms with the Galleon de Manila, also called Galleon de Acapulco or Nao de China - trading ships that crossed the Pacific Ocean from Acapulco to arrive in Manila, Philippines on a yearly basis between 1565 and 1815. The colonies and the Spanish crown received from Asia large quantities of silk, porcelain, medicines and other handicrafts, while the main export of New Spain (Mexico was part of this Spanish colony) was silver; on average fifty metric tons of silver they were transported annually through the galleon.[4] However, this route ended due to the weakening of the Spanish empire and the war of independence in the New Spain, which interrupted the contact between the American and the Asian continent.[5]

The Independence movement and the formation of the First Mexican Empire led to a resetting of foreign relations. The report prepared by the Foreign Affairs Committee of the First Empire and presented to the Sovereign Board of the Governor of the Mexican Empire on 29 December 1821, is about of the future of foreign relations of the empire. By the way, it is necessary to remember that the Philippines was also a Spanish colony like Mexico. In this sense, in the report, three possible scenarios can be identified on the relations with Philippines and in general with Asia. In the first scenario, it was suggested that the Philippines would continue as a colony of Spain, which implied that Mexico definitively suspended its relations with the Philippines. In the second scenario, it was suggested that the Philippines would become independent from Spain, which would allow intergovernmental agreements with Mexico.

The last scenario, referred to the possibility that the Philippines would join Mexico, which would imply commercial advantages, such as the circulation of Mexican silver in Asia or the manufacture of vessels in the Philippines to maintain the commercial flows between Mexico and Asia. In addition, it would imply Asian migrations – Chinese migration, mainly– to colonize the territories of Texas and Alta California, as well as the incorporation of the Mariana Islands to have an intermediate scale in the commercial route between Mexico and the Philippines.[6]

Based on the above, although there was interest from the Mexican Empire (1821-1824) to develop relations with Asia, it was not possible to promote maritime trade or the colonization of Northern Mexico with Chinese settlers, due to institutional incapacity, absence of a strong government and the lack of unity in the independent country. In 1824, after the overthrow of the First Mexican Empire, the first

Constitution of Mexico established a form of government as a federal republic. However, throughout of the nineteenth century, Mexico faced great political instability, foreign interventions from the United States, Spain, France and Great Britain, scarce economic development and a lack of national unity; therefore, Mexico's relations with Asia were lost.[7]

Until the Porfiriato – a period of Mexican history during which power in Mexico was under the control of the military Porfirio Diaz between 28 November 1876 to 25 May 1911 – México's relations with Asia were promoted, mainly with China and Japan. The main objective of establishing diplomatic ties with China was to find a market for Mexican silver exports, import Chinese products and boost flows of Chinese migrants to colonize northern Mexico.[8] Mexican diplomats like Matías Romero considered ways to attract Chinese migrants to work in mines and on the construction of railroads, key sectors of Mexico's economic development at the time.[9]

The negotiations for an agreement between Mexico and China began in 1881; however, the negotiation process was long and intermittent because of the difficulty of maintaining a more fluid communication between both governments.[10] Until 14 December 1899, Wu Ting Fang, plenipotentiary minister of the government of the Qing Dynasty of China in the United States and Manuel de Aspiroz, plenipotentiary minister of Mexico in the United States, officially signed the *Treaty of Friendship, Commerce and Navigation* between China and Mexico to establish formal diplomatic relations.[11] The enforcement of the treaty in 1900 did not bring about a radical change in the relation; at the governmental level, the Sino-Mexican relations were restricted to the opening of representations in both the capital cities of Mexico and Beijing.[12] In addition, although the treaty addressed commercial aspects, there was no increase in trade. On the other hand, the migration of Chinese to Mexico increased, and they became the fourth group of foreigners in Mexico, representing more than 11 per cent of the population in the country.[13]

In the first half of the twentieth century, relations between Mexico and China were strained due to the beginning of the Mexican and Chinese revolutions, Japanese expansion and the tensions that this would generate in the Pacific region. During this period, three themes prevailed in this bilateral relationship: 1) the mutual recognition of the governments following their respective civil wars; 2) the claims for damages suffered during the Mexican Revolution; and 3) the growth of Chinese migratory flows into Mexico. The last theme was undoubtedly one of the issues that dominated bilateral relations in post-revolutionary Mexico, as it led to persecution of the Chinese during the 1920s and 1930s. From the 1920s, and for at least until the mid 1930s, xenophobia was exacerbated, whether encouraged by government agencies or by pressure groups entrenched in power. This manifested in different forms, such as the killing of 303 Chinese in Torreón, Coahuila in northeastern Mexico, which occurred on 15 May 1911, the establishment of pro-race groups in Sonora, also in northern Mexico, the mass expulsion of Chinese and the prohibition of marriages between Mexicans and Chinese.[14] There was also the publication of a book written by José Ángel Espinoza in 1931 entitled *The Chinese Problem in Mexico*, according to which, the Mexican race would be weakened by mixing with Chinese that induced the federal government to contain immigration as its central objective.[15]

The persecution of the Chinese can be explained by several factors. One is the 1929 crisis, which involved the expulsion of Mexicans from the United States who could not find employment upon their return to their home country. At this time, Asians were prevented from entering the United States, so they were stranded in northern Mexico. The Chinese were blamed for the unemployment of the Mexicans and persecution intensified. However, other populations of foreigners in Mexico, such as Guatemalans or Spaniards were not persecuted, so the cause of the persecution against the Chinese was related to racism.[16] During this period, Mexico behaved in a paradoxical manner; on the one hand, Mexicans persecuted and killed Asian people, encouraged by the governors of the northern states due to popular ignorance and racism, while Mexico was defending China in the League of Nations before the Japanese invasion.[17]

Another relevant issue in this period was the question of recognition, which both governments faced. The recognition of Mexico depended on the recognition of the United States to the government of Yuan Shikai, which occurred in April 1913 and the Mexican government concurred in May of that same year. For its part, China recognised the government of Mexico of the then President Adolfo de la Huerta in 1920. When the government of China changed in 1922, it was no longer a relevant issue for Mexico, allowing relations to continue without touching the issue of recognition.[18]

During the 1940s, the bilateral relationship deteriorated further due to the problems of regime changes, mutual recognition, racism, erroneous diplomatic conduct, lack of material interests and denunciation of the basis of the treaty base.[19] The treaty of 1899 was officially repealed in August 1944, as the Chinese government intended to create a new treaty of friendship and commerce of a very general nature. The main purpose of this was to eliminate the extraterritoriality clause.[20]

After the triumph of the Communist Party on 1 October 1949 in mainland China and the consequent founding of the People's Republic of China (PRC), the Mexican government continued diplomatic relations with the government of the Republic of China that was established in Taiwan.[21] Although the Mexican government did not formally recognise the PRC, during the government of Adolfo López Mateos (1958-1964) there was an approach to the PRC. During this period, Beijing carried out an intense worldwide diplomatic campaign in search of recognition through 'cultural diplomacy', which consisted of invitations to political leaders, opinion leaders and artistic groups to visit the PRC, among those include Vicente Lombardo Toledano, Lázaro Cárdenas, Emilio Portes Gil, Fernando Benítez, and others.[22]

The strategy created general interest in Chinese culture, and led to articles, books and travel accounts. In addition, the Centre for Studies of Asia and Africa was opened in El Colegio de México. This helped to counteract the negative feeling directed towards the Chinese in the first decades of the twentieth century. On 7 December 1963, the Economic and Commercial Exhibition of the People's Republic of China was held in Mexico, which resulted in a few economic exchanges, such as a deal to export cotton to mainland China.[23] Nevertheless, the government headed by Gustavo Díaz Ordaz (1964-1970) 'hardened the vigilance and controlled the exchanges with communist countries',[24] which showed a lack of continuity in the Mexican government's actions.

The Mexico-United States relationship played a part in the establishment of Mexico's relations with the People's Republic of China. Following the warming of relations between China and the United States and the readmission of the former to the UN and its Security Council, Mexico changed its official recognition from Taipei to Beijing on 14 February 1972.[25] This led to the establishment of political, economic and cultural relations with mainland China. The relationship that was established was based on a comprehensive

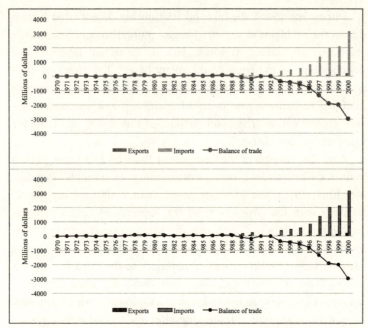

Figure 1: Trade between Mexico and the People's Republic of China 1970-2000. Source: Prepared by the author with data from the International Monetary Fund, http://data.imf.org/regular.aspx?key=61013712 [accessed 7 July 2018]

approach that supported the development of political contacts, economic and commercial expansion, and diversified cooperation.[26]

Since the establishment of diplomatic relations with the PRC, the main objective in the bilateral relationship was to strengthen the political and economic ties between both nations. In 1972, Mexican President Luis Echeverría made a state visit to China. Because of Echeverria's presidential visit to China, the first Commercial Counsel of Mexico was established at the Mexican embassy in Beijing,[27] which proves that Mexico sought to strengthen economic relations and commercial with China. Although trade increased between both nations, which was favourable to Mexico, it was not significant (see figure 1 for details of the increase in trade since the establishment of diplomatic relations.). This situation prevailed throughout the eighties and Mexico managed to maintain a trade surplus until 1987.[28]

Regarding cultural relations between both countries, Mexico established the Special Program for the Teaching of Spanish to Students of the People's Republic of China, sponsored by the Secretariat of Public Education and developed by El Colegio de México, between

1974 and 1987.[29] In addition, in 1978, the Chinese and Mexican governments established the Sino-Mexican Mixed Commission for Cultural and Educational Cooperation.[30] Another interesting case is the opening of the Centre for Oriental Studies of the Universidad Nacional Autónoma de México (UNAM) on 21 July 1966.[31] In 1967, the Centre for Oriental Studies department offered a Bachelor of Arts degree in Oriental Studies, also one of the Center's periodicals was the yearbook *Asia*. In 1973, the centre changed its name to Afro-Asian Studies Centre; however, after a short time, it ceased to exist.[32]

At the end of the 1980s and during the 1990s, the diversification of international relations, including those with Asian countries, was promoted again. At this time, the rapprochement with the United States and Canada deepened, which resulted in the signing of NAFTA. This led to the concentration of economic relations between Mexico and the United States. At the same time, the government of Carlos Salinas de Gortari developed its interest in the Pacific region. Regarding Mexico's relations with China in the 1990s, Haro, León and Ramírez explain that the Mexican government encouraged economic opening. This produced uncontrolled entry of products originating in Greater China (China, Hong Kong and Taiwan) in the early 1990s to Mexico.[33] From then on, the trade balance that had previously been favourable for Mexico changed, giving rise to one of the most relevant characteristics of the relations between Mexico and China in the twenty-first century - the trade deficit for Mexico as shown in figure 1.

At the end of the century, the administration of Ernesto Zedillo sought to deepen the relationship with the PRC with the National Development Plan of 1995-2000.[34] He stated that Mexico 'will seek to establish closer ties with the People's Republic of China, in order to multiply opportunities for commercial exchange with that nation.'[35] Since then, one of the prominent issues in the relationship has been the growing trade deficit for Mexico. Other events that stand out from the relationship during this period are President Zedillo's visit to China in November 1996. During the visit, the Chinese government recognized Mexico's support for the One-China Policy, the Mexico's position on the Tibet issue, the non-interference in human rights issues in China, as well as Mexico's support for China's entry into the World Trade Organization (WTO).[36] On the other hand, the Mexico-China friendship parliamentary group was established on 30 June 1995, and the Mexican Senate arranged the first meeting of the Mexico-China

Policy Consultation Mechanism in October 1996.[37]

However, since the 1980s, in commercial terms, there have been growing tensions between Mexico and China. Faced with the growing trade deficit of Mexico with China and the lack of competitiveness of the Mexican economy to confront the Chinese, the government of Carlos Salinas de Gortari (1988-1994) began to raise tariffs to Chinese products entering Mexico.[38] This situation continued in the following Mexican administration, during the presidency of President Zedillo (1994-2000). At the end of February 1995, the Mexican government temporarily increased (35 per cent on average) the tariff rates applied for bicycles, footwear, tools, yarns and fabrics, toys, appliances and electrical equipment, clothing, organic chemicals, iron and steel valves, among other merchandise. Faced with this situation, the Chinese government showed dissatisfaction and complained about unfair Mexican tariff rates.[39]

THE RELATIONSHIP OF MEXICO WITH THE PEOPLE'S REPUBLIC OF CHINA IN THE 21ST CENTURY: BETWEEN CHANGES AND CONTINUITIES

Currently, in diplomatic terms, Mexico has a permanent mission in the People's Republic of China with an embassy in Beijing as well as consulates-general in Guangzhou, Hong Kong and Shanghai.[40] China has permanent mission in Mexico City and one consulate-general in Tijuana.[41] Xu Shicheng highlights that one of the aspects that distinguish relations between Mexico and China is that the top leaders of both countries have made mutual visits and have maintained frequent contacts.[42] The Mexican presidents Vicente Fox, Felipe Calderón and Enrique Peña have all made state visits to the People's Republic of China. Between 2000 and 2017 Mexico and China signed 98 agreements, especially in economic matters (50 agreements).[43] However, the trade deficit persists and the low foreign investment from China questions the variety of agreements signed and the realities of establishing them.

Regarding economic relations in the period 2000-2017, 59 per cent of the total trade that Mexico made with Northeast Asia was with China, 24 per cent with Japan and 17 per cent with South Korea, which shows dominance of the trade with the PRC. It is the second largest global trading partner of Mexico, while Mexico is China's largest trading partner in Latin America.[44] However, the gap between the first trading partner of Mexico (United States) and the second partner (China) is still very wide (see figure 2).

The total amount of exports from Mexico to China during the period from 2000 to 2017 was US 57.369 billion dollars, while exports from China to Mexico amounted to US 672.076 billion dollars, which represented a deficit for Mexico of US 614.707 billion dollars, which shows that the deficit has continued to grow from the late 1980s. Enrique Dussel explains that the high trade deficit reflects a worrying structural problem: the technological backwardness of Mexican products compared to Asian products, which means the trade deficit for Mexico is not only in quantity but also in the quality of Mexican exports.[45]

To detail the quality of Mexican exports, when reviewing the main goods that Mexico exports to the People's Republic of China, they are mainly mineral products, while importing intermediate and capital goods. For example, in 2000, 86.5 per cent of exports to China were linked to electronics and the automotive sector, these accounted

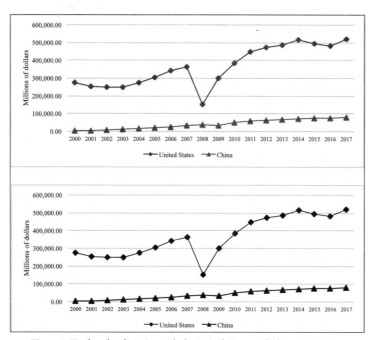

Figure 2: Total trade of Mexico with the United States and China 2000-2017.
Source: Prepared by the author with data from the Ministry of Economy, *Foreign Trade. Statistical Information and Tariff*, https://www.gob.mx/se/acciones-y-programas/comercio-exterior-informacion-estadistica-y-arancelaria?state=published [accessed 8 July 2018]

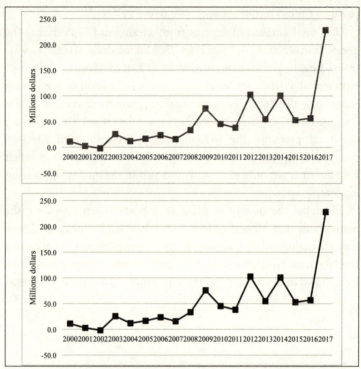

Figure 3: Chinese foreign direct investment to Mexico 2000-2017.
Source: Prepared by the author with data from the Ministry of Economy, *Secretariat of Economy, Competitiveness and Normativity. Official statistics of FDI flows to Mexico*, https://www.gob.mx/se/acciones-y-programas/competitividad-y-normatividad-inversion-extranjera-directa?state=published [accessed 9 July 2018]

for less than 30 per cent in 2010 and during this last year, minerals, particularly oil and copper in various forms and other raw materials generated more than 53 per cent of exports to China.[46] It shows a change in the structure of Mexican exports to China, which goes from exports of high added value to exports of raw materials. China has also changed the products it offers for trade, seeking now to export high technology and value-added products. On the other hand, from 2000 to 2017, Chinese Foreign Direct Investment (FDI) amounted to 899.3 million dollars (see figure 3). Notwithstanding the above, the Chinese exports to Mexico do not compare with the Chinese investments that arrive to Mexico, practically Chinese investments are non-existent.

During the 2000-2017 period, China invested mainly in manufacturing industries, followed by mining, financial services and insurance, commerce, and information in mass media (see figure 4).

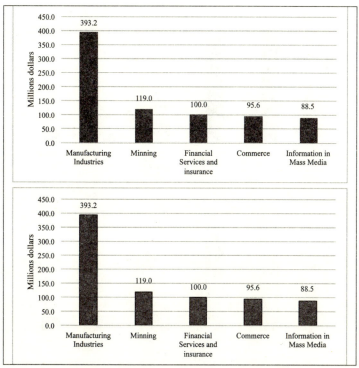

Figure 4: Chinese direct foreign investment by sector 2000-2017.
Source: Prepared by the author with data from the Ministry of Economy, *Secretariat of Economy, Competitiveness and Normativity. Official statistics of FDI flows to Mexico,* https://www.gob.mx/se/acciones-y-programas/competitividad-y-normatividad-inversion-extranjera-directa?state=published [accessed 9 July 2018]

Regarding the geographical distribution of Chinese FDI in Mexico, of the 32 states that make up the Mexican Republic, the state receiving most Chinese investment was Jalisco, followed by Mexico City, Colima, Tabasco, and Chihuahua. As can be seen in figure 5, most of the investment was directed towards the centre and north of the Mexico.

The relationship between Mexico and China experienced moments of understanding and conflict. During the period of 2000-2006, relations were cordial and characterised by the exchange of visits at the highest level and discussions in international forums.[47] For example, the Mexican president, Vicente Fox visited China in June 2001 and returned to participate in the meeting of leaders of the Asia Pacific Economic Cooperation Forum (APEC) in October 2001. Interparliamentary contacts were maintained and there were reciprocal visits by officials from Mexico and the PRC.[48]

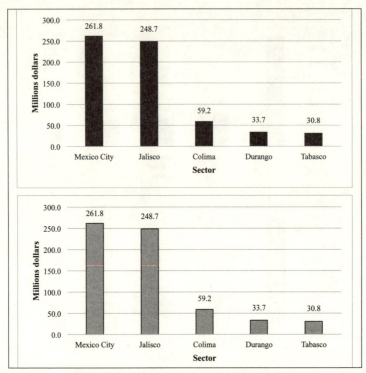

Figure 5: Total Chinese investment by state 2000-2017.
Source: Prepared by the author with data from the Ministry of Economy, *Secretariat of Economy, Competitiveness and Normativity. Official statistics of FDI flows to Mexico*, https://www.gob.mx/se/acciones-y-programas/competitividad-y-normatividad-inversion-extranjera-directa?state=published [Consulted: July 9, 2018]

One of the achievements of this period occurred in 2003 during the visit of Premier Wen Jiabao to Mexico when China and Mexico officially announced the establishment of the Strategic Partnership. Premier Wen described this as 'a new phase in the development of bilateral relations.'[49] Subsequently, in August 2004, the China-Mexico Permanent Binational Commission was created, which was designed to support commercial, educational, cultural and technical-scientific matters, as well as provide a platform for political consultations.[50] Since then, six meetings of this commission have been held. Another relation that was established in 2004 was the Grupo de Alto Nivel (GAN) composed of Ministry of Economy of Mexico and the Ministry of Commerce of China.[51] The objectives of this group are:

Strengthen commercial and investment relationships.

Promote a greater exchange of information to prevent and combat illegal trade.

Promote Mexican exports to China.

Deepen the mutual understanding of the industrial and trade policies between both parties.

At the end of the six-year period in 2006, the Undersecretary of Foreign Affairs of Mexico, Lourdes Aranda inaugurated the Mexican consulate consulate-general in Guangzhou in February 2006. According to Cornejo, this province in 2005 represented a third of China's foreign trade, with a value of 428 billion dollars, not much less than the total trade of Mexico. The establishment of this consulate was due to the relevance of this region in the trade between Mexico and China, and it became an important institutional support to the commercial relationship between both countries.[52]

In the following six years (2006-2012), President Felipe Calderón made a state visit in 2008 during which time he signed several agreements. During the meetings of the Binational Commission, two joint action programs were adopted for the periods 2006-2010 and 2011-2015. The programs set specific commitments in the field of policy, economic-commercial, customs, inspection and quarantine, science and technology, culture and sports, education, agriculture, communications and transport, tourism and social development and overcoming poverty.[53] In principle, these plans seek to propose concrete actions based on specific objectives, to achieve results that benefit both countries on a long-term basis and do not focus solely on economic relations. However, Mexico-China relations require more consolidation. Some significant challenges in the relationship are correcting the trade imbalance that has been unfavourable for Mexico and finding ways to attract greater Chinese foreign investment.

On the other hand, the Binational Commission and the GAN are not the only political mechanisms that seek to improve relations with the PRC. On 17 September 2009, the Mexico-China Strategic Dialogue was established, with the objective of analysing in greater depth various issues on the bilateral and multilateral agenda. These issues include the global economy, climate change, and the reform of the United Nations. So far, five meetings have held on a biennial basis in 2009, 2011 and 2013, 2015 and 2017.[54] In addition, the Permanent Dialogue Forum was established between the Mexican Congress and the National People's Congress of China in 2010, seeking to build a privileged framework for dialogue, exchange and parliamentary cooperation.[55] The purpose is to strengthen bilateral relations and raise solutions to long-term challenges. What is striking about these mechanisms is that they operate outside the scope of the Ministry of Foreign Affairs.

In the current sexennial (2012-2018), there seems to be an interest in improving and deepening relations between these two countries.[56] In the framework of the State visit President Xi Jinping made to Mexico in 2013, both leaders agreed to elevate bilateral relations to an Integral Strategic Partnership. In 2014, the program that established for this project was based mainly on cooperation in the political, commercial, financial and investment spheres.[57]

Despite these bilateral mechanisms, relations between the two countries during this century have also faced challenges. In the 2000-2006 sexennial, there was an incident due to the Dalai Lama's visit to Mexico in October 2004. The Mexican government did not know how to handle this situation. The various Mexican institutions responsible for directing and executing Mexico's foreign policy – the Presidency, the Ministry of the Interior and the Ministry of Foreign Affairs, and the Congress – did not know how to determine the conditions for receiving or not receiving the Dalai Lama. The Chinese government perceived this visit as a violation of the neutrality of the Mexican position on the Tibet issue. [58]

In an echo of what had happened in the 1930s, some social sectors in Mexico have projected an attitude of animosity towards the Chinese community, blaming the Chinese for job losses and identifying them as a threat in commercial competition. Undoubtedly, during the government of Felipe Calderón (2006-2012), tensions with China intensified and as Cornejo points out, the Calderón government inherited from the previous administration a very negative reaction towards China, encouraged by statements of the president and high public officials and the intensification of commercial conflicts.[59] One of the first events that strained the relationship was in January 2007, when the president of Taiwan flew over Mexican territory to assist at the inauguration of the President of Nicaragua, Daniel Ortega. For the return flight of the Taiwan president, the Mexican government requested that he not pass through Mexican territory again. This situation caused the Taiwanese government to accuse the Chinese government of pressuring the Mexican government to make that decision. For its part, the Chinese embassy in Mexico refused to confirm whether it had pressured the Mexican government. However, this error denotes the lack of communication between the agency in charge of foreign relations in Mexico and the Ministry of Communications and Transport.[60]

Another event that negatively affected the bilateral relationship occurred between May and April 2009 when a group of Mexicans was quarantined in China from the outbreak of Swine Flu Mexico. Hence, 'media coverage exacerbated the substrate of anti-Chinese perception that exists in the country.'[61] The Mexican press exacerbated the feelings against the Chinese, for example, *La Jornada* (Mexican newspaper) mentioned that China had undertaken a 'hunt' because of the first case of influenza in Hong Kong and it had arbitrarily retained the group of Mexicans, noting that the Chinese government had discriminated against them because they were Mexicans.[62] Regarding this event, President Calderón made a statement that touched a sensitive point for the government of China: Government transparency. As a result, the Chinese government closed its consulate in Mexico for two weeks, temporally suspension of the direct flight and withdrew country conditions and the status of guest country in the International Food Hall in China in 2009.[63]

Another event that distanced Mexico from China occurred in September 2011, when the Dalai Lama made another visit to Mexico and President Felipe Calderón held a private meeting with him, which caused great displeasure to the Chinese government. According to the then Foreign Ministry spokesperson, Ma Zhaoxu, 'this act [represented] a gross intervention in the internal affairs of China, wounds the sentiment of the Chinese people and damages relations between China and Mexico.'[64]

During the administration of Mexican President Enrique Peña Nieto (2012-2018), there have also been unpleasant moments in the relationship between Mexico and China, despite the fact that one of the main foreign policy objectives of that government was to consolidate China as a key in the diversification of Mexico's economic ties with the world.[65] One of this moment is related to the exhibition centre in Cancun, Quintana Roo, named Dragon Mart, which sold Chinese products. The project was presented to local and federal authorities in 2011. The initial investment was around US $180 million dollars but, only 10 per cent was Chinese capital, and in 2013, the project was approved. However, in 2014. the Mexican government canceled the project arguing violations to environmental laws.[66] The problem with this project was that it received severe criticism from Mexican society, which denoted an anti-Chinese sentiment with newspaper headers like 'Why do we say no to Dragon Mart?', 'Dragon Mart Cancun: the destruction of the Chinese monster arrives in Mexico', reflecting such perception.[67]

Another similar situation was the bidding for the construction of the high-speed train from Mexico City to Querétaro. The public bidding procedures were published in august 2014. Most of the companies that participated in the bidding stated that they could not bid because there was too little time to comply with sophisticated requirements.[68] On 3 November 2014, the Mexican Ministry of Communications and Transportation announced the winner as the consortium formed by China Railway Construction Corporation, China Railway Construction Corporation International, CSR Corporation Limited, all associated with four Mexican companies: Constructora y Edificadora GIA, Prodemex, GHP Infrastructure Mexicana and Constructora Teya.[69] Three days after winning the bid and just a few days before President Peña Nieto was to make an official visit to China, Mexico canceled the project.[70] The revocation of the contract upset the Chinese government and the Chinese companies who said that Mexico's decision to cancel the agreement to build the train was surprising and that they requested a compensation for the costs it had incurred to participate in the bidding.[71]

MEXICO-CHINA RELATIONS IN THE TRUMP ERA AND THE MEXICAN PRESIDENTAL CHANGE: OPPORTUNITIES AND CHALLENGES

After examining the state of bilateral relations between Mexico and China in the twenty-first century, we can note that while relations in political terms have consolidated, the most important challenges lie in economic terms. As Jorge E. Navarrete points out, there is mutual appreciation due to the number and frequency of high-level political encounters among political leaders, respective heads of state, ministers and other government officials. These interactions include *ad hoc* scenarios outside of conferences, meetings and other multilateral, global or interregional meetings.[72] However, although political relations with China are institutionalised to a high degree, there are several bilateral mechanisms which foster trade. China and Mexico have signed multiple agreements jointly.

There is a perception that despite the various mechanisms and agreements put in place to support the relationship, these have not been sufficient to solve the existing problems[73]. Francisco Javier Haro and Rosángel Hernández Mendoza warn that the great advances made in terms of institutionalisation of the relationship have not caused a significant improvement in communication between the governments of Mexico and China.[74] They question the achievements and show the limitations of these mechanisms and agreements. As the former Mexican ambassador to China, Julián Ventura Valero, points out that the political dialogue should continue both annual presidential meetings in the capitals and in the framework of international meetings to provide timely follow-up to the agenda of priorities. Likewise, the exchange of visits by high-level officials should continue to be promoted and the periodicity should be maintained in the meetings of bilateral mechanisms, such as the Binational Commission and the various high-level groups.[75]

On the other hand, the economic problems in the relationship between Mexico and China that continue are:

Mexico's huge deficit in bilateral trade.
Insufficient scientific-technological cooperation and academic exchange.
The scarcity of reciprocal investments between China and Mexico.[76]

Currently, there is uncertainty in the international economy. For Mexico, one of the most important variables is the renegotiation of NAFTA. Faced with this uncertainty, the need for economic diversification has begun to gain strength in political discourses. For example, the deputy general director of the Mexican Foreign Trade Business Council (COMCE), Jorge López Mortón said that the bilateral crisis with the United States allows Mexico to diversify its exports, especially to Asia.[77] It is a propitious moment to promote trade and investment diversification; however, it is worth asking: what will happen when relations with the United States improve? Will policies and actions aimed at diversifying continue? Or will only short and medium-term measures be implemented?

Undoubtedly, the discourses of economic diversification for Mexico are focused on Asia, particularly China. Many stakeholders, from the President of the Republic Enrique Peña Nieto, to businesspersons, academics and representatives of subnational governments, have called for the strengthening of ties with Asia.[78] As mentioned above, in 2013 the relationship was raised to the level of 'Integral Strategic Association', and as a result of this association, in September 2013, the Grupo de Alto Nivel sobre Inversión (GAN-I) was created and headed by the Secretaría de Hacienda y Crédito Público (SHCP) of Mexico and by the National Development and Reform Commission (NDRC) of China. The GAN-I has introduced a planning approach and joint identification of priorities in the investment dialogue[79].

In October 2013, the Grupo de Alto Nivel Empresarial Mexico-China (GAN-E) was established, as an advisory group to the presidents, that incorporates representatives of 28 outstanding state and private companies of both countries, with the mandate to identify actions that take advantage of the potential of the bilateral economic relationship.[80] One of the first achievements of the GAN-I was the establishment of the Binational Investment Fund Mexico-China, consisting of contributions totaling US 1.2 billion dollars from the sovereign banks the China Investment Corporation, the China Development Bank and the Mexican Development Bank in November 2014.[81] During the period from October 2013 to November 2017, the GAN-E met five times. At its last meeting, topics such as financial services platforms, cooperation in electricity and clean energy, infrastructure, oil and gas, trade facilitation and foreign investment, telecommunications and information technologies were discussed.[82]

In September 2017, in the framework of the Summit of Emerging Economies and Developing Countries that took place in the city of Xiamen, China, Presidents Enrique Peña Nieto and Xi Jinping discussed the advances in the bilateral relationship, highlighting:[83]

Entry of Mexican products into the Chinese market, including pork, tequila and berries.
Participation of Chinese companies in the exploration and extraction of Mexican hydrocarbons.
Installation in 2014 of the Mexico-China Binational Fund, which, according to the leaders, has strengthened investment flows.

In 2016, the Industrial Bank and Commerce of China (ICBC) and the Bank of China started operations in Mexico. China Southern Airlines commenced operating the Guangzhou-Vancouver-Mexico City flights, the first Chinese airline to establish a passenger route to Mexico.

Chinese investments in Mexico have been minimal, although in 2017 there was a large increase of Chinese investments (see figure 4). Ambassador Ventura and Meléndrez point out the investment of companies between Mexican and Chinese in the respective markets showing a growing dynamism. Some Mexican companies such as Bimbo (food), Gruma (food), Kuo Group (industrial chemicals), Softek (technologies of information), Interceramic (materials for homes and offices), Metalsa (auto parts) and Alfa, through its subsidiary Nemak (auto parts), are expanding their presence in China. In the same way, Chinese manufacturing companies are establishing in Mexico due to the advantages offered by the Mexican market and its access to the main international markets through its network of free trade agreements. Some examples that stand out in this context are Lenovo (computers), Huawei (telecommunications), ZTE (telecommunications), Minth (auto parts) and Hisense (appliances), and the recent purchase of Sharp Electronics Mexico, S. A. de C. V.[84]

The Mexican government has shown interest in increasing Chinese investments, focusing on two aspects. The first is through instruments such as financial institutions that give confidence to Chinese investors in Mexico; the second, focuses on identifying projects with attractive characteristics for Chinese companies to encourage investment. Derived from the structural reforms that were carried out during the Enrique Peña Nieto administration, new investment opportunities have been generated in hydrocarbons, energy, gas, telecommunications and infrastructure projects, among others. An example is the participation of the consortium led by Sinohydro in the construction of the Chicoasén II hydroelectric plant in the state of Chiapas.[85]. The Chinese also seem to be interested in having a greater role in the Mexican economy. The head of the Industrial and Commercial Bank of China (ICBC) unit in Mexico, Yaogang Chen states, 'If some investment projects in the United States do not occur, there must be someone to invest ... if Chinese companies think it is profitable, they will invest.'[86]

In February 2017, Giant Motors and Grupo Financiero Inbursa announced an investment of US 4.4 billion dollars to create a Chinese car manufacturing plant for JAC brand in Ciudad Sahagún, Hidalgo. The Chinese company BIAC Motor, which is already a client of ICBC, has been selling cars imported from China in Mexico since June 2016, and seeks to build a factory to produce gasoline and electric cars. According to Sergio Ley López, president of the Business Section for the Asia and Oceania region of the Mexican Business Council for Foreign Trade, Investment and Technology (COMCE), several Chinese companies are interested in capitalizing 900 Mexican companies dedicated to trade, manufacturing, industry and services in Mexico City, the State of Mexico, Jalisco and Baja California.[87]

One of the cases that stands out due to its rapid growth in the Mexican market is the Chinese company Huawei. The firm arrived in the Mexican telecommunications sector in 2002. Ten years later, it ventured into the smartphone market, and now occupies sixth place in market share in Mexico with 4.4 per cent, behind Samsung (34.6 per cent), Apple (14.3 per cent), LG (13.5 per cent), Motorola (8 per cent) and Alcatel (6.5 per cent), according to figures from the Competitive Intelligence Unit[88].

Despite the growing tensions with the United States, and the calls to diversify Mexico's economic relations and look towards China, the Mexican government does not yet have a long-term plan to achieve this goal. None of the presidential candidates currently under consideration have presented concrete objectives and actions to consolidate relations with the Asia-Pacific region. In order to strengthen bilateral relations between Mexico and China, Mexico needs to carefully consider its next steps.

Recommendations

To give substance to the diversification of external relations, it is necessary to design a foreign policy of the state and not of central government, that is, to transcend the change of government, in which the different levels of government (vertical and horizontal) and other sectors collaborate, including the private and academic sectors and civil society in general. This should focus on the promotion and achievement of the development of the country, as well as to increase the autonomy and position of Mexico in the international scenario. It is important to know the international, regional and national context for the definition of a State project with a short, medium and long-term vision, to ensure the continuity of actions or, where appropriate, an evaluation that allows adequate rethinking.

Other actors have to be included in the decision-making process and the definition of interests and objectives close to Mexican society. This requires the participation of the federal, local and sub-national executive power of the legislative power (deputies and senators), businessmen and academics - not only for the formulation of foreign policy, but also to design solutions aimed at solving Mexico's internal problems, which currently limit Mexico's more active participation in the international scenario. In addition, this will allow a greater rapprochement and knowledge of the countries with which Mexico maintains ties, and will enhance the interest and opportunities of Mexicans abroad.

There are various agreements and mechanisms in place but economic, cultural and social relations have not led to actions that are more decisive. Therefore, and with regard to the presidential elections due to be held in July 2018, the next Mexican administration should make full use of these existing bilateral instruments and mechanisms aimed at improving Mexico's understanding with China, through dialogue to reduce differences and strengthen cooperations.

Mexico must improve its export structures, for this it needs to improve its industrial capacity, since some proposals suggest that Mexico should continue exporting products from the primary and secondary sectors such as automobiles and auto parts. However, this would maintain a situation of dependence on Asian exports. In effect, the business of high-tech products with greater added value should be stimulated. As proposed by Arturo Oropeza, Mexico requires a leap in technology, which requires investment in science and technology.

Another way to improve understanding between Mexico and the PRC is through expanding the knowledge of both parties; culture provides an important pathway for achieving this. Some actions are already being carried out in this sense; however, the image that Mexicans have about China is still full of prejudice. It is important to increase the exchange of people and information and it is necessary for Mexican officials working in the foreign service to have a broad knowledge of the internal and external policy, economy, social and cultural aspects of the countries in which they work.

Understanding these countries requires the acquisition of quality knowledge. In Mexico, there are several universities, which have programs focused on the Asia-Pacific region, particularly these programs have specializations in Chinese studies. There is El Colegio de México (which particularly focuses on China), the National Autonomous University of Mexico (which has the Centre for China-Mexico Studies known as Cechimex), the University of Colima, the University of Guadalajara, the Autonomous University of Nayarit and the Autonomous University of Nuevo León, to name a few. These universities should promote more research with an interdisciplinary approach to identify the characteristics of the countries of Asia, as well as their strengths and weaknesses and thus generate a Mexican foreign policy aimed at this region more in line with reality. The role of the academic sector is very important in the development of international relations, both in collaborating with the government for the development of foreign policy and the dissemination of related information.

Knowledge about the PRC should not be limited to small groups, such as specialized academics or students who are interested in that country. Knowledge should be expanded in Mexican and Chinese societies because there are inaccuracies and prejudices on both sides. An important element is the language; more and more Mexicans are interested in learning Chinese, so the teaching of this language should be promoted for the public by encouraging the centres to offer courses in Chinese language and guarantee a quality learning experience. We can only hope that the change of administration in Mexico and the tensions in the relationship with the United States will contribute to strengthening the relationship between Mexico and China.

About the author

Edith Incin holds a degree in International Relations from the Faculty of Political and Social Sciences of the National Autonomous University of Mexico. Since August 2018, she is the Movility Coordinator in the Internationalization Office of the Universidad Anáhuac México.
E-mail: incinedith@gmail.com

Endnotes

1 See 'Importaciones y exportaciones por principales países socios. Anual de 1993 a diciembre de 2017', *Ministry of Economy*, (accessed 7 July 2018). https://www.gob.mx/se/acciones-y-

programs/comercio-exterior-informacion-estadistica-y-arancelaria?state=published and 'Informes estadísticos sobre el comportamiento de la IED en México que son presentados por la Comisión Nacional de Inversión Extranjera (CNIE) anual de 2017', *Ministry of Economy*, (accessed 7 July 2018). https://www.gob.mx/se/acciones-y-programas/competitividad-y-normatividad-inversion-extranjera-directa?state=published [translation mine]

2 'Comercio Exterior. Países con Tratados y Acuerdos firmados con México', *Ministry of Ecnomy*, (accessed 7 July 2018). https://www.gob.mx/se/acciones-y-programas/comercio-exterior-paises-con-tratados-y-acuerdos-firmados-con-mexico?state=published [translation mine]

3 Jannet López, 'México, a diversificar y reforzar lazos: Peña', *Milenio*, (Mexico), 24 January 2017, http://www.milenio.com/politica/mexico-a-diversificar-y-reforzar-lazos-pena [translation mine]

4 Javier Mejía Cubillos, 'El fin del Galeón de Acapulco: un análisis desde el neoclasicismo', *Simposio Mercados y mercaderes en los circuitos mercantiles hispanoamericanos 1780-1860*, (Mexico: Segundo Congreso Latinoamericano de Historia Económica, 2-5 February 2010), p. 14, (accessed 7 July 2018). https://www.researchgate.net/publication/242725377_El_Fin_del_Galeon_de_Acapulco_Un_Analisis_desde_el_Neoclasicismo [translation mine]

5 Francisco Javier Haro, José Luis León and Juan José Ramírez, 'Asia,' Mercedes de Vega Armijo (ed.) *Historia de las relaciones internacionales de México, 1821-2010* (Mexico: Secretaría de Relaciones Exteriores-Dirección General del Acervo Histórico Diplomático, 2011), p. 56. [translation mine]

6 Juan Francisco de Azcarate, *Un programa de política internacional* (Mexico: Secretaría de Relaciones Exteriores-Dirección General del Acervo Histórico Diplomático, 1932), pp. 36-41. [translation mine]

7 Haro, *Asia*, p. 63.

8 Ibid., p. 75.

9 Romer Cornejo, "México y China. Ironías y perspectivas de su relación" in Blanca Torres and Gustavo Vega (eds.), *Los grandes problemas de México: Relaciones Internacionales* (Mexico: El Colegio de México, 2010), p. 593. [translation mine]

10 Haro, *Asia*, p. 76.

11 Xu Shicheng, "Los chinos a lo largo de la historia de México" in Enrique Dussel Peters and Yolanda Trápaga Delfín (eds.), *China*

y México: implicaciones de una nueva relación (Mexico: UNAM-Fundación Friedrich Ebert-Instituto Tecnológico y de Estudios Superiores de Monterrey-La Jornada Ediciones, 2007), p. 60. [translation mine]

12 Eugenio Anguiano Roch, 'Relaciones México-China en su perspectiva histórica' in Enrique Dussel Peters and Yolanda Trápaga Delfín (eds.), *China y México: implicaciones de una nueva relación*, (Mexico: UNAM-Fundación Friedrich Ebert-Instituto Tecnológico y de Estudios Superiores de Monterrey-La Jornada Ediciones, 2007), p. 29. [translation mine]

13 Cornejo, 'México y China, p. 595.

14 Ibid., p. 596.

15 Haro, *Asia*, p. 105.

16 Cornejo, 'México y China', p. 596.

17 Anguiano, 'Relaciones México-China', p. 34.

18 Haro, *Asia,* pp. 80-84.

19 Ibid., p. 204.

20 Cornejo, 'México y China', p. 597.

21 Haro, *Asia,* p. 210.

22 Cornejo, 'México y China', p. 598.

23 Cornejo, 'México y China', p. 599.

24 Anguiano, 'Relaciones México-China', p. 38.

25 Cornejo, 'México y China', p. 600.

26 Arturo González, 'Relaciones entre México y China: pasado reciente y perspectivas' in Alicia Girón, Aurelia Vargas and Guillermo Pulido (eds.), *China y México. Un diálogo cultural desde las humanidades y las ciencias sociales* (Mexico: Universidad Nacional Autónoma de México, 2015), p. 297. [translation mine]

27 Xu Shicheng, 'China y México: cuarenta y dos años de relaciones diplomáticas. Una mirada retrospectiva y prospectiva desde China', in Alicia Girón, Aurelia Vargas and Guillermo Pulido (eds.), *China y México. Un diálogo cultural desde las humanidades y las ciencias sociales* (Mexico: Universidad Nacional Autónoma de México, 2015), p. 277. [translation mine]

28 Haro, *Asia*, p. 435.

29 Cornejo, 'México y China', p. 602.

30 Shicheng, 'China y México', p. 280.

31 Marisela Connelly, 'Desarrollo de los estudios chinos en México'

in Alicia Girón, Aurelia Vargas and Guillermo Pulido (eds.), *China y México. Un diálogo cultural desde las humanidades y las ciencias sociales*, (Mexico: Universidad Nacional Autónoma de México, 2015), p. 36. [translation mine]

32 Ibid., p. 37.

33 Haro, *Asia,* p. 436.

34 National Development Plan is the official document of national planning in accordance with the provisions of Article 25 of the Mexican Constitution.

35 'Plan Nacional de Desarrollo 1995-2000', *Presidencia de la Rep*ública, 20, accessed J8 uly 2018. *http://zedillo.presidencia.gob.mx/pages/pnd.pdf* [translation mine]

36 Cornejo, 'México y China', p. 606.

37 Ibid., p. 607.

38 Haro, *Asia,* p. 439

39 Ibid.

40 'Consulates of Mexico abroad', *Secretaría de Relaciones Exteriores, https://directorio.sre.gob.mx/index.php/consulados-de-mexico-en-el-exterior* [translation mine] (accessed 8 July 2018)

41 'China-Mexico', *Embajada de la República Popular China en México, http://mx.china-embassy.org/esp/zmgx/t1248625.htm* [translation mine] (accessed July 8, 2018).

42 Shicheng, 'China y México', p. 275

43 "'nforme de labores de la Secretaría de Relaciones Exteriores 2000-2017/2', *Secretaría de Relaciones Exteriores,* 17 vols. [translation mine]

44 'Economic Relationship', *Embajada de* México en la República Popular China, *https://embamex2.sre.gob.mx/china/index.php/es/la-embajada/relacion-economica* [translation mine] (accessed July 8, 2018).

45 Enrique Dussel, 'Una década de conocimiento de la economía china en México. Síntesis y retos', in Alicia Girón, Aurelia Vargas and Guillermo Pulido (eds.), *China y México. Un diálogo cultural desde las humanidades y las ciencias sociales* (Mexico: Universidad Nacional Autónoma de México, 2015), p. 315. [translation mine]

46 Dussel, 'Una década de conocimiento', p. 84

47 Romer Cornejo, 'México y China: Diplomacia, competencia económica y percepciones' in Humberto Garza, Jorge A. Schiavon and Rafael Velázquez Flores (eds.), *Paradigmas y paradojas de la política exterior de México: 2000-2006* (Mexico: El Colegio de México-Centro de Investigación y Docencia Económicas, 2010), p. 353. [translation mine]

48 *Secretaría de Relaciones Exteriores, Segundo informe de labores 2002 (Mexico: Secretaría de Relaciones Exteriores, 2002), p. 15 [translation mine]*

49 Shicheng, 'China y México', p. 277.

50 Cornejo, 'México y China: Diplomacia', p. 354.

51 Gabriela Cedillo Pérez, 'Grupo de trabajo de Alto Nivel México-China', *China Today,* 14 April 2011. http://www.chinatoday.com.cn/ctspanish/se/txt/2011-04/14/content_351033.htm [translation mine]

52 Cornejo, 'México y China: Diplomacia', p. 355.

53 Secretaría de Relaciones Exteriores, *Cuarto informe de labores 2010,* (Mexico: Secretaría de Relaciones Exteriores, 2010), p. 84, *http://sre.gob.mx/images/stories/doctransparencia/infolab/4infolab* [translation mine]

54 Secretaría de Relaciones Exteriores, *Informes de labores de la Secretaría de Relaciones Exteriores 2009, 2011, 2013, 2015, 2017,* 5 vols. [translation mine]

55 Carlos Jiménez Macías, '40 años de relaciones diplomáticas entre México y China' in Enrique Dussel (ed.), *40 años de la relación entre México y China: acuerdos, desencuentros y futuro* (Mexico: UNAM-Facultad de Economía, 2012), p. 28. http://dusselpeters.com/53.pdf [translation mine]

56 Rafael Fernández de Castro and Diego Cándano, 'Propuestas para que México descifre a China', in Enrique Dussel (ed.), *La relación México-China: desempeño y propuestas para 2016-2018* (Mexico, UNAM-Cámara de Comercio de México en China-Centro de Estudios China-México-Unión de Universidades de América Latina y el Caribe, 2016), p. 23. [translation mine]

57 'Mexico and China strengthen political dialogue and advance their comprehensive strategic partnership', Secretaría de Relaciones Exteriores, https://www.gob.mx/sre/articulos/mexico-y-china-fortalecen-dialogo-politico-y-avanzan-en-su-asociacion-estrategica-integral?idiom=es [translation mine] (accessed 11 July 2018).

58 Cornejo, 'México y China: Diplomacia', p. 356.

59 Romer Cornejo, 'La Relación de México con China, de la política

del desconcierto al acercamiento diplomático', in Humberto Garza Elizondo, Jorge A. Schiavon y Rafael Velázquez Flores (eds.), *Balance y perspectivas de la política exterior de México 2006-2012* (Mexico: El Colegio de México-Centro de Investigación y Docencia Económicas, 2014), pp. 223-246. [translation mine]

60 'China, Taiwan and Mexico, in the midst of diplomatic mess', *El Universal* (Mexico), 13 January 2007. http://archivo.eluniversal. com.mx/notas/399912.html [translation mine]

61 Romer Cornejo, 'La Relación de México con China', p. 233.

62 David Brunat, 'China aísla a 50 viajeros mexicanos', *La Jornada* (Mexico), 4 May 2009. http://www.jornada.unam.mx/2009/05/04/ politica/013n1pol [translation mine]

63 Romer Cornejo, 'La Relación de México con China', p. 233.

64 'La reunión entre Felipe Calderón y el Dalai Lama molesta a China', *Expansión en alianza con CNN* (Mexico), 10 September 2011, http://expansion.mx/nacional/2011/09/10/ la-reunion-entre-felipe-calderon-y-el-dalai-lama-molesta-a-china?newscnn1=%5B20110911%5D [translation mine]

65 Presidency of the Republic, *Plan Nacional de Desarrollo 2013-2018*, (Mexico: Presidency of the Republic), p. 148, http://pnd.gob.mx/ [translation mine]

66 Enrique Dussel, 'Chinese Investment in Mexico: The contemporary context and challenges', *Asian Perspective*, 40, (2016), p. 640. http:// www.dusselpeters.com/114.pdf

67 Ibid.

68 Ibid., p. 641.

69 "México indeminizará a CRCC y su consorcio", *Milenio* (Mexico), 10 November 2014. http://www.milenio.com/negocios/mexico-indemnizara-a-crcc-y-su-consorcio [translation mine]

70 Enrique Dussel, 'Chinese Investment', p. 641.

71 Milenio, 'México indeminizará a CRCC.'

72 Jorge Eduardo Navarrete, 'Algunas ideas para reanimar el diálogo político bilateral', in Enrique Dussel, *La relación México-China: desempeño y propuestas para 2016-2018* (Mexico, UNAM-Cámara de Comercio de México en China-Centro de Estudios China-México-Unión de Universidades de América Latina y el Caribe, 2016), p. 18 [translation mine]

73 Rafael Fernández de Castro and Diego Cándano, 'Propuestas para que México descifre a China', in Enrique Dussel (ed.), *La relación*

México-China: desempeño y propuestas para 2016-2018, (Mexico, UNAM-Cámara de Comercio de México en China-Centro de Estudios China-México-Unión de Universidades de América Latina y el Caribe, 2016), p. 25. [translation mine]

74 Francisco Javier Haro Navejas and Rosángel Hernández Mendoza, 'Viaje al oeste. La Asociación sino-mexicana: una responsabilidad funcionalista', *Foro internacional*, 56, No. 1, Mexico, El Colegio de México, (April-June 2016), p. 431. http://forointernacional.colmex.mx/index.php/fi/article/view/2320/2310 [translation mine]

75 Julián Ventura Valero and Rodrigo Meléndrez Armada, 'Relaciones económicas México-China: una agenda de oportunidades', *Revista Mexicana de Política Exterior*, No. 108, Mexico, Instituto Matías Romero-Ministry of Foreign Affairs, (2017), p. 46. https://revistadigital.sre.gob.mx/index.php/49-numeros-anteriores/183-rmpe-108 [translation mine]

76 Shicheng, 'China y México', pp. 281-282.

77 Anabel Clemente, 'México debe diversificar comercio y Asia es opción, consideran embajadores', *El financiero* (Mexico), 9 March 2017. http://www.elfinanciero.com.mx/nacional/mexico-debe-diversificar-comercio-y-asia-es-opcion-consideran-embajadores.html [translation mine]

78 To mention an example, Graco Ramírez, president of the National Conference of Governors (Conago), announced a working tour of China to establish an economic cooperation agenda and to deepen the bilateral relationship. He also pointed out that the Conago members intended to diversify Mexico's trade relations in light of the changes planned by US President Donald Trump. See 'Los gobernadores irán a China para buscar inversión en México', *Expansión en alianza con CNN* (Mexico), 24 March 2017. http://expansion.mx/nacional/2017/03/24/los-gobernadores-iran-a-china-para-buscar-inversion-en-mexico [translation mine]

79 Abraham Zamora Torres, 'Oportunidades de inversión en México: infraestructura y ZEE' in Enrique Dussel (ed.), *La relación México-China: desempeño y propuestas para 2016-2018* (Mexico, UNAM-Cámara de Comercio de México en China-Centro de Estudios China-México-Unión de Universidades de América Latina y el Caribe, 2016), p. 49. [translation mine]

80 Ventura and Meléndrez, 'Relaciones económicas México-China', p. 40.

81 Ibid., p. 42.

82 'Concluye la V reunión anual del Grupo de Alto Nivel Empresarial México-China', *Gobierno de la república*, (accessed 13 July 2017). https://www.gob.mx/promexico/prensa/concluye-la-v-reunion-anual-del-grupo-de-alto-nivel-empresarial-mexico-china [translation mine]

83 'México busca diversificar mercados y revisa con China avances en comercio, inversión y turismo', *Aristegui Noticias* (Mexico), 4 September 2017. http://aristeguinoticias.com/0409/mexico/mexico-busca-diversificar-mercados-y-revisa-con-china-avances-en-comercio-inversion-y-turismo/ [translation mine]

84 Ventura and Meléndrez, 'Relaciones económicas México-China', p. 40.

85 Zamora, 'Oportunidades de inversión en México', pp. 43-44

86 'El banco chino ICBC ve oportunidades de inversión en México por presión de Trump', *Expansión en alianza con CNN* (Mexico), 24 March 2017. http://expansion.mx/economia/2017/03/24/las-politicas-de-trump-unen-a-china-y-mexico [translation mine]

87 Enrique Hernández, 'Compañías de China llegan de manera silenciosa a México', *Forbes* (Mexico), 4 January 2017. https://www.forbes.com.mx/companias-de-china-llegan-de-manera-silenciosa-a-mexico/ [translation mine]

88 Isaid Mera, Max Chafkin and Joshua Brustein, 'Huawei, y el sigiloso plan para "comerse" el mercado en México ... y el mundo', *El financiero* (Mexico), 9 April 2018. http://www.elfinanciero.com.mx/bloomberg-businessweek/huawei-quiere-venderte-todo-para-tu-smartphone-y-no-solo-un-telefono [translation mine]

YOUNG SCHOLAR ESSAY

Rewriting The Future:
The Conflict And Compromise Of China's Script Revolution

BY ATHENA RU

ABSTRACT

The purpose of this article is to analyse the conflict and compromises involved in the transition from traditional Chinese characters to *pinyin* and simplified characters from the 1920-1960s, the significance of the Chinese script revolution, as well as the short and long-term consequences this entailed for both China and the world. Falling behind to other people is undoubtedly an unpleasant feeling. But falling behind to the rest of the world, as China had experienced, was a historical circumstance of self-loathing and pity. After the Opium Wars shattered China's well-being – economically, politically, and socially – the Chinese desperately desired change in the form of a new written script, as language was viewed as the harbinger of revolution. Although China faced a period of internal struggle regarding the need to modernise their language in line with the rest of the world by replacing traditional characters with *pinyin* (the romanised system for the Chinese written script), the conflict between the scholars' idealistic efforts for a phonetic world language and the reality of China's predicament was effectively compromised in the 1960s by the Chinese government's push to implement simplified characters as the standard form of writing and *pinyin* as the annotation. Indeed, simplified characters and *pinyin* modernised China by promoting a common tongue (*putonghua*), making education more accessible, and spreading and preserving Chinese culture.

INTRODUCTION

It cannot be denied that language is crucial to the development of any country and the success of humanity itself, as it facilitates communication, aids education, and promotes culture. At the same time, language reflects and shapes one's identity; speaking your native language evokes a sense of belonging in a community – a feeling all humans naturally crave. These characteristics of language are clearly evident given China's current exponential rise to power. Dubbed as 'the world's next superpower', China's long march to modernisation came at the cost of a battle that lasted half a century for a common vernacular language. Although China faced a period of internal struggle regarding the need to modernise its language in line with the rest of the world by replacing traditional characters with *pinyin* (the romanised system for the Chinese written script), the conflict between the scholars' idealistic efforts for a phonetic world language and the reality of China's predicament was effectively compromised in the 1960s by the Chinese government's push to implement simplified characters as the standard form of writing and *pinyin* as the annotation. Indeed, simplified characters and *pinyin* modernised China by promoting a common tongue (*putonghua*), making education more accessible, and spreading and preserving Chinese culture.

HISTORICAL BACKGROUND

In order to analyse the Chinese script revolution, the events leading up to this must be considered carefully, because they were the main reason why China fell into disparity over language. Firstly, the Opium Wars signalled the beginning of a barrage of unfair treaties, territory loss, and political upheaval. Wang Shu Lian (王树连), a cartographer at the Institute of Surveying and Mapping, summarises, 'The British invasion of China in 1840 is known as the First Opium War ... From 1857 to 1860, the British and French waged the Second Opium War ... In 1895, the Qing government signed the humiliating and shameful Treaty of Shimonoseki with Japan'.[1] The Treaty of Shimonoseki forced China to pay a war indemnity of 200 million Kuping taels (Chinese currency) and cede the Liaodong Peninsula to Japan. Unfortunately, this treaty was only one of countless others; previous losses include the Treaty of Nanking, which stipulated Britain would claim Hong Kong, and the Treaty of Aigun, which gave Russia 600,000 square kilometres of Chinese land. Humiliated by their constant defeats, the Chinese descended into despair and developed radical mindsets. They believed China fell behind to the rest of the world – politically, technologically, and socially. Immediate change became the zeitgeist of thought and action. Language was one of those pivotal reforms.

CONFLICT

The conflict involved in language reform revolved primarily around whether or not to abolish the traditional Chinese characters (Figure 1)

Figure 1: Horse in Traditional Character Form

Figure 2: Horse in Pinyin Form

and replace them with the phonetic system of *pinyin* (Figure 2). Wu Yu Zhang (吴玉章), a Chinese politician, educator, and former president of Renmin University of China, lamented, 'Chinese [traditional] characters are the product of an ancient and feudal society … This is an obstacle to literacy for the people and is no longer suitable for the present era.'[2] Similarly, Ma Xu Lun (马序论), minister of education and chairman of the Committee for Studying the Reform of the Chinese Written Language declared on 5 February 1952, 'Our written language must … take the direction of phoneticization common to all the languages of the world.'[3] Wu Yu Zhang and Ma Xu Lun's views were shared by the majority of Chinese scholars and linguists who believed China would achieve modernisation through the elimination of the old script. Essentially, these idealists blamed Chinese characters as the reason for their country's humiliation. However, the plans were driven by impulsivity and although Chinese scholars put immense work into creating *pinyin*, the reality was that there simply was not enough time, the plans were driven by impulsivity, and the people could not adjust to a phonetic system. Qian Xuan Tong (钱玄同), a Chinese linguist, stated at the National Language Unification Conference, 'Reformations like this cannot be achieved in a short duration of time … We must not wait until the phonetic alphabets (*pinyin*) successfully carry out reformation.'[4] Simply stated, *pinyin* cannot 'successfully carry out reformation' in a short period of time. Qian Xuan Tong makes clear that the situation in China was dire and the Chinese needed an effective language system without delay – a feat impossible with only *pinyin*. Additionally, Xue Er (雪饵), a historian who specialises in the late Qing dynasty, explains, 'As they witnessed China floundering in a swamp of fatal crisis, their tenacious sense of mission and patriotism as well as their scanty but fanatical worldviews formed a great contrast, and entailed the inevitable consequences.'[5] Xue Er frankly states the problem: the idealistic desires of Chinese scholars for the implementation of *pinyin* conflicted with China's unfortunate reality. Finally, even Wu Yu Zhang (吴玉章) admitted, 'The Chinese are not accustomed to phonetic spelling; in fact, in the past, there were very few educated people and even fewer were those who understood ... phonetics.'[6] Blinded by their quixotic and radical thoughts, the reformists ignored what China really needed: a simpler writing system and a pronunciation guide to help aid the learning process.

Compromise

In the end, the Chinese government decided to simplify traditional characters (Figure 3) and implement *pinyin* as the official annotation, thus resolving the conflict between the Chinese scholars' idealistic desires for a phonetic system and China's conflicting reality. In 1958, Chinese Premier Zhou En Lai (周恩来) proclaimed the script revolution to be a priority for China, 'Current tasks of reforming the Chinese written language involved the simplification of the Chinese characters, popularisation of the common speech and the drawing up and putting into practice of the Scheme for a Chinese Phonetic Alphabet.'[7] At last, China reached a consensus on language reform.

Figure 3: Horse in Simplified Character Form

Short-term effects of compromise (*pinyin*)

The short-term significance of this compromise is seen as *pinyin* that aided the Chinese government in achieving their original goal of modernisation through the promotion of the common tongue known of *putonghua*. Since China covers roughly 9.60 million km, it's no surprise that the vernaculars spoken varied drastically from region to region. David Moser of Chinese Studies at the University of Michigan, explains, 'The dialects are virtually different languages. China was never a unified country in terms of its culture.'[8] Although there is merit in cultural diversity, a unified spoken language was imperative for China to modernise and improve the efficiency of communication.

For instance, Wang Jun writes in the 1991 *Journal of Chinese Linguistics Monograph Series* commissioned by the Institute of Applied Linguistics and The Chinese Academy of Social Sciences, 'Popularization of Putonghua, demand of a national norm of language in the interest of increasing the efficacy and accuracy of information transmission are one of the imperative items in modernisation projects of our country.'[9] In his statement, Wang Jun directly addresses the 'imperative' role of *putonghua* in increasing efficiency across China. The only way in which leaders and citizens alike can share and understand ideas and issues is through a unified language – now possible due to the implementation of *putonghua*. But of course, it cannot be forgotten that *pinyin* is the reason for *putonghua's* existence; the pronunciation of *putonghua* is based on *pinyin*. John Wells, Emeritus Professor of Phonetics at University College London, stated in a 1996 lecture, 'The principal reason for using phonetic transcription is easily stated. When we transcribe a word or an utterance, we give a direct specification of its pronunciation ...This is obvious when we consider a language ... such as Chinese, with a non-alphabetic orthography, whose written form generally does not give any direct information about pronunciation.'[10] Although Wells did not mention *pinyin* specifically, he clearly affirms just how invaluable a phonetic system is. Notably, as Chinese characters do not give any indication of the pronunciation, learners can only painstakingly assimilate the pronunciation based on shape.

However, because of the creation of *pinyin*, which is a phonetic system that 'transcribes' the characters, learners can reference *pinyin* and pronounce *putonghua* easily. This, in turn, promotes *putonghua*, which unifies and ultimately modernises China. All of this is nicely summed up by Britannica, which offers a modern and recent outlook on *pinyin*, 'The gradual acceptance of *pinyin* as the official transcription used in the People's Republic of China signalled a commitment to promote the use of the Beijing dialect as the national standard, to standardise pronunciation across areas that speak different dialects, and to end the confusion in romanising and alphabetising Chinese characters.'[11] Britannica explains how *pinyin* 'standardised pronunciation' so that the citizens of China could communicate more easily. At the same time, *pinyin* achieved what other attempts to alphabetise Chinese characters could not: providing a simple pronunciation system suitable for the uneducated Chinese people. Thus, it cannot be denied *pinyin* modernised China through promoting a standard way of communication known as *putonghua*.

SHORT-TERM EFFECTS OF COMPROMISE (SIMPLIFIED CHARACTERS)

Likewise, simplified characters allowed China to modernise by making education more accessible. The initial problem was that traditional characters caused blurs in printing, which hindered the production of books and other forms of text. Specifically, in 1977, Chin Chuan Cheng, Professor Emeritus of Linguistics at University of Illinois, reflected, 'because of their numerous strokes, complex characters usually cause blurs in printing.'[12] Fifteen years later in 1992, Zhou You Guang (周有光), a member of the Chinese Character Reform Committee, recalls, 'From 1956 to 1987, there were ... over 700 billion books published in Mainland China ... 200 billion copies of magazines printed ... [and] the total number of newspaper copies accumulated to 200 billion. These publications are printed in simplified characters.'[13] Since the Internet had yet to be invented, education depended primarily on textbooks, and if textbooks contained blurs, students would face immense difficulties in learning.

Therefore, simplified characters made educational supplies such as textbooks more accessible for the uneducated people by increasing the production of publications. Naturally, this engenders a smarter workforce that can carry out modernisation campaigns in China more efficiently. Additionally, the benefits of simplified characters are further supported by statistical data showing the decline of illiteracy rates when simplified characters were implemented. UNESCO provides statistical data that shows the decline of adult illiteracy in China from 1949 to 2000. When the Chinese government took control in 1949, the illiteracy rate was at a detrimental 80%, and by 2000, the rate was 9.08 per cent – an astounding drop of about 71 per cent over 51 years.[14] The correlation implies that simplified characters helped educate the Chinese. These statistics corroborate the increasing number of publications (mentioned above); as more books were published in simplified characters, people had increased access to resources, hence the fall of illiteracy rates. Finally, Chelala César, a journalist at *The Globalist*, concludes, 'it is clear that using simplified characters has been a powerful tool in improving the literacy rate of a great number of Chinese.'[15] Chelala César supports Professor Chin Chuan Cheng and the UNESCO data demonstrating that simplified characters modernised China by greatly assisting in education.

However, a recent controversy emerged when it was found that Taiwan boasts one of the highest literacy rates in the world despite continuing to use traditional characters. Chunman Gissing, Independent Educator of Chinese, Greater Seattle Area, and former assistant principal at the International School of Beijing, asserts, 'A quick google search on literacy rates of Chinese population over the age of 15 ... gives a chart indicating the growth of the rate from 1982 at just over 65 per cent ... and yet Taiwan continues to use traditional form of Chinese characters.'[16] The effects of simplified characters may now seem fictitious, but Rana Mitter, Director of the University China Centre and Professor of History and Politics of Modern China offers an explanation to Taiwan's high literacy rate:

> Under Mao, the state took on a much more directed role in areas such as education – mass literacy campaigns for instance. While Taiwan was also an authoritarian state at this time, there may not have been so much explicitly political weight placed behind literacy.
>
> I think there may be another factor about Taiwan. Taiwan's middle class had had a Japanese colonial education until 1945. Japanese has always used complex characters (as it does today).[17]

Mitter gives an alternate perspective on education in Taiwan; the effects of Japanese colonialism on a relatively small group of people (in comparison to China) that allowed them to use traditional characters and still have a high literacy rate. Therefore, given the different situations in mainland China and Taiwan, different systems of writing were needed – simplified characters suited mainland China while traditional characters worked for Taiwan.

LONG-TERM EFFECTS OF COMPROMISE (SIMPLIFIED CHARACTERS)

The long-term significance of simplified characters is that it preserves Chinese culture. Zhang Ri Pei, faculty of the Shanghai Education and Scientific Research Institute explains, 'The basic tendencies of the evolution of Chinese characters are: an expansion in quantity [of characters], a divorce from complicated and figurative pictographs, and becoming more abstract and simple. This made writing and

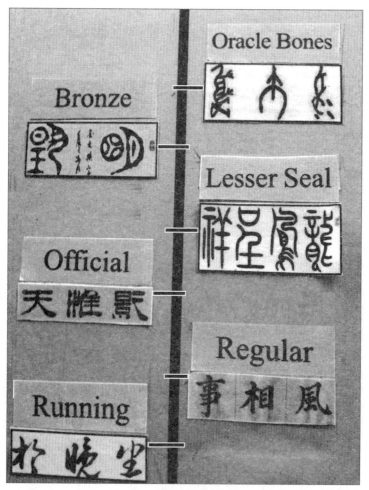

Figure 4: Evolution of Chinese Characters

reading more convenient.'[18] In short, Zhang Ri Pei clarifies that the characters naturally condense and become simpler over time. As simplified characters are part of a natural evolutionary process (see Figure 4), traditional culture was never lost in the first place and is in fact, preserved.

Therefore, not only do simplified characters aid education, but they also modernise China without causing it to lose its traditional culture. Furthermore, simplified characters abide by traditional principles of character-building. Robert Cheng, Professor Emeritus at University of Hawaii who specialises in character morphemes, states in the *Journal of Chinese Linguistics*, 'In spite of sociolinguistic changes,

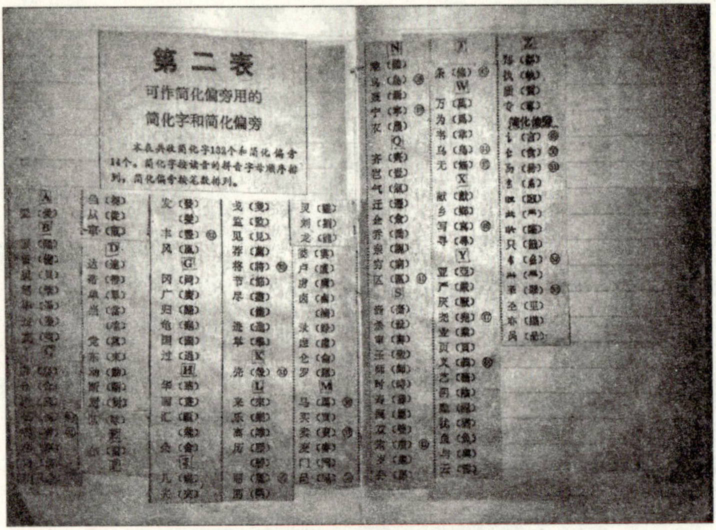
第二表
可作简化偏旁用的
简化字和简化偏旁

Figure 5: Second Version of Simplified Characters

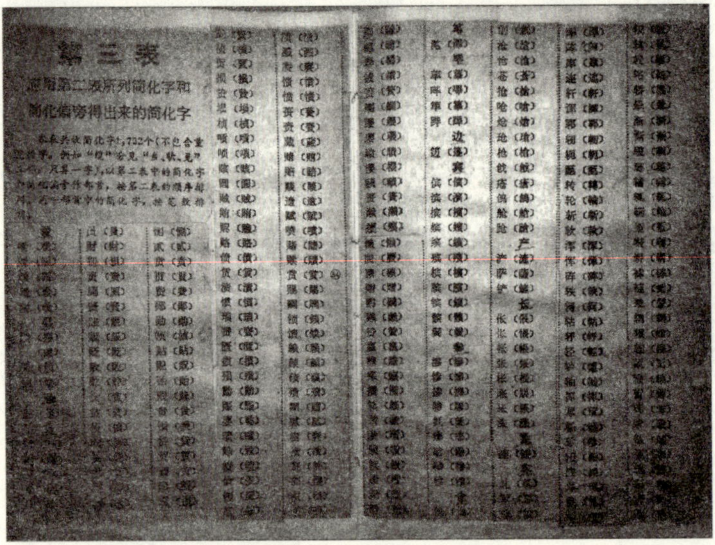
第三表
应用第二表所列简化字和
简化偏旁得出来的简化字

Figure 6: First Two Pages of Third Version of Simplified Characters

the basic principles for forming new characters or selecting existing characters for new usage as presented in the 1900-years-old 六书 (Six characteristics of Chinese characters) remain more or less the same.'[19] Critics who argue simplified characters result in a loss of traditional Chinese culture ignore the fact that they were originally created in accordance with the traditional principles of character-building.

Therefore, Professor Cheng affirms that simplified characters do not cause the loss of Chinese culture.

Finally, because people complained the second version of simplified characters (see Figure 5) were too 'simplified', the Chinese government abolished it and implemented a third version (see Figure 6). Mr. Li Renyu, a retired professor from Tongji University recalls, 'Some of the characters in the second simplification scheme were too "simplified." The meaning was lost and we [the people] did not use them in our daily life. Thankfully, the committee decided to only simplify the words that were suitable for simplification. Thus, the third version (published in 1986) was born, which is the one we use today.'[20] The Chinese government recognised that some characters were unnecessary and immediately abolished them. Thus, current simplified characters preserve traditional Chinese culture because the ones that veered off from the intended simplification process were rightfully abolished and replaced with more suitable forms.

Recently, experts have posed an interesting question: given China's current high literacy rate, is there still the need for simplified characters? The literacy rate among people 15 years and older in China in 2010 was reported by UNESCO to be at a staggering 95.12 per cent.[21] Moser claims, 'It is a myth that the Chinese cannot live without the characters.'[22] He argues from a utilitarian perspective that China is literate enough to abandon the characters. Nevertheless, it cannot be forgotten that without the characters, there would be a loss in culture and identity. Asmaa Ibrahim, a journalist at British Council, refutes:

> Characters are visually beautiful and often poetic and can give the learner a useful insight into the Chinese mind. However, unlike the alphabet, which represents only sounds, each Chinese character has a unique meaning ... [while] Chinese names are also related to cultural beliefs. Some Chinese people believe that the number of strokes used to draw the characters in a name can affect the good fortune of a person ... The Chinese script has thousands of characters, and many Chinese people prefer unique and special names.[23]

Due to the fact that Chinese characters have close ties with cultural beliefs and identity, its existence is necessary for maintaining China's unique heritage and lifestyle (which would have been lost if *pinyin* completely replaced the characters). Thus, simplified characters are a prominent aspect of Chinese culture that reflects society.

Long-term effects of compromise (*pinyin*)

Another equally prominent long-term significance is *pinyin's* involvement in the promotion of Chinese culture. Specifically, foreigners can now utilise *pinyin* to easily learn Mandarin Chinese. Doris Zhao, a Mandarin teacher at Concordia International School Shanghai, explains, '[Foreigners] ... can only learn to read the words after they learn *pinyin*... Because Chinese characters are like pictographs, there must be a *pinyin* system to annotate the characters if you want students to memorise the pronunciation. Otherwise, there is no way to memorise each character's pronunciation purely based on the character form.'[24] Notably, Zhao directly mentions the immense benefit of *pinyin* for foreigners. By providing a romanised pronunciation of the characters, *pinyin* helps foreigners to understand and remember a phonetic alphabet more easily than a pictograph. After all, memorising the shape of more than 2,000 characters is much more time-consuming than memorizing the 26 alphabet letters of *pinyin*. Therefore, *pinyin* serves as a bridge between China and the rest of the world, thus facilitating globalisation.

Additionally, *pinyin* connects with the digital era. Chunman Gissing shares her conversation with Zhou Youguang, the father of *pinyin*, 'communication via writing language is mostly done by typing ... [Mr. Zhou Youguang and I] text a great deal to communicate and [he] said that texting benefited from the invention of *pinyin*, which he was instrumental in developing. Texting also popularises *pinyin*, so it is a win-win situation.'[25] If one were to only text on phones by drawing out each character, it would be incredibly time-consuming. As for computer keyboards, since they almost universally consist of letters of the English alphabet, it would be impossible to type simplified characters without *pinyin*. Therefore, the long-term significance of *pinyin* is evident given people now live in a digital era where communication is primarily done through typing.

Lastly, the British Council reaffirms the importance of learning Mandarin Chinese in the twenty-first century, 'With the rapidly changing international picture, languages such as Mandarin Chinese are becoming strategically important to the United Kingdom and internationally. Mandarin Chinese is one of the priority languages for the Foreign and Commonwealth Office and additional diplomatic posts are being created in China reflecting its growing economic and strategic importance.'[26] This secondary source is highly relevant as it explained why being able to speak Mandarin Chinese is crucial in terms of business and politics. As China increasingly grows in power, the demand for the ability to speak Mandarin rises too – for business and political reasons. It is preferable for foreigners to learn Mandarin in the quickest and most efficient way possible. Thankfully, *pinyin* and simplified characters enable this. Therefore, it cannot be denied that simplified characters and *pinyin* preserve and globalise Chinese culture.

Conclusion

Without a doubt, the conflict between Chinese scholars' efforts for an entirely phonetic vernacular system and the reality of China's predicament was effectively compromised by the Chinese government's push to implement simplified Chinese as the standard form of writing and *pinyin* as the annotation in the 1960s. Given undeniable evidence, simplified characters and *pinyin* modernised China by promoting a common tongue (*putonghua*), making education more accessible, and spreading and preserving Chinese culture. In this regard, the Chinese government's endeavours were highly successful and effective. In fact, the aftermath of the Chinese script revolution is conspicuous today, which can be seen from the sheer number of simplified character and *pinyin* users. Moreover, China now stands as one of the most modernised and powerful nations in the world. Indeed, changing the vernacular language has helped alter China's fate from an isolated, floundering nation to a contender for the title of the 'world's superpower.'

About the author

Athena Ru is a rising junior attending Concordia International School Shanghai in China. Her team won first place in the group exhibit category in National History Day China finals. She enjoys pondering over philosophical questions in her spare time and also holds a black belt in Taekwondo.

Email: Athena2021191@concordiashanghai.org

Endnotes

1 王树连, '历史上的中国版图', *China Surveying and Mapping*, 2005, no. 4: 28–33, http://kns.cnki.net/KCMS/detail/detail.aspx?dbcode=CJFQ&dbname=CJFD2005&filenameZCHZ200504013&v=MTQ3NTBSdEZ5N21WYnJBUHk3RGRMRzRIdFRNcTQ5RVo0UjlWDFMdXhZUzdEaDFUM3FUcldNMUZyQ1VSTEtmWmU=.

2 吴玉章, '利用拼音字母帮助扫盲和推广普通话', 1959, no. 6: 1–3. doi:10.16412.

3 Constantin Milsky, 'New Developments in Language Reform'. *The China Quarterly*, 1973, no. 53, pp. 98–133, http://www.jstor.org/stable/652509.

4 姚婧, '从《废除汉字采用新拼音文字案》看钱玄同所谓'汉字革命'', *Journal of Language and Literature Studies* 29, 2010, no. 19, pp. 94–97, http://kns.cnki.net/KCMS/detail/detail.aspx?dbcode=CFJD&dbname=CJFDN0911&filename=YWXK201019044&v=MDc2Njl1ZHVG3ZrVkx2SlBEclRaYkc0SDlITnBvOUJZSVI4ZVgxTHV4WVM3RGgxVDNxVHJXTTFGcNVUkxLZlo=.

5 雪珥, '百年前的"文字大跃进"', 2009 November 28, finance.qq.com/a/20091128/001572.htm.

6 Milsky, 'New Developments in Language Reform', pp. 98–133.

7 Ibid.

8 David Moser, e-mail message to author. 5 February 2018.

9 Jun Wang, 'Language Interaction In China', *Journal of Chinese Linguistics Monograph Series*, 1991, no. 3, pp. 159–84, http://www.jstor.org/stable/23827038.

10 John C. Wells, John. 'Why Phonetic Transcription Is Important', *Malsori: Phonetics (Journal of the Phonetic Society of Korea)*, 1996, 21 (31), pp. 239–42, http://www.phon.ucl.ac.uk/home/wells/whytranscription.htm.

11 The Editors of Encyclopædia Britannica, 'Pinyin Romanization', *Encyclopædia Britannica*. Encyclopædia Britannica, Inc. 25 April 2011, http://www.britannica.com/topic/Pinyin-romanization#ref161966.

12 Chin-Chuan Cheng, 'In Defense of Teaching Simplified Characters.' *Journal of Chinese Linguistics* 5 (2), 1977, pp. 314–41, http://www.jstor.org/stable/23753021.

13 周有光, '切音字运动百年祭.' *Language Planning* 5 (May 1992), pp. 34–35. doi: 10.16412/j.cnki.1001-8476.1992.05.015.

14 Tiedao Zhang, 'Literacy Education in China', 2006, *UNESCO*,

http://docplayer.net/storage/49/25399815/1526824879/698gb_
SHioO6OIQhss3r0g/2539981.pdf.

15 César Chelala, 'China: Language Simplification to Increase Literacy?'
The Globalist, 22 February 2016, www.theglobalist.com/china-
literacy-language-society/.

16 Chunman Gissing, e-mail message to author, 11 January 2018.

17 Rana Mitter, e-mail message to author, 22 January 2018.

18 张日培, '汉字的历史选择', 光明日报, July 2009, kns.cnki.net/
KCMS/detail/detail.aspx?dbcode=CCND&dbname=CCNDHI
S&filename=GMRB200907010112&uid=WEEvREcwSlJHSldT
TEYzU3EycEhlOEdQQVRtUG5zUUZ1RG9VanhLUEFiYz0=$
9A4hF_YAuvQ5obgVAqNKPCYcEjKensW4ggI8Fm4gTkoUKa-
ID8j8gFw!!&v=MjE2MDlNT1VLcmlmWnU1dkZDdm5VTC9
JS1ZzZElpRFpiTEc0SHRqTXFJOUVaT29PRGhOS3VoZGhua-
jk4VG5qcXF4ZEVl.

19 Robert Cheng and 郑良伟, 'Taiwanese Morphemes in Search of
Chinese Characters', *Journal of Chinese Linguistics*, 6 (2), 1978, pp.
306–14, http://www.jstor.org/stable/23752837.

20 Renyu Li, in discussion with the author, 6 February 2018.

21 UNESCO Institute for Statistics, 5AD. 'China', *UNESCO*, https://
en.unesco.org/countries/china.

22 Moser, e-mail message to author, 5 February 2018.

23 Asmaa Ibrahim, 'Chinese: Complex Tones and Characters,
Streamlined Grammar', *British Council*. British Council, 2014,
http://www.britishcouncil.org/voices-magazine/chinese-complex-
tones-characters-streamlined-grammar.

24 Doris Zhao, Doris in discussion with the author, 16 January 2018.

25 Chunman, e-mail message to author, 11 January 2018.

26 Teresa Tinsley and Kathryn Board, 'Languages for the Future', n. d.,
British Council, https://www.britishcouncil.org/sites/default/files/
languages-for-the-future-report.pdf

BOOK REVIEWS

When True Love Came to China
Published: 2015, Hong Kong University Press
BY LYNN PAN

REVIEWED BY DAGMAR BORCHARD

IS ROMANTIC LOVE a universal concept or a Western cultural construct? What do Chinese mean when they talk about love? Does the word 'love' mean the same in all cultures regardless of the language? Lynn Pan addresses these questions in her latest book on the concept of romantic love in China. 'We don't put much store by love, you hear the Chinese say of themselves, not in any tone of self-depreciation but a matter-of-factly. In one sense it is true: except among a small minority, romantic love is not felt to be of overriding importance in the choice of whom the Chinese marry.' Through a historical, literary, biographical and comparative approach, this well written study shows how the notion of love shifted with the rejection of arranged marriages and concubinage. It tells the story of how the concept of romantic love was slowly adopted and embraced by the Chinese in the early twentieth century.

For centuries before that, in China, all marriages were arranged either by parents or go-betweens and no Chinese chose their own spouse on the basis of romantic love. So for the Chinese, for a long period, love was not always essential for a marriage. It was only in the years following the May Fourth Period and the new Cultural Movement, which questioned the validity of the old Confucian traditions and the rigidity of the traditional family system, that ideas of liberty, democracy and rationalism from abroad slowly gained ground and changed at least the intellectuals' notion of what could be the precondition to a successful and modern marriage. The idea of choosing a partner based on your heart was so radical that even a new word had to be created in Chinese - *lian`ai*.

Pan reminds us that the debate of loving in the Western tradition was central to the modernisation efforts that China experienced in the first half of the last century. It was one of the answers Chinese intellectual vanguards found to the question of how China could overcome its backwardness. Pan describes the love stories by the most prominent Chinese writers such as Hu Shi, Lu Xun, Yu Dafu, Xu Zhimo, Shao Xunmei as well as famous women writers such as Eileen Chang and Ding Ling, all of whom lived much of their love life through the early twentieth century. Against this background, Pan reveals how the notion of love shifted in China with the rejection of arranged marriages and concubinages in favor of free and individual choice, monogamy and the Western model of romantic love. Pan details the real-life dilemmas of these intellectuals as nearly all of the men had to negotiate an arranged marriage with a wife back home in the remote countryside and a 'true' love in the city. Most of them had children with their arranged marriage wives, though only Lu Xun lived up to his new ideals and refused to consummate his arranged marriage. In 1925, he fell in love with his student Xu Guangping. The two lived together and had children, although in the eyes of the family, she remains a concubine.

The famous reformist Liang Qichao knew that revolution would lead to reform in society as he asserted that to renew the people, one needed to create a new fiction. A novelist wanting to write about man-woman relationship would inevitably turn to The *Dream of the Red Chamber* as a model. So Pan starts her analysis with two of China's own classics on love, the *Peony Pavillon* and the *Dream of the Red Chamber*. But as Liang had criticized, these novels only encouraged debauchery. So Chinese writers entangled with romantic love would rather turn to great Western love stories like Dumas' *Camellia Lady* or Goethe's *Werther* in their more or less aptly translated versions in Chinese. Some of the then much debated novels are now quite forgotten as Rider Haggard's *Joan Haste*, which in China became an influential model of romantic passion.

Pan took the title of her book out of the short story 'Stale Mates' from her favorite Chinese writer Eileen Chang, whom she characterises as 'hopelessly romantic.' In a famous letter to a friend, Chang wrote in 1969, 'To this day, we Chinese don't know much about love, and even our love stories don't often tell about love. Practically everybody was married and had children before ever hearing of love.' Chang subtitled her famous piece 'A Short Story Set In The Time When Love Came To China', which Pan echoes skillfully in the title she took for her own book, the Chinese translation being *It happened in the May Fourth Period*.

The coming of true love to China is a story without a happy

ending. Pan summarises in her last chapter where she analyses Ding Ling's *Sophie's Diary*, a landmark in the evolution of modern Chinese womanhood. Ding Ling, in real life, had to make compromises to the social forces of revolution to an extent that she had to betray her former independence and pursuit for love. Communist leaders were Confucianists in a new gown as romantic love should always come second to the devotion of the party and to a couple's ideological compatibility.

ABOUT THE REVIEWER

Dagmar Borchard is an independent researcher, journalist and photographer based in Shanghai since 2011. She holds an MA in Sinology and graduated in law from Volljuristin. She has been working as a lawyer in a German law firm since 2003. She is a regular contributor to several German journals and has been co-editing the German journal *das neue China* in which she writes a column about the latest developments in Shanghai.

BOOK REVIEWS

Half the Sky: Conversations with Women Artists in China
Published: 2016, Piper Press
BY LUISE GUEST
REVIEWED BY NIAMH CUNNINGHAM

AS WITH ALL OTHER aspects of global life, China has a greater impact today than it did 30 years ago. But Chinese artists, especially women, are still relatively unknown. Luise Guest tries to tackle this shortfall in knowledge with an intriguing and well-presented look in her book *Half the Sky*.[1] At 224 illustrated pages, the book highlights the works, sometimes bizarre, yet always thought-provoking, about the gender in China that Mao claimed 'held up half the sky.' Anyone who has visited China know women do more than that and the 30 artists featured in the book keep the sky from falling in ways you can barely imagine.

Guest knows her subjects and has a gift of bringing the reader on a journey with her. Take for instance the chapter titled '*Nüshu*.' This is an obscure traditional female language used in the remote areas of Jiangyong County, Hunan province. The outside world discovered this language in the 1980's just as it was fading out. The slanted script stitched on fans, handkerchiefs and clothbound books was given to brides to show marriage as a terrible fate. Nüshu allowed women to articulate their sorrow and anger at the stoic endurance of suffering expected of them and so the emphasis is more on duty at the expense of individual desire reinforcing Confucian sensibilities of obedient submission to familial authority.

Artist TAo Aimin's series Women's Book (2008-2010) used wooden washboards collected from hundreds of rural women over many years. Tao has collected over a thousand of these artefacts of female history and has recorded the details of each owner. Tao Aimin doesn't see herself as a feminist artist although she is sensitive to the idea of female destiny and it is humanity of male and female that is important to her. Tao has scrolls and books with traces of ink on washboards and marks made by the act of printing that suggests mountains and misty waterfalls of literati landscape painting. By choosing Nüshu as her calligraphy, Guest writes of Tao, 'She inserts a language invented by anonymous, unlettered rural women into the rarefied canon of the Imperial Scholarly tradition, bringing a largely unacknowledged female history into the light of day.' (page 168)

Another artist in the Nüshu category is performance artist Ma Yanling. Also a photographer and painter, Ma Yanling's *Suitcase Series* (2001) shows the artist tightly bound with silk ribbon as she crams herself into small cupboards and suitcases. 'These metaphors of bondage and confinement are feminist expressions of dissent in a country where dissent can come at a high price.' (page 171)

Neither is the book heavy in its focus. The cover of the book is adorned with Bu Hua's *AD 3012* (2012) and the back cover is her work *Brave Diligent.* (2014) Bu Hua along with Cui Xiuwen and Cao Fei are highlighted in the first chapter 'Alter Egos and Avatars' offering worlds of paradox filled with humour, wit and pathos but also with tones of increasing levels of anxiety. 'Distanced from the collective past, they have embraced the pluralist possibilities of the present whilst remaining clear- sighted about its dangers.' (page 32)

While discussing the use of textiles, Guest states the importance of acknowledging the doubts expressed by the artists about what a twenty-first century Chinese feminism might be. Artist Gao Rong denies any feminist intent in using the materials and techniques of domestic labour. Her work transforms banal objects into hyper real textile sculptures such as a sink full of dirty dishes, the carefully embroidered dirt and a deboned fish, and the exquisite suds, which could be Limerick lace. A different kind of stitching is done by Lin Jingjing where she has sewn through canvas which has been printed and/or painted. One of Lin Jingjings projects is *Color of Memory* where she asks complete strangers to tell her three things: their most painful memory; an object they associate with it; and the colour it evokes. Lin stitches the object named by the person on to the canvas before applying paint, representing memory as something tangible but always partially obscured. Some of the stories were so heart-breaking that Lin was uncertain about continuing the project. A woman loses her three-year old daughter in a shopping mall and the child is never seen again, presumably kidnapped. Speaking to Lin was the first time the woman was able to recount in twenty years.

Personal and collective memory informs Yin Xiuzhen's work. One work *Collective Subconscious* (Blue), 2007 is made from a minivan cut in half and connected by a concertina- like armature wrapped in a quilt made of four hundred items of discarded clothing collected from friends and relatives. Yin transforms the symbol of private success and entrepreneurship into a public space. The audience sits inside little stools and listens to popular songs of the nineties.[2] 'The choice of material may be at odds with the artists own stated intent ...nevertheless, in their very materiality, each artist embodies their own femaleness as well as reflecting on broader concerns such as environment destruction and the high social cost of progress.' (page 71)

The fourth chapter 'Black as lacquer- Reinventing Ink' looks at how the significance of ink painting and calligraphy in Chinese history continues to resonate with the reinvention of ancient traditions. Ink artist Bing Yi's work spans from meditative miniature contemplations to her vast scale site-specific installations. She has even applied ink from a helicopter for some of her installations. Bing Yi lives and works in an old temple and her work is informed by Buddhist beliefs embodying the notion of eternity.

This book is a companion to anyone who wants to understand the forces driving a sector of the art world that is emerging from the dark corners. Guest deserves our gratitude for being able to shed some light on it.

——◇◇◇——

Endnotes

1 People's Daily (online English)
http://en.people.cn/90001/90776/90882/6778815.html
2 Gao Rong denies feminist intent in using materials of domestic labour and Lin Jingjing says her act of sewing has nothing. to do with 'women's work'.

ABOUT THE REVIEWER

Niamh Cunningham is an artist working in Beijing since 2010. She has been actively engaged in cross-cultural projects in China co-curating the annual *Irish Wave* exhibitions in Beijing and Shanghai (2012-2016). She was also the Beijing co-curator of the *Intimate Transgressions* exhibition in October 2015 .